Player Piano Treasury

Player Piano Treasury

SECOND EDITION

BY HARVEY ROEHL

THE SCRAPBOOK

HISTORY

OF THE

MECHANICAL

PIANO

IN AMERICA

AS TOLD

IN STORY

PICTURES

TRADE JOURNAL

ARTICLES

AND ADVERTISING

VESTAL, N.Y. 13850

Library of Congress Card Catalog Number for the Second Edition 73-77327
ISBN 0-911572-00-7

Printed in the United States of America

Cover artwork for this book was adapted by Brian A. Williams
from an original QRS Music Roll advertisement which
appeared in the December 1922 issue of Asia Magazine.
Permission for its use granted to The Vestal Press
by QRS Music Rolls, Inc., Buffalo, N.Y.

Frontispiece art work by Ted Robinson

Contents

Preface

The ever-accelerating pace of technical developments during the middle years of the Twentieth Century is one that leaves anyone who thinks about it quite overwhelmed. Advances in all fields of technology are literally so staggering that it is a monumental task even to keep abreast of developments in one field—let alone get a comprehensive view of what goes on. Accomplishments which take place today with very little notice were beyond the wildest dreams of most men just short years ago. Although there are those who claim to wish for a return to the "good old days" when life was simpler and less hectic, the fact is that in most ways the old days really weren't so good.

But certainly one of the unfortunate aspects of our pell-mell rush toward greater material accomplishments is that many very wonderful and fascinating things are developed that get passed over so quickly that they soon are forgotten. Such is the case with the player piano and all its variations. The vast player piano industry which for three decades caused the atmosphere to be permeated with mechanical music has for all practical purposes been dead since 1925, victim mainly of the radio and the phonograph. The public has long since forgotten it . . . but like many another industry, when it was a thriving giant it brought forth devices which were not only miraculous in their day, but seem so even today when we take a look at what was done.

Who of today's generation has heard a reproducing piano?

Who of today's generation has seen or heard the violin-playing machines of the Hupfeld organization or of the great mechanical and electrical wizard, Henry Konrad Sandell?

Who of today's generation has heard of the fabulous family of coin-in-the-slot entertainers of the roaring twenties, the one-machine bands known as orchestrions?

Or for that matter, how many of today's youngsters have ever pedaled an ordinary player piano?

Probably in no other field of endeavor have so many men, working mainly as individuals, produced so many contraptions and gadgets as were built by those who devoted their lives to the production of music by mechanical means. Students of the history of the player piano are constantly amazed at the devices which were contrived and offered to the public, gadgets which occasionally were produced in large numbers but more often appeared in only a handful of production pieces and therefore have had even more reason to become forgotten. And the men who promoted the sales of these machines and gadgets to the public were no less ingenious than the inventors in their striving to capture a bigger market and in so doing to gain a larger fortune.

We might laugh today at some of the advertising and sales gimmicks of yesteryear, as those of future generations will do when they review what was done in the Mid-Twentieth Century.

A comprehensive treatment of the entire field of mechanical piano music is quite impossible in a book this size. In fact, it is quite impossible! Because so many devices were produced in small shops, and because so many never reached the market place in quantity, and because written records in the piano industry are all but non-existent, the research required to do an absolutely complete work becomes a formidable obstacle.

But it is possible to go back through the years and get a very good idea of what went on, and to see most of the better known devices that came out of the era. As in the case of reading a book on automobile history one must imagine himself jogging along a dirt road with all the discomforts of home, so must our reader use his imagination, for the printed page cannot sing forth with the magnificent music made by the many machines pictured here. Fortunately, in recent years many phonograph records of still-existing machines have been marketed, so that anyone wanting to hear them may now do so in his home. In addition, a number of fine public collections of restored machines of all types are open around the country for the benefit of those who not only wish to hear, but to see and to feel a part of what were — as far as the player piano is concerned — the "good old days."

This book represents the efforts of many people dedicated to keeping alive the spirit of this by-gone era, through their collections not only of machines but of literature about them, much of which has been loaned for reproduction here. Specific acknowledgments are made in the work, but special thanks must go to Carl Baxter, Paul Eakins, Larry Givens, Stan Peters, Durrell Armstrong, Edwin A. Link, and Oswald Wurdeman for major contributions to this effort. Thanks also are made to Professor Lloyd Hartman for his critical review of the manuscript material.

HARVEY N. ROEHL
Vestal, New York

September 1961.

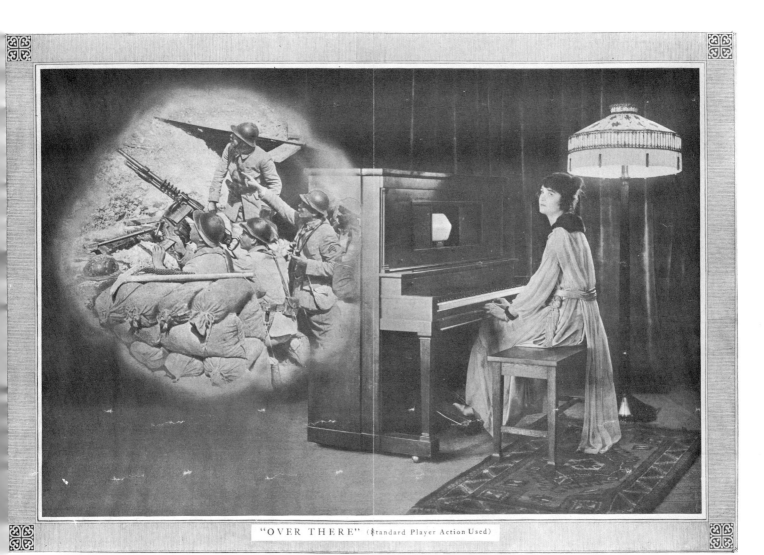

"OVER THERE" (Standard Player Action Used)

Foreword to the Second Edition

Over ten years have elapsed since PLAYER PIANO TREASURY entered the literary scene, and during these intervening years a tremendous amount of interest has developed in automatic pianos, orchestrions, band organs, and other types of mechanical music makers. It was inevitable that much new historical material would be uncovered during this period; so much so, in fact, that it would be impracticable for any new edition of this book to pretend to cover it all.

The author is exceedingly proud of the fact that the first edition seemed to spark much of today's interest in the field, and if his early efforts have caused other historians to dig deeper than he has been able to do, we're all better off for these new discoveries.

The second edition of this work has been motivated not so much by a requirement to up-date it, as by the purely mechanical reason that its success has caused it to be printed in large quantities. The oblong shape of the original volume caused no end of production difficulties, and it finally became necessary to re-format the entire volume for this reason alone!

Acceptance of this, however, gave the chance to correct a few historical inaccuracies that evidenced themselves, as well as to add a much-needed index and to re-set the manuscript in a larger type-face for easier reading.

There was one, and only one, reason for this book to come into existence in the first place, and that was the author's pure and simple enjoyment of all types of mechanically-reproduced piano music. This enjoyment has never diminished in the 10 years since issuance of the first edition of PLAYER PIANO TREASURY, and it is especially gratifying that the great interest which has developed in the years since then have meant that literally thousands of these historically-precious instruments have been saved which otherwise might have gone into oblivion.

The author's fondest wish would be that readers of this book will get as much fun from reading it as he has had in assembling it.

Harvey N. Roehl
Vestal, New York 13850

Rhapsodies In Wrapping Paper

The question, "who invented the player piano?" is like "who invented the automobile?" There just isn't any clear-cut answer, for as in the case of that auto, the credit must be divided among a number of pioneers in the field; undoubtedly many similar ideas were conceived independently by different individuals at about the same times. But we do know that in 1863 a Frenchman named Forneaux patented what appears to be the first player operating on pneumatic principles. This he called the "Pianista," and it formed the basis of practically all later developments in the field. According to Alfred Dolge, who published his monumental work "Pianos and Their Makers" in two volumes, dated 1911 and 1913 (and in so doing preserved for mankind an intimate story of the world's great piano builders through his first-hand dealings with many of them), the Pianista was first exhibited in America at the Philadelphia Exposition in 1876. As the picture shows, it operated by means of a hand crank which produced the vacuum to work a set of "fingers" which in turn played the keyboard of an ordinary piano.

Dolge, himself, is an important figure in American piano history, for he foresaw the immense commercial possibilities in the market. To capitalize on them he built large factories in what is now Dolgeville, New York, to make piano felt and to mass produce sounding boards from Adirondack spruce at a price which individual piano manufacturers could not possibly

match. (Dolgeville was originally called Brockett's Bridge, but the townspeople changed it in honor of their leading citizen.)

He eventually became a leading supplier to the trade for almost all piano components, and he established factories on the West Coast as well. Not only a great industrialist but a humanitarian, he was a pioneer in good personnel relations with his workmen, and all shared in the profits of the enterprise. Dolge recognized that men, like machines, must be replaced and he put into effect pension plans over a half century before industry in general was forced to recognize this need.

But like many another businessman, Dolge over-extended his financial resources, and shortly after the turn of the century lost everything. We are fortunate that he did take advantage of his dealings with the world's great piano makers and wrote of them. His writings on the development of the player piano are just about the only objective history of the early activities in that field.

Dolge suggests that one R. W. Pain was probably the first who built a pneumatic self-playing piano (that is, a completely self-contained unit) in his 39-note instrument built for Needham and Sons in 1880. Later, in 1888, he built a 65-note electrically operated piano, and this probably was also the first of its kind.

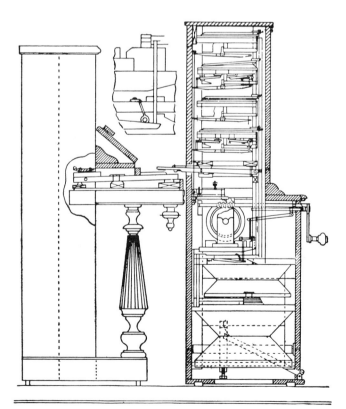

Fourneaux's Pianista

Alfred Dolge (signature)

"More Fascinating Than Golf"

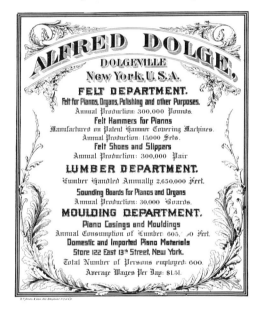

JOHN McTammany, a veteran of the Civil War, went to his grave proclaiming that he was the one true inventor of the player piano, and two books authored by him were published in an attempt to get everyone to agree with his position. During his lifetime he did a lot of work in the field of paper-played reed organs in addition to his efforts in the piano field, and there is no doubt that he did make significant contributions to the art. He is buried at Canton, Ohio, where his headstone proudly states that he was the inventor.

But whether he was or not, it is a fact that he was never able to capitalize on his work to any great degree, and he died in meager surroundings in 1915.

John McTammany patented in 1868 certain devices pertinent to automatic organ construction, which in effect were improvements over Forneaux' designs.

Elias Parkman Needham invented the upright action used in reed organs, which made possible all their later improvements. He originated the idea of the perforated sheet of paper passing over a reed chamber

ELIAS PARKMAN NEEDHAM

which allowed the escape of musical tones as the perforations passed over the reed opening. This idea was protected by fifteen patents, which he sold to the Mechanical Orguinette Company, later to become the basis of the Aeolian Corporation.

In 1886 George B. Kelly developed the slide-valve wind motor, and this device eventually became universally adopted as the type of motor to be used to cause rotation of the drive spool for paper music rolls in player pianos.

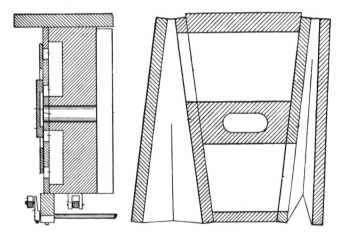

George B. Kelly's Wind Motor with Slide Valves, 1886

Merritt Gally, in 1881, patented a device which, while it never became an important factor in itself, did lay the groundwork not only for the later American Electrelle playing device which was marketed from around 1910 to 1915 by the American Piano Company, but also for all modern electric typewriters. The essential feature is the cam, which when impressed lightly upon a rotating roller, causes a large force to be exerted against a lever — in his case, a lever the other end of which depressed a piano key, and in the typewriter, a typebar which prints a character.

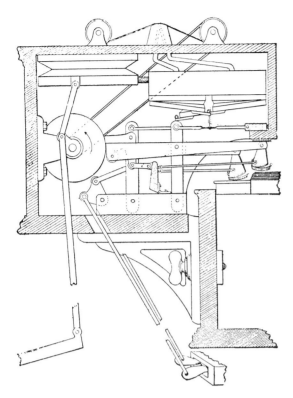

Merritt Gally's Player Mechanism, 1881

In 1891 William D. Parker of Meriden, Connecticut received a patent assigned to his employer, the Wilcox and White Company, for a combination manual and paper-roll-operated piano, but the first commercially successful automatic product of this company was the Angelus Orchestral cabinet-style player, patented in 1897.

This machine contained not only the playing mechanism for a piano but also reeds in the manner of the then highly popular reed organ, so the operator could truly have an "orchestral" offering!

But of all the efforts in commercializing the possibilities inherent in the player piano, the most credit must go to William B. Tremaine and his son, H. B. Tremaine. Quoting directly from Dolge:

"William B. Tremaine, born in 1840, entered the piano business in 1868 as a member of the firm of Tremaine Brothers. A man of restless disposition, cultured and versatile, he seized upon opportunities whenever presented. When Mason J. Mathews had his orguinette ready for the market, Tremaine organized in 1876 the "Mechanical Orguinette Company" and marketed these automatic instruments by the thousands. (*Note:* This machine was a small reed organ which played from a paper tune sheet; it was about the size of a small table model radio.) Later on the "Celestina" (an enlarged Orguinette) was introduced with considerable success, and in 1883 the Aeolian Organ was brought out. Acquiring in 1888 the patents and stock in trade of the Automatic Music Paper Company of Boston, Tremaine organized the Aeolian Organ and Music Company, manufacturing automatic organs and music rolls. Success crowning his efforts, he purchased in 1892 all the patents owned by the Munroe Organ Reed Company of Worcester, and in 1895 introduced the "Aeriol" self-playing piano.

"W. B. Tremaine was the founder of the business (in America) of manufacturing automatic playing musical instruments. Before the advent of the "Pianola" there was neither competition nor encouragement from the piano trade, and it required a man of keen foresight and courage to meet these conditions and make a success of the business, as he did, up to the time of his relinquishing it to his son.

"In H. B. Tremaine (his son, b. 1866) we meet the new element in the business world. The thorough education which he had enjoyed had trained his mind in logical reasoning, supporting his large vision for utilization of modern inventions and discoveries on a large scale. Tremaine had the great advantage that he had nothing to forget. He also knew how to apply all that he had learned in relation to modern economics. When he, in 1899, took charge of the business of the Aeolian Company as President, he surveyed the situation as it presented itself. His father had laid a good foundation. Votey had perfected his Pianola. How to exploit what he found, to its fullest extent, was the problem for Tremaine to solve. Believing with the enthusiasm of youth the almost boundless commercial possibilities of the new automatic appliances for musical instruments, he knew that success was only obtainable if adequate capital could be combined with the manufacturing and selling organization then at his command. So strong was his faith, so plausible the plans which he had worked out that he did succeed in interesting men of affairs, and obtained capital by the millions for the furtherance of his ambitious plans. Backed by this abundant capital, he lost no time in setting his machinery in action. The advertising campaign for the Pianola, which he inaugurated immediately, stunned the old-timers in the piano trade. Dire disaster was prophesied by many, but Tremaine knew his cards, his carefully laid plans did not miscarry, and no one today (1911) denies him the credit of having blasted and paved the way for the popularity of the player piano. Like all great leaders, Tremaine has the talent to pick the right man for the right place. He found an able assistant in Edward R. Perkins, who joined the Aeolian forces in 1893 at the age of 24. Perkins exhibited such ability and strength that he

H. B. Tremaine, President of the Weber Piano Co., Under Whose Able Guidance the High Ideals of Albert Weber, Founder of the Company, Are Rigidly Maintained

E. S. Votey

was entrusted with the responsible position of vice-president and general manager when the greater organization was completed.

"William E. Wheelock came into the fold as President of the Weber Piano Company in 1903, and is now in charge of the financial department as treasurer of the corporation.

"Tremaine understands the economy of high-priced labor. When he wanted to build the best player pianos he secured the services of Pain, Votey, Kelly, and others of ability. Just as soon as he was ready to enter the piano field proper, he associated with the Weber and Steck pianos, and finally made a combination with the house of Steinway for the exclusive use of the Pianola in their instruments. Knowing that large capital can be economically applied only under conditions of increasing returns, which again are possible only with relatively large markets, he branched out and went into the markets of Europe, Asia, South America, and Australia. For the stimulus of the home market bidding for the patronage of the wealthy, Tremaine built Aeolian Hall, in the very heart of New

MUSIC

The Pianola solves the problem of music in the home. Its production was the crowning achievement of musical activity in the century just closed.

Within the home, where there is a Pianola, music reigns supreme, and every member of the household may be a performer. The piano is available to all. In its rhythmic tones the busy man forgets his cares. The hostess finds relief from thoughts concerning entertainment for her guests; and happy young folks respond with feet or voice and in a dance or song find wholesome recreation underneath the family roof.

Of music man never tires. Every new example of the art awakens new emotions in his breast. One piece may lose its freshness, but with the next comes back, enhanced, the pleasure of the first.

The owner of a Pianola need never fear it may grow tiresome. The music for it has no limit. Its repertoire, enormous in extent, magnificent in variety, absolutely precludes such a possibility.

Eight thousand one hundred and thirty-one pieces at present, and new selections added monthly at the rate of two hundred and fifty, makes a collection such as the world has never heretofore seen brought together.

In view of this, how apparent it is that one can never tire of the Pianola.

The Pianola's self is not the question. The music it makes possible is the consideration, and every new selection renews again the novelty and freshness of the instrument.

Without the Pianola what possibilities are hidden within the piano?

Before the Pianola came, how very few there were who even caught a glimpse into the grand world of harmony. Toiling laboriously to reproduce a small part of the great compositions of the masters, even the best pianists were sadly limited.

The iron rules of technique, the inexorable necessity of long hours spent in daily practice, forbade *pianists* the pleasure of roaming at will throughout the world of music. To all the rest of human kind the masterpieces of the grandest art that is known to man were buried treasures.

This is what the Pianola does for man.

To those who never yet have felt the fascination of pouring forth the best emotions of their souls in music, or those who *used to play*, but have been weaned by other cares from practice, it brings a joy that any time before it came the wealth of all the world could not have bought.

The music of the world is free to all.

For those whom classic pieces interest, Scarlatti, Bach, Haydn, and old Händel have written oratorios and fugues. Unhappy Schubert speaks to them in the sweet tones of Rosamunde. Beethoven, master of masters, thrills alike the listeners and the performer with his Appassionata or beautiful Fifth Symphony.

Chopin bemoans the fate of Poland in his Nocturnes or breathes the fiery valor of his countrymen in Polonaise. Mendelssohn, Rubinstein, Moszkowski, Liszt, all help to weave tone-pictures for ear and mind alike to revel in.

For other tastes, where settings of the stage have served

to spur the fancies of their favorites, great Wagner comes and, lifting them aloft above the clouds, transports them to the mighty Halls of old Walhalla, in Ride of Walküres, or takes them to the cool, green depths of classic Rhine in Nibelungen Ring.

Verdi, Mascagni, Suppé, and Gounod have all bequeathed to man a wealth of melody, each tone of which is precious to the lover of the opera.

To owners of the Pianola, both this and music of a lighter strain is possible. A waltz by Strauss, a Sousa march, a song, a rag-time hit, a part of Florodora are ever at his call, and always fresh, not needing practice.

The most gifted pianist the world has ever known has but a small fraction of this repertoire.

The Pianola is the universal means of playing the piano.

Universal, because there is no one in all the world, having the use of hands and feet, who could not learn to use it with but little effort.

To operate it is simplicity itself.

Adjustable to any piano, the Pianola stands before it when in use, and plays the keys with tiny, felt-tipped fingers.

The striking of the notes of the selection, in proper time and place, is no concern of the player. This is correctly done by perforated rolls of paper (the form in which the music for the Pianola comes).

The player's only task is to decide how slow or how fast the notes shall sound, how loud or how soft he wants them, also he uses the sustaining-pedal. Three little levers serve to impart the player's wishes to the Pianola. On these his fingers rest.

Should the air be familiar, the player's taste will dictate the expression. But if it is strange or difficult, a very simple set of markings on the moving music-roll direct the proper movement of the levers.

A little child can do all this and give correct expression to the compositions played.

Simple it is, but in its simplicity it is musically artistic. Paderewski, Hofmann, and other great artists find pleasure in the Pianola and use it because they can so perfectly control the elements which go to make up "expression."

The Pianola thus is found to be a pleasure-giving instrument for all, both tyro and musician, enabling them to play on the piano with absolute correctness and with human feeling.

More could not be asked of mortal ingenuity.

Less never would have served to place the Pianola where it stands to-day—the greatest and most widely popular of musical inventions, the only practical solution of, and the Royal Road to Music in the Home.

The Pianola can be seen and played at our new exposition-rooms, Fifth Avenue and Thirty-fourth Street, New York, and at the warerooms of any of our agents throughout the country, and a personal opinion formed by both the novice and the skilled musician upon the benefits to be derived from its assistance.

A handsomely illustrated and descriptive brochure (catalog X) will be sent to those desiring information by mail, and all questions answered through our correspondence department.

The price of the Pianola is **$250.** Purchasable by monthly payments if desired.

THE AEOLIAN COMPANY
AEOLIAN HALL
Fifth Avenue and Thirty-fourth Street, New York

York's fashionable quarters, engaging the best artists to demonstrate the value of his products at the elegant auditorium. In 1903 he organized the Aeolian, Weber Piano and Pianola Company, capitalized at $10,000,000 and controlling subsidiary companies: The Aeolian Company, The Orchestrelle Company (London), The Choralion Company (Berlin), The Aeolian Company Ltd. (Paris), The Pianola Company Proprietary, Ltd. (Melbourne and Sidney), the Weber Piano Company, George Steck and Company, Wheelock Piano Company, Stuyvesant Piano Company, Chilton Piano Company, Technola Piano Company, Votey Organ Company and the Universal Music (roll) Company. These companies give employment to about 5,000 people scattered all over the world. The total capital employed under the direction of H. B. Tremaine amounts to $15,000,000, which is more than the capital invested in the entire organ and piano industry of the United States in 1890.

"The remarkable results achieved by Tremaine within so short a time can be accounted for by the fact that he learned from history what others had to learn from the dreary school of experience. As an observant student, he saw the potentialities of mechanical appliances for musical instruments and knew how to develop them. A genius as an organizer, he believes in a combination of capital and brains, division of labor and responsibilities, and adequate compensation for all. He has proven that a higher education is not a hindrance for advancement, but a necessity for progress in industrial, commercial, or financial pursuits. He has made his record in breaking the path for the new school of industrial revolutionists in the piano industry. A pioneer of the most forceful, aggressive type, he is withal of a gentlemanly and most retiring disposition, shunning publicity to an unwarranted degree.

"How rapidly the player piano is forging to the front, with almost irresistible force, is clearly demonstrated by the tremendous growth of such factories as seem to know how to serve the public best."

What Dolge says of Pianola advertising — that Tremaine literally stunned the rest of the industry with it — can be appreciated from the four-page ad reproduced on the previous page. This appeared in a 1902 COSMOPOLITAN, in *two colors!* Not that colored advertising was new, but the idea of using it in piano advertising certainly was.

The impact of the Pianola on the market can also be appreciated from the fact that while this was actually a trade name, copyrighted and registered by one company, the name caught on so well that for all practical purposes it became a generic term applied to all types of piano players, much in the manner of "Cellophane" or "Victrola" in later years in their respective product areas. And as is the case with all successful products, many others came along to get their share of the market . . . and while dozens of other "cabinet" or "push-up" players appeared, probably the ones best known are the Angelus, built by Wilcox and White, and the Cecilian, built by the Farrand Organ Company.

The advertising for these machines fails to point out that they usually played only sixty-five notes of the normal 88-note piano scale, and that this, in turn, meant that the original composers' scores all had to be rearranged — (and in many cases mutilated) — to fit this range. But even the sixty-five notes were enough to bring some semblance of artistry into the home, and while these cabinet-style piano players are very

IT'S ALL IN THE BELLOWS

THE pianist produces his effects upon the piano by means of muscular force, exerted by his fingers. In the piano-player, air takes the place of muscle; that is, the mechanical fingers of the piano-player are actuated by air.

The bellows must provide the performer at all times with a reserve power, which will enable him to accent a note; to swing instantly from the softest pianissimo to the heaviest fortissimo or vice versa. It is because the patented bellows construction in the

CECILIAN PIANO=PLAYER

makes it possible for the performer to do these things surely and easily at all times that the Cecilian is to-day far superior to any other piano-player on the market.

Inside of the big operating bellows of the Cecilian is a small bellows. When the pedals are worked, both parts of this compound bellows are immediately put into action. As the air with which the smaller bellows is filled must escape into the larger bellows, you will readily see that the large bellows must first be exhausted before the small bellows comes into play.

The small bellows thus provides a reserve force which continues to operate the player without any loss of power, after the force of the big bellows has been exhausted. This peculiar and patented bellows construction in the Cecilian, gives the performer the utmost freedom for individual expression and enables him to produce the most delicate effects in tone coloring, with an absolutely non-mechanical touch, and also makes it possible for a woman to operate the Cecilian without fatigue.

The Cecilian can be attached to any piano, and with it any one can play any music without previous experience or musical knowledge. The price is $250.00. Easy payments if desired. Write for booklet.

FARRAND ORGAN COMPANY, Dept. H

PARIS, FRANCE   DETROIT, MICH.   LONDON, ENGLAND

The PIANOLA

The Pianola in use in connection with Grand Piano

9

The Needham Paragon

A Song Without Words

NEEDHAM PIANO & ORGAN CO.
96 Fifth Avenue, New York

Little boys or girls operating a player piano or cabinet player always had an appeal which was exploited by a number of manufacturers in their advertising. But while everyone likes little boys and girls, this type of thinking had much to do with later difficulties of the industry. Not only were children not inclined to learn to operate the instrument properly so as to make something approaching pleasant-sounding results, but the ease with which even poor-sounding music could be made destroyed their incentive to want to learn to play by manual means. Most piano dealers agree that the poor market in the 30's and 40's resulted not so much from depression and war as the fact that a whole generation of people had simply not learned to play the piano itself.

Oddly enough, the advent of television in the 1950's did not, as many prophets of doom forecast, kill off what was left of the industry, but conversely did a great deal to stimulate it. The opportunities youngsters had to see real performers in action caused many to want to learn, with the result that the market reached new highs.

rare sixty years later, they served a tremendous purpose in introducing mechanically produced music to the public during their brief period of popularity.

And the reason that they were popular for only a few years — from around 1900 to 1905 — is simply that in spite of their intrinsic worth they were, nevertheless, a clumsy contraption — clumsy to move up to the keyboard to play (great care was necessary so as not to break off the wooden fingers), a nuisance to have to take away when one wanted to play the piano by hand, and worst of all, a device easily ignored and forgotten when once moved away from the piano. So it is not surprising that very early in the game, efforts were made to eliminate the player as a separate unit and to build its features directly into the piano itself.

No doubt the most famous incident concerning youngsters and player pianos is that of the Katzenjammer Kids in the early days of that comic strip. Salvaging a player from a wrecked ship, but finding no music, the ever-resourceful Kids solved the problem by cutting up Swiss Cheese into strips!

The Angelus

representatives invite you, informally, to your own concert.

The name of nearest representative mailed immediately on request. A fine piano and an *Angelus* are ready for *your* inexhaustible repertoire.

You will not be disturbed and may sit and play as long as you wish without being under the slightest obligation to purchase.

¶ Our beautiful souvenir art calendar showing the musical instruments of different periods, from the lyre of the Egyptians to the grand piano of to-day, reproduced with absolute faithfulness to detail, in dainty water color facsimile on heavy art paper (10 x 12¾ inches), ribbon tied, will be mailed for twenty-five cents (stamps or coin) and mention of this publication.

Purchased by Royalty and the World's Greatest Musicians. Send for booklet

THE WILCOX & WHITE CO.

Established 1876   MERIDEN, CONN., U. S. A.

Another of the great pioneers in the player piano industry, Melville Clark, was one of the first to market pianos and their players as a complete unit, and was also about the first (1902) to build a player unit to operate the entire 88-note range of the piano. Clark was a prolific inventor who secured many patents in the field — notable of which was the transposing device which permits a player piano to operate in a number of different keys, obviously a great boon to the accompanist of vocal music.

During this period a gradual transition was being made from the 65-note roll to the full 88-note player roll, and pianos and cabinet players were marketed which had the capacity of handling either size. Of course some manufacturers were non-conformists with these, and Melville Clark felt obliged to produce at least one model which would handle five different sizes of rolls! Needless to say, this chaotic condition of a lack of standardization of rolls was an obvious hindrance to the health and progress of the industry. Fortunately, at a convention of manufacturers at Buffalo, New York in 1908 an agreement was reached on roll practices which insured interchangeability among pianos of practically all makes.

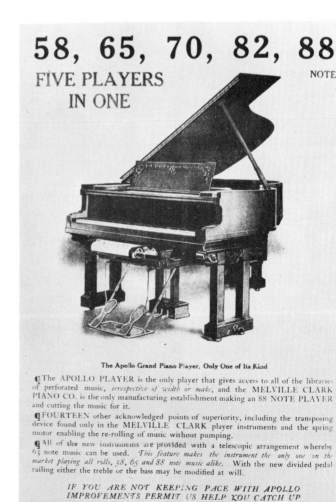

The AEOLIAN COMPANY
ANNOUNCES THE NEW
PIANOLA PIANO
"The First Complete Piano"

Combining in a single compact instrument an upright piano of the highest grade and a Metrostyle Pianola

Prices **$500** to **$1,000.** Purchasable on moderate monthly payments. Pianos of all other makes taken in exchange at fair valuation.

THE PIANOLA PIANO represents an entirely new thought in musical instruments. Its advantages over the accepted type of pianoforte are so manifest that thousands of pianos heretofore satisfactory to their owners are destined to be disposed of to make room for this Twentieth Century production.

The Pianola Piano is, first of all, *a perfect piano.* It may be played by the fingers on the keyboard in the usual way. In tone, action, durability, and appearance, it leaves nothing to be desired.

But, most important of all, it contains *within its case* a complete Metrostyle Pianola—the latest and best of all piano-players. The change from hand-playing to Pianola-playing takes no more time than is required to slide back a panel in the front of the case and insert a perforated roll of music. There is nothing to move up in front of the keyboard, as the Pianola mechanism occupies the heretofore unused space within the pianoforte.

The Pianola Piano is the first piano which may be *enjoyed by every one*—irrespective of any previous knowledge of music—from the very moment of its installation. *It is the one piano which it is certain will not stand idle, no matter into whose home it may go.*

Illustrated Book Given to Inquirers
SOLD BY
The Oliver Ditson Co., Boston
John Wanamaker, New York and Philadelphia
Juelg & Co., Baltimore and Washington
S. Hamilton, Pittsburg
Geo. P. Bent, Chicago
The Estey Co., St. Louis
Sherman, Clay & Co., San Francisco
The W. G. Woodmansee Piano Co., Cincinnati
The J. T. Wamelink & Sons Piano Co., Cleveland
Junius Hart Piano House, New Orleans
F. J. Schwankousky, Detroit
THE WILCOX & WHITE CO.,
Main Offices and Factory - · Meriden, Conn., U.S.A.

Testimonial from the celebrated composer of "Cavalleria Rusticana," "Amico Fritz," "Iris," etc.:

"The Angelus is a wonderful virtuoso-pianist, and at the same time an excellent organist.

"Thanks to its marvellous means of expression, it can give the complicated pieces more *life and soul* than any other instrument of its kind is able to give.

"Bravo to the inventors."

(Signed) PIETRO MASCAGNI.

The Player Comes Of Age

Mrs. Neurich —"Yes, My Daughter Has a Great Foot for Music"

By 1910 the American public didn't have to be sold any more on the idea of the player piano — the instrument was here to stay, or at least so it seemed! The monumental step forward accomplished by standardization of roll sizes and perforation spacing set the stage for the great mass penetration of the market, where the hucksters and the peddlers could make their great play. It was no longer a question of whether or not to buy a player — rather the question now was what kind to buy. For by this time, the technical development of the ordinary foot-operated player had reached its plateau, and any improvements made upon the mechanisms of players after this date were mostly in the class of minor refinements. As a matter of fact, the machine introduced by Hardman, Peck and Company in 1957 was for all practical purposes mechanically identical with most players built in 1910. This is not to say that there wasn't real effort to make improvements; it merely is to repeat the well-known fact that for most manufactured products selling to mass markets, one best way of building the article usually evolves as a result of simple economics.

Naturally enough, of course, through the years various manufacturers came up with wondrous gadgets and gimmicks to assist in the sales of their machines, and of course they were all touted with catchy descriptive adjectives and fancy names. Some of these were sold as accessories, as noted later, but plenty of them were part and parcel of the pianos themselves.

Emerson's *AccompanO* permitted the singer to operate his own accompaniment by manipulation of

16

a switch at the end of a cable. Aeolian's *Metro-style* and *Themodist* gave the pianist some control of expression and speed; Wilcox and White's *Phrasing Lever* and *Melodant* offered similar possibilities. Melville Clark's *Transposing Mouthpiece* permitted the piano to be played in several different keys, and of course this device was eventually almost universally adopted throughout the industry. The Apollo pianos, also made by Clark, boasted a mechanical arrangement of the operative mechanism which permitted the striking force to be exerted downward on the keys, allegedly giving the touch more of a "human quality." They also had a spring re-wind motor which wound up as one pedaled through a roll, storing energy which then re-wound the roll without further human effort. According to the ads, this latter device "saves you work." Evidently the ad-writers for this concern were intentionally or otherwise ignorant of the most elementary principles of high school physics!

The name Pianola which was controlled by Aeolian caught on so well that inevitably there were a host of other names conjured by imitators, many of whom tried to capitalize on the suffix "OLA," and most of the rest of whom worked "TONE" into the name in some manner. In the best tradition of our Madison Avenue advertising people of the modern generation, no doubt many men stayed awake nights to come up with what today seem like perfectly absurd names for their machines. In 1911, for example, we find the TECHNOLA and the AERIOLA, the first a medium-priced piano and the second a medium-priced, cabinet-style player, both of which were produced by

piano Company itself, established in 1903 by R. W. Lawrence, remained for years a strong factor in the player business, making only player pianos.

The AUTOLA, a catchy name implying both Automatic and Ola, was used by the Horace Waters Company of New York City, and the ARTISTANO, somehow implying automatic artistry, was the name applied to machines made by the A. B. Chase Company of Norwalk, Ohio. By 1913, the AIR-O-PLAYER was marketed by the Briggs Piano Company of Boston, as was the CONCERTONE of the Mansfield Piano Company of New York, to say nothing of the CONVERTOLA, put out by the Columbus Piano Company of Columbus, Ohio, the VIRTUOLO of Boston's Conway Company, the MANUALO of the Ellington Company of Cincinnati, the ELECTROVA (a coin-operated machine) of the company of the same name, the DULCITONE and the RESOTONE, both of the Cable-Nelson Piano Company of Chicago,

subsidiary organizations of the Aeolian Company. The AUTOTONE was produced by Hardman, Peck and Company. The CROWN-COMBINOLA, by the George P. Bent Company of Chicago, was evidently meant to imply a combination of the Crown piano and a player unit. The INTERIOLA, manufactured in this period by Ricca and Son of New York City, obviously was named to make it clear that the player unit was in the interior of the piano and not a separate unit. The AUTO-GRAND, AUTO-PLAYER, and PIAN-AUTO were all names used by the Krell Company to make it apparent to the prospective purchaser that here was truly music in an automatic form. The PIANISTA, a cabinet player manufactured by the AUTOPIANO Company, was of course a direct usage of the name coined by Forneaux for his very earliest of this type of machine in 1863. The Auto-

THE IMPROVED AMERICAN PLAYER ACTION

SECTION OF WIND-CHEST WITH FRONTS REMOVED

ALL VITAL PARTS ACCESSIBLE FROM THE FRONT

Note the Stroke Regulating Screws, Lost

Motion Screws, Valves, Pouches, Bleeds

AMERICAN PLAYER ACTION CO.   2595 Third Avenue
New York City

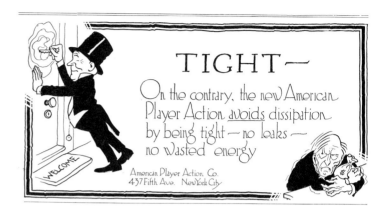

TIGHT—

On the contrary, the new American Player Action *avoids* dissipation by being tight — no leaks — no wasted energy

American Player Action Co.
437 Fifth Ave. New York City

ARTROLA
Player Action

For installation in any make of piano. Especially adapted for use by manufacturers and dealers desirous of *converting* straight and 65 note players into UP TO DATE 88 NOTE INSTRUMENTS.

Dominant Features:
**Responsiveness   Simplicity
Durability   Accessibility**

FULLY   GUARANTEED

Artrola Player Co.
Gen. Offices: 506 Republic Bldg.
CHICAGO

N. B. Manufacturers also of ARTROLA VARNISH REJUVENATOR for the *eradication* of hair-check, blemish, blister, etc., and ARTROLA VARNISH REMOVER.

The CECILIAN

New Style Primary and Secondary Pneumatics and Wind Chest—made all of Metal and in one piece.

The only piano-player whose mechanism is **made of metal** instead of wood and leather.

In **every** Piano-Player there are 65 primary and 65 secondary pneumatics, or bellows. (See illustrations at bottom of page.)   These 130 pneumatics operate the wooden fingers which strike the keys of the piano.

In all Piano-Players **except the Cecilian** these pneumatics are made of wood and leather, and the constant changes in the weather, from hot to cold, from wet to dry, etc., cause them sooner or later to split or leak, and then the Player must be repaired.

Ask the man who owns one if this is not so.

In the Cecilian Piano-Player the primary and secondary pneumatics, and also the wind chest, are built of steel, brass, and phosphor bronze, and consequently are never affected by atmospheric or climatic changes of any kind, and practically do away with all necessity for repairs.

Furthermore, the Metal Action of the Cecilian enables it to give a more perfect musical performance than anything heretofore accomplished by any Piano-Player.

The Metal Action is now put into the Cecilian (cabinet) Piano-Player, the Sohmer-Cecilian, and the Farrand-Cecilian pianos.

FULL PARTICULARS SENT ON REQUEST

OLD STYLE
PRIMARY PNEUMATIC
MADE OF WOOD AND LEATHER

The
FARRAND
COMPANY,
DETROIT,
MICH.

London, Eng.
Paris, France.

OLD STYLE
SECONDARY PNEUMATIC
MADE OF WOOD AND LEATHER

the TONE-OLA built by the Hasbrouck Piano Company of New York, the AERO-TONE of Kelso and Company, New York, and the STERLITONE of Derby, Connecticut's, Sterling Piano Company. And Autopiano's SYMPHOTONE, Price and Teeple's SYMPHONOLA (made in Chicago), Pflueger Brothers PLAYOLA, and the MARVEOLA of New York's Weser Brothers — the latter obviously connoting a marvelous mechanism. Someone even built a PURE-A-TONE!

And in this period also came the PLAYOTONE, made by the Autotone Company (in turn controlled by Hardman Peck), the PRIMATONE, made by Foster-Armstrong of East Rochester, New York, the MELODISTYLE (evidently an electric machine) made by Milwaukee's Waltham Company, Gulbransen's DUO-CONCERTO (used in grands exclusively), the PLAYAPIANO put out by the Lawson Piano Company of New York, Lindenberg's WONDER-TONE made in Columbus, Ohio, and the VACUOLA (a reference to the fact that player pianos operate by

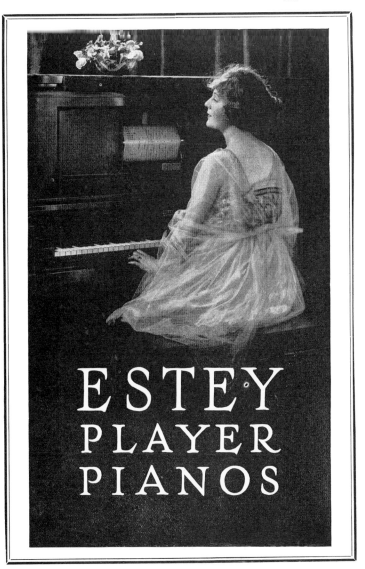

vacuum), an action made by the Ballou-Dart Piano Player Company of Hartford, Connecticut.

Other names worthy of mention are the PISTON-OLA, a British make which used small pistons instead of bellows, or pneumatics, to operate the keys, the SOLOTONE put out by the Schaff Company of Huntington, Indiana, the REPRO-PHRASO of Chicago's Story and Clark Company, to say nothing of the MELL-O-TONE and the PLAYERNOLA of New York's Becker Brothers!

Yet with all this odd assortment of names, there undoubtedly were scores more, for a standard trade practice has always been for some manufacturers to market unlabeled pianos through department stores and other merchants, who, in turn, would dream up their own special name to stencil on the fallboard above the keys.

Undoubtedly the two most famous trademarks in the history of mechanical music are the Victor Dog and the Gulbransen Baby. Not only were the pages of the *Saturday Evening Post* and other popular magazines adorned with both of them, but every well-equipped dealer in either line had a papier-mache model of either the dog, the baby, or both adorning his show window.

As it is with the great organizations of the mid-twentieth century selling television, automobiles, cigarettes, and any other consumer product one can name, the success of the concern depends mainly on its merchandising ability and not so much on inherent basic differences in product. Here the merchandisers really came into their own; the inventors had had their play. And typically, each organization lined up behind its particular gimmick for sales appeal — some relied on catchy adjectives, others on the fact that "anyone could play." Gulbransen leaned heavily on the curious line to the effect that unless your friends somehow saw the player roll, they would think you were really playing the piano yourself! Others (notably Autopiano) featured endorsements, assuming that somehow the fact that the Pope or the Shah of Persia or the Japanese Royal Family liked their player piano would influence the public to buy their brand. Melville Clark even published a letter expressing the delight of the Dowager Empress of China with her machine! Of course, if you didn't care for the brand endorsed by royalty, you were sure to find one favored by the latest movie matinee idol of the day.

Gulbransen Trade Mark.

Easy to play—easy to sell— easy to keep in good order.

Nationally priced — nationally advertised — nationally esteemed.

GULBRANSEN
Player-Piano
GULBRANSEN-DICKINSON CO., 3242 W. Chicago Avenue, CHICAGO

There was never any shortage of gadgets to help the piano dealer push sales of players. More ambitious concerns bought Bowen or Atwood loaders for their Ford cars and had their salesmen take them right out to the farmyards of America to deliver their pitch! Others depended on gimmicks right in the display rooms, like the Moto-Playo bench which could be used to assure the customer that he could indeed produce music with no manual effort whatever.

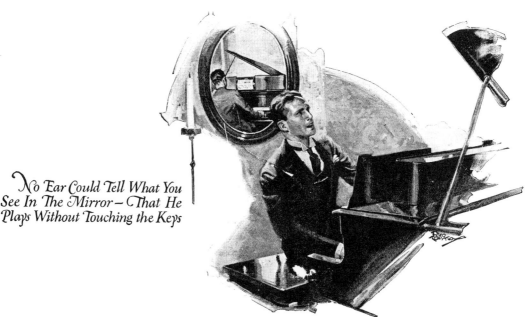

No Ear Could Tell What You See In The Mirror—That He Plays Without Touching the Keys

The Biggest Thrill in Music is playing it *Yourself*

And now even untrained persons can do it

IN MUSIC as in every human activity, it's your own participation that rouses your emotions most.

It's the ball you drive down the fairway yourself that stirs your blood.

It's the song that you sing yourself that touches your heart.

It's the number that you dance yourself that entrances you.

And this human trait is even more pronounced in the music that you play.

There is rapture in listening to the playing of others; but in playing yourself there's the thrill of personal creation, the hush of ineffable sweetness, and the flight of joy to heights no other music can attain. It is here you find your supreme inspiration.

Only Piano of Its Kind

We admit that it seems incredible that untrained persons can play like this—can play by roll, equal to playing by hand. Indeed it would be impossible were it not for the Gulbransen Registering Piano, the only instrument of its kind in the world.

For neither ordinary player-pianos, nor reproducing pianos can give you complete control of the keys, the same as in hand playing. The Gulbransen alone does this.

Hence you can play not "mechanical" music, but human music, with the human expression—the Time,

You can play better by roll than many who play by hand

And you can play ALL pieces while they can play but a few

the Touch and the Tone Volume that you yourself impart to it.

You can play a piano solo correctly, accenting the melody and chords.

You can play dance music in perfect time and rhythm.

You can play an accompaniment for voices or instruments, subduing the melody to a whisper, pausing for the singer, and playing only the bass or lower register.

Why Pianists Own It

You could not do more if you played by hand than you can do by roll on the Gulbransen. And you could not play so many pieces.

That's one reason many pianists own the Gulbransen Registering Piano, notwithstanding that this same beautifully toned instrument is made without the roll-playing action.

Pieces they study, they can play by hand. More difficult compositions by Chopin, Rachmaninoff and others of the masters—they can play by roll.

Then there are many who cannot read a single note of sheet music who play by roll on the Gulbransen beautifully, easily and inspiringly. Who accompany artists who would not sing to "mechanical" music—whose only exception to hand-played accompaniments are those played by roll on the Gulbransen Registering Piano.

This Free Book
"Your Unsuspected Talent"
Will Surprise You

Mail us the coupon today for our new illustrated book de luxe—"Your Unsuspected Talent—Its Discovery and Enjoyment." It reveals a Treasure Trove of musical compositions. It shows the joys of playing them at home.

With this book comes the address of the nearest Gulbransen show room where you can see and play all Gulbransen models—Grand and Upright.

Mail the coupon now—Indoor Months are here. Let music make home gay.

Gulbransen Suburban Registering Piano, $530

Style S, same model in a straight Piano, $330

The New Gulbransen
GRAND
As a Straight Piano, $785
As a Registering Piano, $1275

National Price—Suitable Terms

Gulbransen pianos are sold at the same cash price, freight prepaid, throughout the United States. For your protection, we stamp this price on the back, where you can read it. And Gulbransen dealers are prepared to deliver any model, Grand or Upright, for a small cash payment—balance to suit the purchaser. A reasonable allowance will be made for your present piano, if you own one.

Four Upright Models—Community, $450, Suburban, $530, Country Seat, $615, White House, $700; Straight Grand, $785; Registering Grand, $1275.

The Nat'l Association of Piano Tuners recommends that all pianos be tuned twice a year. Your Gulbransen deserves this care.

GULBRANSEN
The *Registering* Piano

SEND THIS COUPON
to Gulbransen Company, 3232 Chicago Ave., Chicago
for Color-Illustrated Book De Luxe
"Your Unsuspected Talent—Its Discovery and Enjoyment"

Name_____

Address_____

City_____ State_____

☐ Check here if you own a piano and we will send you form enabling us to estimate value.

"Easy to Play"

Gulbransen Trademark

The Piano that Plays Itself

THERE are many social occasions in most homes where a self-playing piano run by a small electric motor will add a great deal of enjoyment.

The Harmonist Self-Playing Piano, technically known in our Blue Book as "Style P,"* is made in two forms.

In one form it is a complete piano. The only difference between it and an ordinary upright piano is in the attachment of the player at the right, underneath the keyboard. The illustration shows this attachment closed. The small picture shows it opened. Here the perforated music is inserted. A small electric motor inside the piano operates the music, which is played automatically, with expression, furnishing music for small dancing parties, receptions, luncheons and other social things where **real** music is wished without the attention of a pianist or an operator upon a piano player. The piano itself is in appearance an ornament to the finest home. It can be used as an ordinary piano to be played upon by hand in the ordinary way without any change whatever. The other form is that of a cabinet piano player, similar to the Harmonist Foot-Power Piano Player, with the exception of the electric attachment. This player can be moved up to any piano, the wire attached to an ordinary light socket, and it will play the Harmonist music automatically, giving it its proper expression. In this style the expression is subject to the control of the operator by disconnecting the automatic device, using the lever to do so.

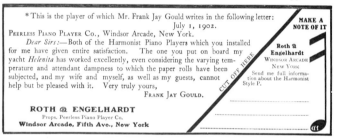

Either of these forms of the Harmonist will prove a welcome addition to every home, fraternity chapter house, lodge room, social hall, ballroom or any place, private, semi-public or public, where good music, accurately rendered, will add to the festivity of the occasion. You may have the automatic player built into any make of any piano you desire, or have it furnished in our own piano, which we recommend for both its musical qualities and its artistic appearance.

---

* This is the player of which Mr. Frank Jay Gould writes in the following letter:

July 1, 1902.

PEERLESS PIANO PLAYER CO., Windsor Arcade, New York.

Dear Sirs:—Both of the Harmonist Piano Players which you installed for me have given entire satisfaction. The one you put on board my yacht *Helenita* has worked excellently, even considering the varying temperature and attendant dampness to which the paper rolls have been subjected, and my wife and myself, as well as my guests, cannot help but be pleased with it. Very truly yours,

FRANK JAY GOULD.

ROTH & ENGELHARDT
Props. Peerless Piano Player Co.
Windsor Arcade, Fifth Ave., New York

MAKE A NOTE OF IT

Roth & Engelhardt
WINDSOR ARCADE
NEW YORK

Send me full information about the Harmonist Style P.

CUT OFF HERE

Please mention McClure's when you write to advertisers.

MELVILLE CLARK

—The MAN and His WORK,

The APOLLO-PIANO

THE ORIGINAL 88-NOTE PLAYER

ANTONIUS STRADIVARIUS made a better violin because he knew the violin. Melville Clark knows the player piano. In the music trades his personal supremacy in the field of pneumatics is unquestioned. Recently the entire player piano industry paid a remarkable tribute to his genius in adopting the 88-note (complete keyboard) principle, which for eight years was exclusively an Apollo feature.

Other Apollo features (invented and patented by Melville Clark) are:

Apollo Human Touch—The pneumatic fingers of the Apollo 88-Note Player Piano strike DOWN on TOP of the keys, just as the human fingers do in manual playing. Other players strike UP on the sticker of the action, or UNDER the keys at the back. Both of these methods are unnatural and are the cause of the unnatural, mechanical music produced by other player pianos.

Apollo Self-acting Motor—A patented motor that runs the music roll and rewinds it without pumping or electricity. Other players are equipped with air motors which necessitate tiresome pedaling. The Apollo's self-acting motor costs five times as much to manufacture as the old style leather-and-wood air motor.

Solo-Apollo Accenting Device — The latest triumph of Melville Clark and the climax in the development of the Apollo Player Piano toward an ideal. The Solo-Apollo actually emphasizes the melody as a virile idea of the composer, and as he intended it to be emphasized.

More Apollos In Use—Notwithstanding the Apollo costs $25 to $50 more than ordinary player pianos, there are more 88-note Apollo Player Pianos and Piano Players in use than all other similar instruments combined.

There are only three player pianos made that can even lay claim to being artistic. Write for descriptive literature and a simple, sure method by which you can decide the player piano question.

Melville Clark Piano Co., 434 Steinway Hall, **Chicago**

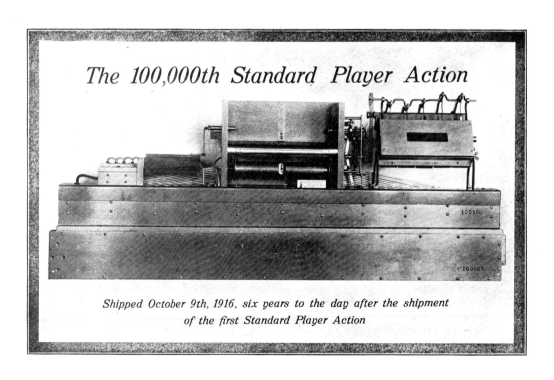

The 100,000th Standard Player Action

Shipped October 9th, 1916, six years to the day after the shipment of the first Standard Player Action

The Graduation Gift

Recent reductions in the price of pianos has made the Player-piano a very popular graduation gift this year.

There is not one other gift which will give your daughter so much real, permanent pleasure and lasting happiness as a Playerpiano.   Music makes the home attractive for young folks. The home with music is a Mecca for young people.

Now is the time to buy your Playerpiano.   Prices are lower today than they have been since pre-war days.

Our Playerpianos are equipped with the famous Standard Player Action, which contains numerous features not found in ordinary Playerpianos.

THE MUSIC SHOP

500 Broad Street   **Corner Starr Avenue**

(Mats of this Ad supplied upon request)

"Let's Get Away from Home"

Comforts of Camp?

Comforts of Home

LET'S get away to the great open spaces, where men are men and women get wild, and bugs are bugs, and skeeters are skeeters, and rain is rain; where you get caterpillars in your sandwiches and ants in your sugar and sand in your shoes. Let's sleep on a damp mattress between damp sheets spread on the bosom of Mother Earth, with nothing between us and the pure air, and the sweet wet rain and the singing stinging flies, but a sheet of canvas.

Let's do this. And then let's go back home to where men can be comfortable and women can be happy; where bugs and flies are taboo; where rain can't affect us; where we and our food can be kept clean; where we can enjoy a pleasant and profitable evening with the Player-Piano and books and newspapers, and where we can go to sleep in a snug, clean, dry bed.

Let's have a *Good* Home to return to — a home with *Music* — with a PLAYER-PIANO. We'll find pleasure in the contrast between the rough and the smooth.

STANDARD PNEUMATIC ACTION COMPANY

W. A. Mennie, Pres.

638 West 52nd Street   New York City

Of course, if the prospect already had a piano, perhaps he could be sold an attachable player action which would convert his instrument from the old-fashioned hand-played variety to the very latest in piano vogue! Or if he had a player already and he had bought his share of rolls, he might be a prospect for a FLEX-A-TONE, a Kazoo, or some other noise-maker to embellish his repertoire.

Then, too, every player owner was a prospect for a KLEERNOTE tracker bar pump. Since players are vacuum-operated devices, they suck all kinds of dirt and lint into the small holes in the brass bar over which the paper roll passes, and this was the perfect device to keep them clean and operating properly.

World War I occurred just before the peak of popularity of the player piano. Advertisements suggest that the military services placed some value on these machines as morale builders among the troops, although official military history is vague as to use of grand pianos located by the trenches, as the Behning people would have us believe!

Milton "Invisible"
88-note Player
Library Mission Model
Art Finish

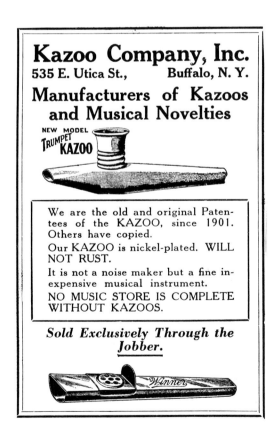

Home and Memories

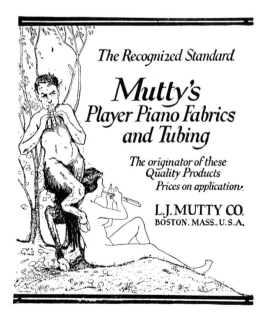

THREE MORE AUTOPIANOS ON BOARD U. S. S. "DELAWARE"

First-Line Battleship Now Equipped With Six Autopianos—Latest Sale of Three Instruments Made by Charles S. Norris, Autopiano Representative in Boston, Mass.

The satisfactory service which the Autopiano, manufactured by the Autopiano Co., New York, has given the officers and men of the U. S. Navy was again manifested last week when three of Autopiano Co. in that city. The instruments were three of the very latest models which have been produced.

The U. S. S. "Delaware," which was built in

The U. S. S. "Delaware," Now Equipped With Six Autopianos

these instruments were purchased for use on the U. S. S. "Delaware." This makes a total of six Autopianos now in use on this battleship, the first three having been purchased some time before the war, but are still in good condition and being used daily.

The sale last week was made by Chas. S. Norris, of Boston, Mass., representative of the

1907, is one of the battleship fleet of the United States Navy and has a displacement of 20,000 tons. During the war it was one of the vessels in the squadron which for nine months patrolled the high seas with the British grand fleet under the command of Admiral Beatty. Since its return to this country it has been stationed in Boston harbor.

The placing of the three new Autopianos on the "Delaware" adds to the long list which have already been sold for use on the various vessels of the U. S. Navy, many of which have been on ships which have seen active service during the war. The test to which these instruments are subjected by their being taken from place to place in various climates and exposed to the atmosphere of the sea at all times gives proof of their durable construction and ability to stand up under any and every condition.

Through the Ages ~ Music Endures

STANDARD PLAYER ACTION

"I *like* my music lessons"

FROM the very first music lesson, a player piano equipped with the Standard Player Action encourages children in the study of music. Through a set of educational music rolls the Standard Player Action can be of assistance in learning to play the piano manually and in simplifying the music-teacher's work. And while the musical education of your children is in process, you have at the same time a wonderful player piano that enables you to play all of the world's best music with the skill of a talented musician.

The Standard-equipped piano brings to every member of the family the pleasure that comes in producing music to fit their own moods and tastes, their own impulses and emotions. This is made possible by the exclusive and patented features of the Standard Player Action. The flexible striking finger gives the human touch. The patent Standard Tracker keeps the rolls in place, insuring perfect reproduction. A special method of air-tight construction brings out the full beauty of the piano's tone. Accent and expression devices encourage individual interpretations.

REGARDLESS OF WHAT PLAYER PIANO YOU BUY, INSIST ON THE STANDARD PLAYER ACTION

The Standard Player Action is simple, smooth in action, and of extraordinary durability. Its superiority is proved by the fact that the manufacturers of 125 different makes of pianos have chosen the Standard Player Action. Look for the big "S" on the pedals.

The Standard Player Action is sold by music dealers everywhere in a wide range of prices, convenient terms if desired. It is guaranteed for five years.

Write for handsome new booklet, *The Heart Appeal of Music*. It will be sent free. Standard Pneumatic Action Company, 648 West 52nd St., New York City.

> STANDARD PNEUMATIC ACTION CO.
> 648 West 52nd St., New York City
> Please send me your free booklet, *The Heart Appeal of Music.*
> Name......................
> Street......................
> City.............State........

Tuners, You Will Enjoy Working With the

Story & Clark
Repro-Phraso

It is always a pleasure to work with and tune a fine instrument' for your work when finished is a source of real satisfaction to both you and the instrument's owner.

There is no other instrument quite like the Repro-Phraso. It is a perfect personal reproducing piano, equipped with special new patented devices that permit of the finest effects. Beautiful expression is obtainable, and the melody sings out with bell-like beauty against a soft background of accompaniment.

If you have not yet seen the Repro-Phraso, be sure to visit the nearest Story & Clark dealer for a personal examination. If you're in New York at the Music Industries Convention in June, *visit the Story & Clark display!* Full information will be furnished you soon, as to place, room numbers, etc.

The Story & Clark Piano Company

315-317 South Wabash Avenue   Chicago, Illinois

ETUDE

"Come, lassie and lad, be blithe and glad,
And away to the May-pole hie,
For every fair has a partner there,
And the players standing by"

Put it out on the lawn for the May Dance~The

STORY & CLARK MINIATURE PLAYER PIANO

Is so small you can easily move it around anyplace

Only
four feet
two inches
high
Finest quality
of tone

Ideal size
for
the small
apartment
or
home

This new model~containing all the exclusive features for which Story & Clark instruments are noted ~is another one of those fine creations which has maintained the leadership of Story & Clark in the manufacture of fine musical instruments since 1857

Priced within reach of every home

The Story & Clark Piano Company
Chicago

New York   Brooklyn   Philadelphia   Pittsburgh   Detroit

The ANGELUS DIAPHRAGM PNEUMATIC and the HUMAN FINGER

The Diaphragm Pneumatic when in action or "striking" is filled with buoyant air, which gives a resilient touch, just like the human finger. Note the absence of creases or corners, which insures greater durability.

DIAPHRAGM PNEUMATIC INFLATED FOR STRIKING

THE Diaphragm Pneumatic is the only means ever devised to give the real human touch. When in action it is an air inflated cushion, with the same firm but resilient and buoyant touch that characterizes the human fingers. All other pneumatics are collapsed when in action, withdrawing from them the buoyancy of the air, resulting in a hard, mechanical touch. The

Diaphragm Pneumatic

is an exclusive feature of the

The Bellows Pneumatic is worked by an exhaust; that is, when it strikes a note the air is entirely withdrawn from it, which causes it to collapse with a hard staccato touch, in no way resembling the pliancy and flexibility of the human finger.

BELLOWS PNEUMATIC WITH AIR EXHAUSTED FOR STRIKING

ANGELUS

and together with the famous Phrasing Lever (patented) and the wonderful Melodant (patented) have made the ANGELUS pre-eminently *the* artistic piano-player.

KNABE-ANGELUS   EMERSON-ANGELUS   LINDEMAN & SONS-ANGELUS   ANGELUS PIANO
The Peerless Knabe Piano   The sweet-toned Emerson   The original and celebrated Linde-   An excellent piano made
and the Angelus.   Piano and the Angelus.   man Piano and the Angelus.   expressly for the Angelus.

THE WILCOX & WHITE CO.,   **MERIDEN, CONN.**
Pioneers in the Piano-Player Industry

ANGELUS HALL   REGENT ST.   LONDON

STEGER
The most valuable piano in the world

¶ Pre-eminently artistic, of superb musical worth, the Steger piano is the perfect realization of the critical desires of a famous family of piano makers.

¶ Steger Pianos and Player Pianos are shipped on approval to persons of responsibility. Write for Steger Style Brochure and convenient terms.

STEGER & SONS
PIANO MANUFACTURING COMPANY
Founded by John V. Steger, 1879
Steger Bldg., Chicago—Factories at Steger, Illinois

YOU'll Like Gulbransen Music, too

No happier folks anywhere — no family group more closely knit together — no home life more delightfully congenial and enjoyable than where the entertainment centers around a Gulbransen!

In the tens of thousands of Gulbransen homes — ask the fathers and mothers. Ask the sons and daughters. Young or old, all say the same about it. All have the same warm feeling for it. Good piano music speaks in language everybody loves and understands. There's no age limit to enjoyment of the Gulbransen!

Children take to the Gulbransen naturally, eagerly, enthusiastically. It's so easy to play. To sing their school songs to Gulbransen accompaniment — "Columbia," "Sweet and Low," "Sleep Kentucky Babe" — is such fun. Quickly and easily mastered Gulbransen In-

struction Rolls stir their interest in music — encourage and sustain it — where tedious finger practice and long months and years of study only dull it.

Grown-ups prefer the Gulbransen because Registering Piano music is so superior, so distinctive. You play it with so much of musical *feeling* and *expression.* The only music you can honestly compare it with is exceptionally fine hand-playing.

If you do not know the difference between the Gulbransen Registering Piano and ordinary player-pianos, investigate. Take the children with you when you do. Their intuitive young minds will help you detect the difference in a hurry!

Write us for form on which to describe your present piano. We will then tell you its trade-in value. No obligation. Or, send for name of nearest dealer. The most convincing test of a Gulbransen is to put your feet on the pedals and play it.

GULBRANSEN COMPANY
3232 West Chicago Avenue · CHICAGO

HARPER'S MAGAZINE ADVERTISER.

WHAT more delightful gift, or what better time to give it! The full enjoyment of all music, for all time, in

The ANGELUS PLAYER-PIANO

In the development of the ANGELUS PLAYER-PIANO a most significant advance has recently been made, giving still greater emphasis to the fact of its complete supremacy. Where with all other instruments the player must rely for the correctness of the music upon faulty or incomplete methods of roll-marking, the ANGELUS performer now has the *Artistyle* system of expression characters to guide his playing. This new method of roll-marking is the most effective aid to the production of good music in that it makes the way easy, even for the novice, to render a selection in a manner which must satisfy and delight the most critical of listeners. The *Artistyle* system of expression characters, the *Melodant,* the famous *Phrasing Lever* and other expression devices are all exclusive features of the ANGELUS instruments.

Hear and Play the ANGELUS instruments yourself. Write us for address of your nearest representative and free booklet.

THE WILCOX & WHITE CO.

MERIDEN, Conn. *Established 1876.* Regent House, Regent St., LONDON.

If you are interested in a Player Action that can be installed with complete satisfaction in any size piano, old or new,

get in touch with the

Chicago Player Action Company

W. N. Van Matre, Pres.

ROCKFORD   ILLINOIS

Our famous Player Piano spells the biggest opportunity for the wide-awake Merchant.

The AUTOPIANO International Achievements—
Its Remarkable Expression Capabilities and Durability—

The Unequalled Advertising and Selling Aids which characterize our proposition—make it the one Player to concentrate on and to push vigorously.

Let us place before you the unusual possibilities our Player Piano offers for you.

THE AUTOPIANO COMPANY

R. W. LAWRENCE, President
12th AVENUE, 51st and 52d STREETS
NEW YORK CITY

AUTOPIANO COMPANY, THE. Incorporated under the laws of the State of New York; capital stock, $1,000,000, fully paid up. Financial and commercial standing of this corporation is unquestioned. Officers: Paul Brown Klugh, president; F. E. Edgar, vice-president and sales manager; Emil Neff, treasurer; William J. Keeley, secretary. The company was one of the first concerns to put on the market a successful interior player-piano, the first having been shipped in 1904. It is said that there are twice as many Autopianos in use as any other player-piano. The Autopiano Co. occupies its modern six-story plant on the Hudson River and extending from Fifty-first to Fifty-second streets, New York. It is the largest factory in the world devoted exclusively to the manufacture of player-pianos. The Autopiano is conceded by experts to be one of the best player-pianos in the trade. The piano itself is of first-class construction; the tone is rich and clear; the case designs are artistic and built with special regard to player-piano requirements. The material used in the Autopiano is the best obtainable; the labor employed is the pick of the industry; the methods applied are the most modern and up to date known, and the executive personnel would be considered unusual in any industry. The player action is noted for its simplicity and durability, containing many exclusive patented features and embodying the very latest and most effective devices. This company manufactures the Autopiano in several attractive styles, and also the Autopiano Grand, the Autopiano Electric, and the Autopiano Welte-Mignon. The fame of the Autopiano is world-wide. It is sold in almost every American country and throughout Canada, in the Alaskan gold fields, in Mexico, South America, the Argentine, as well as in Europe. Autopianos have been shipped to India, China, Siberia, Japan, the Philippines, Australia, Africa, Persia, Egypt and Cape Colony, Ceylon, Korea and many other "out of the way" countries. The Autopiano has received the highest awards at the following expositions: Grand Highest Award, Alaska-Yukon-Pacific Exhibition, 1909; Grand Prix, Rotterdam, Holland, International Musical Exhibition, 1909; Gold Medal, Manchester, England, Industrial Exhibition, 1910; Gold Medal, Manchester Coronation Exhibition, 1911; Highest Award, Appalachian Exposition, Knoxville, Tenn., 1911; Gold Medal, Second Insular Fair, Porto Rico, 1911; Gold Medal, Festival of Empire, London, England, 1911; Grand Prix, International Exposition, Petrograd, Russia, 1911; Gran Premio, International Exposition, Turin, Italy, 1911; Gold Medal, International Exhibition, Leeds, England, 1912; Grand Prix and Diploma of Honor, Anglo-American Exhibition, at London, England, in 1914; Gold Medal and Diploma of Honor, International Exposition at Lyons, France, 1914. The State Commissioners of more than twenty States officially selected the Autopiano for their respective State Buildings at the Panama-Pacific International Exposition, San Francisco, Cal., 1915. The New Mexico and Washington State Buildings of the Panama-California Exposition, San Diego, Cal., 1915, also officially selected the Autopiano. In addition to this practically universal selection at these last two named expositions, the Autopiano received at the San Francisco Panama-Pacific International Exposition the following awards: (1) Medal of Honor; (2) Gold Medal; (3) Silver Medal; and at the Panama-California Exposition at San Diego a Diploma of Honor and a Gold Medal. Among the other notable triumphs achieved by this splendid player-piano are a beautiful Gold Medal and the Order of St. Sylvester from the late Pope Pius X, the White Cross of Merit and Royal Appointment from His Majesty, Alphonso XII., King of Spain, and two Gold Medals and Royal Appointments from His Imperial Majesty, Ahmed, Shah of Persia. The Autopiano is also official purveyor to the royal families of Japan and is in the palaces of Prince Shidinadva and Prince Ito; this distinction is also enjoyed in Korea, where Prince Ye of the reigning dynasty has an Autopiano in his palace. There are Autopianos in the homes of Puccini, the composer, and Victor Herbert, who have expressed their appreciation of this instrument. Among many other famous musicians who have endorsed the Autopiano are Luisa Tetrazzini, Mary Garden, Alice Verlet and Federico Carasa. The officers and crews of more than one hundred vessels in the United States and foreign navies have purchased and use these instruments. The manner in which they stand up under all sorts of climatic conditions and hard usage incident to life on shipboard is strong evidence of their great durability. Abbé Lorenzo Perosi, leader of the famous Sistine Choir of Rome, and director of all music used in the Catholic Church, has honored the Autopiano Co. with a testimonial as to the artistic quality of this remarkable instrument. The most recent of all Autopiano achievements was the appointment of the Autopiano Co. as official purveyors to the Holy See by His Holiness Pope Benedict XV. This latest appointment means that the Autopiano is pre-eminent at the Vatican. The Autopiano is also extremely popular in the U. S. Army. Seven were recently shipped to be used at Fortress Monroe; and an order was received recently for 75 Autopianos to be shipped to various army encampments throughout the United States, bringing the total of Autopianos in use in the United States Army to about 150. The Autopiano line of upright player-pianos consists at present of the style S, Studio Model; Style G, Grand Prix Model; Style P, Soloist Model; Style O, Conservatory Model; Style E, Concert Model, and the Exposition Model.

No Better Pianos Made At These Low Prices

J. L. MITCHELL, Manager,
Music Department

Tone is the final test of quality in any musical instrument. Design, materials and workmanship must all be of the best if the tone is to be satisfactory. Deficiency in any one of these three factors may offset the other two.

Because we know this to be true, we set rigid standards for the materials and workmanship used in all our musical instruments. They are made by manufacturers of long experience and unquestioned reputation for quality.

Dollar for dollar, we believe you will find finer tone quality in the instruments shown on these pages than in any other instruments obtainable in this country. And you will find our prices to be uniformly from 25 to 50 per cent lower than prices on the same quality instruments sold elsewhere. Remember that Tone is the Test. Don't judge by the low price—try the instruments. You are safe under our guarantee.

J. L. Mitchell

$10.00 Down
$15.00 A Month
No Interest

Anyone Can Play the Windsor—No Musical Training Needed
Easy Action, Perfect Expression and Control

Give yourself and your family the supreme satisfaction which comes only from making music—not from merely listening to it. Put this fine Windsor Player Piano into your home; play your favorite selections yourself, whenever you want them. Easy action; superb tone; perfect expression exactly as you wish it to be. Beautiful rubbed bright finish on veneer of genuine Mahogany, Walnut or Quarter Sawed Oak. Has full metal plate. Bushed tuning pins. Genuine wool felt hammers. Strong brass hinges and pedals.

You would pay at least $50 more for a player piano of this quality elsewhere. Plays any standard rolls; transposing device; finest workmanship throughout. Generous terms without interest. Height, 54 inches; width, 60 inches; depth, 28½ inches. Bench and rolls included.
See "Estimated Freight Charges" below. Shipping weight, complete, 835 lbs. Use Easy Payment Order Blank No. 1 on Page 613.

267 D 27—Mahogany...........$398.00
267 D 28—Walnut............. 398.00
267 D 29—Oak............. 398.00
Shipped from Factory near Chicago

The Windsor without Player Action

The same fine cabinet work as above without the player action. Height, 54 inches; width, 63 inches; depth, 26 inches. Bench included. Shipping weight, 760 pounds. Easy Terms of $10 down and $10 a month. Use Easy Payment Order Blank No. 1 on Page 613. See "Estimated, Total Freight Charges" below.

267 D 2—Mahogany...........$284.00
267 D 3—Walnut............. 284.00
267 D 4—Oak............. 284.00
Shipped from Factory near Chicago

$10.00 Down
$15.00 A Month
No Interest

Our Finest Windsor Player Piano

Remember that your investment in a Windsor Player Piano is not for today or tomorrow. This Supreme Windsor contains a lifetime of pleasure and entertainment, for every member of your family. Resonant, sweet singing tone; perfect expression control; automatic tracking device; balanced pedals for easy playing; player mechanism of most modern type, all tubes of fiber covered metal. Compare it with any player piano retailing for $100 more.

The handsome, graceful case is built up layer on layer. It can not warp and endanger the tone of your Windsor. Veneer of genuine Mahogany, Burl Walnut or Quartered Oak,

rubbed to a French polish. New Empire top does away with the disfiguring top hinge; Strong piano hinges and pedals of solid brass, genuine ivory keys. Height, 54½ inches; width, 60½ inches; depth, 28 inches. Bench, cabinet and rolls included.
See "Estimated Freight Charges" below. Shipping weight, complete, 880 pounds. Use Easy Payment Order Blank No. 1 on Page 613.

267 D 68—Mahogany.........$485.00
267 D 69—Walnut............. 485.00
267 D 70—Oak............. 485.00
Shipped from Factory near Chicago

$25.00 Down
$15.00 A Month
No Interest

Beautiful Windsor Baby Grand Piano
Priced Below the Usual Retail Price of an Upright

This wonderful Windsor Baby Grand Piano has been the choice of many music lovers who wanted only the best for their homes. A truly fine musical instrument possessing a rare quality of tone. Deep, resonant bass; clear, singing treble; easy responsive action; and a design and finish that will excite the enthusiastic approval of all who see it. Yet the price of this masterpiece—the baby grand she has always wanted—is little more than you would have to pay elsewhere for a good upright piano. And only $25 will place it in your home, with generous terms and not one cent of interest.

Your living room or music room affords ample space for the Windsor Baby Grand without the slightest appearance of crowding.

It is only 57 inches wide and 57 inches long. Try it in your home for thirty days liberal guarantee. You are taking ab no risk. Bench included.

Double veneered with your choice uine Mahogany or Walnut, satin finish.
See "Estimated Freight Charges" Shipping weight, complete, 1080, poun Easy Payment Order Blank No. 1 613.

267 D 58—Mahogany, satin finish $
267 D 59—Mahogany, high polish
267 D 60—Walnut, satin finish
267 D 61—Walnut, high polish
Shipped from Factory near Chic

Free with Windsor Player Pianos

With No. 267 D 27-28-29—ten Music Rolls and Bench.
With No. 68-69-70—ten Music Rolls, Music Roll Cabinet and Bench.

30 Days' Free Trial of Any Windsor in Your Home

When writing to advertisers kindly mention Harper's Magazine.

Sir Harry Lauder, Scotch Comedian, Praises Performance of Gulbransen Registering Piano

Sir Harry Lauder, Famous Scot, Poses for Photograph with R. H. Nimmo and the Latter's Sons, Hamilton and A. Nimmo, in Front of the Establishment of Messrs. Nimmo & Sons, Music Dealers, Wellington, New Zealand

A. G. Gulbransen

SIR HARRY LAUDER, famous singer of Scotch songs, recently visited the store of Messrs. Nimmo & Sons, dealers in Gulbransen instruments in Wellington, New Zealand, where he heard a demonstration of the Gulbransen registering piano.

During his stay in Wellington he returned to the store twice and listened to demonstrations staged at his request.

Sir Harry was loud in praise of the Gulbransen registering piano. On one of his visits to the store he posed for the photograph that is reproduced above. The photograph was autographed and sent to the Gulbransen Co., Chicago.

39

THE NEW AUTOPIANO GRAND NOW INTRODUCED.

Autopiano Co., Through the Medium of a Most Elaborate and Handsome Catalog, Presents the Latest Addition to Its Line—One of the Smallest Instruments of Its Kind.

The Autopiano Co., Fiftieth street and Twelfth avenue, New York, announces this week the Autopiano grand. This instrument is to be made in three distinct styles, known as styles GA, GB and

Autopiano Grand, Style "GA."

GC. This grand is one of the smallest made in the world. It is four feet eight inches in length and four feet six inches in width. It can be furnished in mahogany with polished or art finish and Circassian walnut in art finish on special orders.

All the features of the Autopiano upright, which

is internationally known, may be found in this player grand. The expression controls are the same and permit the most delicate phrasing. The pedal action is also practically the same as that of the

Autopiano Grand, Style "GB."

upright and is well known for its ease of operation. The same durable construction which is found throughout all the instruments manufactured by this company will be found in this new addition to its line.

Practically the entire player mechanism is out of

sight underneath the body of the piano. The only difference in comparison with an ordinary grand piano is that the lyre is made in the form of a box and the ...., ... the keybed, where it may be conveniently pulled out or pushed back with great ease.

Simplicity has been the watchword in constructing the player mechanism for this grand piano and all the regulation features are where they may be reached with ease.

Another important feature is the size of the instrument which permits its use in places where space is at a premium, and therefore brings the player grand within reach of persons of moderate means, or who have not purchased a grand because they have felt that they did not have the space required for it.

In announcing this player grand the company has issued a most elaborate and attractive catalog showing the different styles. The booklet is printed in blue and brown, and the decorations are in keeping with the high standard of the product.

On the front page is shown a number of medals and insignias which have been bestowed upon the makers of the Autopiano by crowned heads and others.

Following a short and snappy introduction there are presented illustrations of the new Autopiano grand in its various styles. Two views of each style are given, one showing the player mechanism open for playing and the other closed. The illustrations are printed in an attractive sepia tint and each is set in a dainty illuminated border of blue and sepia.

The new catalog is a volume that is a credit to its compiler and well worthy of the new Autopiano product.

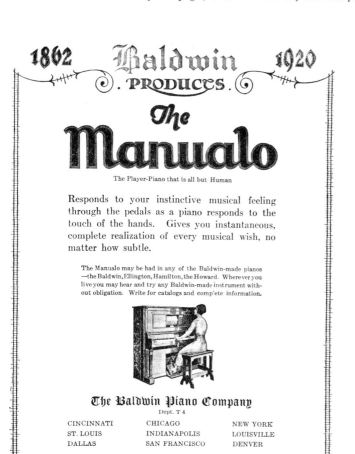

MUSIC WILL HELP YOU

To Harmonize

Yourself with your condition
Your work with your pleasure
Your family with your home

MUSIC will help you to live your life so as to get the *most out of it*, to do your work so you can put the *most into it*, and it will help *every* member of your family as it helps you.

We have just passed through strenuous times. Music carried us over the rough places, kept our hearts up and our nerves steady. The whole nation worked with a will, worked together and accomplished its purpose to the rhythm of music. And the rhythm of music will never pass out of our lives. It will be waiting for us at the end of a hard day's task.

It will bring us rest when rest is what we need. It will add to our gaiety when we want the brightness to sparkle. It will fill the empty chair when we are lonesome. It will bring us quiet contentment, rich enjoyment, solid comfort according to our desire and the need of the moment.

Yes, it will help every one of us over stony paths and along the broad highway. And it will help each member of our family, for it develops that community of interest, that bond of unity so valuable *to a family* or *to a nation.*

See that music brings its blessings to *you* and *your* family.

Buy a piano, a player-piano or a phonograph and you will increase your efficiency and your pleasure, the contentment of your family and will brighten the atmosphere round about you.

MUSIC in the Piping Times of PEACE

Copyrighted, 1919
L. W. Fairchild, New York

— THE MYSTERIOUS CHRISTMAS PACKAGE —

— THE PACKAGE OPENED —

The Mysterious Christmas Package

It was moved in with as great stealth as its weight and bulk would permit. It was wrapped about with a covering that hid its real shape. The men handling it, supervised by Father Jones, made as little noise as possible in getting it into the living-room. But sharp eyes and ears, kept awake by thoughts of Santa Claus, heard strange sounds, and peeping through the window saw a strange sight, and then went to bed fully mystified.

But what a glad surprise there was for everyone when the mysterious big package was opened Christmas morning, and revealed a Playerpiano.

And what a happy man was Father Jones at the end of the day when every-one declared that this "Christmas with music" was the happiest one the Jones family had ever had.

At the dinner table

Without any assistance on your part the wonderful Telektra will play your piano with perfect musical expression while you and your guests are gathered around the dinner table. You may turn to the transmitter at any time and by a mere turn of the wrist vary the interpretation to suit either your guests or your own particular musical fancies. Regardless of where in the house your piano may be situated, this distinctive Telektra feature enables you to easily and comfortably enjoy the luxury of the most artistic piano playing while you "let good digestion wait on appetite and health on both."

The best known electrically operated home players in the early days of the player industry in addition to the Electrelle were the two put out by the Tel-Electric Company of New York. These were the Tel-Electric ($350) and the Telektra ($450) both of which were attachments to be put on existing pianos, either grand or upright, and both of which were operated from thin sheet brass music rolls placed in a special control box which could be moved from place to place at the end of a cable. The machines were made in Pittsfield, Massachusetts, and one of the selling points in their advertising was "the one player that convalescents and elderly folks can operate." The company was organized in 1905 by John Forrest Kelly, who was one of the first college-trained electrical engineers in America. He received the Ph.D. Degree from Stevens Institute of Technology in Hoboken, New Jersey, in 1881. A one-time associate of Thomas Edison, he did much fundamental work in development of alternating-current systems for transmission of electricity. He was one of the founders of a company which formed the foundation of the giant General Electric facility in Pittsfield, Massachusetts.

This Bank of Electro Magnets, one for every note, is the only attachment necessary to transform your piano into the most artistic of player pianos. The Telektra transmitter is attached to this bank of magnets by a small invisible cord which may be of any desired length. There is no part of the Telektra inside the piano.

This Piano is equipped for the Telektra Piano Player. Note the absence of bellows, tubes, valves, etc. Nothing to get out of order—nothing that damp weather can effect. The small attractive box under the keyboard is attached by an electric cord, which may be of any length, to the Telektra player itself.

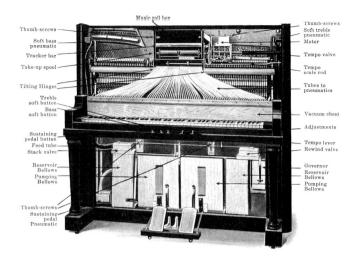

Music roll box

Thumb-screws
Soft bass pneumatic
Tracker bar
Take-up spool
Tilting Hinges
Treble soft button
Bass soft button
Sustaining pedal button
Feed tube
Stack valve
Reservoir Bellows
Pumping Bellows
Thumb-screws
Sustaining pedal Pneumatic

Thumb-screws
Soft treble pneumatic
Motor
Tempo valve
Tempo scale rod
Tubes to pneumatics
Vacuum chest
Adjustments
Tempo lever
Rewind valve
Governor
Reservoir Bellows
Pumping Bellows

Above is a representative Pneumatic Player Piano. Compare its complicated mechanism of bellows, tubes, valves, screws, levers, buttons and adjustments of various kinds with the simplicity of the Telektra-ly equipped piano shown opposite. Tuning often requires the removal of a part of this mechanism.

Why the Telektra construction is superior--

Contrast the Telektra and the pneumatic player. The latter is a mystic maze of bellows, wheels, tubing, valves and intricate mechanism, ready and willing at all times to get out of order, and decidedly expensive to repair.

The Telektra consists of two parts, the player itself or transmitter and a small box containing a bank of electro-magnets that is attached to the under side of the piano keyboard, each one of these magnets operating a single key. This small and attractive box containing the bank of electro-magnets, the only part directly attached to the piano, is connected with the transmitter by a small invisible cable which may be of any desired length. The current from the transmitter vitalizes these magnets and the keys are depressed, depressed with a soft, velvet-like touch or with thunderous force according to the strength of the electric impulse which the person playing has under his absolute control.

The pneumatic player is operated by tiresome pumping of treadles; the motive power of the Telektra is electricity—your feet have nothing to do. With the pneumatic player for piano effects, pump gently, but not too gently or the tone will die; for forte passages, pump hard; for fortissimo effect, pump very hard. For pianissimo effects with the Telektra use less

current, for full-toned effects use more current, all governed by a mere turn of the wrist.

The pneumatic player plays from the interior of the mechanism; the Telektra most closely approximates the finger touch, playing in a natural way directly from the keys. It is brains and fingers that count in artistic piano playing. The Telektra supplies electric fingers, in action wonderfully like human fingers. One's attention is not divided between head, hand and foot work. The feet are idle, the mind is free.

The pneumatic player uses music rolls cut in paper, that have a tendency to tear, warp and swell and that require complicated mechanism to make them track properly. The Telektra uses practically indestructible music rolls cut in a metal ribbon thinner than paper. They cannot shrink or swell. Damp weather has no effect on them. The expression is cut into these rolls as indicated by the composer, to be used or not as you may elect. They are economical in cost and are rewound by electricity.

The Telektra may be attached to your own piano regardless of its make, age or style in a few hours' time in your own home. While electricity is the motive power of the Telektra, electric current is not necessary in the home. Batteries are furnished.

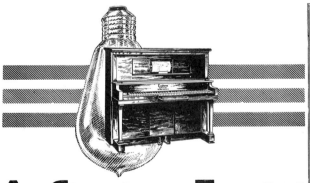

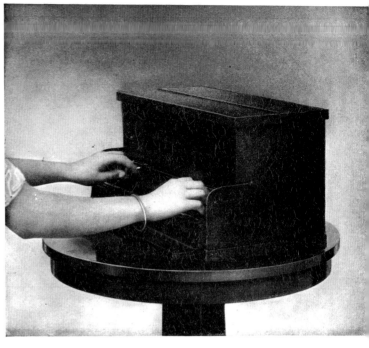

Three ways of playing the Telektra

The Telektra at Sea

The fact that the Telektra has been in successful operation for several years on a number of the big ships of our navy, as well as on various private yachts, proves that the unique mechanical features and wonderful musical qualities of this most artistic player are totally unaffected by the damp sea air. Being made of thin metal, the music rolls cannot shrink or swell, warp or tear, and for this reason alone make the Telektra the only suitable player for the seashore home. Under every condition of temperature and atmosphere the Telektra performs perfectly. For the city home, the summer bungalow, or the yacht, the Telektra is the one practical player.

There are three distinct and different ways in which the Telektra may be played. First, the entirely personal way by which you may put your own interpretation into any composition. A mere pressure of the finger, or a turn of the wrist controls every shade of expression. You may bring out the theme or melody, accent notes, subdue the treble or bass and control the tempo and the pedals. Second, the entirely impersonal way by which you may let the Telektra play entirely without your assistance. In this case the music roll itself puts in all the expression. Third, a combination of the first and second by using the expression cut into the roll, but modifying it to suit your particular fancy. No other player offers these advantages nor has any other player such marvelous control of expression as the Telektra.

The development of electrically operated pianos has opened an attractive opportunity for the exploitation of electric service. Although, of course, no great increase in the use of electrical energy is to be anticipated directly as a consequence of this development, the indirect benefits of one more application of electricity in the household—and particularly one which is so close to the home life of the entire family—must not be overlooked. Central-station interests are, therefore, not losing sight of the electric piano as a means of widening the use of electrical energy. Many companies have installed electric pianos in their display rooms and are receiving the co-operation of piano manufacturers in the demonstration of the instruments.

Recently representatives of the National Piano Manufacturers' Association and members of the merchandising committee of the Commercial Section of the N. E. L. A. conferred to discuss methods of furthering the use of electric player-pianos. A number of electric pianos will be operated for the benefit of the members of the above-named committee when it meets in New York on Dec. 10. Artists will be present at this meeting, and members of the committee will have an opportunity to hear the rendition of well-known works by electricity and by hand. The instruments will also be utilized to accompany violinists and singers and an electrically operated graphonola. The committee session will take place in the afternoon, but in the evening a number of these instruments will be operated before the meeting of the New York Electrical Society, in the Engineering Societies Building, which will be open to the public.

The Modern Electrical Piano a Triumph of Musical Expression

ELECTRICAL WORLD
DECEMBER 4, 1915

As the result of numerous refinements and improvements in electrically operated pianos and their auxiliary apparatus, great artistic possibilities have been opened up, placing the modern electric instrument far ahead of the ordinary foot-pedal player in both artistic expression and, of course, in an entirely different class from the early electric pianos. Delicacy of expression, uniformity in tempo and rhythm, and fidelity in shading possible with no other mechanical player, can be attained by the latest electric pianos when the hand-played rolls of master performers are used. The instruments are especially well adapted for use in accompaniment work. Moreover, where volume and carrying power are required, as in auditoriums or dance halls, two or more electric pianos may be operated in synchronism.

The latest electrically operated pianos or accessories may be divided into three groups, the first two of these groups including auxiliary apparatus which may be attached to play ordinary pianos already in use, and the third including the so-called electrically driven player-pianos. Of the two types of electric apparatus for pianos already in use, one is exemplified by the "Telektra," shown in Figs. 1 and 3, in which the control mechanism and rolls are inclosed in a separate cabinet (Fig. 3), which may be placed at a distance from the piano itself, and the second by the "Flexotone-Electrelle," illustrated in Fig. 2. This auxiliary apparatus often proves especially attractive to persons who are attached to their own pianos for sentimental reasons. The motor for operating an "Autopiano Electric," which is of the player-piano type, belonging to the third group as above classified, is illustrated in Fig. 4.

The "Telektra" consists of two parts, the player itself, or transmitter, and a small box containing a bank of elec-

tromagnets attached to the under side of the piano keyboard, each of the magnets operating a single key. The bank of electromagnets is connected with the transmitter by a light cable, which may be of any desired length. Energy is taken from an ordinary lighting socket and is utilized to operate an 0.25-hp. motor-generator set, which delivers the 14-volt direct current used for control purposes. The music rolls used in the transmitter are of brass. Eighty-eight fingers, corresponding to the eighty-eight keys of the piano, rest on this brass roll. When the tip of a finger falls in a slot of the roll it trips and closes the circuit to the corresponding magnet, energizing the magnet and causing it to pull down the key. Twelve other fingers are utilized for controlling the expression. Magnets are also employed for controlling the pedals. The "Telektra" is made by the Tel-Electric Company, 12 West Thirty-third Street, New York.

The "Flexotone-Electrelle" has been brought out by the American Piano Company, Fifth Avenue and Thirty-ninth Street, New York. The apparatus consists of a suction blower operated by a 1/30-hp. motor, a tracker bar over which the music roll passes, and a bank of magnets which are attached to cork shoes resting on a revolving shaft. In the tracker bar are eighty-eight holes, each of which controls one of the keys of the piano. Inside the tracker bar is a series of silver fingers which are brought into contact with silver-tipped screws whenever perforations in the music roll pass over the holes in the tracker bar, admitting currents of air which force the silver fingers against the silver-tipped screws. These pneumatic impulses close the circuits and energize the magnets, which in turn cause the cork shoes to come in contact with the revolving shaft. The shoes are kicked out and they pull the tapes which are connected to the whippens and throw the hammers against the piano wires. Expression is controlled by means of a flexible rail divided into four sections upon which the hammers rest. Keys are provided to control this rail in such a way that the distance between the hammers and the strings can be instantly changed, not only on the whole keyboard, but also on any part of the keyboard. The speed of the roll is controlled by means of a friction clutch.

The "Autopiano Electric," which is an instrument of the player type, is operated by a universal 110-volt motor, which propels a bellows feeder concealed within the player. The instrument is equipped with a safety valve, making over-pressure impossible. A special accenting lever called the "dynatone" makes possible all tonal contrasts, the manufacturer declares, and covers a wide range of dynamic effects. An automatic re-roll automatic motor stop and automatic re-play device form part of the equipment. Player treadles are also provided, so that the instrument may be used where there are no electric circuits. The manufacturer points out that the "Autopiano Electric" really comprises four instruments in one—a piano, a player with treadles, a player without treadles,

and a "self-operating" instrument. Ordinary eighty-eight-note rolls may be employed with this player-piano, which is being made by the Autopiano Company, Twelfth Avenue and Fifty-first Street, New York.

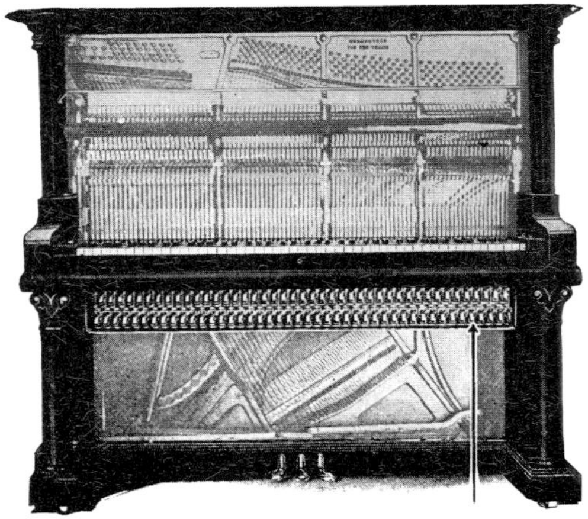

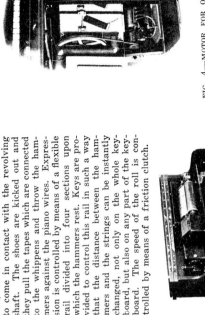

FIG. 4—MOTOR FOR OPERATING PLAYER-PIANO

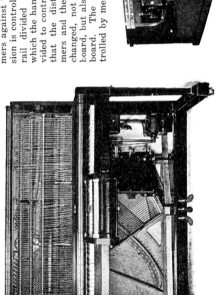

FIG. 3—METAL ROLL IN SEPARATE CABINET

FIG. 2—PIANO OPERATED BY SUCTION BLOWER AND BANK OF MAGNETS

FIG. 1—PIANO WITH BANK OF MAGNETS BENEATH KEYBOARD —OPERATED FROM ROLL IN SEPARATE CABINET

Music Means Health

A NEW word has been born to our language. "MELOTHERAPY." It seems to be an astounding blend of Coueism and—Music.

Dr. Gustave Gayer is the exponent of this remarkable cult and the interesting part of it is that his experiments are proving there is a foundation of truth to everything he says.

Briefly, this is the idea: Music has peculiar curative powers. It works on the body through the mind, the soul, the delicate, responsive membranes of the mind. It effects the nerves. It will not cure all human complaints but it most assuredly will relieve a great many popular conditions, which often baffle physicians.

According to the facts in the case, every home should have a Playerpiano, just as one would have a family physician.

And certain types of melodies should be employed for different kinds of complaints. In the chart, for example, we find the following:—

INSOMNIA		NEURASTHENIA	
Cradle Song	*Brahms*	Simple Aveu	*Thome*
Melody	*Dawes*	Sous la Feuillee	*Thome*
Mighty Lak' a Rose	*Nevin*	La Chinquantaine	*Gabriel-Marie*

DYSPEPSIA		HYSTERIA	
Humoresque	*Dvorak*	Elegie	*Massenet*
Vale Bleu	*Margis*	Dream	*Bartlett*
Serenade	*Moszkowski*	Love Song	*Flegier*

Music, according to Dr. Gayer, is the strongest force in the world to use with suggestion, because it is vibratory—it expresses all human emotions, it is in itself, healing. The next time you have an attack of indigestion, make yourself comfortable and have a friend play something on your Playerpiano. It's not such a bad idea, at that.

The Point of View

The Foot-Driven Player and Its Power-Driven Rival—Two Widely Divergent Views on the Future of the Player, Which Sum Up the Principal Points in the Discussion as to Which Type of Instrument Will Eventually Be Supreme

What are we going to do about the foot-driven player-piano? Are we going to lose interest in it? Are we going to conclude that its day is done? Or if not, what relation is it to bear to its newer and now so prominent rival, the power-driven player?

These are not questions concerning which one should adopt a dogmatic attitude. It is quite easy to take snap judgments in such matters, but snap judgments are, worth simply nothing. We need careful discussion and clear understanding. For if one thing is more certain than another, it is that the player business is approaching an important and possibly critical epoch in its career.

The importance of the questions at issue between the foot-power and the electric-power players does not depend upon any apparent excitement throughout the trade. Despite the conceded merits of various types of reproducing pianos, there is no evidence that the trade is considering the advisability of throwing the foot-driven player overboard. But there is much evidence going to show that retailers are confused by rival claims and are uncertain as to the course they should pursue in the immediate future.

The Review believes that the player trade must take its normal course of development, that it cannot be forced into any unnatural course without disaster, and that it remains for those who are capable of forming good judgments to decide for themselves what direction they had better take.

But it is proper to do what can be done to assist in the formation of correct judgments; and to the end we have secured two impersonal expressions of opinion, which between them appear to sum up the two sides of the case quite completely. The result of reading what follows should be to render the formation of a fair judgment much easier. To perform this service, rather than to dogmatize, is the object of the present "review":

THE DAY OF THE ELECTRIC

By an Eastern Dealer

"You can sum up the whole argument about the future of the player-piano, in my judgment, by saying that the electric player with or without reproducing features, is destined to sweep the board within a few years. The American People have been pretty badly fooled on the player-piano. Fifteen years ago, when we still had the old-fashioned cabinet player attachment, a big and costly attempt was made by several manufacturers to get the people interested in learning to play the player well, and in cultivating music through it. The attempt was a failure all around and the player-piano never has been well played by the people and never will be satisfactory to them as long as they have to work it themselves.

"It would be different if the majority of our people were musical. But everybody knows they are not. They like music, but they want to have some one play and sing for them. They don't want to do it themselves. Of course, I do not mean that no one wants to play the piano or the violin, or to sing. There are thousands and tens of thousands of teachers of music and tens of thousands of students; but these all together make up only a very small proportion of the whole people. The mass of the people are not interested in the kind of music they have to make by themselves. That is my point.

"Now, when we can come to the people with a player-piano that they can play by the mere turning of a switch, we have something that can be called popular. Most people these days are in touch with electric current, and virtually all of them in the cities are fixed so that they can use an electric player if they have one. If we can give them an electric self-playing piano that will rattle off the latest stuff without any bother, then we can catch many thousands who will not bite half so readily at some instrument they have to pump and work at; especially as the hand-played roll and the expression control of the electric make a pretty good musical result quite sure, without any trouble.

"I don't think the foot-driven player is dead yet, of course, for we still sell them and many people prefer them. But I think that as the use of electric current becomes more and more nearly universal, the people will take more and more to the electric and less and less to the foot-driven instrument. The fact is that the player-piano exists for entertainment and not for education. With some gratifying exceptions, the people don't want to be educated and will not thank you for educating them, or trying to do so. They want to be amused and that is all.

"So I think I want to see a moderate priced electric player on the market, that is not full of special features, but can be sold to anybody on the same terms as the ordinary foot-pumper. I want it to be reliable and simple, not easy to get out of order, and above all not too expensive. I don't care for the very high-class electric as a proposition for the mass of the people. That is all right for the cultured But the plain people are not cultured. Yet they do want amusement; and want it without trouble.

"There is, of course, a big field for the high-class electric of the reproducing kind. The people who have culture and can appreciate the best in music ought to have the finest there is; and so far as I can see they are likely to get it. There will be no trouble in selling as many of the fine reproducing players as can be turned out by manufacturers.

"But I think that the moderate-priced electric is, at least, equally important, and I believe that the future of the player business rests largely with it."

MUSIC
Brings Happiness
—:—

Note the contrast between these two homes. In one there is a "straight" piano, but none who can play it,—everyone feels dull and stupid. But in the home downstairs is a Player-Piano. Just note the difference. A PLAYING PIANO IS A PAYING PIANO. -:- -:- -:- -:- -:- -:-

STANDARD PNEUMATIC ACTION COMPANY

W. A. MENNIE, *Pres.*

638 West 52nd Street

New York City

A suggestion to Parents

The charts on the following pages make it clear that by the end of the twenties the player piano was for all practical purposes a dead issue as far as the American public was concerned. Of course, there were a few machines built in the early thirties, and the late model Ampico Reproducing grand pianos were built as late as 1936 and perhaps even later on special order. A few hundred of the Ampico spinet model reproducers were built in the very late thirties, but this was the last of any players in America until the Aeolian Company introduced its key-top Pianola in 1950.

As the picture indicates, this was an attachment which merely had to be lifted onto the keyboard of any piano in order to operate. In spite of the obvious clever design of the unit, evidently it was not sufficiently satisfactory from a sales standpoint to cause history to repeat itself, and it was soon withdrawn from the market.

The next serious attempt at revival came in the mid-1950's, when the Gribble Music Company of Kansas City introduced the "Magic Fingers" to the music world. Like the 1950 version of the Pianola, it was an attachment which could be used with any

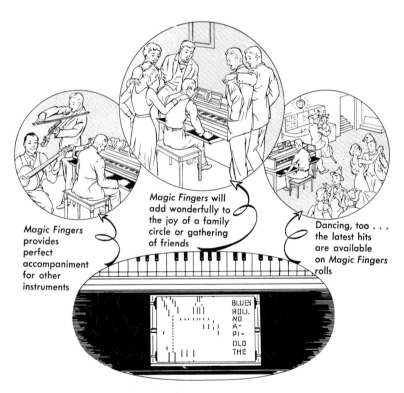

Magic Fingers provides perfect accompaniment for other instruments

Magic Fingers will add wonderfully to the joy of a family circle or gathering of friends

Dancing, too . . . the latest hits are available on *Magic Fingers* rolls

There is no limit to the selection of classical and popular numbers available for Magic Fingers. It plays standard player rolls, thousands of which are available in music stores throughout the world. Lyrics are printed on Magic Fingers rolls, so you may sing as you play. The operation of Magic Fingers is simple. Slide out the drawer, insert a roll, press the switch, close the drawer and enjoy the music Magic Fingers plays so perfectly.

Magic Fingers *is* amazing, not only as a new, live medium of entertainment, but also as a well-perfected, thoroughly tested masterpiece of construction. There are no maintenance problems. Magic Fingers on your present piano, or as a complete innerplayer unit on the new piano of your choice will give you years of trouble-free enjoyment. Plan now to bring this new world of delightful music into your home.

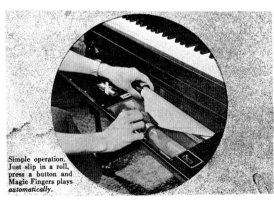

Year	1909	1914	1919	1921	1923	1925	1927	1929	1931	1935
Total number of pianos produced	364,545	326,274	341,652	221,210	347,589	306,584	218,140	130,973	51,370	61,198
Total value	$58,493,846	$56,311,863	$95,823,444	$66,267,751	$104,362,578	$93,676,977	$67,210,775	$37,998,695	$12,780,746	$11,668,531
Upright, with player	34,495	84,456	166,091	101,534	170,549	143,831	76,447	17,336	1,692	418
Upright, reproducer			11,488	5,309	12,658	5,476	4,096	1,445	146	
Separate player attachments	10,898	6,493	25,292	8,160	8,304					
Baby grands with players	21	831	1,195	348	1397	5287	490	384		
Baby grand reproducers			839	2,261	5,372	7,597	7,223	5,905	168	
Parlor grand players			12	21	106	156	42	42		
Parlor grand reproducers			113	1432	2631	2543	1182	2165	311	
Automatic and electric		3,622	3,511	3,374	4,539	4,303	5,974	9,727		
Total reproducers			12,440	9,002	20,661	15,610	12,501	9,515	625	
Total players, all types	45,414	95,402	208,541	122,439	205,556	169,193	95,454	36,504	2,171	418

All figures reported by the U. S. Department of Commerce. Blank spaces represent data not available.

HARDMAN-DUO

piano, but it required a number of hours of labor to affix it, wherein it became permanently mounted under the keyboard. The Magic Fingers was a cleverly designed unit, and was in fact engineered by the Midwest Research Institute. It was aggressively merchandised by its promoters, but for a variety of reasons was not successful.

It suffered from the one problem common to many otherwise salable products — high cost of manufacture. A player device almost inherently requires much hand labor, and the nature of the distributive process being what it is, by the time an article of this type reaches the ultimate consumer there are only a limited number willing to pay the price. Other possible reasons why it did not succeed were the limited manufacturing experience of its promoters and the fact that many technicians were reluctant to do the work required to install it on pianos.

In the face of two recent failures, then, it seemed to many observers that the chance of success of the Hardman Peck Duo, introduced in 1957, was indeed a limited one. But this time the public had money to spend on what appeared to be a well engineered apparatus, and in spite of a $1300 price tag, a fair sized market developed for the piano. It was so successful, in fact, that still another version under the old Pianola name was introduced late in 1960 — a 64-note spinet, selling for just over $1,000.

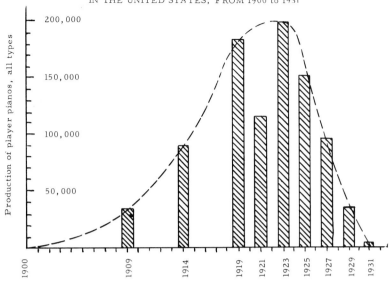

The curve represents the level of popularity of the player piano; total production in this period was about 2,500,000 machines of all types. The drop in production in 1921 was a result of the post-World-War-One business recession.   Source: U.S. Department of Commerce.

During the 1960's other manufacturers jumped into the field, to take advantage of the growing "nostalgia" market, and as the second edition of this book is prepared, perhaps as many as five or six thousand player pianos are being sold each year in the United States. Some operate on pneumatic principles just as in the old days, while others have seen fit to take advantage of new developments in electronics as a means of transferring the holed-sheet to the struck-note.

Certainly no one believes that history will repeat itself to the extent that players will again be as popular as they were in the twenties, but the fact is that a lot of people like these things, and to the extent that the public can be persuaded to part with its money, mechanical music will again return to the scene.

Just how well the marketers and hucksters performed their task of peddling mechanical music to the American public may be judged by the figures on the previous page, which were compiled from data supplied by the United States Government Bureau of the Census. Since the information on manufacturers is not collected each year, it is not possible to make a complete table. Furthermore, in certain years where only one manufacturer was producing a particular type of item, his production figures are not shown because government policy is not to release figures which would reveal the output of a specific company. This would seem to help explain the lack of any figures on grand piano production in the thirties.

Some interesting facts are revealed, nevertheless. The curve of total player production seen here of all types indicates clearly that the peak of production came in 1923, five years after the end of World War I, and that a few short years after this, the industry was just about out of business. One reason is that the phonograph industry was making serious inroads on the market for pianos and players in the late teens and early twenties, but most authorities acknowledge that the radio — which only really began to amount to something in the mid-twenties — was the real cause of the rapid drop in player sales.

Of course, it is interesting to note that sales of coin-operated and automatic pianos did not follow the pattern of the home player. The fact that prohibition was in full swing in the twenties made their market bigger each year, right up until the market crash in 1929. After all, no speakeasy worthy of the name was without its automatic piano! Of course, for that matter, neither was any well-equipped house of ill-repute without such a machine, supplied with music rolls of quick, snappy two-minute tunes to stimulate a fast turnover of trade. Unfortunately, government statistics fail to reveal any clues as to the extent of this usage!

Of course in their desperation to reverse the curve of sales of home pianos, many tricks were tried by the makers. Some built pianos with phonographs inside. Others, like Weydig, built radios in the cabinets in an obvious attempt to follow the old maxim, "If you can't fight 'em, join 'em."

But, if there was any thing within its control which spelled the eventual doom of the industry it was the fact that too few voiced the opinion that here, at last, was a means of bringing real music into the home, and that the person who took the time to learn how to operate a player properly could indeed make very fine music with it. True, most of the manufacturers recognized the need for selling music, not gadgets, but for the most part the dealers — those with whom the public comes in contact — were content to sell the machines to American homes strictly on the basis of getting something sold. The public had little opportunity to learn how to operate properly the machines they bought, with the result that the mechanically produced music they made soon wore pretty thin.

In an attempt to do something about this, player piano playing contests were staged as a means of stimulating interest in proper operation, but they failed — as did all the other schemes — to change the market picture.

Alfred Dolge, writing in 1909, foresaw the need for proper education of the public in player piano operation.

"As time passes on, the beauty and scope of the player piano will be appreciated in the same ratio as people learn to perform upon it properly. Teachers must be trained to give instructions on the player piano just as manual piano playing is taught at the present. It not only requires practice, but earnest and intelligent study to learn the use of expression and accentuating devices, and more especially to master the pedalling, because, after all, the secret of proper shading and phrasing in rendering a composition depends mainly upon the artistic use of the pedals. The "touch," this all-controlling factor in producing the various shades of tone on the piano, is controlled by the pedals almost entirely."

George M. Steger, Piano Merchant of Peoria, Ill., Suggests Plan for Player-Piano Contest for Amateurs

Points Out That Series of Contests Under Direction of Music Merchants in All Parts of the Country Will Serve to Awaken Interest in Players and Music Rolls and Teach Owners How to Play the Instruments Properly

PEORIA, ILL., Oct. 5.

GEORGE M. STEGER, piano merchant of this city is one of the most progressive members of the trade in this State. He is active in the Illinois Music Merchants Association, in the National Association of Piano Tuners and in every movement that tends to uplift the industry.

Mr. Steger, in common with many other dealers, realizes that interest in the player-piano must be quickened and he believes the rekindling can best be accomplished by enlisting the support of every player-owner in the country. To get this support he proposes a player-piano contest, open to any owner of a player-piano who uses the instrument simply as a means of entertainment. Not only would this awaken interest but it would afford an opportunity for those who own player-pianos to learn how to play them, Mr. Steger points out. He is convinced that one of the drawbacks to player sales is that a large percentage of owners do not know how to operate the instrument to get really musical results.

"I have talked with many dealers and we have discussed several ways of increasing player sales—restoring its one-time popularity—and of these ideas none seems to me to hold the potency of the amateur player-pianist contest," Mr. Steger said to a representative of THE MUSIC TRADES. "The details of the plan are not entirely worked out but in a general way this is the idea: The dealers in each city first will hold player-piano contests. These contests would be advertised in the local newspapers and each dealer could send invitations to the owners of player-pianos on his books to participate. The local contests would

be announced in advance to give the contestants an opportunity to brush up on their playing. This would serve to renew interest in the player and in the roll departments.

"The winners in the local contests would then compete in country or district contests. The winners in these would be eligible to enter the state contests, and the state contests' winners would play in a national contest. This national contest could be staged as a feature of a national music industries convention.

"Since the contest would have for its object the increasing of interest in music and the making of it, it would be considered of news value by the daily papers. The advertising of the local dealers would carry news of the plan and it could be pointed out that anybody with an aptitude for music could easily become a master of the player-piano. This would develop sales while the contest was in progress. It goes without saying the manufacturers of player-pianos would be interested in and would support such a movement. The manufacturers have been doing many things to keep up player interest. New designs, new finishes, etc., have been brought out. Some manufacturers have introduced splendid color combinations and beautiful period models and have produced instruments of small proportions. The player-roll manufacturers have urged the buying of player-pianos in their advertisements but none of these things will offset the feeling of customers who, because they never have been taught how to operate their player-pianos, either never play the instruments or play them improperly, to the disgust of the neighbors.

"The dealers in Peoria are ready to try out the player-pianist contest and, from talks I have had with dealers in other cities, I believe the idea would quickly take hold if advocated."

Standard Playerpiano Phonograph

THE Standard Playerpiano Phonograph, the first announcement of which was made in the *Standard Player Monthly* for March, has caused widespread comment.

This device permits manufacturers and dealers to sell a playerpiano and a phonograph in the same playerpiano case. The phonograph is built on the player action at the left of the spool box and is invisible in the playerpiano except when the left panel in the top frame is open to receive the record.

This playerpiano phonograph is equipped

Standard Playerpiano Phonograph Installed in Player. Left Panel is Open, Exposing Phonograph

with a Meisselbach spring motor. We consider this the best and most reliable motor for the purpose. It is especially designed to do most efficiently the work required and all of the gears and pinions and even the frame itself is especially heavy. Nothing but cut gears are used. The worm gear is hand made and the fibre gear in which the worm runs is especially cut to give the best results. The sulpho-bronze bearings, micromic adjustments and nickel trimmings place this motor at the head of its class.

The turntable in this phonograph runs nearly vertical but is set at such a plane that it absolutely prevents the record from falling over.

The tone-arm is especially designed to give a full, round, deep tone, free from the scratch that is so annoying in many phonographs. It is of the universal type and with its black die-cast base, swings freely on its pivot bearings. The tone arm is so balanced that the needle runs firmly and smoothly along the sound waves.

In the selection of the sound-box, great care was taken to select one that gives a pure, rich, full tone. The sound-box will not easily get out of adjustment and will give the best results on all styles of records.

The spool box acts as a tone chamber for the phonograph. The horn, which carries the tone waves from the tone arm to the tone chamber is made of wood. The phonograph will play any record manufactured. By simply turning the sound-box or reproducer you can play either laterally-cut or vertically-cut records.

The playerpiano case does not have to be mutilated in any manner in order to receive this playerpiano phonograph. The only restrictions involve the use of a three-panel top frame. This is necessary because a left panel must be provided to open and expose the turntable to receive the records.

Of course, the playerpiano is fundamental and of first importance but this new invention permits dealers to sell their customers two instruments in one—a playerpiano and a phonograph.

Standard Pneumatic Action Co. Player Piano Playing Contest Awakens Interest of Trade

W. Sinclair Duncan, Springfield, Mass., Tuner, Writes His Experiences—Says Dealers Can Increase Player Sales by Proper Demonstrations — One Player Owner Thought Bass and Treble Buttons Were Dummies

WITH the contest inaugurated by the Standard Pneumatic Action Co., New York, in which prizes were awarded at the Tuners' convention, Chicago, to tuners best able to demonstrate the player-piano, a matter of vital consideration to the music trade has been started, in the opinion of dealers and tuners. That this is recognized is evident from the following letter received by the Standard company from W. Sinclair Duncan, a tuner of Springfield, Mass.:

"If there is anything that I can say or do to help you in your campaign for better players and more business, or anything for me to say how you like you are at liberty to mention it in the manner you see fit," Mr. Duncan prefaces an interesting incident.

"A customer recently told me that the way in which I operated the player-piano was a revelation. She had never been aware of the wonderful effects that could be produced on a player, for no one had ever told her how to do it. She even thought that the soft bass and treble buttons were dummies.

"I told her that she had a technical musical giant at her command and that she could make it do her bidding. I was waiting for her to say how she liked to play her songs and dances. She must be the dictator, not it.

"Now, I have been on the selling end of the business, as well as the tuning end, and I will give you some facts and results from experience in this connection. I was at one time a tuner in a large piano department. The manager told me to see if I could adjust the stock of three players so they would stay right for a day. He didn't like them; said they were too mechanical—hurdy gurdies. He said nobody would buy them, and he had only sold two or three. There were a number of salesmen, but neither they nor the manager knew anything of music. When a prospect came in they put a roll of jazz or ragtime and ground it out—that was all there was to it.

"Of course, these players didn't sell. Customers had heard too often the tune of the jay with a monkey and organ.

"I remonstrated with these salesmen and told them they never could sell players with that kind of music and playing. They laughed when I put on a classic and broke up the tempo; but my playing drew people from all over the store. They thought there was some great pianist performing. They were very much surprised when they found the music came from a player-piano, and said they had never heard such good music from a player before. They asked what make of player it was.

"I told the manager that if he wished to do a player business he would have to let his players be heard and let their remarks as they got nearer:

"After about three months' entreating I was permitted to move a player with a Standard player action and in fine shape onto a small balcony in the center of the store. It was a Saturday afternoon and a full house. I had a program of the best classical numbers to bring out the capabilities of the player, and I knew them and my player from A to Z.

"Very soon the interested ones came climbing up the steps to the balcony where there were seats, and I could hear their remarks as they got nearer:

"'Why, it's a player-piano! I would not have believed it. I never heard one like that before. It doesn't sound the least bit mechanical.'

"There they sat, stood and crowded around the whole afternoon, and I frequently had to stop playing and answer questions. I handed likely customers over to the salesmen in waiting, and the department had the good fortune to book three good sales from that experience. Needless to say, we have had recitals on many afternoons since that time; and having been made manager of the department, I was careful to see that no one should be allowed to demonstrate a player unless he were thoroughly competent.

"I collected fifty of the most attractive selections produced and kept these rolls ready at all times. They were rolls that would show the wonderful possibilities of a player and which the novice would make to sound attractive when he was shown how.

"Now, tradesmen, this is the player question multiplied to its greatest drawing capacity. The experiment has grown into an immense reality today."

55

INTRODUCING

The Newest
Musical Instrument of the Century!
The completely new, all-electric/electronic

SEEBURG
SERENADA PLAYER PIANO

The only modern instrument of its kind that plays like a living artist!

When the marvels of Space-Age technology are applied to a fine piano like the Seeburg, something wonderfully exciting happens! Here is a player piano that *actually sounds as if a live performer is at the keyboard*. No old-time mechanical tinkle, no soulless heavy beat! You actually hear the whisper of a pianissimo, the crash of a forte, the accents in a rippling arpeggio, just as they are played by a living artist. All the subtle shadings of tonal intensity that make a live performance so distinctive are built into Seeburg piano rolls, and reproduced faithfully by the instrument! This is made possible by Seeburg's new, patented electronic action (see reverse side)—a thrilling departure from the "horse and buggy" systems still used by other manufacturers. In striking realism, in beautiful styling, in fun and enjoyment for the family, the Seeburg Player Piano has no equal. Try it for yourself and see!

The Superb Seeburg Serenada
shown in French Walnut

Only the Seeburg has this new kind of playing system—all-electric/electronic—for long life and serviceability!

So new and revolutionary it's patented! This is the electric "heart" of Seeburg's new key-activating system. Electric impulses activate rods which push upward *under* the rear of the keys to make them strike the piano hammers in the regular way — just as when you play an ordinary, non-player piano. The *degree* of push, and the working of the pedal, are controlled by the Seeburg piano rolls — enabling the piano to play loud or soft and achieve life-like performance quality. You can actually watch the pedal move by itself!

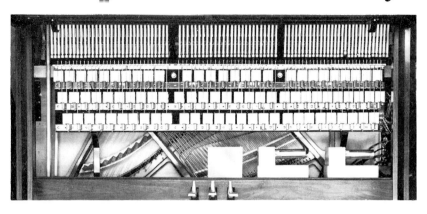

...plus these 8 exclusive Seeburg features for your enjoyment:

1.
AUTOMATIC EXPRESSION

Programmed in the piano roll and faithfully reproduced by the player piano. Gives the music the full range of dynamics —from the softest pianissimo to the loudest fortissimo— that a living artist can achieve on the keyboard.

2.
AUTOMATIC SUSTAINING PEDAL

Gives the music continuity and flow—provides for the artistic *blending* of tones necessary for life-like performance. Forever does away with the choppy, thumpy sound so characteristic of mechanical instruments. Seeburg's Automatic Sustaining Pedal responds to the pedal programming that is built into the great majority of music rolls, old and new.

3.
QUIET OPERATION

No wheezing, puffing or pounding of old-fashioned bellows or pneumatic air supply! No need to pump air at all — by pedals or with an electric motor — because all this has been *eliminated* from the Seeburg! Seeburg's all-electric/electronic operation is as modern as the Space Age, provides all the power needed for Balanced Intensity (see point 4 on this page), and does it *quietly*.

4.
WIDE RANGE BALANCED INTENSITY CONTROL

Intensity level regulator automatically compensates for number of notes being played to maintain perfect tonal balance throughout the entire dynamic range. It maintains this balance whether the piano plays whisper-quiet or thunder-loud.

5.
AUTOMATIC START, RE-ROLL, SHUTOFF, AND REPLAY

Only the Seeburg has *all* of these convenience controls that add to your pleasure in operating the piano.

6.
PRECISION TEMPO-CONTROL

Allows you to play music at any of *eight standard* playing tempos. In addition, an exceptionally slow *educational speed* permits *learning* to play the piano through music rolls.

7.
PLAYS ALL MUSIC ROLLS — OLD OR NEW

Though designed for new music rolls with expression built-in (see feature #1, above), the Seeburg player piano will also faithfully reproduce some older-type rolls. And you'll hear them as you've never heard them before!

Naturally, the Seeburg also may be played manually just like any other piano, because it is a superb piano in its own right. The electronic playing mechanism has no effect on manual playing.

8.
REMOTE PLAYING

The Seeburg Player Piano is available in two forms: One has the spool-box holding the music-roll *built into the case* of the piano. The other has the spool-box *outside the piano in a separate unit* that is attached to the piano via a cable. This allows you to operate the piano from anywhere in a room.

Remote Spool-Box

STYLES, FINISHES AND DIMENSIONS
The Superb Seeburg Serenada All-Electric/Electronic Player Piano is available in a wide combination of wood finishes and styles.

PIANO DIMENSIONS:
Length, 57¾ inches; depth, 26½ inches; height, 37 inches. Matching bench available.

Contemporary		Transitional	
PSCSM1-WAS	Walnut	PSTRM1-WAS	Walnut
PSCSM1-FWS	French Walnut	PSTRM1-FWS	French Walnut
PSCSM1-CHS	Cherry	PSTRM1-CHS	Cherry

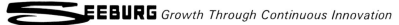

SEEBURG *Growth Through Continuous Innovation*

Musical Instrument Division, The Seeburg Corporation, Chicago, Illinois 60622

The Seeburg Serenada and the WurliTzer instruments shown here are interesting examples of developments of the middle 1960's. The Seeburg can trace its origin to the Wood and Brooks "Electrachord", which in turn can find its basis for existence in the fact that most people want to do things "the easy way."

It is a fact that modern electronic organs are easier to handle than a piano, in the sense that an untrained person can with a few lessons produce acceptable music, whereas this is not possible with the piano. Few adults bother to study piano for this reason; fewer still ever become proficient artists! Most pianists start as children, or they don't start at all.

The development of "chord organs", wherein the mere pushing of appropriate buttons in the bass produces the proper chord to go with a melody note played by the right hand, opened up a big market from adults who could not or would not take the time to learn to play by traditional methods. Sales of these music makers furthered the plight of piano manufacturers who were hard-pressed for business, and who hated to see the organ people take any of it away from them.

The "Electrachord" was an attempt to answer this competition. Developed by a young electrical wizard named Lee von Gunten, it was literally a series of push buttons wired to electric solenoid coils, such that a would-be pianist could have a whole set of bass chords at his command merely by using a single finger at the appropriate spot on a tiny bank of these buttons located near his left hand. The Wood and Brooks Company, makers of piano actions, marketed the device— or at least tried to market it—but for some reason it was completely unsuccessful in the market-place. It is not clear if this was due to poor sales efforts on the part of the piano manufacturers, or if piano dealers were simply wary of another electric "gadget" hung on a piano.

It was a simple matter to take the Electrachord one step further, and have a complete set of solenoids to operate the entire piano, and have them triggered in turn from holes in a paper roll. This scheme was taken up by the Seeburg Corporation, and Mr. von Gunten joined the staff of their research and development laboratory to carry on the work. It was designed to have several levels of expression, in a manner reminiscent of the Recordo expression scheme used decades earlier. The holes in the music roll were read by wire brushes, in a manner not unlike the Mills Violano-Virtuoso, of which more later. Considerable work was done on music rolls of Mylar instead of paper, but it would work on either.

The instrument performed well enough in the laboratory that Seeburg saw fit to show it at the trade show in Chicago, where it got a lot of attention. For some reason, however, the company elected not to put it on the market. It may have been that the decision was based on technical matters, or perhaps the market picture seemed unclear to the management. But in any event, today the Seeburg Serenada remains one more curiosity which, like hundreds of devices in similar years, never got "off the ground".

In the meanwhile, Dale Electronics of Yankton, South Dakota, was hard at work on their new player scheme. One of their developments was a piano-top player similar in concept to many which have gone before it in history (not one of which has ever been commercially successful), but the scheme was adapted to spinet-style pianos and the WurliTzer Corporation took it on.

It is an interesting combination of electronics and pneumatics. A vacuum is used to perform the function of reading the holes in the paper, just as in the "old days", but the valve which is actuated by the vacuum as it vents from the brass tracker bar through the note-hole in the paper to the atmosphere, serves only to

complete an electric circuit. From there, a solenoid is actuated to strike the piano key, as it did in the Seeburg unit.

The author had the interesting experience of being asked to service a new player sold by a local piano daler, which was agreed to because a return favor was owed the seller. Imagine the chagrin of the would-be technician who, upon arriving on the scene in a Chinese restaurant armed with vacuum guage, rubber tubing, glue, pneumatic cloth and related materials, discovered that what he really needed would have been in the nature of a vacuum-tube volt-meter, an oscilloscope, a bundle of wire, a soldering gun, and a spare transistor or two!

No More Pumping!
No More Bellows!

Say "goodbye" to player-piano fatigue! No more huffing and puffing as was often the case with the old-type systems. Now, a compact electronic circuitry has taken over. You just sit back and enjoy the music along with the rest.

Bring back the good old days with the special RINKY TINK control

Enjoy the nostalgic sound so popular in the "Roaring Twenties." RINKY TINK gives you that fascinating, tinny sound so much in vogue during the days of the plush movie palaces and the Mighty Wurlitzer Theatre Organ!

The fun maker that everyone can play!

WURLITZER
PLAYER PIANO

Play it like a regular piano . . . or let it play itself—electronically

Fun becomes contagious and the party suddenly begins to swing—the moment you plug in your Wurlitzer Player Piano and slip a music roll into the player unit. Of course, if you wish, it can be played manually like any regular piano. Either way you'll appreciate the rich, full tones. Simple to operate, easy to use, the Wurlitzer Player Piano is perfect for parties, dancing, or just listening. It's really *two* perfect pianos housed in a beautifully wrought cabinet. Just for the fun of it, why not sit down to a Wurlitzer Player Piano!

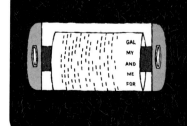

Just slip on a roll! Reads music, plays music with electronic fingers

**Italian Provincial P102-P102E in fine-grained walnut
matching bench available**

A Product of Aeolian Corporation

88 NOTE SPINET, PLAYER-PIANO

MUSETTE is the best of both worlds—a fine piano for students or musicians—and a player piano for fun and parties that everyone can play! No experience necessary. This rich-voiced responsive instrument with its full, 88 note keyboard, is a delight to play and hear. Trim and compact—only 57½" wide, 39½" high, 27¾" deep—it is scaled for today's rooms. Five gracious styles to suit any decor. Choice of Walnut or Cherry. (Over 1000 AEOLIAN Music Rolls available for every taste, from Beethoven to Country Rock, most with printed words for sing-alongs.) Complete hand and foot controls for widest personal expression in tempo, volume, bass or treble accent and special, old-time "rinky-tink" effect. Choice of 5 keys for easiest sing-along or play-along. MUSETTE is truly the instrument for everyone, the family music center.

Re-Enacting the Artist

The STEINWAY DUO-ART

REPRODUCING PIANO

Alfred Dolge proposed that persons should be trained to play a player piano properly, by proper use of the pedals. What he was driving at was that if the operator of an ordinary pedal-played player piano merely pushes the pedals at a uniform speed and amount of force, the musical output will indeed sound un-musical. However, by varying his footwork, the same operator can achieve a remarkable degree of musical "expression" from the ordinary player piano — and people should be trained, just as they are trained to play by hand, in order to gain fine music from this type of instrument.

Historically, it is clear that Dolge's suggestions (and he was certainly not alone in his protestations of how player pianos were operated by most owners) were not taken seriously by the public. Even today, when these machines are the subject of serious hobby interest, the number of persons who can make truly musical results from them — as compared with purely mechanical effects — is very limited.

But this human failing provided just one more avenue for clever inventors to go to work, to see if they couldn't come up with a completely automatic way of putting into the reproduction of player music all the phrasing, shading, rubato, touch, and other forms of musical interpretation of the actual human artist. The problem was first licked by the Germans, and around the turn of the Century two such devices were put on the market.

These were the "DEA", perfected by the Hupfeld organization, and the "Welte-Mignon", developed by M. Welte and Sons. Both of these firms had a long history in the field of automatic music, so it was perhaps a natural that they would be pioneers in this highly specialized field. Welte orchestrions — automatic orchestras — had in some cases grown to enormous size, and this accounts for the name "Welte Mignon" or "Small Welte" as applied to pianos of this new character. Only the Welte was marketed to any extent in America, and this effort started around 1907.

Pianos having the capability of "reproducing the expression" of the human artist became known as "reproducing pianos", and their invention led to the rather remarkable situation of the artistry of practically all the prominent pianists who lived during the next thirty years having their efforts captured on paper rolls such that today we can hear them play, precisely as they did years ago . . . and all this many years prior to the time the phonograph was capable of much more than recording squeaks and squawks!

Edwin Welte.

LESCHETITZKY PLAYING FOR
"THE WELTE-MIGNON"

I must consider this invention, which is known under the simple, unobtrusive name of "WELTE-MIGNON," to be really wonderful, and can only express my regret that this marvel was not known one hundred years ago. How much would "youth and age" have learned from it! What happiness there would be in being and remaining young, that we might harvest the fruits of this wonderful invention for all time!

THEODOR LESCHETITZKY.

One might say that the reproducing piano differs from the ordinary player piano in the same way that color television differs from black and white. They both can play the notes, but how one springs to life as compared with the other! Even today, in an age when scientific marvels are commonplace, the capability of a mechanical device to re-create the beauty and charm of an actual human performance at the keyboard is startling to those who have the privilege of hearing one of these instruments for the first time. The pell-mell rush of the human race to achieve greater and better things is such that the rise and fall of the reproducing piano in the marketplace took place in only about twenty years, and only in the 1960's did hobbyists start in earnest to delve into the wonders that had gone practically un-noticed for the previous 30 years.

The big difference between the reproducing piano and the ordinary player piano is that when the music roll is made originally (normally by an actual artist playing) extra holes are punched into the music roll which "record" the expression of the artists efforts. The piano on which the roll is played has various con-

CLAUDE DEBUSSY

CLAUDE DEBUSSY, most strikingly original of modern French composers and leader of the impressionists in music, began as a pianist. He was prepared for the Paris Conservatory by Mme. de Sivry, a pupil of Chopin; was admitted at the early age of eleven, continued to study piano with Marmontel, and won many prizes. He was born near Paris in 1862, and died in that city on March 26, 1918. To hear his own playing of his piano pieces is a rare treat.

"It is impossible to attain a greater perfection of reproduction than that of the 'Welte-Mignon' apparatus. I am happy to assure you in these lines of my astonishment and admiration at what I heard."

Welte-Mignon Cabinet Player, William and Mary Model, with spool box open, showing position of Artists' Record Roll

EDVARD GRIEG

NORWAY'S greatest composer, Edvard Grieg was also a pianist of remarkable poetic individuality, and as such made many successful professional tours of Europe. He was born at Bergen, in 1843, and died there in 1907. He was one of the most original composers of the nineteenth century, and his shorter piano pieces (known to every music-lover) are among the most charming and beautiful works of their kind.

"This ingenious invention, 'The Welte-Mignon,' or the idea to use the electrical power in the service of the intelligence, struck me with admiration; it surpasses all other essays in the way of artistical pianos."

RÖNISH-HUPFELD

Triphonola

Similar in appearance to above, is a Pedal-Electric Reproducing Piano, which may be operated either electrically or by means of the pedals.

May be purchased by small Quarterly or Monthly Payments.

The DUOPHONOLA and the TRIPHONOLA.

We now come to the more recent developments in the Player world, the so-called Reproducing Pianos. We have mentioned above that the **Hupfeld Duophonola and Triphonola,** with the aid of the ordinary electric light current, can reproduce the performance of the great Pianists. This result is of course only attained by using a special type of Music Roll on which the performance in question is faithfully recorded. Before going into further details concerning the Player action, it may be as well to give a short explanation of the method by which this record is obtained.

Instead of taking the score, the manufacturer engages a pianist of recognised ability and distinction, who is capable of performing a composition in a way to satisfy even the most punctilious critic. The artist is informed that it is desired to obtain a reproduction of say, a Nocturne of Chopin. He seats himself at the piano, and performs his nocturne precisely as he would do were he performing at a concert in the presence of a critical audience. He gives rein to his emotions and plays the composition as he feels that it should be played. He introduces into his playing all the rallentando, accelerando, rituendo effects, and nuances which go to make up an artistic as compared with a mere mechanical performance.

The making of the actual record is a perfectly simple matter. Every note of the piano is connected by an electric wire to a corresponding row of pencils which are superimposed on a strip of paper revolving on a drum. Every time the artist strikes a note, the corresponding pencil is brought into contact with the paper. So long as the artist keeps his finger on the note, the pencil produces a line on the paper. Immediately he releases the note the pencil leaves the paper and the line is brought to an end. It will thus be seen that if the pianist strikes a chord with even the slightest arpeggio effect, this is immediately reproduced on the pencil record. When he plays a scale each note is reproduced just that length of time during which the artist holds his finger on that particular note. If he makes a pause on any one note, so is this shown on the record by the extra length of pencil line resulting from this pause. Should he accelerate a certain passage, so will this be recorded by the shortening of the pencil lines. When he has finished the composition, the strip of paper with the pencil lines is taken from the drum of the reproduction instrument, and wherever the pencil lines are visible the paper is perforated. From this " Master Roll," rolls to an unlimited number can be manufactured.

The touch or dynamic force is recorded by means of a separated pneumatic contrivance which records the force with which each note is struck by the Pianist. This record is then combined with the record of the tempo explained above, by the addition of extra side perforations at the margin of the Roll. These are generally called the expression perforations. *

It is not proposed to give a long description of the technical working of these expression holes. It is sufficient here to explain that they control the touch of the Player action in precisely the same way as the human operator does through the pedals of the Solophonola. From the lightest shades of pianissimo to the heaviest fortissimo the original touch of the Pianist is recorded.

We can now visualise a performance by the Duophonola or the Triphonola. Imagine, for example, we want to hear the Ballade in G minor played by Busoni. The Roll is inserted, the button is pressed and immediately a veritable miracle is performed. The opening phrase of this monumental work swells out with all the majesty and force that the Great Master, Busoni, could give to it. We hear his interpretation of one of the world's masterpieces. On the Duophonola or the Triphonola you can actually hear Grieg play one of his own compositions. In short, The **Hupfeld Reproducing Piano** brings the world's greatest composers and performers into your own home. In lighter vein you can have Jazz and dance music. And what better accompaniment to dancing in the home than that of a full-toned Piano? Remember, it is the instrument itself you hear, not a mere distorted reproduction Press the button, the music you want is there. At the end of the piece, the Roll, without your moving a finger, will re-roll itself automatically, ready for another performance. Such is the Reproducing Piano!

---

* In this connection it is interesting to note that with many if not all Reproducing Players except the Hupfeld, there are no additional expression perforations on the margin of the Roll. The holes at the end of the scale, that is the extreme bass and treble, are used for expression purposes, with the result that the notes at both ends are dumb. The Duophonola (and of course, the Triphonola) plays every note on the score and the original record need never be faked as is the case with other Players.

trol devices which respond to these coded holes in the music roll, and put the expression back into the playing.

The means by which this can be accomplished are by no means simple, and the fact that it was accomplished at all by gadgeteers and experimenters before the days that scientific methodology had entered industry in general makes the extreme sophistication of the typical reproducing piano all the more remarkable. A number of systems eventually hit the market, all of which are beyond the scope of this book as far as technical details are concerned . . . but technical manuals are available for most of them for the benefit of the serious student. (see bibliography, end of book)

But back to the history of the builders. The Welte organization of Freiburg, Germany, was started by Michael Welte in the first half of the 19th Century, as an outgrowth of clock-manufacturing. He is given credit for having perfected the first "orchestrion" of any consequence, that being the name applied to a machine which can best be described as a "mechanical orchestra."

These enormously expensive devices of extreme complexity can best be described as playthings for the wealthy, although many of course found their way into places for public entertainment. Early versions were operated by pinned cylinders of ponderous dimensions, much in the way of Swiss cylinder-type musical boxes.

Edwin Welte, a grandson of Michael, worked with his brother-in-law Karl Bokisch on the problem of the reproducing piano, and by 1903 they had succeeded in getting the various composers and artists of their day to sit down and make paper music rolls which would record their particular brand of piano technique.

As the years went on, practically all the great artists of the day recorded at one time or another for either Welte or Hupfeld, and many of these interpretations were later adapted for American-made machines of other types. But not only were the pianos capable of playing back the reproducing rolls exceedingly costly, in terms of the average person's income, but the rolls themselves had staggering price tags. The 1912 Welte-Mignon roll catalog of several hundred numbers lists many rolls costing $10, $15, and up to $17 each, and some much more, considering that very often compositions had to be divided between two and three rolls owing to their length. Little wonder that today these original German-made Welte machines are scarce. Not many people could afford them in their day, and those people of means who could do so undoubtedly were the types who could afford to discard the instruments as soon as they tired of them.

Some Welte mechanisms were placed in American-made pianos, and the experience of hearing some of this early music in a magnificent piano such as the Mason & Hamlin is not easily forgotten by connoisseurs of this type of device.

Welte's assets in America were seized by the Alien Property Custodian with the entrance of America into World War I. After that conflict it established a manufacturing operation in Poughkeepsie, New York, even after having licensed rights to its original patents to the Auto-Pneumatic Action Company, a division of Kohler and Campbell Industries, in America. In the twenties they made cabinet-style piano players similar in operative principle to the early-day push-up players, but the market for these was always a limited one. Welte made its last reproducing instrument in 1931, and Edwin Welte died in 1957 at the age of 82, after having in his lifetime seen the entire span of popularity of the reproducing piano take place.

It is rather surprising that no American concern managed to produce a reproducing device until as late as 1913; perhaps none had been really perfected,

DUO-ART PIANOLA PIANO, THE.—The Duo-Art Pianola Piano is the reproducing piano manufactured by The Æolian Company, New York. This remarkable instrument was introduced to the public during the fall of 1913 and is the latest and greatest contribution by The Æolian Company to the automatic piano art. The Duo-Art (that is, representing two arts—the art of the performer and the art of the interpreting pianist) embodies three instruments in one: pianoforte, player-piano and reproducing piano. This instrument represents years of development by The Æolian corps of experts and inventors in continuation of earlier important inventions of the same company, including the Metrostyle and Themodist. The Metrostyle, a very remarkable invention, won the respect and indorsement of all the great composers and artists for the Pianola, the trade-name by which The Æolian Company's player-pianos are designated. The Themodist, another exclusive Æolian invention, enabled the Pianola automatically to voice the theme in the music roll so as to sound over the accompaniment. The Duo-Art Pianola Piano has been enthusiastically indorsed by leading artists and musicians of this country and Europe, and many of the great pianists such as Paderewski, Hofmann, Bauer, Ganz, Grainger, etc., have contracted to record exclusively for this reproducing piano. The Duo-Art has appeared as soloist with many of the leading orchestras of the country, having played a complete concerto in Æolian Hall, New York, accompanied by the New York Symphony Orchestra, conducted by Walter Damrosch. Also at Philadelphia with the Philadelphia Symphony Orchestra, conducted by Leopold Stokowsky; with the Chicago Symphony Orchestra, conducted by Eric DeLamarter, and with the San Francisco Symphony Orchestra, Alfred Hertz conducting. This last concert was one of the regular series given by the orchestra, the Duo-Art having had the unique distinction of being substituted in place of the living artist. The remarkable patented mechanism of the Duo-Art reproduces not only the notes, tempo, phrasing and attack, but also every tone gradation precisely as originally played and recorded by the artist, including all the dynamics of his rendition with the innumerable gradations from pianissimo to sforzando, all crescendos and diminuendos, whether of abrupt or extended length; also all pedal effects of the artist in the use of the sostenuto and soft pedals; also all other expression effects so true to the individuality of the respective artists who recorded the original Duo-Art rolls that their style and identity is unmistakably to be recognized in their performance by the Duo-Art Pianola. In short, the Duo-Art music rolls embodied in the Duo-Art Pianola Piano reproduce the individual manner and musical personality of the recording artists in a truly remarkable manner. The artist's original master record is made automatically as he plays on a specially devised recording Duo-Art piano, the artist playing the composition by hand on this piano in the characteristic manner which he desires to record, and the automatic mechanism recording in the form of perforations in a moving sheet not only all of the notes but all of the artist's expression effects, including tempo, rhythm, dynamics and pedaling, exactly as played. As soon as the artist has finished his performance, the perforated music roll recording his rendition is immediately available for insertion in the Duo-Art piano to reproduce the original performance. In this way the leading artists have permanently recorded for all time their characteristic piano interpretations, and these are available for the enjoyment of all users of the Duo-Art piano in a rapidly growing catalogue which already includes over eight hundred Duo-Art rolls. The Duo-Art is incorporated in such leading pianos as the Steinway, Weber, Steck, etc., both in grands and uprights.

Mr. and Mrs. I. J. Paderewski listening to one of Mr. Paderewski's Duo-Art recordings

George Gershwin

GEORGE GERSHWIN, who records his piano playing exclusively for the Duo-Art, was born in Brooklyn, N. Y., on September 26, 1898. When he was thirteen years old his mother bought a piano and decided that young George must learn to play it. A new and hitherto undreamed of world was opened to him. He learned rapidly and well, the best of his early teachers being Charles Hambitzer, who gave him his first lessons in harmony and his first real reverence for music, but who died before his pupil had gone very far. Later he studied harmony with Eduard Kilenyi, and after that took some work in composition with Rubin Goldmark, for early in his piano lessons he had begun to dabble at writing. When sixteen he went to work as a "song plugger" for a music publisher, often playing piano all day for vaudeville acts and far into the night at cafés. This led to his engagement to play for the chorus rehearsals of various musical shows. Meanwhile he kept trying his hand at composition, until, in 1918, with "I Was So Young and You Were So Beautiful," he found himself launched as the author of a popular song hit. Since that successful start his work has shown a steady advance.

Duo-Art Records by George Gershwin

(See also, Supplementary Catalog of Dance Music)

RHAPSODY IN BLUE, Part II: Andantino and Finale *George Gershwin* 68787 1.75

BEYOND question George Gershwin's "Rhapsody in Blue" is the most imposing and the most important composition thus far achieved by anybody in the jazz idiom. Its title is particularly appropriate, for it is freely rhapsodic in form and it makes plentiful and effective use of the contrasting discords which the jazz artists call "blue notes." It is really a Concerto in Fantasia form for Piano and Jazz Orchestra (the first of the kind ever written). It was commissioned by Paul Whiteman, and had its first performance at Mr. Whiteman's now historic concert, in Aeolian Hall, New York, on February 12, 1924, with the composer at the piano.

Everybody who takes any interest at all in American music will want to hear this Rhapsody. It is a remarkable work, from every point of view. It has a throbbing, pulsating vitality, and a glamour of great popular appeal. It discloses a genuine melodic gift—novel, individualistic and fine; an astonishing skill in handling the new harmonies produced by American jazz bands; a still more noteworthy ability in the invention and manipulation of striking rhythms; and a happy facility in the arrangement of form.

It has been said that delicacy, even dreaminess, is a quality that Gershwin alone brings into jazz music. Something of this phase of his talent is shown in the impressively beautiful theme of the *Andantino*, beginning the Second Part of the Rhapsody incorporated in the present Duo-Art Record of the composer's own brilliant and masterly performance. And this finely expressive theme itself demonstrates his command of melodic ideas quite as convincingly as the Finale shows his ability to pile up a powerful and thrilling climax.

SO AM I (Ballad from "Lady, Be Good!" With Words) *George Gershwin* 102625 1.25

The DUO-ART

The Aeolian Company, makers of the Pianola, for more than a quarter of a century, have been recognized as the world's greatest force in the development of musical instruments. Their supreme achievement is the Duo-Art Reproducing Piano.

This splendid instrument offers more to music lovers than any piano ever before made. It offers them the satisfaction of owning the finest Grand or Upright the market provides—a Steinway, Steck, Wheelock, Stroud or the famous Weber.

The Pianola action affords the individual a means of playing the piano and giving artistic expression to his own ideas of music.

And it brings the playing of the most gifted pianists of all time into the home—their performances reproduced with the naturalness of which only the Duo-Art is capable.

THE AEOLIAN COMPANY

NEW YORK   LONDON   PARIS   MADRID
SYDNEY   MELBOURNE

or perhaps the manufacturers were convinced that no market really existed until that time. However, the Steinway Duo-Art Pianola was introduced in that year, as a result of a contract which had been made between the Aeolian Corporation and the Steinway Company in 1909. Aeolian purchased pianos in special cases from Steinway, and then proceeded to install their newly-perfected Duo-Art reproducing mechanism in them. In succeeding years these mechanisms were also installed in the makes actually built by Aeolian; these were for Weber, Steck, Wheelock, Stroud, and Aeolian pianos, in that order of quality and price, for the American market. Many Steinway models were made in special Art-cases with much ornate woodwork and the least costly of any of the models produced was around $4500; other pianos in the line could be had for prices closer to one-third that much.

As in the case of the Welte, this also meant that only the wealthy could afford reproducing pianos, and that the market was always bound to be a limited one. But rolls were made for much lower selling prices (a Duo-Art roll was high if it brought $4) in an attempt to capitalize on the possibilities of this part of the market. Again, as in the case of Welte, the Aeolian Corporation induced as many of the great artists of the day to play for them as it possibly could, and then it made double use of these person's names through all kinds of endorsements . . . and following the example set earlier by Tremaine, plugged its new wares through tremendous advertising campaigns. Of course a discerning reader can detect a note of similarity in all the endorsements; it is hard to believe that many of these people actually said what was printed!

Victor Herbert

THE contributions of Victor Herbert to both serious and light music form an important chapter in the history of art in America. He was America's best-loved writer of music. And he was thoroughly and typically American both as a man and as a musician, notwithstanding that he was born in Dublin, on February 1, 1859 (he was a grandson of Samuel Lover, the famous Irish novelist), and that he received his musical education in Germany, where he was a student for twelve years. He came to America in 1886 and began his career here as first 'cellist at the Metropolitan Opera House in New York. Successively leading 'cellist in the orchestras of Theodore Thomas, Anton Seidl, and the New York Philharmonic, he won nation-wide celebrity as an artist of the highest rank. Then he achieved still greater reputation as a conductor. Meanwhile he had begun to compose.

In 1893 William MacDonald, the manager of the Bostonians, persuaded Mr. Herbert to try his hand at light opera, offering him the libretto of "Prince Ananias," and the emphatic success won by that work determined his future career as a composer. For thirty years, with amazing fertility of invention, he produced successful operettas at the rate of at least one a year—and became the most prolific and the most successful of American composers. Victor Herbert died in New York, on May 26, 1924.

A Duo-Art Record by Victor Herbert

WHEN YOU'RE AWAY. From "The Only Girl" 57667 1.75

Mr. Herbert here recorded his own interpretation of a very attractive number from one of the most popular of his many musical comedy successes, "The Only Girl." Lovers of the best light music will find this a delightful record-roll.

THE WORLD'S FOREMOST PIANISTS
Record Their Playing Exclusively For
THE DUO-ART
Reproducing Piano

"I CONGRATULATE you again on the production of the Duo-Art Piano. For acquiring a broad, musical education, it is undoubtedly the most perfect and really great medium. This instrument is, without question, greatly superior to any other of its kind, and I shall be glad indeed to have my playing reproduced with such fidelity."

I. J. Paderewski

"My Duo-Art rolls correctly reproduce my phrasing, accent, pedaling, and are endowed with my personality. They are my actual interpretation with all that implies. One thing is certain; in the reproduction of my playing, the Duo-Art is so far superior to any other instrument of its kind there can be no real basis for comparison."

Josef Hofmann

On these pages are pictured a few of the world's most famous pianists who record their playing exclusively for the Duo-Art. The significance of their choice does not require emphasis. The supremacy of the Duo-Art is world-wide.

THE AEOLIAN COMPANY

"In fidelity of reproduction, in brilliancy, power, delicacy, quality and variety of tone the vast superiority of the Duo-Art over all similar instruments is now definitely established. I am most happy to avail myself of such a wonderful means of leaving to posterity a record, as nearly perfect as can be conceived, of my interpretative art."

Harold Bauer

"I CONSIDER the Duo-Art Piano a most important and valuable means for musical development. The pianists' interpretations are works of creative art, as truly as are the writings of the composer. The Duo-Art Piano by bringing the fruits of the pianists' creative genius before countless people is destined to fill a high mission in the musical life of the future."

Ossip Gabrilowitsch

The Duo-Art was installed up until the mid-thirties, when the economic conditions of the day forced a merger between the Aeolian Company and the American Piano Company. Rolls continued to be made during the depression years, and there was much interrelationship between the AMPICO reproducing piano activity and the Duo-Art, no doubt resulting from the fact that everything was then under one roof.

Today authorities disagree as to whether the Duo-Art reproducing mechanism could replace human artistry as satisfactorily as would the other pianos produced in this country with that presumed capability, and various technical theories are advanced supporting one position or the other. What really counts in the end is the judgment of serious students of piano music, and not that of the technicians . . . and there is plenty of evidence to show that when all is said and done, the results can be equally good from well-regulated instruments.

Regardless of technical differences and their alleged influence on the musical results produced by the pianos in which it was contained, the Duo-Art reached the market early, it always had a good share of the market, and it was right there until the bitter end when all reproducing pianos, along with the more conventional players, finally lost out as the price of progress.

YOUR NEW OPPORTUNITY TO KNOW THE WORLD'S GREAT MUSIC

An interview with Rudolph Ganz, the eminent Swiss pianist, regarding

The Duo-Art Pianola

Rudolph Ganz

WHEN Mr. Ganz grips your hand in an introductory clasp, your instant impression is of a man's man—a keen, virile personality free from the taint of morbidity so often associated with high artistic ability.

He is a composer of fine achievement. His songs and compositions for piano and orchestra are widely performed.

Possessed of remarkable power as an interpretative artist, his popularity as a concert pianist is growing with a rapidity that he well deserves.

Mr. Ganz is the well balanced, well informed type of musician whose sincere and authoritative statements cannot be taken lightly by the public.

"THE degree of pleasure you derive from the music depends largely upon your musical associations. Let any person of good taste and intelligence listen regularly to fine music beautifully interpreted and presently he is an enthusiastic music lover."

Mr. Ganz's grave, good humored manner of speaking and the hint of a twinkle that is always lurking about the corner of his eyes betray him for what he is—a big, jovial optimist, a fine, wholesome-minded artist who believes simply and earnestly in his art.

"You think then," I said, "that people who consider themselves unmusical are merely those who haven't heard plenty of great music played so they can derive pleasure from it?"

"Yes," he replied, "and so it is that artists, if they live up to their ideals, are accomplishing more than entertainment in their concert work

—they are imparting to their audiences music knowledge and comprehension —their interpretations of the musical scriptures are aiding the hearers to a new and broadened capacity for musical pleasure and understanding.

"And now the time has come," continued Mr. Ganz, "when every pianist must awaken to a new responsibility—a new and greater opportunity. By the developments of the past few years the pianist's field has been extended immeasurably."

"You are speaking, perhaps, with your recent experience with the Duo-Art Pianola in mind?" I suggested.

"THE Duo-Art Pianola, yes. The reproducing piano brings the artist into intimate contact with the people in their homes—he is to become a part of their daily lives instead of remaining the casual stranger of the concert hall. His message of music is made generally available by the Duo-Art."

"You seem to have a very definite confidence in the ability of the Duo-Art to accurately reproduce your playing."

"Well, I must confess that at first I doubted. But now that I have heard my finished records, I have nothing more to ask—these records are my own performances. Anyone who has heard me play would instantly recognize these reproductions."

"DO YOU intend that statement to apply to the Duo-Art reproductions in all respects? Do you, for example, consider that we have faithfully duplicated your tone production?"

"Surely! I have had no difficulty in getting the tone results I wanted in the records. The climaxes are worked up just as I played them. The distinction between voices, between theme and accompaniment, are practically perfect. The intonation and crispness of phrasing add the last convincing touch of personality and the tone-production pleases me much. If anyone criticizes it, they criticize my playing," said Mr. Ganz, smiling.

"And tempo and phrasing?"

"AH! they are perfect—true to my performance. My typical rhythmical characteristics, my rubati, my most personal ways, are exactly duplicated. I have been much interested also in the pedal results. By careful editing, the tone color and sustained effects secured by the pedal may be even more fully developed than in the spontaneous performance at the keyboard.

"Thorough work in recording and editing may well bring the interpretation as reproduced by the Duo-Art Pianola to a point where it challenges the artist's performance in the concert hall. When playing in concert so many circumstances and conditions may influence results. In recording we make our own conditions—even choose our moods. So the Duo-Art should present the pianist at his best."

THE DUO-ART PIANOLA

THE Duo-Art Pianola is the highest modern development of the pianoforte.

It is primarily a piano of conventional type—a Steinway, Weber, Steck or Stroud, with all the fine tonal qualities that distinguish these well-known instruments. The action and keyboard for hand playing are identical with other pianos of the same make.

IT is a player-piano of truly remarkable capacity, providing the Pianolist with easy and complete control of every phase of musical expression possible upon the pianoforte. It is an instrument of such broad artistic possibilities that it will interest not only the layman but also the experienced musician who will find in it the enjoyment of a limitless repertory.

AS a reproducing piano— as an instrument for re-creating the interpretations of

the great artists of the pianoforte, it is truly revolutionary in its attainments. Guided by the wonderful Duo-Art records, the Duo-Art Pianola actually repeats in every shading of tone and tempo the pianist's original performance.

AEOLIAN representatives in every principal city of the United States are prepared to demonstrate this wonderful new instrument. We invite you to write for address of representative nearest you and an interesting Booklet of the Duo-Art. Please address Department E 11.

Steinway Duo-Art Pianola
Other models are the Steck, Stroud and famous Weber. Moderate prices.

THE AEOLIAN COMPANY, AEOLIAN HALL
29 WEST FORTY-SECOND STREET · NEW YORK CITY
Makers of the Aeolian-Vocalion, largest manufacturers of musical instruments in the world.

Mr Ganz (at the right) engaged in editing Duo-Art Records. This work of retouching and revising the recorded interpretations gives them the last degree of perfection that the artist can impart.

"Instead of feeding upon concert memories, those who love music may actually hear their favorite interpretations whenever they wish. This new and closer contact between artist and audience is to me the most fascinating possibility of the Duo-Art.

"A WHILE ago the Swiss Ambassador in Washington, who is a friend of mine, purchased one of these instruments—and at his request I tried a number of them and chose the one which was to be sent him. In writing him I said—'It is with pleasure that I look forward to being in your home indirectly, for with this new instrument I can have the privilege of playing for

you whenever you like, even though I am not with you in person.'

"And that is exactly the way I feel about it—you see! What a delight to be able to think that you are part of the artistic life in so many homes.

"THAT is the wonderful thing The Aeolian Company has accomplished: to take the concert pianist from the concert hall into the home."

▼ ▼ ▼

I have read the above interview in print and find it a true report of my statements.

71

Weber Duo-Art in Mussolini's Palace, Rome, Also in Elysee Palace of President of France

Instruments Supplied Through Aeolian Co., London, Which Notifies Aeolian Headquarters in United States by Radiogram — Signed Photograph of Mussolini Presented to H. B. Tremaine, President of Aeolian Co.—Sale Featured in the Aeolian Window Display, New York

Aeolian Hall, New York, Window Trim, Featuring the Weber Duo-Art in an Italian Period Model by Zaiser, and Personally Signed Photograph of Mussolini Which Was Presented to H. B. Tremaine, President of the Aeolian Co.

As previously mentioned, early in the history of the Aeolian Company a great music hall was erected in a fashionable district of New York City by H. B. Tremaine, in order to garner the trade of the wealthy. This soon proved inadequate, and in 1926 the *New Aeolian Hall* was erected, a magnificent structure in which all the various instruments sold by the company were displayed in showrooms decorated in accordance with different architectural periods. Since grand piano sales in the 'twenties (when everyone was rich, on paper) were as apt to be made on the basis of promoting a beautiful piece of furniture, rather than a musical instrument, it was popular to have a particular line of pianos available in many period styles — William and Mary, Louis XVI, Italian Renaissance, Georgian, Duncan Phyfe, Indo-Grecian-Gothic, Early Peoria and what-have-you. The new Aeolian Hall was able to provide the proper settings for these new sales efforts.

THE world famous Weber Duo-Art reproducing piano has been supplied to His Excellency Signor Benito Mussolini for his palace in Rome. A similar instrument has also been furnished for the Elysee Palace, the official residence of the President of the French Republic, Paris.

These instruments were installed by the Aeolian Co. of London, which sent this information recently to the Aeolian headquarters in New York by radiogram.

The acceptance of the Duo-Art by these two rulers of Europe is gratifying to Aeolian officials in view of the fact that the Duo-Art is already treasured by other members of royalty and presiding heads in different European countries. Prominent among the latter, who have long been admirers of the Duo-Art, are Her Majesty Queen Mary of England, His Royal Highness the Prince of Wales, Their Majesties the King and Queen of Spain, Her Majesty the Queen of the Belgians, and Her Majesty the Queen of Norway. The Duo-Art is also greatly appreciated by His Holiness Pope Pius XI. This instrument was likewise much admired by Leo XIII.

Sales Featured in Advertisements

The Aeolian Co. has capitalized the placing of the Weber Duo-Art in the palaces at Rome and Paris mentioned above in page advertisements which have already appeared in New York newspapers. These are illustrated with a picture of a period model Weber Duo-Art grand, the coat of arms of Italy and also of France, and a reproduction of the radiogram from the Aeolian Co. of London, which reads as follows:

"We are gratified to advise you that we have supplied a Weber Duo-Art grand piano to His Excellency Signor Benito Mussolini for his Palace in Rome. We have also supplied a Weber Duo-Art grand piano to the Elysee Palace, the official residence of the President of the French Republic in Paris."

This advertisement is captioned "World Wide Appreciation of the Duo-Art Reproducing Piano." The following is an excerpt from the advertisement:

"The radiogram reproduced herewth tells of two notable additions to the impressive list of distinguished patrons of the Aeolian Co. in whose homes Duo-Art reproducing pianos have been installed.

"The steadily increasing popularity of the reproducing piano is confined to no country nor people.

Everywhere throughout the world, men and women of discriminating musical taste are purchasing Duo-Art pianos and availing themselves of the means this marvelous instrument affords to gratify their love of music and further increase their familiarity with and understanding of all that is best in the divine art."

Following this there is a brief description of the Duo-Art reproducing piano, and a statement that the Duo-Art is available in the Steinway, Steck, Wheelock, Stroud, Aeolian and the famous Weber.

H. B. Tremaine, president of the Aeolian Co., has been presented with a personally autographed photograph of Mussolini. The inscription reads: "Al Signor H. B. Tremaine. Complimenti. Roma, 5 Giugno, 1926. Mussolini."

This photograph, as well as reproductions of coats of arms of Italy and France, in colors, were advantageously used in a window display at Aeolian Hall, New York, which featured the Weber Duo-Art reproducing grand piano in the Italian period model by Zaiser. Many passersby stopped to admire this handsome piano and also to examine closely the signed photograph by Mussolini, which was presented to Mr. Tremaine.

Among the members of royalty and rulers in Europe who already are patrons of the Duo-Art, in addition to those mentioned previously, are the following: Her Majesty the late Queen Alexandra of England, Her Late Majesty Queen Victoria of England, H. R. H. Prince Henry, K. G.; H. R. H. the Princess Royal, H. R. H. the Princess Victoria, H. R. H. the Duke of Connaught, K. G.; H. R. H. the Princess Henry of Battenberg, H. R. H. the Princess Louise, Duchess of Argyll; Her Late Majesty the Empress Alexandria Feodorowna of Russia, Her Majesty the ex-Dowager Empress Marie Feodorowna of Russia, Her Majesty the Dowager Queen of Italy, His Late Majesty King Carlos of Portugal, His Majesty the ex-King Ferdinand of Bulgaria, His Late Majesty Abdul Hamid, Sultan of Turkey; His Late Majesty Abbas Pascha, Khedive of Egypt; His Late Majesty Musafer-Ed-Din, Shah of Persia; His Late Majesty Chulalongkorn, King of Siam; His Majesty Prajadhipok, King of Siam; His Majesty Mir Mahmid, Khan of Bluchistan; H. S. H. the Sultan of Jahore, H. S. H. the Marajah Jamsahib of Nawanajar, H. R. H. Prince Purachatra of Siam, Prince Gustav of Denmark, Prince Heinrich XXXI of Reuss, H. R. H. the Crown Prince of Sweden, His Highness Principe Buancompagni of Switzerland, ex-President Dr. Jose Figuero Alcorta, Argentine; ex-President Sr. Don Jose Batalle y Ordonez, Uruguay; Prince Temistocle Della Vedova, Italy.

INTERVIEW WITH PERCY GRAINGER ON DUO-ART PIANOLA

Interesting Views of Noted Australian Composer-Pianist Reproduced in Form of Advertisement by the Aeolian Co. This Week—An Instrument of Broad Possibilities

The Aeolian Co. carried an effective advertisement in this week's newspapers, featuring an interview with Percy Grainger, the talented Australian composer-pianist, anent the Duo-Art Pianola. Mr. Grainger, who has made a number of rolls for the Duo-Art library, has achieved remarkable success and fame both here and abroad. His musical writings have received world-wide recognition, and the following interview is one of the finest tributes which could be accorded a musical instrument:

"If people sometimes are listening to music, and sometimes taking part in it, we shall have better musicians, much keener listeners—and greater enjoyment in music!"

Mr. Grainger thus epitomized for me his idea of music at its best.

"Why," I asked, "do you require that people take part in music as well as listen?"

"I feel that quicker, clearer understanding comes that way," he replied. "If a man plays a bit himself, he better appreciates what the musician is trying to do. But just as making music sharpens our wits and our taste for hearing it, so listening to fine music feeds and stimulates our musicianship."

"Then surely our Duo-Art Pianola is quite your ideal of a musical instrument for the home," I suggested.

"Yes—quite," said Mr. Grainger, "I am frightfully interested in the Duo-Art. I play it as a piano, and sometimes as a Pianola. Does the idea of a pianist using a Pianola seem odd to you? Well, you know, I am thinking of doing some compositions for the Pianola. From the viewpoint of the composer, it is a very interesting instrument, with perhaps broader possibilities even than the piano.

"And, of course, we do not lose sight of the third faculty of the Duo-Art. When I am en tour, my mother may have it to reproduce my records, and for the time, I am with her in spirit—the Duo-Art reproductions are so vividly like my playing.

"On the whole, the Duo-Art is quite wonderful indeed—one of the greatest marvels I have found in your remarkable America."

"You sincerely think that the Duo-Art reproduces from your records so accurately as to satisfy one so well qualified to judge critically as your own mother?"

"Yes, surely. And when I myself hear the records which I have played at my best and then edited and corrected until they are my fullest musical expressions, I think to myself —'Ah, on the days when I play like that I am very well pleased.' "

"This is quite a fine thing you are saying for the Duo-Art, Mr. Grainger—tell me, do you mean to go on record with the statement that the Duo-Art actually simulates your art even in such subtle things as gradations of touch and tone quality?"

"That is a very legal sounding query, if you

understand what I mean," replied Grainger, smiling—"yes, I think the Duo-Art simulates every phrase of my work, rhythm, tone and all the rest. With reference to rhythm particularly, I am amazed at the absolute accuracy with which the instrument reproduces the artist's most personal characteristics."

"You have found record-making an exacting task, then," I suggested, "each detail must be so carefully considered in order that the finished record may be you at your best."

"Extremely interesting, yes, and exacting—but very valuable too. My mother, who has always been my inseparable companion and advisor, the other day remarked upon my improved interpretation of a work which I present frequently in recital. 'You play that differently and much more tellingly these last few days,' she said, 'has anything occurred to give you a new point of view?'

" 'I've been hearing my interpretation on the Duo-Art Pianola—I have been playing the part of the audience, listening to my own work. The improved interpretation is the result of a new kind of self-criticism,' I replied.

"The Duo-Art actually has helped greatly in study and practice," he went on, "for obviously as one sits at the keyboard it is impossible to know how some effects reach the audience."

Mr. Grainger slid deep down in his chair and sat thoughtfully quiet for a few moments. "I quite sincerely think that the Duo-Art Pianola is going to do great things for music. Artistic interpretations by great musicians make musical classics clear and comprehensible—and entertaining to the layman. With these fine interpretations presented so widely by means of the Duo-Art, the result must be a rapidly advancing taste in music—a quickly increasing interest in music.

"The musical world surely owes much to the Aeolian Co., for you with your high ideals and your very liberal spirit have added a distinct impetus to the advancement of musical art."

THE NEW AEOLIAN HALL
*Gold Medal awarded by the Fifth Avenue Association
for the best building erected during 1926*

The DUO-ART is not only a magnificent piano, endowed with ability to reproduce playing, but is as well
a really fine piece of furniture.

Not to be outdone by the Aeolian Company of New York, the American Piano Company — the combine manufacturing the Mason & Hamlin, Knabe, Marshall and Wendell, Haines Brothers and Franklin pianos, produced its own reproducing mechanism and named it the AMPICO.

While the Ampico was first marketed around 1913, the company chose to make its first formal introduction to the public through a demonstration held at the Hotel Biltmore in New York City, October 8, 1916. Leopold Godowsky was the demonstrating pianist, and he played certain numbers himself, and then let the piano alone repeat his work by playing pre-recorded rolls — a show designed to convince even the most skeptical of the true capabilities of the reproducing piano in re-interpreting the efforts of the artist.

This was not the first, nor the last, demonstration of this sort. It was, in fact, a rather routine thing for the companies selling these machines to stage demon-

HARVARD UNIVERSITY ORDERS THE CHICKERING GRAND AMPICO

Instrument Is Installed in Division of Music for Use in Appreciation of Music Courses

Harvard University, through its division of music, has recently ordered from the Ampico Corp. a Chickering grand Ampico for use in its music classes.

The Ampico, which will be the sole reproducing piano of Harvard University, was selected by Professor

Music Division Building at Harvard University, Recently Equipped with the Ampico

Walter R. Spalding, the head of the music division, and will be used principally in the appreciation of music courses, conducted by Professor Spalding and Assistant Professor Edward Ballantine.

"The division of music at Harvard has long enjoyed an enviable distinction among universities for the high standards it has maintained in scholarship and musicianship, as well as the completeness of its housing and equipment," says an authority. "It is therefore a significant tribute to the Ampico that it should be chosen for the music courses of this institution."

strations of this nature, and they were done all over the country at one time or another, with various artists participating. Some of these were solo affairs, some with more than one pianist being involved, and often a whole orchestra was accompanied by a piano strictly untouched by human hands during its performance.

All the makers of reproducing pianos plugged hard at two items in their advertising campaigns: the fact that they were used and enjoyed by prominent and wealthy people, and the fact that this type of machine could be used in schools of music as a definite aid to teaching, in terms of being able to reproduce the artistry of actual pianists in a manner that the phonographs of the day could not hope to attain.

Credit for the invention of the Ampico goes to one Charles Fuller Stoddard, a somewhat eccentric mechanical wizard who lived between 1876 and 1958.

Largely self-taught, he worked at a variety of occupations before becoming involved with the player piano, and one of these jobs served him well as it was as a development engineer with the American Pneumatic Service Company, makers of dispatching systems for parcels, mail, and other commodities. A number of patents on pneumatic devices were assigned by him to this company while in its employ.

According to Larry Givens, author of "Re-Enacting the Artist", (a story of the Ampico reproducing piano) Mr. Stoddard's tender sensibilities were affected by hearing a very mechanical-sounding player piano around 1910, and he set out to do something about it. His efforts led him to the development of what was to become the "Ampico", and he was engaged by the American Piano Company to carry out these efforts, at a substantial salary.

CHARLES FULLER STODDARD
Inventor of the Ampico.
December 26th, 1876 — April 29th, 1958

THE BARDINI
Italian Renaissance Art Reproducing Grand

CUSTOM BUILT THROUGHOUT, ALL CARVING BY HAND, ON SOLID WALNUT
DESIGN—AN AUTHENTIC REPRODUCTION OF AN EXISTING FLORENTINE ANTIQUE
Action—Schulz Aria Divina or Welte-Mignon (Licensee)

THE Art pianos, of which the Bardini is illustrated, mark a new achievement for American wood-carving. Designed for the M. Schulz Co. by a great Italian artist, each is an authentic reproduction of a museum piece. The series includes Italian, French and Spanish designs elaborately executed. No finer piano cases have ever been attempted in America.

Ruainooo Group Elects Banker to Directorate

November 18, 1917

THE PIANO PLAYED ITSELF.

Harold Bauer's "Duo-Art" Roll Interpreted with Orchestra.

The Aeolian Company made a unique demonstration last evening in Aeolian Hall of their Duo-Art Piano, in which they had the assistance of the New York Symphony orchestra, conducted by Mr. Walter Damrosch. The program contained orchestral pieces with a pianoforte concerto, accompanied by the orchestra. Only, instead of a pianist, the concerto was played by the automatic action of the Duo-Art roll in a grand piano. It was a reproduction of Mr. Harold Bauer's interpretation of Saint Saen's G minor concerto. Mr. Bauer himself was in Chicago. Mr. Damrosch followed it as he would a player of flesh and blood, and created some amusement by his occasional close scrutiny of the moving keys of the keyboard and his success in "coming out even" with the roll, after the pianist had had a pause which was filled in by the orchestra.

The orchestra began with the overture to "Oberon," and after the concerto two of Mr. Percy Grainger's folksong arrangements were played.

There was a remarkable audience present in which musicians and pianoforte makers were conspicuous. The achievement of the Duo-Art roll and the orchestra together — an achievement which is perhaps unique — aroused great interest.

BIG JERSEY TRACT TO BE PLANT AREA

... of Singer Property at ...abeth Bought as Site ...r Industrial Park

... of New Jersey's indu ...ndmarks wil be redeve ... an industrial park.

... half of the Singer Se ...chine Company's la ...t facilities in Elizabe ... acquired by the int ... now operate the El ... Terminal in Kear ...rty was sold by ...chine manufactur ...s part of a $10,0 ...ion program. Si ...he rest of the p ... own use. ...roject, to be kr ...zabeth Indu ...ated at the ...bull Street. ...mpasses for ... nine major ... many at ...ll of whicl ...,000 squa ...e. ... range in ... e storie ... units ... 5,000 ...ll run ... re fo ... deve ...rial ... by ...at ... c ... ic ... ti ...

... New Yo ... a mile from th ... Industrial Park will ...ty-four piers that ...modate ocean shippi

Railroad tracks a plant are being sl buildings in the Inc

Manhattan ... Aide PIANO PLAYS AS 'SOLOIST'

With Metropolitan Orchestra and in Comparison with Leo Ornstein

Before a remarkable audience of musicians and pianoforte makers yesterday in Carnegie Hall, and on a stage decked as rarely before with some hundreds of flags of America and the Allies, the American Piano Company gave a demonstration of the Ampico Reproducing Piano, not only as "soloist" with orchestra, but with the artist "recorded," who was Leo Ornstein. The orchestra of the Metropolitan Opera House conducted masterfully by Arthur Bodansky, assisted by special permission of the Metropolitan Opera Company.

Mr. Bodansky and his ninety players made an interesting start on their own account, in Beethoven's third "Leonore" overture, with the distant trumpet calls reduced to a faintest echo from the cloakrooms of the hall. The only other number, aside from the final encore—an Ornstein solo record of the "Liebestraum" of Liszt, was that for which all present had assembled, the favorite D minor concerto of Rubinstein for pianoforte and orchestra.

Mr. Ornstein at first sat quietly on the stage while, in popular phrase, "the piano played itself." Two motors, as the instrument's inventor explained, spurred a Knabe concert grand during the first movement of the concerto, reproducing in power and speed, in all dynamic gradation and tonal shading, the artist's interpretation. The sense of personality in touch and tempo was only visibly modified, a change of sight, not of hearing, when the power was switched off and Ornstein himself took the keyboard to finish the two remaining divisions of Rubinstein's concerto.

Harold Bauer last November was "Heard" on another instrument, with another orchestra, the New York Symphony, when Bauer was actually in Chicago.

DATA

... in ... ut ...

... in ... d ... by ...ed ... in ... e tre ...tic d ...me ... last ... nman ...ing b ... autom ... n mov ... relat ... The ma ...a proc ... contra ...uipmen ...ace for ...dividua ...e mach ... At the ...anies ar ...quipmen ...heir owl

Among ...cently op ... two by t ...ness Mac ... of them ... feet in t ... on the A ... at Fiftie ... has 5,7 ... Broadwa ...tains a ... headquai ...enue and

Two Nation ... opened ...country ...using 1 ... space. ... America ... Wall Stra ... An ...ner ... The c ...en- ...eds

RS

AMST ...

Closing quotations
K U 544½
...mster Rubber 127½
...llton Tin ...462
...ll Maats ...a172½
...ndelsverein .139
...ll-Am Line .164¾

...ner Sh Un 179½
Phillips Gloe .1214½
Royal Blast F 902
Royal Dutch a142.3
Unilever 891
aQuoted in guilders

Dominion
75. Royal 1
74, and Loe
Canadian Av
Canadian B:
both were o.
Hollinger rose
metals eased.

S. Aluminum Output Off

Primary aluminum production the United States totaled ,427 short tons in January, 1, compared with 165,504 in preceding month and 164, in January, 1960, according he Aluminum Association.

COMPANIES ISSUE EARNINGS FIGURES
PAPER ... RS EYE NEW METHODS

The success in the market-place of this device brought great fortune to his employer and to him, and to his everlasting credit music lovers of today may hear and enjoy the artistry of some of the greatest pianists who have ever lived — completely free from the mechanical imperfections which Mr. Stoddard set about to eliminate.

Another important name in the Ampico development process is that of Lewis B. Doman, whose involvement was largely with the construction of the piano action itself which for the major number of years of the Ampico's tenure was done by the Amphion Piano Player Company of Syracuse, New York. Mr. Doman was involved with the Maestro Company of Elbridge, New York in the construction of an early-day piano player; this organization formed the basis of Amphion of which he became chief engineer. After the production of the Ampico was removed to East Rochester, New York in the mid-twenties, Mr. Doman — who was an accomplished musician as well as a technical wizard — proceeded to develop and started to manufacture a paper-roll pipe organ player, attachable to any pipe organ, called the "Artona". Only two of these units had been sold when the advent of sound movies and the stock market crash combined to squelch this market.

In 1924, Mr. Stoddard brought to the laboratories of the American Piano Company one Clarence Hickman, who had been previously employed by the U. S. Bureau of Standards. Hickman was perhaps the first technical person hired in the piano industry who enjoyed the distinction of having earned a Doctorate in Physics, in his case from Clark University in 1922.

Dr. Hickman set out to bring true scientific methodology to the piano laboratory, and a fine formal educational background combined with his inherent inventive genius resulted in the creation of an entirely new Ampico reproducing mechanism which was first introduced to the market late in 1928. This became known as the "Model B", and it represented the highest state of sophistication ever achieved in the art of reproducing the actual playing of human artists. Special music rolls were prepared for this model, but the refinement of the device was so outstanding that music rolls for both Model "A" and Model "B" instruments are interchangeable with practically no noticable affect on the music.

The "B" mechanism was installed in grand pianos only, and only into the middle 1930's. Unfortunately, their introduction to the market came so late that they were never produced in substantial quantity, and ones in good condition are rare today. This fact is

particularly distressing considering the magnificent renditions of which these pianos are capable. Fortunately, the rebirth of interest in mechanical pianos of all types has caused enthusiasts to be alert as to the value of the Ampico B in particular, and chances are that practically all those remaining in existence will be preserved for the enjoyment of future generations.

Of course the time of arrival of these machines on the market coincided closely with the stock-market crash and the advent of the great depression, with the result that the prices took quite a tumble from what reproducing pianos had previously cost. The Marshall and Wendell 4-foot, 8-inch small grand, for example, was actually priced at $995, a figure more in line with

The American Piano Company

makes Another Important Announcement

THE NEW AMPICO

...in a Baby Grand

$995

[$300 LESS THAN EVER BEFORE]

Sponsored by Chickering · Built by Marshall & Wendell

*What fun to dance to the brilliant music of the greatest pianists
the world has ever known!*

A few months ago we announced the wonderful new Ampico that plays a whole delightful program, or throughout dinner without interruption or the necessity of changing a roll.

Now still another new and extraordinary development, this same new Ampico in a mahogany baby grand at $995—the answer to thousands of music lovers who have longed for the joys of Ampico ownership, but have thought it beyond their means.

Only by the collaboration of three of the world's foremost groups of piano craftsmen—Chickering, Marshall & Wendell, Ampico—is it possible to offer a handsome, sonorous, full-toned Ampico Grand at $300 less than ever before.

The influence of Chickering—America's oldest builder of pianos, and world famous for the glorious Chickering tone—is clearly evidenced in the golden voice of this new Ampico Grand. Marshall & Wendell—founded in 1836, today achieving new fame in the designing of pianos for small rooms and the creating of beautiful period models—have contributed the early American case design which makes this new Ampico so distinguished a furniture-piece.

And from the makers of the Ampico comes that wonderful invention which preserves for all time the playing of great pianists, exactly recreating even the most delicate bits of their pianistic shading.

Indeed, this new Ampico offers you immeasurably greater value, immeasurably greater enjoyment than any other equivalent purchase might bring.

Can you think of a finer Christmas gift for your family and yourself? There isn't any!

By playing a delightful program or throughout dinner without changing a roll, the new Ampico allows you to enjoy selection after selection without stirring from your chair.

It reproduces exactly, upon the piano itself, the playing of the world's greatest artists, it is the only instrument which does so.

It is the supreme means of creating piano music. It is unrivaled in its artistry—unrivaled in the deep and satisfying pleasure which it affords to its listeners.

The development of this, the finest musical instrument in the world, is typical of the many important contributions which the American Piano Company has made to the music-loving public.

Typical also of the thoroughness with which the American Piano Company seeks to serve the needs of the American people, is the fact that the new Ampico is offered not simply in one model, but in 25; that there are not simply a handful of brilliant Ampico recordings to entertain you, but 2500.

The resources of the American Piano Company, the discoveries made during its 21 years of research in its laboratories, the skill and science of its piano-craft, the ideals of its workmen, are unique and matchless; and unique also is its long association with the builders of the Mason & Hamlin, acknowledged the finest of all pianos; the Knabe,

Day by day the Ampico pleasantly brings to your own children all the numerous benefits of noble music.

official piano of the Metropolitan O□□a Company; the Chickering, America's oldest □□no; the J. & C. Fischer, eagerly sought by th□□ally discriminating people both here and ab□□ac. he Marshall & Wendell, noted for its beau□□ period styles; the Haines Bros., chosen b□ 1□ conservatories.

Each of these pianos is the fine□ i □ ts price range. Indeed, no matter what price□ou □refer, an instrument of the American Piano □om□ny will bring you far richer tone and gre□□e outward beauty than will any other make at □e □e price.

With the Ampico, these superb ins ru□□s range from $750 up. Without the Ampic□□□ 375 up. Slightly higher west of the Rockies □□venient terms will be arranged by your deal□□ a generous allowance made for your old piano□o matter what its make. For complete Ampico □□talogue, write to the American Piano Company □ 84 Fifth Avenue, New York City.

MASON & HAMLIN · KNABE · CHICKERING

J.&C. FISCHER · MARSHALL & WENDELL · HAINES BROS · THE AMPICO

THE RECORDING INSTRUMENT ⌃

The record of the notes and tone coloring are taken down on the right-hand sheet in the form of pencil marks. The dynamic record, on the left, comes off the instrument without anything showing on the sheet. After it is put through a development process, marks indicating the measurement appear. These marks are then identified into pairs which are measured by a scale divided into one hundred and twenty parts; each part represents one-tenth of the difference in loudness discernible by the average ear. After this is done the measurements are transferred to the note sheet giving a figure at the beginning of each note which tells to an unbelievable accuracy just how loud that note was struck by the recording artist. The recording instrument is connected by means of electrical circuits to the recording piano located in another room where the artist plays the original music

WRONG NOTES ARE ELIMINATED

A painstaking checking with the sheet music eliminates wrong notes which were accidentally struck by the pianist

⌃ EVERY DETAIL IS MEASURED

Here the myriad dots and lines of the recording are examined and measured in the process of translating them into music-roll perforations which control the reproducing mechanism in the piano, and give a performance which clearly possesses even the emotional qualities of the original playing. Operators examine and measure every detail set down in the recording of a person's playing. One of the most interesting operations is the analysis of the tone quality which is made possible by indications showing the speed with which the dampers move up and down in the operation of the damper pedal. The reproduction of "half pedaling" and other subtle tone effects is made possible by a system of extending certain note perforations, which cause their tones to sing through from one harmony to the next, thereby giving effects identical with those which the original artist contrived to put into his playing

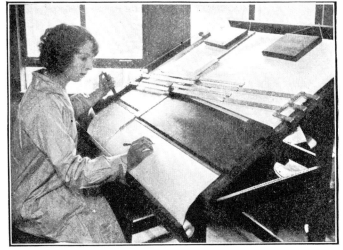

TRANSFERRING MEASUREMENTS

Unraveling the maze of figures in a dynamic record and transferring them to the roll is made extremely simple by an ingenious device

HAND PERFORATING PILOT HOLES

Hand-perforated holes at each end of the line indicating the position and duration of the notes guide the automatic stencil-making machine

Recording the Soul of Piano Playing

A RECORDING instrument, lately perfected by the Ampico Research Laboratory, accurately reveals the physical basis of those finer emotional qualities which mark the inspired performances of the great masters. A record taken on this instrument of the playing of an everyday pianist clearly shows the mediocrity of his performance as compared with that of one of the foremost great artists. That lovely liquid singing quality of tone—which is so rarely heard even in the great recital halls; that bel canto which subdues an audience to the point of making them regard the dropping of a pin as a misdemeanor; and a cough as a states prison offence; and

other effects, heretofore regarded almost as manifestations of the soul of the artist, are being analyzed for mechanical reproduction through the record music roll. This delicate recording instrument measures accurately the length of time it takes the hammer to travel the last eighth of an inch before it strikes the string, and from this measurement the exact loudness of the tone produced can be easily calculated, 416 hundred-thousandths of a second being required to produce the softest note and 51 hundred-thousandths for the loudest. About 60 times more energy therefore is expended in striking the loudest note than when producing a whispered pianissimo. Some

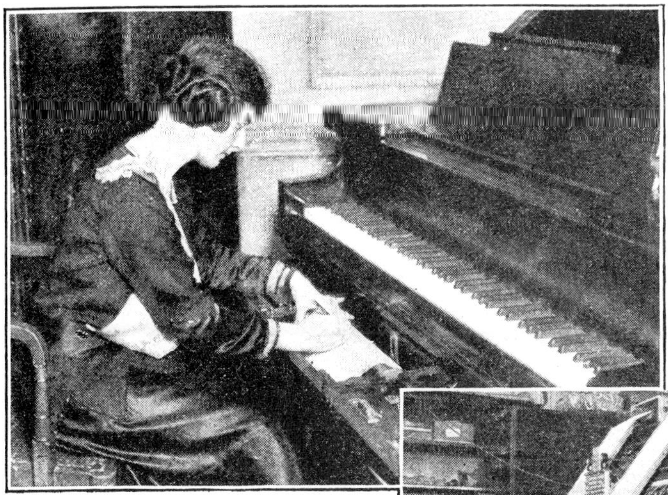

FIRST HEARING OF RECORD ↑

The first time a record is heard is when it comes from the automatic stencil-making machine. With only pilot perforations at the beginning and end of each note as guides, this machine has simultaneously cut a trial and a finished stencil. The stencil is three times the length of the trial record. An operator who is a finished musician takes the record at this stage and carefully examines every detail of the performance, checking up the result of the various stages in the long process of its completion. After the corrections indicated during this rigid inspection have been made, the record is an exact duplicate of the artist's playing, even in the smallest detail of light and shade, and is now ready for the artist to hear. Upon hearing the record, the artist becomes his own critic and if any further change is to be made, it is in deference to his wish to alter his performance

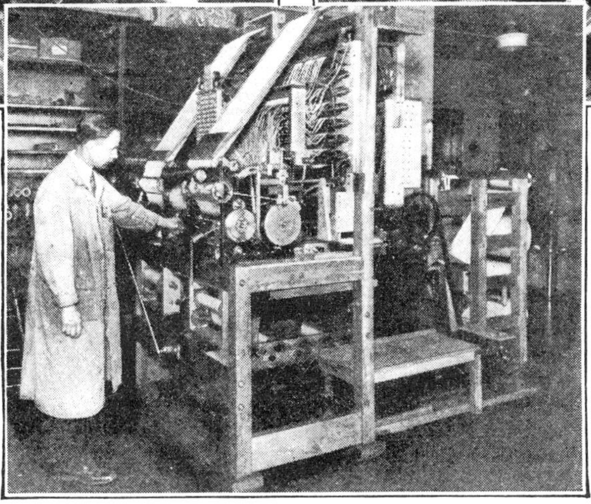

AUTOMATIC STENCIL MACHINE

This remarkable piece of automatic mechanism, which all but thinks, took more than five years to design and construct

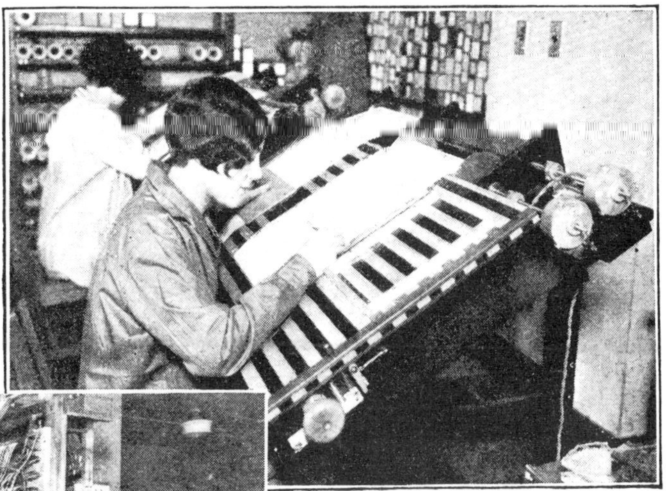

↑ **STENCIL CHANGES**

A special table over which the record and the stencil pass at the right proportionate speeds facilitates the making of any changes in the stencil which the artist has indicated in the record after hearing its performance. Usually the changes suggested by an artist have to do with dynamic where he accented a note too much or too little or where one phase had too much or too little contrast with another. He seldom touches the rhythm or the tone coloring. In a dance record, the rhythm is automatically checked and corrected in the stencil machine. After alterations are made the machine makes duplicates from this stencil and these in turn are used in the manufacture of the finished music rolls used in the reproducing piano. The actual music-cutting machines are duplex, cutting 30 rolls at a time in two groups of 15 each at the rate of three and one-half feet of finished record per minute of operation

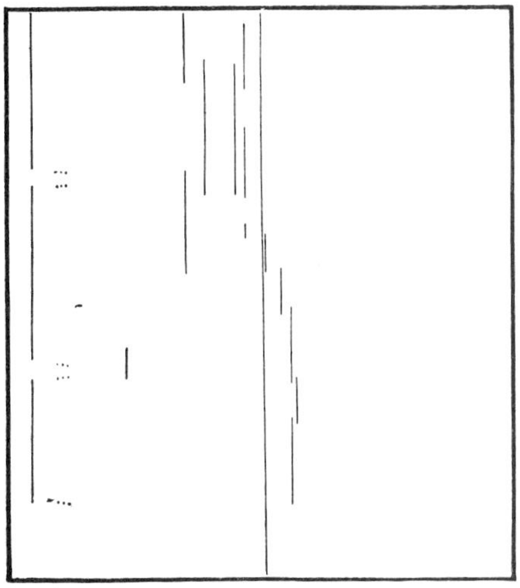

ORIGINAL RECORDING

Here are shown the pencilled lines of the notes, pedaling, and speed of the dampers

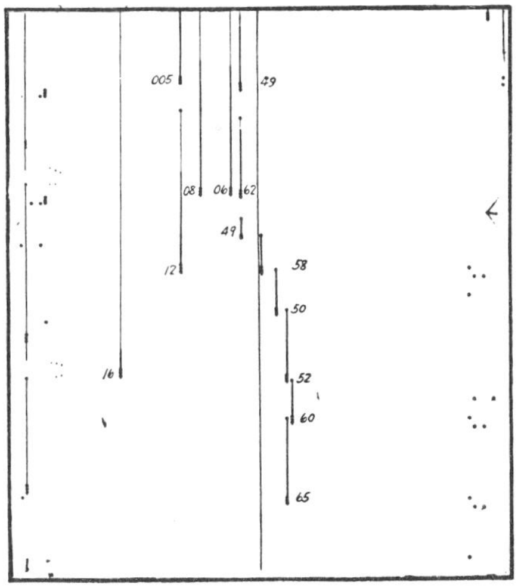

COMPLETED MASTER

It has the dynamic figures, tone coloring extensions and expression perforations

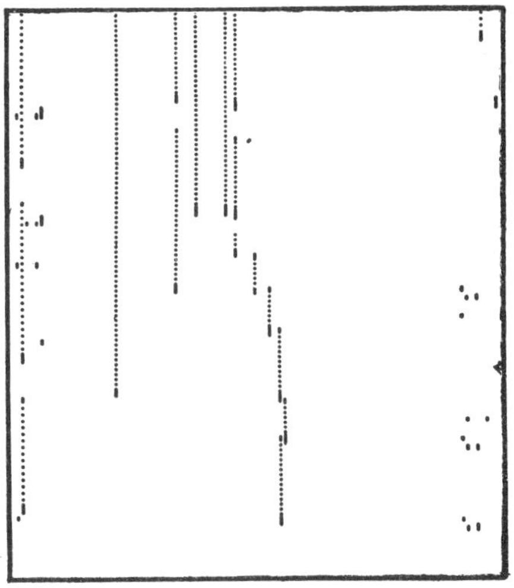

FINISHED PRODUCT

The record as it comes from automatic stencil machine, ready for first hearing

Revealing Idiosyncrasies of Artists

interesting side-lights are shown in the playing of great pianists by this super-accurate method of recording. One artist who produced an exceptionally beautiful quality of singing tone was found to co-ordinate his hands and pedaling to the almost incredible accuracy of one fiftieth of a second. We sometimes hear a performance which sounds perfect. Apparently there is not a flaw existing in the playing. Records of such performances when analyzed sometimes reveal unbelievable faults. One example, which to the ear showed the most remarkable control of dynamics, beautifully graduated melody, and an accompaniment played with almost inaudible softness and smoothness, revealed when submitted to the tests of an uncompromising measuring machine, a grossly faulty rhythm in the accompaniment. This shortcoming was not discernible in listening to the playing because the accompaniment was too soft to define the positions of the various notes. The records measure technical ability with uncanny accuracy. The marks of the pencil points of this soul-searching machine show exactly the control the pianist has over his fingers; whether his dynamics are nicely balanced or ragged; if his tone is good or bad; and even whether his playing has feeling or is cold. The performance is figuratively put under a microscope.

Ampico in the Chickering Grand Constructed
Specially for Jackie Coogan, Screen Star

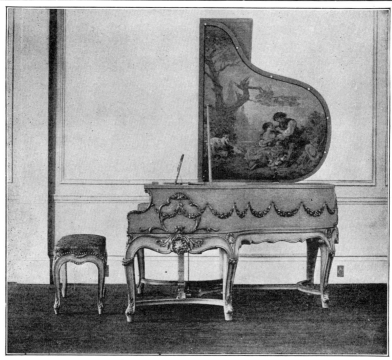

The Ampico in the Chickering Grand Just Shipped from Boston to the Southern California Music Co.
for Jackie Coogan, Famous Juvenile Film Star

BOSTON, May 4.

CHICKERING & SONS have just shipped to the Southern California Music Co. of Los Angeles a beautiful Ampico grand specially designed and executed on order from the parents of Jackie Coogan, famous screen star.

This instrument is finished in old ivory and gold, with the inside of the lid handsomely decorated in colors by Sutton. It required ten months to complete this piano, which, from the very start, was constructed for its famous owner. The main body of the case is in old ivory enamel, the garlands and carved decorations being entirely of gold with the high lights burnished.

DELCAMP is musical to his fingertips, an artist whose playing presents a rare, spontaneous quality and a sympathy with the compositions he chooses to interpret, which gives his artistry its peculiar charm.

He was a successful leader of a theatre orchestra at fifteen which led to the adoption of a musical career. His instruction was received chiefly at the Combs Conservatory of Music in Philadelphia, of which he is a graduate.

He has secured for himself a place in the foremost rank of pianists playing popular music and the sentimental ballads which are so important a part of the lighter music of the day. He records exclusively for the Ampico.

Two of the most popular artists who played for the Ampico were Adam Carroll (left, above) and J. Milton Delcamp. The information on Delcamp is from the elaborate Ampico Music Roll catalog printed in 1925, while Carroll's picture along with that of Ned Wayburn, the famous dance master, appeared in a 1926 issue of *Music Trade Review*. Both Wayburn and Alexis Kosloff of the Metropolitan Opera Company made extensive use of reproducing piano rolls in the teaching of dancing, as earlier illustrated. Another famous series of dance instruction rolls was that sponsored by Ted Shawn and Ruth St. Denis, the great ballet and modern-style masters of the art.

J. Milton Delcamp

Becomes So Engrossed in the Ampico That
He Neglects to Perform His Literary Work

Alexander Wolcott, Dramatic Critic of the "New York World," Takes Time, Between Inserting Music Rolls, to Write a Eulogy of the Ampico That Conveys His Ardent Admiration in a Unique Manner

JUST recently a New York dramatic critic made a discovery about the Ampico that becomes one of the highest — if not the highest — indorsements of this world famous reenacting instrument. Briefly, he discovered that the Ampico music is so fascinating it keeps him from performing his regular literary work.

Alexander Wolcott is dramatic critic for the "New York World." Besides attending premieres in Broadway theaters and writing reviews of the performances, he also contributes daily news articles about actors and current plays. At least, he did do this daily without interruption until—the Ampico entered his home.

All is changed now. Music from the extensive Ampico library is the order of the day in Mr. Wolcott's home. He says that he has found it irresistible — this reenacting instrument that plays the recordings of the world's great pianists with all of the subtle nuances and artistic finish that they display when appearing in person on the concert stage. And the literary work—that daily stint, a column wide and a column long — is becoming second to the Ampico.

This Mr. Wolcott has expressed in an indorsement of the Ampico that is cherished by the Ampico Corp. officials for its uniqueness, and which he supplemented by an explanation in person. The indorsement reads as follows:

"Will you make arrangements to remove at once the Ampico installed here in my quarters? I shall miss it acutely for I am used now to the luxury of having my twilight filled with Rachmaninoff's playing.

"But everyone flocks here to play the instrument at all hours of the day and night; and, whereas at first the illusion of social success this gave me was agreeable, it has since dawned on me that I never will get any work done while this beguiling attraction remains on the premises."

The receipt of this letter was followed by a personal conversation with Mr. Wolcott.

"Remove the Ampico from my home?" he parried

The Ampico in the Studio of Alexander Wolcott, "New York World" Dramatic Critic. So Fascinating Does Mr. Wolcott Find the Ampico That Its Reenacting of the World's Best Music Makes Serious Inroads Into His Working Hours

the salesman who had expressed a willingness to do anything possible to please the new Ampico owner, and who had the opening sentence of Mr. Wolcott's letter in mind when he spoke to the dramatic critic. "I'd like to see you or your company or anybody else take my Ampico away. No, sir, nothing doing. Oh, that letter of mine? Don't let that worry you in the least—no, sir, not in the least. It's just my way of expressing how delighted I am with the Ampico."

---

what ordinary upright player pianos of high quality had brought a few short years previously.

Music for the Ampico was manufactured as late as 1941, but only in very limited quantity compared to what earlier years had seen. This is especially regrettable considering that some of the very finest music rolls ever produced were the later ones, particularly the "long-play" rolls (up to 30 minutes) which would fit only the late-model Ampico piano, with the result that original rolls of this type are now exceedingly scarce. However, developments in the early 1960's were such that many of these are again available through perfection of copying machines owned and operated by various individuals throughout the United States, so that today there is no need for an owner

of an Ampico piano to be deprived of having in his music library some of the finest music ever perforated.

Since the Ampico and the Duo-Art mechanisms were available for use in pianos made only by the Aeolian Corporation and the American Piano Corporation, there naturally existed a market among all scores of independent piano manufacturers for a reproducing mechanism which they could put in their pianos. To meet this demand a number of other types were developed and promoted, but the only one which ever got a share of the market worth mentioning was the Welte (Licensee), manufactured by Kohler Industries of New York City, which controlled the Auto Pneumatic Action Company, the Standard Pneumatic Action Company, and others. This apparatus was, as

Ampico Featured as "Accompanist" for Dancing at Ampico Week in Wanamaker Auditorium, New York

Ned Wayburn, Authority on Stage Dancing and the Charleston, Who Indorses the Ampico

AMPICO WEEK in the Wanamaker Auditorium, New York, is an established institution in music circles in the New York metropolitan territory, attracting each fall capacity audiences to hear the best in music as interpreted by the Ampico.

This year the availability of the Ampico as an accompaniment for dancing was featured. This is a new field for the Ampico and was ably demonstrated at the annual convention of dancing instructors held in New York recently.

The various programs given on different days of the week featured dancers from some of the best known schools of modern and stage dancing in the country. Prominent among these were artists from the Wayburn School and the Mason Dancers.

Adam Carroll and Paul Rickenbach were starred on the program for the first day of Ampico Week at the Wanamaker Auditorium. Both of them are individually famous as pianists and both are Ampico artists.

Music by these artists, as interpreted by the Ampico, was also billed for the third day of the demonstration, when Wayburn School dancers again demonstrated their terpsichorean ability.

Werner Janssen was billed on Tuesday and Thursday. On the former day the Wayburn dancers again appeared and numbers by the Mason Dancers featured the program on Thursday.

The program for the concluding day of Ampico Week

Adam Carroll, Ampico Artist

at the Wanamaker Auditorium was a delightful one. The Ampico was featured as accompaniment for the Mason Dancers. Edna B. Bloom was also accompanied by the Ampico. Edgar Fairchild and Ralph Rainger were also on the program.

The Ampico as accompanying instrument for dancers has been indorsed by a number of the leading instructors in ballroom and stage dancing. Among these is Ned Wayburn, exponent of the Charleston. In his studio in New York the Ampico has a prominent place. Of the special Ampico roll for the Charleston he says:

"I just received the 'Ned Wayburn Original Charleston Instruction Recording,' and after playing it for all of my instructors and having them follow the chart, they, as one, indorsed it as a 100 per cent Charleston dance instructor, through the aid of the Ampico."

Alexis Kosloff, director of the Metropolitan Opera House ballet, in a letter to the Ampico Corp., says:

"My Ampico recordings for instructing fancy and interpretative dances have reached my studio and I hasten to compliment you on carrying out my ideas to the letter. We tried them at once on the new Ampico recently purchased, and had several beginners follow the No. 1 recording. Now they are anxious for an Ampico to follow up their studio work in practice at home, for the method is exactly the same as I teach here every day."

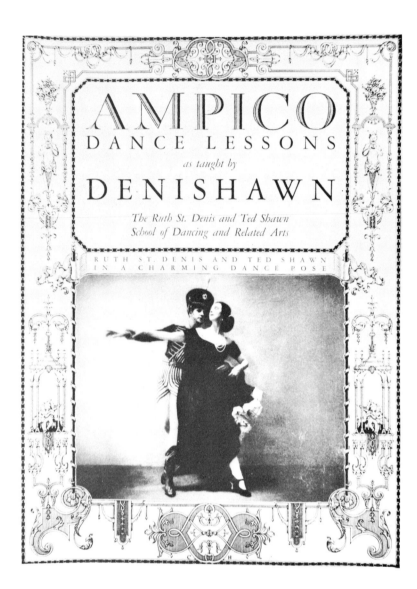

Knabe Ampico Used by University of California in Music Appreciation Classes and for Lectures

The Southern Branch of the University of California at Los Angeles, Which Has Purchased a Knabe Ampico for Its Music Department

THE southern branch of the University of California, located at Los Angeles, is the latest of the important educational institutions to add the Ampico to its teaching equipment.

A superb Knabe has just been installed by the Fitzgerald Music Co. The handsome college building in which the music classes are held is shown in the accompanying illustration. It stands in a beautifully landscaped campus, and with its mantle of ivy and splendid portico presents a picture of unusual charm.

The Ampico is used in the music appreciation classes and lectures, which are illustrated with the recordings of the great pianists and composers which the Ampico offers.

the name implies, a modification of the original German-developed Welte mechanism, both as to simplicity of construction and roll size.

The licensee mechanism was at one time installed in well over a hundred different makes of pianos in the United States, and the rallying call of its advertising — common to all makes in which it was installed — was "The Master's Fingers on Your Piano."

Notable among other reproducing mechanisms were the Solo Carola, the Artecho, the Apollo, the Angelus Artrio, the Aria Devina, and the Celco. The Artecho and the Apollo were mechanically the same, and both were developed by the American Piano Company — the former for sale to independent piano manufacturers, and the latter a name used by Wurlitzer when it adopted the device. The Solo Carola, if we may judge by the advertisement from *Scientific American,* was certainly an interesting technical approach to the problem of reproduction, but evidently it never sold in any quantities. The Angelus Artrio was used in the Hallet and Davis, Conway, and Merrill pianos built by the Conway Music Industries, a holding organization similar to, but smaller than, either Aeolian or American. The Celco reproducing medium was obtainable in Chase, Emerson, and Lindeman pianos.

Reproducing pianos had one outstanding characteristic, and that was cost — the mechanisms were inherently complicated and involved much hand labor for their construction. This opened up a market for sort of an "in-between" device — a player mechanism not really a reproducer, but more than an ordinary player—and somewhere between them in cost to the buyer. These were generally classed as "Expression Pianos," and examples are any of the machines designed to play "Recordo" rolls as produced by the QRS Company. Machines of this type were generally limited to some five degrees of expression, applied to the entire keyboard, whereas true reproducing pianos could produce amounts of expression anywhere from sixteen steps to infinite variation, within the range of the volume of the piano, applied individually to bass and treble sections, with perhaps further control of a theme or melody, as well as control of accentuation.

Music rolls for reproducing pianos were alleged to be "hand-played" by the originating artists, but the fact is that most such rolls were created by a multiple process wherein the pianist played the notes and the expression information was "edited" into the roll. Generally a sort of "musical secretary" would be present when an artist was recording; he would make notations on a musical score in accordance with the

These are the Phantom Hands of a thousand celestial pianists, their glorious genius preserved forever, through the miracle of Welte-Mignon reproduction

Only one in a thousand knows what a Reproducing Piano really is

FEW people know how a reproducing piano differs from a regular foot-operated player piano. But the difference is vast. The latter plays certain musical notes, punched into a player roll. The only expression possible is that which the operator gives through the use of levers.

The Reproducing Piano is an electrically operated instrument that reproduces the playing of great pianists. Not only does it play the musical notes, but it also brings forth every touch in technique, every subtlety of expression and tone color, in fact, you hear the *actual playing* of a master musician.

The Reproducing Piano was invented twenty years ago. It was the Welte-Mignon. Ever since it has remained supreme. After hearing it once you will be convinced that no other mechanism has been devised that records and then reproduces a pianist's playing with such

absolute fidelity. None other gives the perfect "Floating Crescendo," that ultimate touch of genius that makes faultless reproduction possible.

And in these twenty years the master pianists of the world have preserved their art in over two thousand master records. The Welte-Mignon Library can never be equalled. Many of the artists will never play again, but their phantom hands will live forever through their Welte-Mignon records.

The Welte-Mignon* is built into almost every famous make of piano, your own favorite among them, either Grand or Upright. Its artistic value cannot be pictured or described any more than can a musical composition. But it can be *heard* at any good piano store.

A brochure explaining the Welte-Mignon* in greater detail will be sent to you upon request. Address the AUTO PNEUMATIC ACTION CO., 12th Avenue and 51st Street, New York City.

> *The Welte-Mignon* brings such masters as these into your home—*
> D'Albert, Busoni, Carreno, Conradi, Danziger, Dohnanyi, Gabrilowitsch, Ganz, Grieg, Lamond, Leschetizky, Lhevinne, Mero, Paderewski, Saint-Saens, Samaroff, Scharwenka, Schelling, Bloomfield-Zeisler.

(Licensee)

Hear it—in comparison. There's a nearby dealer

*This modernized Welte-Mignon is LICENSED under the original Welte patents

Perhaps you ask, "What is the 'Welte-Mignon'?" It is a separate mechanism which, installed in a grand or upright piano, plays the instrument in exactly the same way that some talented musician played when he made the master reproducing roll. The Welte-Mignon* in a piano is practically invisible and does not interfere with manual playing. A few of the many pianos now equipped with the Welte-Mignon* are listed below:

Acoustigrande	Hardman	Ivers-Pond	Kurtzmann	Sohmer
Baldwin	Hazelton	Kranich & Bach	Mehlin & Son	Stieff

The Ampico in the Chickering in Italian Renaissance Case, Hand Carved in Italy. This beautiful instrument was on display at Chickering Hall during the Convention

W. C. Heaton, President, Auto Pneumatic Action Co.

New Foot-Propelled Welte-Mignon (Licensee)
Action Quickly Finds Friends in the Trade

THE announcement just made by W. C. Heaton, president of the Auto Pneumatic Action Co., of the new foot-operated Welte-Mignon (Licensee) action has caused considerable stir among dealers and manufacturers alike. From all parts of the country inquiries have come to the company's New York headquarters for detailed information about this new and improved foot-propelled player action for upright pianos.

It has long been realized in the trade that although the better type of player action affords full scope for expressive playing and is widely used by people of a certain musical appreciation, nevertheless there exists a still larger class of people who cannot successfully operate the usual type of player, because they lack a true sense of musical values. They have no "ear for music," and for that reason they play atrociously upon pianos equipped even with high grade player actions— actions which, in the hands of a music lover with a natural ear for music, can be made to render delightful service. Hence, too often, potential sales in a neighborhood are killed by someone unable to do justice to the possibilities of the player-piano he has purchased.

To reach the enormous markets of the non-musical and half-musical and to conquer the growing prejudice of the truly musical against the present type of player action, was the chief motive behind the experiments which have been conducted during the last four years by the Auto Pneumatic Action Co.

"In its laboratories, the Auto Pneumatic Action Co. through these years of quiet research and experimentation, has developed a successful adaptation of the unexcelled reproducing powers of the Welte-Mignon (Licensee) electric action to a foot-propelled action for upright pianos," says an official. "To bring the new action within the price range of the player and to make the action pump easily were the two outstanding difficulties which had to be overcome to make this new action commercially desired.

"These have been accomplished most successfully. The new foot-operated Welte-Mignon (Licensee) action is 'fool proof.' Even in the hands of the veriest novice, it would play with beautiful expression, while the difference in price as compared with the usual player action is negligible.

"It is believed the new foot-operated Welte-Mignon (Licensee) action opens an immense new market because of its special features and its popular price, and that it will do this without interrupting the present demand for players among that part of the population professing a more than average understanding of music. In fact, with intelligent selling, this new foot-pump Welte-Mignon (Licensee) action should materially help to stabilize the market for present types of player-pianos by reducing the number who play them badly and who are now destroying the demand for players, and even in some measure for pianos, too.

"The perfected action now announced is a development of the De Luxe pneumatic action designed to reproduce with exact fidelity the original interpretation of the pianist who recorded the music roll. The result is the same faithful effect obtained by the electrically driven Welte-Mignon (Licensee) reproducing action where even the slightest nuances and tone shadings in the playing of the artist himself are faithfully reproduced. The dynamic control is so complete that no guiding line on the music roll is necessary.

"The new action, besides playing Welte-Mignon (Licensee) and De Luxe reproducing rolls, plays the regular 88-note player roll. The reproducing mechanism is thrown into action by the simple shifting of a lever, which is then locked while the reproducing roll is being played.

"The Auto Pneumatic Action Co. has planned production upon this new action in such a manner as to make it available to manufacturers and dealers at a small increase in price over the regular player action, so that the complete piano, equipped with this new foot-operated reproducing action, can be sold at a comparatively slight advance in the retail price over player-pianos of the regular type of corresponding grades of the piano."

Manufacturers and dealers who have examined and tested the new foot-propelled Welte-Mignon (Licensee) action express themselves as enthusiastic over the results the Auto Pneumatic Action Co. has achieved and over the sales possibilities of pianos equipped with it, as shown by the orders the Auto Pneumatic Action Co. has already received.

expression characteristics as the pianist played the piece.

These notations would then be transferred to the form of punched holes on the master music roll which had read the actual notes struck, and the resulting roll would then be played back to the artist on a regular reproducing piano. Decisions would then have to be made by the artist as to whether the expression information was rendering the music in the manner that he intended, and corrections made accordingly. By a process of elimination, the roll would be refined to the point where all were satisfied, and the roll would only then be released for production and sale.

It is also possible for a person who understands how the expression characteristics desired in a musical performance can be coded into holes on the music roll to create an entirely satisfactory product, and indeed most of the Ampico rolls created during the 1930's were done by this means by one Frank Milne who masqueraded under a variety of Nom de Plumes as well as his own name. Many of the finest light and popular tunes produced and sold during this period were arranged by Milne in his own home, and he never even owned a reproducing instrument!

It remained for Dr. C. N. Hickman to develop for Ampico the one great scientific process for recording the actual performances — expression as well as notes — automatically as a piece was played. This was his "spark-chronograph" machine, which took advantage of the fact that the one variable of greatest importance in recording piano expression is the velocity of the piano hammer as it strikes the strings. His machine was able to measure this wonderfully well, but even at that, some human editing was required as described in the *Scientific American* article appearing on these pages. (readers desiring further information on this remarkable device are referred to *Re-Enacting the Artist,* cited earlier and in the bibliography)

FIVE DUO-ARTS INSTALLED IN DENVER SCHOOLS

Two Included the Steinway and Three, the Weber—All Furnished by Knight-Campbell Music Co., Whose Educational Director, Mrs. Cynthia Reynolds, Works in Close Cooperation with Denver School Officials

Scenes in Denver Schools Where Five Duo-Arts Play an Important Part in Musical Education of the Pupils

CONVINCING proof of the value of cooperation is evidenced in Knight-Campbell's recent successful campaign, the immediate result of which is the installation of the Duo-Art in many of Denver's educational institutions.

Mrs. Cynthia Reynolds, director of the Knight-Campbell educational department, has been working in close cooperation with the Aeolian educational department in New York, directed by Franklin Dunham. Outstanding among recent achievements is the installation of three Weber Duo-Art grands in the three beautiful junior high schools of Denver. Two Steinway Duo-Art grands have been added to the equipment of two other large high schools.

These instruments are being used in the auditoriums of the various schools where they form a valuable aid, among other things, in music appreciation and music history courses because of the enormous library of recordings from which the teacher may draw illustrative material.

Mrs. Reynolds and the Aeolian educational department have had the able support in their work of Clarence Campbell and W. W. Bradford. Mrs. Reynolds is alive to the possibilities open in the school and music circles in the Far West. She is convinced that there, as in other parts of the country, is a crying need for this instrument, with its many sided uses, so adaptable to service in the school.

With the Duo-Art the student can study the forms and development of music from pre-Bach days to the present; the development of harmony can be illustrated, and by playing the interpretations of the same compositions by many great artists the student is afforded the opportunity of making comparisons.

Not only in the auditorium and the music room is the Duo-Art of value, but as well in the gymnasium, precluding the necessity of a pianist.

The Duo-Art holds a unique place in musical education today. In the North and South, in the East and now the Far West, it is answering the cry of musical educators, points out a music critic. John Kendel, director of music in the Denver schools, has welcomed its splendid work in educational institutions. Mr. Kendel is probably one of the most progressive directors of school music in the United States, and he views the entire project of Duo-Arts in the schools with the utmost sympathy.

REPRODUCING VERSUS EXPRESSION PIANO

A REPRODUCING piano is the highest expression of the artistic and mechanical genius of the musical instrument industries. These instruments reproduce with absolute fidelity as to dynamics, phrasing and musical expression the playing of the world's greatest pianists. In an earlier edition of the GUIDE, when the reproducing piano was more or less in its infancy, it was stated that these instruments were epoch-making in character and would exert a tremendous influence of an educational nature. This prophecy has been fulfilled.

In the evolution that has taken place in the piano industry there has been the development of the expression piano, which is an improvement over the ordinary player-piano, yet which does not represent the perfection that is embodied in the reproducing instrument. As a result of this evolution there are certain unscrupulous dealers in the trade today who are selling expression pianos as reproducing instruments and thereby offering in a misleading manner an instrument that does not possess the qualities of performance to be found in the reproducing piano.

It is, therefore, the purpose of this article to warn the buying public of the danger that lies before them in the selection of a reproducing piano. They should first bear in mind the fact that there is a decided difference between the so-called expression piano and the reproducing piano.

The principal point of difference between these instruments is that the reproducing piano has the ability to record the playing of the artist so faithfully that in its performance of reproduction it records the exact note with the identical degree of force whenever required by the artist. This perfection in reproduction will not be found in any instrument other than a reproducing piano.

The reproducing piano represents three instruments in one, viz.: the pianoforte, the player-piano and the reproducing piano. Its mechanism is capable of reproducing not only the notes, tempo, phrasing and attack, but it records to the most minute degree every tone gradation precisely as originally interpreted and played by the artist, including all the dynamics of the rendition, all crescendoes and diminuendoes, also all pedal and other expression effects of the recording artist.

Reproducing pianos are now being made available by many of the foremost artistic piano makers of the country. Their rise to eminence has been within the last few years, during which they have won notable triumphs. Many of these instruments have been used as soloists with the most noted symphony orchestras in America. Their generous indorsement by great conductors and great artists has been general and unstinted, and the great musical interpreters of the piano have recorded their playing. Usually these instruments are operated by an electrically driven motor, but they may also be operated in the usual way with foot-power and may be used not only to reproduce the playing of an artist, but also with the ordinary music roll made for the regulation player-piano.

It is not the purpose of this treatise to disparage the expression piano. It is an instrument of artistic ability, but it cannot be accepted as a piano representing the same mechanical and artistic achievement as the reproducing piano.

And while the expression piano does present an agreeable rendition of music adapted for its use, it does not attempt to faithfully record every individual feature of the artist's playing.

For fidelity in reproduction the reproducing piano has no equal. It stands alone in the field of pianofortes and represents the highest achievement in pianoforte manufacture. It is, therefore, important that the purchaser consider carefully, and in every detail the merits of the instrument he intends to buy.

New Angelus Master and Pupil Rolls, Developed by Godowsky, Give Every Piano Learner Advantages of Master's Instruction

New System Just Released Will Prove Great Benefit to Every Dealer—Hallet & Davis Piano Co. at the Forefront of Piano Instruction Movement With This Splendid New Development—Godowsky Personally Assists Every Child in Piano Study Under This New System—Dealers to Benefit by Advertising Campaign and Promotion Material from Company—Idea Designed as Great Aid to Piano Teacher

Leopold Godowsky, World Famed Pianist, Recording at the Angelus Reproducing Studios, Meriden, Conn.

Pictorial Design That Fittingly Illustrates the New Angelus "Master and Pupil" Reproducing Rolls. It Depicts Godowsky Guiding the Hands of the Child Pianist

HAT is the best system of teaching a child to play the piano; that is, teaching the child beyond that degree of elementary instruction that can be given by the group method?

Ask this question of half a dozen piano teachers, and you will get as many answers; the ultimate sum of all the answers being that the best system is any system the best masters use. To compress the information within a sentence—piano instruction is an individual art, the value of which is dependent upon the musical stature of the instructor.

Unfortunately for those who would learn to play the piano, there is an insufficient number of great pianists to give the instruction necessary, and among this limited number of great pianists there are very few who have any time to give to instructional work anyway. A great pianist plays at concerts—he doesn't assist children, no matter how talented. If he once started it he would soon be doing nothing else.

And yet—how are our children to become better pianists without the best quality of instruction?

The Angelus Answers the Question

Now here has long been a genuine musical dilemma, and it is vastly to the credit of the Hallet & Davis Piano Co., New York, that it has at last found a solution. By this solution the Angelus reproducing grand itself becomes the teacher, and a teacher of world-wide

fame. Through this new method the Angelus speaks with the strong, singing tones of Leopold Godowsky, one of the greatest of living pianists, and little children are, in a sense, brought into personal contact with this splendid artist. Godowsky's own hands guide and direct the pupil; Godowsky's own playing is set as a model to copy, and Godowsky himself, via the Angelus, has unlimited time to give to the piano instruction of every child in the country.

Designed as Aid to Piano Teacher

In presenting the Godowsky Master and Pupil Angelus Reproducing Roll it is pointed out that this method is not designed to eliminate the piano teacher from the scheme of things, but rather serve as a strong cooperative force in the relation of teacher to pupil and thereby give the pupil the benefit of specially prepared instruction by one of the most eminent living masters of the pianoforte.

Dealers will at once recognize the value of such a development. "I would like a reproducing piano," the prospective customer often says, "but who will teach my child to play it?" To this the dealer may now answer: "Leopold Godowsky, one of the world's greatest composers and pianists." With such an answer on the tip of his tongue, the sale is already more than half made for the dealer.

Creation Is Godowsky's Own

The plan is Godowsky's own, working in cooperation with Walter C. Hepperla, the dynamic head of the Hallet & Davis Piano Co.

The system is embodied in the new Godowsky Master and Pupil Angelus rolls, preliminary announcements of which have already been made to the trade. Patents covering them are pending.

Forty-two of these rolls are included in the complete set of the first releases of which have just been announced by the Hallet & Davis Piano Co., all compositions by Godowsky, bearing the generic title of "Godowsky Miniatures." Each is a full length Angelus roll, to be used in the Angelus reproducing piano. Each is arranged to give the pupil the personal instruction of the composer. The initial releases will be ready for trade distribution in the near future.

Each roll will be accompanied by the appropriate sheet music, scored as it would be for any musician, and each roll is personally recorded by the great pianist who developed the system.

The rolls are divided into three sections. Carefully following the music, the child plays the roll on the

Angelus. In the first section Godowsky plays the entire composition for the student; then the child who is following the instruction plays the treble to accompany this bass which is played by Godowsky. In the third section the situation is reversed; the instructor plays the treble, while the child plays the bass. Thus the composition is played by the master's hands, the melody being interwoven as only Godowsky can interweave it, while the child observes, and the roll once played in this fashion, the child is free to practise it, following the melody from the notes, observing and remembering how it was done by the master pianist.

To devise a better system would be difficult. Timing, accent, every feature of playing are shown exactly and carefully by the master; the pupil is forced to improve. It is necessary to play well in the last two parts of the roll to follow the playing of Godowsky; and having played well each half of the selection, the pupil can hardly fail to combine them well, under the very eyes, as it were, of Godowsky himself.

Among the forty-two compositions so accurately taught are many already familiar to the musical public: "Processional March," "Arabian Chat," "Tyrolean," "The Miller's Song," "Meditation," "Humoresque" "Barcarolle" and "In Days of Yore" are only a few. They are the result of a special trip to this country made last summer by the pianist, when this system was developed and this group of rolls made.

Dealer to Benefit by This Teaching Method

This new teaching method and the accompanying rolls are covered by patents pending; the announcements of the Hallet & Davis Co. are still being sent out, and

---

LEOPOLD GODOWSKY, the master artist who developed the new teaching method described in the accompanying article, says of it: "This is my personal piano instruction system, and I am glad to say that the Angelus reproduces my playing with absolute fidelity. It is not designed to wholly teach the pupil but rather to augment the work of the teacher. By no means is it intended to eliminate the teacher."

"THIS system," says Walter C. Hepperla, president of the Hallet & Davis Piano Co., "offers dealers an unequalled opportunity. Never before have merchants been able to say to prospective reproducing piano purchasers what they can now say: 'We will send one of the greatest living pianists into your home to assist you in the study of piano music.' We are very happy that the Hallet & Davis Piano Co. is able to offer piano merchants and the public such a long step in advancing piano instruction. This new teaching method and rolls are covered by pending patents."

A Musical Miracle

The *SOLO CAROLA* INNER-PLAYER
the Most Marvelous Musical Invention of the Century

THE perfect Player-Piano has been produced. In fact it was produced two years ago, but it has never been our policy to experiment at the expense of the public. And so for many months this instrument has been tested in every conceivable way.

Over one hundred and seventy-five thousand dollars and eight years of ceaseless labor have been spent in perfecting it.

With this announcement all other so-called "solo devices" become obsolete—or nearly so.

In playing the SOLO CAROLA you cease to be conscious of the feeling that the music is being *ground out*. For this instrument is the *only* one that has complete solo control. You experience then, the thrill and pleasure of playing a composition pianistically—perfectly.

The Principle of the Solo Carola

Like many great inventions, the mechanism of the SOLO CAROLA is simple.

If you place your foot upon the so-called "soft pedal" of a piano and then strike downward upon a key, you cause a hammer to fly forward about an inch, striking a string and sounding a note.

If you next take your foot off the "soft pedal" and strike a second key, the resulting tone will be much louder than the first. Because when you released the pedal the hammer dropped backward to nearly double its former distance from the string. When you again struck the key, the hammer (traveling about two inches this time) struck the wire with greater force, causing a louder tone.

The principle of the SOLO CAROLA is a development of this simple theory.

A piano has eighty-eight hammers. When not in the act of striking a note, all eighty-eight hammers lie at an equal distance from the strings against a bar which is called a "rest rail." In the ordinary piano and player-piano this "rest rail" may be moved to either of two fixed distances from the strings.

In the SOLO CAROLA the mechanism corresponding to the "rest rail" is movable. When you wish to play softly you merely pump softly and the hammers automatically and instantly move up close to the strings. When you wish to play louder you pump slightly faster and the hammers strike from greater and greater distances the faster you pump.

It is simple—it is automatic—it requires no levers to operate.

World's Greatest Manufacturers of Pianos and Inner-Player Pianos

And now the invention that's most important of all. Notice the long vertical openings in the tracker-board, shown in the accompanying illustration. They are called Solo slots. There is one over each note. Each slot is connected with a small bellows which independently controls the position of each individual piano hammer. You will notice that the roll perforations register exactly with these solo slots before the ordinary striking openings (shown underneath the solo slots) are reached. Thus each piano hammer is automatically set in any desired position before the note is struck. Thus you see, in how simple a manner this player produces an infinite variety of solo effects never before approached on any other player-piano.

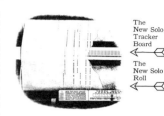

The New Solo Tracker Board

The New Solo Roll

Individual Features

The SOLO CAROLA is the *only* player-piano ever made on which you can strike any of the eighty-eight solo or accompaniment notes either independently or simultaneously with varying degrees of power.

The SOLO CAROLA is the *only* player-piano that eliminates completely the mechanical effect in reproducing music.

The SOLO CAROLA is the *only* player so constructed as to be able to play *every* composition ever written for the piano without mutilation or rearrangement just as it was written and just as great artists play it. The SOLO CAROLA will play any standard 88-note player roll made.

The SOLO CAROLA faithfully reproduces the playing of famous pianists with all their individualities of touch, accent, nuance and rhythm.

In *every* respect the SOLO CAROLA is the most wonderful player-piano that has ever been made. We simply can't help being enthusiastic about it—nor can you when you own one.

Musicians Endorse the Solo Carola

Eminent pianists agree that the performance of the SOLO CAROLA is thoroughly musical and supremely artistic.

Some of the most celebrated pianists now living make records for the SOLO CAROLA exclusively because it is the *only* player-piano which reproduces accurately just what they play—just as they play it.

The SOLO CAROLA will astonish and delight you.

With it you may play the softest, dreamiest waltz or the most thunderous crash of martial music in a way heretofore absolutely impossible with a player-piano.

You have only to see, to hear and to play it yourself to be convinced that the *perfect* player-piano has at last been produced.

The Cable Company

Wabash and Jackson
Chicago

NEW GODOWSKY PUPIL
ROLLS ARE ANNOUNCED

the publicity on this new teaching method is being rushed forward with all possible speed.

A more valuable aid to the child than a set of these instructions could hardly be imagined, for not only does it offer instruction of unparalleled value, but it gives the child as well a chance to hear Godowsky's personal playing of forty-two of his best compositions, an opportunity that both pupil and music lover will appreciate as a treat.

It is for this reason that work on the new system has been so rushed that every dealer may have his supply of the first releases at an early date, and dealers will realize the value of this, for the Godowsky Master and Pupil Reproducing Rolls offer the dealer not only an ideal merchandising item in themselves, but an opportunity to vastly increase his piano business by selling the pianos in which the Angelus is installed.

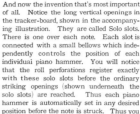

ST. LOUIS THEATER TO HAVE
$7,500 BALDWIN WELTE-MIGNON
GRAND FINISHED IN GOLD LEAF

As thousands of St. Louisans pass through the new Ambassador Theater lobby into the sumptuous auditorium they will hear popular melodies played on the most expensive piano in St. Louis—a $7,500 instrument that has been finished in leaf gold.

The piano is a Baldwin Welte-Mignon (Licensee) reproducing grand furnished the theater by the Baldwin Piano Co. of St. Louis. With it went a large and varied assortment of recordings from the extensive Welte-Mignon (Licensee) library of music—the best known compositions of famous pianists and composers.

This piano will be placed on the mezzanine promenade and at the conclusion of each show will be played

View of the Baldwin Welte-Mignon (Licensee) Gold Piano to Be Installed in the Lobby of the New Ambassador Theater, St. Louis

by a distinguished pianist. At other times, through the aid of music rolls, it will reproduce the compositions of the finest music writers.

The Ambassador is the latest venture of the well known producers, Skouras Brothers, and was completed late in August at a cost of $5,500,000. It is one of the most complete and beautifully appointed theaters in the Middle West.

The Baldwin Welte-Mignon (Licensee) reproducing grand will be located on the grand mezzanine promenade that leads to the upper levels of the auditorium.

———•———

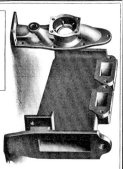

The Evolution of the Music Roll

By Charles F. Stoddard (*Inventor of the Ampico*), Director, Research Laboratory, American Piano Company, New York City

Convention Address

WHEN Mr. O'Meara asked me to talk to you on the subject of evolution, I immediately asked him if he did not realize that many people associate evolution with the monkey, and he replied that there are just as many who associate the music roll with the monkey. I asked him what he meant and he quickly explained that he referred to the music roll that Tony puts in his hand organ while Jocko collects the pennies.

I have a photograph of an old print dated 1657, thirty-seven years after the Pilgrims landed at Plymouth Rock, which shows a beautiful pipe organ operated by such a roll. The entire mechanism was driven by an overshot water wheel. In Latin is a complete description of this organ which tells exactly how the music was laid out. I shall read a translation of the Latin:

> Transfer the Pythagorean melody to the aforesaid phonotactic cylinder. Since the melody consists of 54 times, or measures, the whole circumference of the cylinder should be divided into 54 equal parts; then each part should be subdivided into three parts since each note of this melody equals one-third of a measure. In the figure the heavy lines drawn longitudinally on the cylinder mark the first division into 54 parts, the dotted line shows the subdivisions into three parts. Then transfer to the cylinder the melody and fix the teeth which correspond to the notes in the proper places.

Notice particularly that we have a complete description in 1657 of the exact method of laying out a music roll which was followed up to the first part of the present century.

The little wooden roll filled with pins that Tony puts in his hand organ is made by the selfsame method that was used in the earliest automatic keyboard instruments.

In about the year 1840 we find the first mention of the use of the continuous paper roll which later supplanted the pin cylinder. Claude Felix Seytre of Lyons, France, appears to be the inventor of the perforated paper note sheet. This patent was dated

January 24, 1842. Until about 1850 the only mechanically operated keyboard instruments were organs. At this time, we find Hunt and Bradish in Warren, Ohio, taking out a patent on a little pianoforte controlled by a paper music roll and actuated by a crank turned by hand, so we may safely say that about 1850 was the earliest date of a piano player actuated by a paper music roll. This patent of Hunt and Bradish is accompanied by a drawing of a little piano with only thirteen strings which could be carried around easily under the arm. The illustration shows the crank, but as no monkey is shown I presume it was not carried under the arm or strapped over the shoulder.

The first music rolls which were laid out were merely perforated rolls with the notes exactly as they were shown in the sheet music, thus leaving it entirely to the operator to provide the musical expression. A great many thousands of players were sold which were operated by these crude mathematically laid out music rolls. How well do we all remember having a neighbor who owned one of those piano players! Those owners had a lot of fun trying to put musical expression into those mechanically played notes, but the neighbors suffered a lot of agony.

Generally speaking, the owners of those instruments had about as much idea of music as the old fellow in the country church orchestra who played the piccolo. At one of the vesper services at which the orchestra performed this particular old fellow got the pages of his sheet music mixed so that he was playing the third page while the rest of the orchestra were playing the second page. A distinguished gentleman who sat in the third pew was so upset by the mistake that he could not repress his feelings and in his disgust said right out loud, "the damn fool piccolo player." After the orchestra had completed its selection, the minister stepped to the front of the pulpit and asked the person in the congregation who called the piccolo player a "damn fool" please to stand up. The distinguished gentleman did not stand up, but a little deacon in the back of the church rose and said, "Preacher, may I suggest that you do not try to find out who called the piccolo player a damn fool, but that you try to find out who called the damn fool a piccolo player?"

It was a long time before it became evident that the general public were not musicians. They loved music, but they did not know how to give musical expression. Realizing this, many inventors in the field of the player piano set about to construct various devices which would help the public to give musical expression to those mechanically played notes.

In 1891 R. M. Hunter of Philadelphia conceived the idea of putting a wavy line on the music roll to denote when the music should be played loudly and when softly. This was the first step in the long road traveled in the development of the marvelous present day players. From this important step, the evolution of the music roll took a turn toward producing various effects automatically instead of leaving them to the discretion of the operator of the player piano.

Following Mr. Hunter by nearly ten years, F. L. Young of the Aeolian Company conceived the idea of the *Metrostyle,* which was also a wavy line running the length of the sheet and a pointer attached to the tempo lever, the index end of which reached up to the tracker bar. If the tempo lever were moved so that this index end of the pointer followed the line the various retards and accelerandos and other tempo effects were rendered in musical style.

Some five years later the *Themodist* was invented simultaneously by Mr. Crooks and Mr. Skinner. This improvement in the music roll consisted of inserting supplementary perforations on the edge of the sheet opposite each theme or melody note. These perforations controlled a mechanism which automatically brought out the melody of the piece.

While these later improvements were going on in this country, Edwin Welte in Germany was attacking the problem in an entirely new manner. He was taking an actual record of a musician's playing and reproducing it entirely automatically. Mr. Welte's music roll contained supplementary perforations which controlled the force with which the different notes were struck. His achievement was by far the greatest step forward made up to that time in mechan-

ically produced music. Simultaneously with the development of the *Welte,* there was a similar development made in this country which later was brought out by the American Piano Company and is now known as the *Ampico.*

Sometime after the *Ampico,* came the *Duo-Art,* which was also entirely automatic. These reproducing instruments were all operated by electric motors instead of by foot pedals.

With the advent of the *Ampico,* there came another improvement in the music roll, the development of a means for producing tonal effects which had been, up to that time, regarded by many musicians as not being within the realm of mechanism but were rather, as they liked to express it, "A manifestation of the soul of the performer." This invention consisted of arbitrarily extending the perforations of certain notes in order to carry their tones across from one harmony to another—thereby obtaining precisely the effect which the performer did by his subtle operation of the damper pedal. Numerous patents were applied for and granted to the American Piano Company on this method of obtaining these subtle tonal effects.

The next development in the evolution of the music roll came in the method of recording a musician's playing. Mr. Welte's method was secret, so we cannot know how it was done. The method used in the early days of the *Ampico* was covered by a patent granted about 1912. This consisted of placing electric contacts on the piano key which would indicate on a moving sheet the length of time it took the key to be depressed. We can readily see that it requires a much longer time to depress the key when playing a soft note than it does when playing a loud note. So a long mark denotes a soft note and a short mark denotes a loud note, with various gradations between.

This *Ampico* process of recording, like most of the others, was kept a profound secret. Many people were skeptical about it being possible to record all the delicate shadings that a pianist gave to his playing and they regarded these secret recording processes as "the bunk." Only recently has the American Piano Company decided to break away from this great secrecy and to show what it is doing in the way of recording. There are some recent improvements in the process upon which patents have not been granted, and these of course must for a while be kept secret, but in the main, I will explain how it is done.

Any process of recording which goes in for extreme accuracy entails an unbelievable amount of labor and expense. I have in mind a very wonderful record of Lhévinne's playing of the *Blue Danube Waltz* which took over five weeks to complete, and represented over 100,000 operations. This piece contains 7,915 notes and every note required thirteen or more operations before the record was ready for publication.

Generally speaking, the method employed in making an *Ampico* recording is a complete and thorough measurement of every detail of the playing, reducing the same to terms of simple figures. These figures, which show with great exactness just what the artist does, are then translated into side hole perforations which cause the *Ampico* to give forth exactly the same music as does the artist.

Two records are taken simultaneously of the artist's playing, one of the notes and the pedaling, and the other of the dynamics. The record of the notes consists of penciled marks made on a moving sheet. The exact position of the pedaling is recorded as is also the speed with which the pedal is depressed and released. The dynamic record consists simply of measuring with great accuracy the amount of energy in the hammer just at the instant it strikes the string. It is right at

this point where the secrecy of the *Ampico* method exists, but I may say that the accuracy of this measurement discloses differences in the pianist's touch ten times more delicate than the human ear is capable of detecting.

In the *Blue Danube Waltz,* Shultz-Elver transcription, played by Josef Lhévinne, there are, as I said before, 7,915 notes, and the dynamic force with which Mr. Lhévinne struck everyone of these notes was measured accurately.

The first operation on the note record is a check of each and every single note with the notes on the sheet music to eliminate wrong notes. We call the checking of each individual note with the sheet music one operation, so that in the note check-up of the *Blue Danube Waltz* there were 7,915 operations. This took one operator about three days. While the notes are being checked, there are two operations going on in the dynamic record, one the identification of the marks, and the other the measurement of them. The two sheets are then put on a pantograph table, which makes it very easy for the operator to transfer the figures of the dynamic sheet, which show the loudness with which every note was struck, to the note sheet. This entails another 7,915 operations, making a total of 31,660 operations to this point. The roll is then given to an operator who translates the record of the pedaling into extended perforations which, with the automatic damper pedal of the reproducing piano, control the quality of tone. This is one of the most interesting steps in the process of editing the roll. Now we have a note sheet with a figure at the beginning of every penciled mark telling exactly how loud that note was struck. Another operator then takes the roll and translates these figures into side hole perforations which will control the loudness of every note, so that the performance the *Ampico* will render is exactly as the artist played. This necessitates 7,915 more operations, and on this particular roll required nearly five days of the operator's time.

The producing of subtle tone shading through pedaling is a very important part of the playing of every great pianist. There is full pedaling and half pedaling. Half pedaling is a quick use of the damper pedal which does not wholly cause the strings touched by the dampers to cease sounding. The vibrations of a half-pedaled string continue long after the artist's finger has left the key. These vibrations mingled with those of the notes struck in a harmony immediately following create one form of what is known as tone color. This is one of the subtle things that makes piano playing so wonderful. It is something thoroughly understood and constantly used by the great artists.

Extended marks on the side of the *Ampico* record show exactly where the damper pedals lifted the dampers from the strings and where they were returned. There are also indications which show exactly how fast the dampers were lifted from the strings or returned to them, and how deeply the dampers sunk into the strings.

To solve this troublesome problem of reproducing these subtle tonal pedal effects with a mechanically operated pedal mechanism, the *Ampico* uses a patented process of extended note perforations. We can readily understand that so long as a note perforation is extended, just so long will the key remain depressed and the damper be held off the string, and the string continue to sing or vibrate. If the record of the artist's playing shows that he "half-pedaled" in a given place, and did not damp out certain tones

which had been sounded, the perforations in the music roll controlling these tones will be extended right through that part where the mechanical pedaling damps the strings. We must remember that mechanical pedaling is not "half pedaling," but complete pedaling. The tonal effects obtained by this process of extended note perforations are identical with those obtained by the artist.

I have gone into an explanation of this detail at great length as it is one of the peculiarities of the *Ampico* record which is very often misunderstood. Many times in the record there are as many as eighteen or twenty note perforations being extended at the same time. This makes it appear as if the artist had held down that many notes with his fingers, which would be an impossibility. What the artist did do was to keep that many strings singing by the manipulation of his damper pedal, and in order to give precisely the same quality of tone as the artist did these perforations are extended as we see them in an *Ampico* music roll.

Up to this time no holes have been placed in the record, but it is now ready for the preliminary perforating. This is done by hand. A perforation about one-fourth of an inch long is placed at the front end of all the penciled lines indicating notes, except the very shortest, for which a much shorter perforation is used. A single round hole is placed at the end of each penciled line. With these preforations merely at the beginning and end of the penciled lines the record is now ready to go to the automatic stencil making machine. It must be realized that it has not yet been put on a player, therefore it has never been heard, although more than 71,235 operations have been done on it.

The automatic stencil machine finishes the stencil completely, and a trial cutting with it ready to be heard, in less than an hour and a half. In the old days much of the work of laying out a stencil like this was done by hand, and the *Blue Danube Waltz* would have taken six boys about three days to complete.

The dynamic figures are copied from the original note record into this new trial roll which comes from the stencil machine to guide the editor in the next operation, which is a complete inspection of the roll to see that no errors of any kind exist. After all corrections are made in this proof roll and transferred to the stencil, another cutting is made and the piece is now, for the first time, ready to be heard by the artist.

The record submitted to the artist is a perfect performance, an exact duplicate of the one he gave when making the record.

It is seldom that the artist requests any change. If a change is made, it is not a correction. Hearing the record, the artist becomes his own critic and if a change is made it is to meet his wish to alter slightly his own performance.

The record of the *Blue Danube Waltz* contains about five times as many notes as the average record and it required considerably over 100,000 operations to bring it to completion, but the result fully justified the great effort.

Now we see on looking back that in the beginning the music roll contained only the notes, and the person owning the player was supposed to put in all of the musical expression. The evolution of the music roll has carried it to a highly developed product which leaves absolutely nothing for the owner of the instrument to do but to insert the roll and turn on the switch.

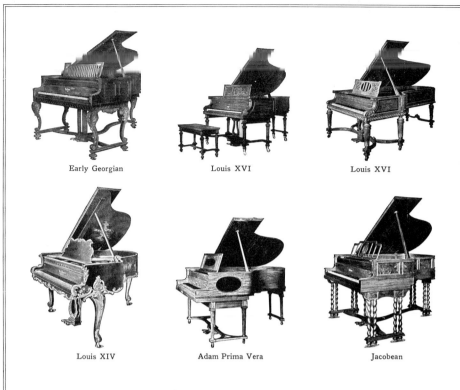

Early Georgian   Louis XVI   Louis XVI

Louis XIV   Adam Prima Vera   Jacobean

Period Case Designs

The Baldwin Piano Company

CINCINNATI   CHICAGO   ST. LOUIS   NEW YORK   LOUISVILLE

INDIANAPOLIS   DENVER   DALLAS   SAN FRANCISCO

The Federal Printing Company, New York

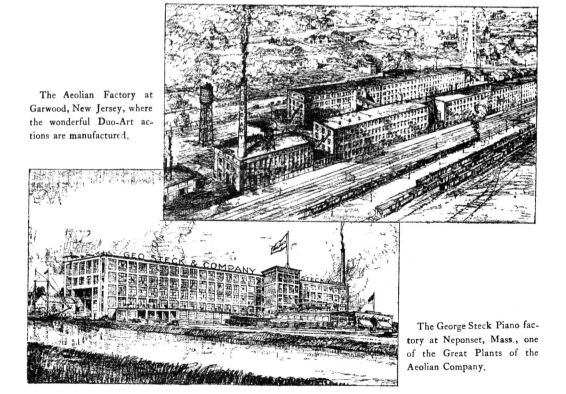

The Aeolian Factory at Garwood, New Jersey, where the wonderful Duo-Art actions are manufactured.

The George Steck Piano factory at Neponset, Mass., one of the Great Plants of the Aeolian Company.

Angelus Reproducing Piano Plays Important Rôle in "Kiss Me Again," a Movie Classic

Scenes from "Kiss Me Again," Classic Feature Film, in Which the Angelus Is Starred

"KISS ME AGAIN," a Warner Brothers classic feature film, directed by Ernst Lubitsch, famous European movie director, boasts of three stars--Monte Blue, Marie Prevost and the Angelus reproducing piano.

It is the opinion of the directors that the Angelus not only "played" its part well but also inspired the other stars to play as they never did before.

The Angelus is also employed in Hollywood as a director. When not playing in a picture it plays on the sidelines. Many a star has, inspired by the Angelus, given a brand of acting otherwise unattainable without the instrument's influence.

The
Electrical Bottom Unit
changes the foot-pumper
to an electric reproducer.

The PRATT READ PLAYER ACTION Co.
Deep River, Conn.

Hear Paderewski play his Famous Minuet on the Wonderful Duo-Art Pianola

MANY people have heard Paderewski's "Minuet, Op. 5, No. 1"—have heard it and been charmed by its beautiful melody and graceful measures.

A comparatively small number have enjoyed the privilege of hearing the master himself play it, with the exquisite feeling, the incomparable skill, of which he is possessed.

Those who have ever enjoyed this privilege do not forget it. For them, hereafter, the lovely tone picture he painted of crinoline and lace, of dainty women and courtly men tripping its stately measures, is ineradicable. Light though it is, Paderewski's "Minuet" is immortal, and Paderewski's playing of it is immortal also.

○○○○○○○○○○

One afternoon, a year or so ago, Paderewski came to Aeolian Hall and played his "Minuet." At a superb grand piano, in a quiet studio and with only one or two listeners, the great artist gave himself to the music. The exquisite melody was inspired by his touch. Rippling tones, now in delicate pianissimo, now in bold sforzando, sang from the pianoforte.

When he finished, no wild tumult of applause burst from a crowded hall, but thousands upon thousands of music-lovers, all unknowing, had been granted the privilege of hearing the performance.

○○○○○○○○○○

It was thus that the Duo-Art record-roll of Paderewski's "Minuet" was made. While the master played, a wonderful machine in another room, connected electrically with his piano, was recording his interpretation. Nothing was lost, nothing changed. The roll, so made, when edited and signed by Paderewski, was not an echo of the performance; hardly to be called a reproduction of it, but was the performance itself in absolute verity.

○○○○○○○○○○

The Duo-Art Pianola is a piano—indeed *the* piano—for the home.

In addition to its marvelous power of reproducing the world's finest playing, it is a regular piano for hand-playing and a *player-piano* of unequalled excellence.

The greatest living pianists are recording for the Duo-Art and its owner may enjoy, at his will, the playing of Paderewski, Hofmann, Bauer, Gabrilowitsch, Ganz, Grainger, Novaes and scores of other virtuosi as well as the best performers of dance and popular music.

Grands and Uprights, in the following celebrated makes—Steinway, Steck, Stroud and famous Weber.

Name of nearest representative and catalog free on request.

The DUO-ART PIANOLA

The AEOLIAN COMPANY
AEOLIAN HALL, NEW YORK CITY
LONDON   PARIS   MADRID   MELBOURNE

Makers of the Aeolian-Vocalion—Foremost Manufacturers of Musical Instruments in the World

THE AEOLIAN COMPANY
29 WEST 42ND STREET
NEW YORK CITY

GENTLEMEN: Kindly send me the illustrated catalog of the Duo-Art.

Name_____

Address_____

The Nickel Grabbers

To the person who likes real razz-a-ma-tazz piano music, nothing tickles the ears more than the variety of music made by the various members of the great family of coin-operated pianos built for use in public places. No sooner had the player piano as such been perfected when far-sighted men saw the possibilities in this field. The first one commercially successful was marketed in 1898, under the name of Peerless, by Roth & Englehardt of St. Johnsville, New York, and of course a number of other firms jumped into this field right away in order to get their share of the market.

Oddly enough, however, the real big market for the coin pianos didn't come along until twenty years later, when with prohibition came the speakeasies, each of which needed some sort of entertainment device. But even if this market hadn't developed, America would have been the richer for one fact — the person considered by many to have been the greatest American composer — George Gershwin — first became interested in piano music as a result of being enchanted with the output of a coin piano at a neighborhood store!

By the middle 1920's, coin pianos were everywhere. A Wurlitzer catalog of the day proclaims to all merchants: "Tell us the nature of your business, and we will tell you the sort of instrument best adapted to your needs. Music may be the one thing lacking in your place of business. This is the time to give this matter consideration and learn how easy a matter it is to install an instrument that will pay your rent and all your overhead and leave your profits 'clean profits.' Just glance over the list of classes of business that received benefits by installing WURLITZER Automatic Musical Instruments . . . Amusement Parks, Billiard Halls, Bowling Alleys, Cafes, Confectionaries, Cigar Stores, Clubs, Dance Halls, Drug Stores, Market Houses, Department Stores, Groceries, Hotels, Lodges, Lunch Rooms, News Stands, Post Card Studios, Railroad Depots, Restaurants, Community Houses."

Probably in deference to alleged standards of morality which perhaps weren't actually very high during the twenties, the two biggest users of coin machines don't appear on this list. Possibly the biggest market of all for coin pianos in this period was in the speakeasies, and undoubtedly this accounts for the fact that sales of coin pianos took a big jump in the mid-20's. Ads for these machines are replete with such references as "The Perfect Piano for Dry Territory" (Seeburg). The other big users of coin pianos, and probably the second largest single factor in the market

Exhibit of J. P. Seeburg Piano Co. a Rendezvous for Thousands of Visitors to Philadelphia Sesqui

Music Hath Charms, as Evidenced by the Throng That Gathered Daily at the Exhibit of the J. P. Seeburg Co., Chicago, at the Sesquicentennial Exposition, Philadelphia. The Other Picture Is a Close-Up of the Seeburg Line of Automatic Pianos and Orchestrions Which Held the Sesqui Visitors Spellbound

PHILADELPHIA, November 27, 1926

THOSE who have visited the Sesquicentennial Exposition will remember the exhibit of the J. P. Seeburg Piano Co., manufacturer of automatic pianos and orchestrions, 1508-1516 Dayton Street, Chicago, long after they have forgotten the latest in hot water heaters, tile, roofing material and whatnot.

The position of the exhibit in the center of Building No. 1, the last of the buildings around the circuit of the grounds, was to its advantage. The visitors, tired long before they entered the structure that housed the Seeburg exhibit, were immediately attracted by the music that issued from the booth and never failed to quicken their steps to drink it in. Refreshed by the music, the visitors would listen for quite a time at the exhibit before they moved on.

At the Seeburg booth the public had an excellent opportunity of viewing the latest in player pipe organs, automatic pianos and orchestrions. Five instruments were displayed. They were the Celesta De Luxe reproducing pipe organ; the Style "L" automatic piano, the smallest instrument; the Style "E"; Style "H" solo orchestrion, and the "Matchless Orchestrion," a small automatic orchestra.

The most popular instrument in the Seeburg exhibit proved to be an instrument never before shown at any similar exposition, namely, the Seeburg Celesta De Luxe player pipe organ. The crowds seemed suddenly to turn in the direction of this sweet pipe organ music. To learn that the instrument was not being played by some renowned organist but entirely automatic proved quite the reverse of their expectation. Their imagination received a further jolt upon observing that the entire mechanism, including all pipes from the deep voiced diapason and the mellow flute to the birdlike quintadena, were contained within a single case just slightly larger than an ordinary piano. They watched the attendant turn off the switch which controlled the automatic device and saw him strike the keyboard. Again they were amazed as they heard the familiar note of a beautifully toned piano. Once more they were attracted by a few motions of the operator's fingers as he pressed certain stop buttons located directly above the keyboard. Gradually they heard the blendings of various pipe organ tones which swelled into the mighty combination of full pipe organ and piano. The strain subsided and his fingers suddenly struck up a beautiful Spanish air intermingling with which could be heard vibrant sounds exactly imitating the soft tinkling of a troubadour's guitar

As the pipe organ music ceased their attention was drawn to other instruments in the booth which were all entirely different, being both automatic and coin operated, intended for installation in public places such as ice cream parlors, restaurants, cafes, billiard rooms. Many had seen such instruments in various places before, but they now realized what advanced improvements had been made.

Directly toward the rear and to the left of the large orchestrion stood the Seeburg Style "E," known under the catalog designation as the "automatic master," containing piano, xylophone and mandolin attachment instruments. This model was provided with a keyboard and could be played either automatically or by hand. It was found that the piano scale of special patented design included the full eighty-eight notes found on the ordinary piano. The case work was nicely done in a beautiful dull finish mahogany provided with a panel of neatly designed art glass flanked on either side by two art lamps. The xylophone played intermittently as called for on the music roll and lent a novelty effect that was quite pleasing.

The Style "L" instrument, which was located to the extreme left of the booth, is one of the smallest automatic pianos built, measuring slightly over four feet in height and only three feet wide, closely resembling an ordinary phonograph case. The beautiful art glass panels harmonized well with the mission oak finish of the case and played the latest music with piano and mandolin attachment. The volume of music from so small an instrument was greatly beyond their expectation and they realized the purpose of this model was to provide a piano of small dimensions for use in places where it was desirable to save space. It was controlled for automatic loud and soft expression and was indeed worthy of a prominent place in the front portion of the exhibit.

Immediately to the right stood the enormous Style "H" solo orchestrion equipped with piano, xylophone, mandolin attachment, and all trap instruments such as bass drum, snare drum, tympani, cymbal, triangle and castanets, with a full complement of sixty-eight wind pipes, giving the effect of violin, piccolo, flute and clarinet. Truly remarkable is this ingenious assembly of scientifically devised mechanisms that plays all of these instruments in concert as well as solo.

Standing more than seven feet in height, its beautiful case added considerably to its attractiveness. Four large art glass panels with metal imitation pipes adorned the upper front part of the instrument directly over the keyboard, further augmented by two hand carved wooden statues reaching up from the front truss supporting a jutting top ornamented with art glass lights and small art glass panels. Admiring visitors remarked about the originality of this excellent case design.

On the right was found a beautiful instrument done in silver gray finish with gold bronze trimmings, the upper panel being beautified by an Oriental design art glass. This instrument was called the "Matchless Orchestrion" and it certainly lived up to its name. In a case not quite five and one-half feet in height and four feet in width were contained eleven different orchestrated instruments, including piano. A program of ten selections appeared behind a clear section of the glass, each selection being announced as played by a small indicator which automatically presented to view a different number each time the piece was played, thereby making it possible to determine the name of the particular bit of music. Beautiful vari-colored lights flashed on and off automatically as the music played, adding further to the beauty and attractiveness of the entire instrument.

Control buttons were provided making it possible to shut off entirely xylophone as well as the drums. Another button controlled the degrees of expression desired from extremely soft to extra loud.

Again it was noted that on this, as on all other instruments, the music roll would rewind of itself and could be made to operate from a remote control any distance from the instrument either by coin or electric contact button. When coin operated it was found that from one to twenty coins could be inserted at a time and the instrument would accurately record each insertion so that the proper number of pieces would be played, according to the number of remittances.

The entire Seeburg display was most attractive and will be long remembered by all who were privileged to visit the exhibit.

were the houses of ill repute. As stated earlier in this work, what better device for stimulating a fast turnover of trade than a coin piano in the parlor with a roll of fast, snappy, 2-minute tunes!

An elderly retired piano salesman once told of his experiences in selling coin machines all over New England, and particularly about one Madam who, two weeks after investing in one of his machines, called him by phone, hopping mad because her piano had stopped working. A hurried service call to her establishment revealed the trouble to be that it had so much money in it that the coin chute was all jammed up tight! The gentleman stated that the most money he ever made in the business in a short time was from sales of the same character made on a two-week trip to Baltimore, a town at one time noted for its activities in this field.

One of the most important firms which dominated the coin piano market was that established by Justus Percival Sjoberg a dozen or so years after the turn of the century. According to one of the music journals of the day ". . . adjoining the manual training high school which Justus P. Seeburg attended when a boy in his native town of Gothenburg, Sweden, stood the Malinjos Piano Factory, where the young man spent considerable time outside of school hours, and made up his mind that when he learned a trade it should be that of piano making. After he finished school he came to this country, and on his arrival sought employment in a piano factory. He was speedily put through the different departments of the factory as his mechanical aptitude and interest in the work became manifest, and soon was known as an expert action finisher and regulator. After six years spent with

STYLE "A"—"The Sturdy Performer
Piano with mandolin attachment.

UNIQUE and attractive. Notable for its simplicity of construction and absolute reliability. New and original scale of seven and one-third octaves, over-strung copper bass, three unison throughout.

Double veneered hardwood, finished in oak or mahogany; walnut at slight extra cost. Art glass panel, design subject to change without notice.

Equipped with automatic loud and soft control; tempo regulator. Uses Style "A", 65-note, ten-selection music roll with the famous SEEBURG automatic rewind system.

Height: 4 feet, 9½ inches; Width: 5 feet, 3 inches; Depth: 2 feet, 6½ inches. Weight, boxed for shipment: 900 lbs.

J. P. SEEBURG PIANO CO.   MANUFACTURERS, CHICAGO

STYLE "B"—"The Artistic Automatic"
Piano with mandolin attachment.

HANDSOME and serviceable. Its appearance is a distinct factor in coaxing its operation. New and original scale of seven and one-third octaves, over-strung copper bass, three unison throughout.

Double veneered hardwood case. Finished in oak or mahogany; walnut at slight extra cost. Full art glass panel in top frame, design subject to change without notice.

Equipped with automatic loud and soft control; tempo regulator. Uses Style "A", 65-note, ten-selection music roll with the famous SEEBURG automatic rewind system.

Height: 4 feet, 9½ inches; width: 5 feet, 3 inches; Depth, 2 feet, 6½ inches. Weight, boxed for shipment: 900 lbs.

J. P. SEEBURG PIANO CO.   MANUFACTURERS, CHICAGO

another factory in this capacity he went with one of the largest concerns in the West in charge of construction of one of their makes of instruments. (It was in this period that he changed his family from Sjoberg as a matter of convenience.)

"In 1895 he went to Rockford, Illinois, and became one of the organizers of the Kurtz-Seeburg Action Company. After a couple of years he sold his interest in the business, and returning to Chicago, became interested in a new company engaging in the manufacture of pneumatic player actions and player pianos. When this company later brought out an electric coin operated piano, Mr. Seeburg was quick to see the opportunity before this type of instrument. He then withdrew and in 1907 organized the J. P. Seeburg Piano Company, marketing the coin-operated output of the company. The business developed so rapidly that he soon decided to engage in the manufacture of electric coin-operated pianos. His associates in the

J. P. Seeburg Piano Company enthusiastically supported him in the move, and factory quarters were secured on Clybourn Avenue, and in a few months the Seeburg electric coin-operated piano made its appearance."

By the mid-twenties Seeburg was producing not only at least nine models of pianos and orchestrions (pianos with additional instrumentation, usually in the form of drums and traps), but also various pipe organs. The most popular of the latter was the Celeste, a combination pipe-organ and player piano made especially for the mortuary trade.

The J. P. Seeburg Company was one concern which managed successfully to shift its efforts to different fields of endeavor when the market for players finally evaporated, and as a result in the mid-twentieth century it is a leader in the building of coin-operated phonographs (juke boxes) for places of public entertainment.

STYLE "E"—"The Automatic Master"

Piano, xylophone, and mandolin attachment.

A MODEL in refinement of case design. New and original scale of seven and one-third octaves, over-strung copper bass, three unison throughout.

Double veneered hardwood case, finished in oak or mahogany; walnut at slight extra cost. Elaborate art glass panel with burnished brass art lamps at each side in top frame, design subject to change without notice.

Equipped with automatic loud and soft control; tempo regulator. Uses Style "A", 65-note, ten-selection music roll with famous SEEBURG automatic rewind system.

Height: 4 feet, 9½ inches; Width: 5 feet, 3 inches; Depth: 2 feet, 6½ inches. Weight, boxed for shipment: 900 lbs.

STYLE "X"—"Expression"

Straight piano, reproducing expression, almost human in accomplishment.

M ASTERFULLY exact. Designed for locations demanding a reproducing instrument—real artistic interpretation. Also constructed for home use when so desired.

Handsome in construction, finished in either oak, dull or bright mahogany, or choice walnut, all double veneered.

Improved scale of seven and one-third octaves, over-strung copper bass, three unison throughout with full metal plate and bushed tuning pins. Selected ivory keys.

Special tempo regulator with graded scale; tracker-bar adjuster; separate "on and off" control located in front of roll chamber; rewind control. Uses specially arranged Style "XP" 4 to 6 selection reproducing roll. Also accommodates all standard 88-note rolls.

Height: 4 feet, 9½ inches; Width: 5 feet, 3 inches; Depth: 2 feet, 6½ inches. Weight, when boxed for shipment: 900 lbs.

STYLE "K"—"Midget Orchestrion"
Case design patented

Piano, mandolin and xylophone.

F ANCY and effective. Beautiful case design; 61-note scale of exceptional tone quality.

Double veneered hardwood case, finished in silver grey, gold trimmings, or regular mission oak. Attractive art glass, electrically illuminated from within. (Design subject to change without notice.)

Automatic loud and soft control; mandolin and xylophone "off and on" controls. Uses Style "A", 65-note, ten-selection music roll with famous SEEBURG automatic rewind system.

Height: 5 feet, 2 inches; Width: 4 feet; Depth: 1 foot, 10½ inches. Weight, boxed for shipment: 800 lbs.

STYLE "KT"

Same as the Style "K" with the added attractiveness of castanets, triangle, and tambourine. Uses Style "G", 65-note, ten-selection music roll.

STYLE "KT SPECIAL"—"The Matchless Orchestrion"

Piano, xylophone, mandolin attachment, bass drum, snare drum, tympani, cymbal, triangle, castanets, tambourine, Chinese block.

B ALL-ROOM favorite. Designed to serve in places requiring the ultra-supreme in automatic orchestral development. Elimination of keyboard reduces instrument to convenient dimensions.

Double veneered hardwood case, finished in silver grey oak with artistic gold trimmings. Oriental art glass, electrically illuminated from within.

Equipped with automatic loud and soft control; special shut-off device for all orchestration instruments; ingenious device for "on and off" flashing of colored lights behind tambourine and drum heads; automatic indicating device, showing which number on music roll is being rendered. Uses Style "G", 65-note, ten-selection music roll, with famous SEEBURG automatic rewind system.

Height: 5 feet, 5½ inches; Width, 4 feet, ½ inch; Depth: 2 feet, ½ inch. Weight, boxed for shipment: 850 lbs.

Salesoffice and Warerooms
209 SO. STATE ST. CHICAGO

STYLE "E SPECIAL"—"The All-Purpose Orchestrion"

Piano, mandolin attachment, xylophone, bass drum, snare drum, tympani, cymbal, triangle, castanets, tambourine, Chinese block.

DESIGNED to serve a dual purpose—that of an automatic orchestrion, and thru the convenience of the keyboard, piano can be manually played whenever desirable.

Double veneered hardwood case, finished in mission oak, or dull mahogany. Service doors in upper panel set with ornamental art glass; burnished brass art lamps at each side; design subject to change without notice. Program holder back of glass.

Equipped with loud and soft control; tempo regulator; special shut-off device for all orchestration instruments. Uses Style "G", 65-note, ten-selection music roll, with famous SEEBURG automatic rewind system.

Height: 4 feet, 9½ inches; Width: 5 feet, 3 inches; Depth: 2 feet, 9 inches. Weight, boxed for shipment: 1100 lbs.

STYLE "G"—"Art Style Orchestrion

Piano, two sets of wood pipes (violin and flute), mandolin attachment, bass drum, snare drum, tympani, cymbal and triangle.

EXCEPTIONAL volume. A wonderful example of the remarkable accomplishment in automatic music. New and original scale of seven and one-third octaves, over-strung copper bass, three unison throughout. Ornamental full iron plate, imported tuning pins and music wire; highest grade imported wool hammers; best grade ivory keys and ebony sharps. Electrically illuminated from within.

Double veneered hardwood case, finished in durable mission oak.

Equipped with automatic "loud and soft" control; tempo regulator; shut-off device for orchestrion effects. Uses Style "G", 65-note, ten-selection music roll with famous SEEBURG automatic rewind system.

Height: 6 feet, 7½ inches; Width, 5 feet, 10½ inches; Depth: 2 feet, 4½ inches. Weight, boxed for shipment: 1300 lbs.

STYLE "H"—"Solo Orchestrion"

Piano; xylophone; 68 pipes, giving violin, piccolo, flute, and clarinet effects; mandolin attachment; bass drum; snare drum; tympani; cymbal; triangle, and castanets.

"MASKED MARVEL." Equal to seven man orchestra. Equipped with patented soft drum control, enabling instrument to render wonderful solo effects.

Double veneered hardwood case finished in mission oak (silver grey finish by special order); adorned with two hand carved wood Caryatids, representing "Strength and Beauty," typical of this combination of excellence in case design.

Tempo regulator; automatic loud and soft controls; uses special Style "H", 88-note, ten-selection music roll with famous SEEBURG automatic rewind system.

Height: 7 feet, 3 inches; Width, 6 feet, 4 inches; Depth, 2 feet, 10½ inches. Weight, boxed for shipment: 1800 lbs.

Popularity of the New Seeburg KT Attested to
by Order for Two Carloads from One Dealer

CHICAGO, Sept. 2. (1925)

THE popularity of the new KT Special, the latest addition to the J. P. Seeburg Piano Co.'s line of automatic instruments, was presaged by the fact that the initial order for the instrument was for fifty.

This came from one of the Seeburg dealers who saw the first KT, which was turned out early in the year. The attractive design, the beauty of the finish and the number of special features won the dealer immediately and the order for two carloads was placed.

The KT Special was brought out about the first of February. Since that time the demand for it has been very brisk and there has been no chance to accumulate stock in spite of the fact that production in this style has been heavy. This style was featured in the company's display at the Drake Hotel during the national convention and the dealers were enthusiastic over it. It has been an outstanding success throughout the year.

Imposing in Proportions

The KT Special is of imposing proportions. It is 48½ inches in width, 24½ inches deep and 65½ inches high. Among its special features are an automatic indicator, which shows what number is being played, and a program holder, placed back of the glass. The finish is especially attractive. It is done in silver gray trimmed in gold, a color scheme which harmonizes with almost any furnishings and at the same time is rich and impressive. It has Oriental art glass of beautiful design and color. The lines of the instrument have great appeal.

Musically the KT Special is exceptional. It has the volume of an average orchestra and the tone quality is excellent. The instruments it contains are the piano, mandolin, xylophone, bass drum, snare drum, cymbals, triangle, castanets, tambourines and Chinese block.

Other additions to the big Seeburg line are soon to be announced. Among these is the new design of the Style L, among the smallest electric pianos in the world, and the E Special.

The company reports that the year so far has been excellent, going well ahead of last year. The promise for the fall is exceptionally bright.

CLEVER ADVERTISEMENT COMES FROM J. P. SEEBURG PIANO CO.

"What You Don't Know" Is Startling Opening of Folder That Shows How Profits Are Made

CHICAGO, June 9.—A novel folder was mailed to the trade last week by the J. P. Seeburg Piano Co.

"What you don't know" is the rather startling message that greets one as the folder is opened and a blue line directs to the next page, which completes the message—"doesn't hurt you—but—"

Then the blue line directs to the next page, which says: "from us you can learn how—"

Right there the turn of the page brings one to a broadside gay with color. Ten Seeburg styles are shown, all done in their natural colors—exact reproductions of the instruments. Across the top of the broadside is a line which tells the dealer that "a Seeburg automatic piano-orchestrion will help your business. A drawing card—brings new customers; a wise investment pays for itself." Then follows this:

"Everyone likes music. Good music makes them stop and take notice. Seeburg automatic pianos and orchestrions play that kind of music. Install one of the instruments pictured on this page and watch your trade grow. People just can't resist good music.

"Every piece of equipment in your place is paid for out of capital. Here is something that pays for itself right out of its own cash box. The public gladly helps you pay for your Seeburg. Why deny them that chance? See the gains others are making."

To prove beyond quibble the statement that Seeburg instruments pay big profits actual records of instruments are given. Among the instances cited are: A Seeburg Style "E" in a Chili parlor in Kansas City earned $1,200 in one year; a Style "A" in a cafe in Atlanta earned in one week $162.50; a Style "H" in a dance pavilion in the little city of Wausau, Wis., earned $40 in three days; a Style "K" in a soft drink parlor in Chicago earned $103 in five days.

"A Seeburg instrument installed in your place of business will pay astonishing profits," comments the folder. "It costs you nothing to find out more about these profit-producing instruments. Just fill in and mail the attached postcard today. Act now—and receive your share of these profits."

The automatic piano which first appeared on the American market was the Peerless, put out by the firm of Roth & Englehardt, of St. Johnsville, New York. In 1908 this became F. Englehardt and Sons, Inc., operated by Frederick Englehardt (together with his sons Alfred and Walter) who had been in charge of the Steinway piano action department for many years. By 1910 this firm was producing 12 models of automatic pianos. In addition to the original model D, there were styles M; 44 (a 44-note piano with no keyboard); DX (which included bass and snare drum, cymbal, and flutes); DM (which included bass and snare drums, cymbal and metalphone attachment); style RR (which used a 20-tune roll), and style A, a large orchestrion.

By 1913 the firm was giving fancy names to its machines, and in its line lists the "Cabaret," the "Elite," the "DeLuxe," and "Arcadian" models, in addition to styles F, V, and the "Trio." The trade journals make no mention of this concern after 1915.

111

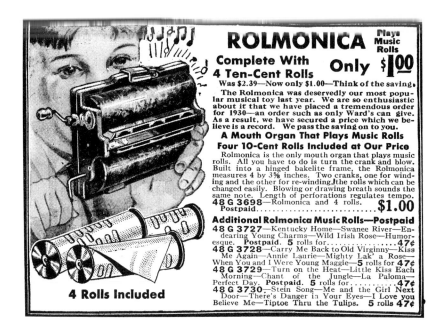
Violin Rhapsodist

Coin-operated Electric Piano
with Violin Pipes, Xylophone and Mandolin Attachment.
Playable by hand or with Perforated Roll.

Rhapsodist Orchestra

A perfect Orchestra, to be operated by Perforated Roll or by hand. A very desirable Instrument for Moving Picture Theaters and other places of Amusement.

NOTICE

Do not confound these two instruments with the ordinary electrically-operated Instruments.

Remember, that either of these Instruments can be played by hand, producing the full Orchestral effect.

If interested, write at once as the demand is heavy and it may take some little time to fill your order.

Orchestration
Full 88 Note Piano, 37 Violin Pipes of the highest quality that perfectly imitate the Violin Soloist, 25 bar Professional Rosewood Xylophone, and Solo Mandolin effect. Three small levers on the side of keyboard enables you to shut off anyone of the effects that you do not wish to play.

Description
Double veneered, mission oak case, with illuminated art glass panels, two illuminated art lamps and beveled mirror, seven and one-third octaves, overstrung full copper wound bass, three unisons throughout. Full iron frame. Brass flange action, German felt hammers. Finest grade ivory keys, polished ebony sharps.

Equipped with magazine slot that plays one to twenty nickels, and our Patented Re-wind Machine that is considered the best on the market and practically eliminates the many troubles others are still battling with.

This instrument is equipped with the highest grade of motor, in either A. C. or Direct Current. Can also be furnished with ten cent slot if so desired, without extra charge.

Orchestration
Full 88 Note Piano, 37 Violin Pipes that are a perfect imitation of the Violin, 25 bar Professional Rosewood Xylophone, Solo Mandolin, Base Drum, Snare Drum, Crash Cymbal and Triangle. Small levers on the right side of keyboard enables you to cut out any of the instruments that you do not wish.
The entire combination of above Orchestra can be played by hand, or Automatically with Perforated Roll.

Description
Double veneered, mission oak case, three illuminated art glass panels, two illuminated art lamps, seven and one-third octaves, overstrung full copper wound bass, three unisons throughout. Full iron frame. Brass flange action, German felt hammers. Finest grade ivory keys, polished ebony sharps.
This instrument is equipped with Automatic Mandolin Attachment.
Our patented Re-wind Machine makes it an automatic wonder. Supplied with either A. C. or D. C. Motor. When playing, automatically the current is turned off and on with an electric switch, we can however supply it with Magazine Slot Attachment, if so desired, without extra charge.

NORTH TONAWANDA MUSICAL INSTRUMENT WORKS
NORTH TONAWANDA, N. Y., U. S. A.

THE case is an Arts and Crafts design, made of fine figured quartered oak, and finished in either early mission, fumed or polished golden oak, double veneered inside and outside.

Two handsome art-glass panels, copper framed in the front, and two richly designed colored glass lamps are attached to the upper front panel.

New and improved scale of seven and one-third octaves, especially designed for high grade instruments of this class.

Overstrung bass and three unisons throughout.

Best quality ivory keys and ebony sharps.

Contains set of solo violin or flute pipes of extraordinary quality and considered by experts to be the closest imitation of the tones of these instruments of anything of the kind on the market.

The mandolin attachment on the piano is so designed as to produce the real tone of a mandolin, and with the pipes, on and off automatically in the perforated music, the monotony usually found in automatic instruments is entirely eliminated, and with the clever expression device, the music is rendered like that of a human artiste of high degree. This instrument is ideal for home use, lodge rooms, dancing, fine ice cream parlors, cafés, etc., also moving picture theatres, as any selection on the music roll may be played at will by using the re-wind and starting buttons in front of the instrument.

Dimensions:

Height, 4 ft. 5½ in.; length, 5 ft. 5½ ins.; width, 2 ft. 5½ in.

Instrumentation:

Piano, seven and one-third octaves, with mandolin attachment, loud and soft pedal.

Set of very fine violin or flute pipes.

Clever automatic expression device.

Fourteen selections on each music roll; two of which are included in the price of the instrument.

When ordering, please give data to the electric power to be used, namely, number of volts and cycles, also phases, so as to enable us to supply the correct kind of electric motor.

Automatic Keyboard Piano
Style "L"

Pianolin "B"—49 Notes

Pianolin "B"—49 Notes

THIS instrument is designed to be used where a keyboard piano is not wanted, and where something on the "Orchestrion" order is in demand. Used principally in moving picture theatre lobbies, cafés, dining halls, restaurants, ice cream parlors and for dancing.

The case is built of fine figured hardwood, and finished in silver gray, mission or any of the soft satin finishes. The colored art-glass upper panels add greatly to the beauty of the instrument when lighted up by the electric lamps inside while playing.

Endless paper rolls, containing six selections each, are used in the PIANOLIN, which has proven to be the most efficient system known for instruments of this size; and the divided tracker bar with wire screen keeps the valves in fine working order, constantly; therefore, trouble is reduced to a minimum or practically eliminated.

The music is arranged for orchestral effect by professional musicians of high standing; and there is no other instrument of this kind that can be compared with the PIANOLIN. There are three six-piece rolls and the electric motor included in the price of the PIANOLIN.

A mute for the violin pipes; a softener for the piano; a coin dropper and a lifter for the top are placed on the outside of the case; so that the music can be made as loud or soft as the owner desires; and the tempo regulator inside governs the speed of it to suit any occasion or purpose.

Dimensions:—

Height, 5 ft. 7 in.; length, 3 ft. 2½ in.; depth, 2 ft. 2 in.

Instrumentation:—

44-note piano with loud or soft pedal and mandolin attachment; 44 violin pipes; representing first and second violins, viola and "cello", or flute pipes, as desired.

Orchestrina—87 Notes

THE case is made of quartered oak, of fine figure and piano finish; with an elaborate top which is supported by three heavy columns in the front; making a massive and fine appearance.

Two bevel plate glass panels or colored art-glass panels are shown in the front; and the lamps inside the case light up when the music is started; making the instrument very attractive.

The tone quality is wonderful in its close imitation of a human orchestra; and the tempo of the music can be governed at the will of the operator; making it play as slow or as fast as needed.

It is suitable for any occasion or location, as it plays dance music, latest ragtime or popular selections, as well as classic overtures; and is very successfully used to furnish good orchestra music in moving picture theatres, dancing academies, hotel lobbies or dining rooms, restaurants, cafés, summer resort pavilions and in private residences.

Operated by electric motor and coin slot which, with two ten-piece music rolls, are included in the price of instrument.

Dimensions:—

Height, 9 ft. 6 in.; length, 6 ft. 4 in.; depth, 3 ft. 8 in.

Instrumentation:—

Consists of 191 sounding notes; representing an orchestra of twelve men. Piano with loud or soft pedal; two first violins; two second violins; viola; "cello"; string bass; first and second clarionets; trap drums with loud and soft stroke; cymbal; castanets and thirteen orchestra bells.

Orchestrina—87 Notes

Please furnish data for electric current—such as number of volts and cycles—when ordering. Book of instructions with each instrument; showing how to start and operate it.

Capitol Bluebird Orchestra

Electrically Driven

Coin Operated

6 ft., 6½ in. High   4 ft., 2 in. Long   2 ft., 6 in. Deep

THE Capitol Bluebird Orchestra is handsomely and solidly designed, being constructed of highest grade quartered oak with art glass panels. It is designed to fulfill the needs of medium sized dance halls, cafes, restaurants, confectioneries, or anywhere high class music is required. It is free from all complicated mechanisms and will stand hard wear unusually well.

Beside the high grade piano there are 45 string-toned pipes representing first and second violins, viola and 'cello, mandolin and orchestral bells, castanets, and the sweetly singing bluebird occasionally chirps in an accompaniment.

The Rolls used in the Capitol Bluebird Orchestra are made in our own plant at North Tonawanda, N. Y., by expert musicians who are masters in their calling. Each roll contains twelve separate pieces. Every month a bulletin listing the new orchestrations is sent to each instrument owner so an up-to-date repertoire may be maintained.

This instrument is ready to be played when received and may be instantly connected with any electric current. It will never require attention.

THE CAPITOL

"Music is the Life of the Nation"

PIANO and **ORGAN CO.**

Incorporated

251 West 34th Street   New York City

'Phone Longacre 7660
7661

It is Just Like a REAL Jazz Orchestra

This 1922 Capitol Jazz Concert Orchestra will

Crowd Your Place   Increase Your Business   Double Your Profits

SOMETHING ENTIRELY NEW!

Attention

YOU want more business. This Jazz Orchestra will get you more business. People passing your doors will stop to listen to the sweet music and will drop in —spend their money and come again and again with their friends, which means—Big Crowds—Big Business—Big Profits.

Don't Delay — Every day you are without this trade winner, you are Losing Business.

This Capitol Jazz Orchestra is a 1921 Invention—entirely different from the old style electric pianos and organs you have seen in the past. This is a Real Musical Instrument that plays with Human Expression that the people want and enjoy.

Everybody Loves This New Orchestra

This Orchestra will Advertise Your Place

This Orchestra will Double Your Business

Notice!
If you have an old piano or organ, we will gladly take it in exchange.

This Handsome Jazz Orchestra Interprets
Classical and Operatic Music with the Same Human Effect

It Pays for Itself

IN order to introduce this new Orchestra we will install it in your place at practically no expense.

Your customers will go wild about it and never stop dropping nickels into it to hear it play and in that way it will pay for itself.

If you cannot call, mail today the enclosed post card and we will tell you how you can get this wonderful business getter so that it costs you practically nothing.

Mail back the enclosed Postal and we will send you full Information FREE.

The Berry-Wood write-up appeared in a trade journal during the year 1913. Note the statement at the end which points out that the company "enjoys the distinction of using strictly high grade pianos." This is indicative of a rather common trade practice of the day, wherein the makers of coin pianos often actually did not construct the basic pianos, but purchased them from other concerns. They, in turn, would then proceed to add to them the player mechanisms, coin-handling devices, the drums, traps, and other instruments in the orchestrion models, and if necessary, to build extensions on the cases to house the various pieces of apparatus.

If the coin-piano manufacturer was prosperous enough to be able to order pianos made to his specifications, then he might have his name cast into the metal plate which supports the tremendous tension of the piano strings. If not, then in all likelihood a separate cast name plate would be bolted over the existing name plate, and to the serious collector who is involved in restoration of coin pianos, this often becomes a clue as to the true history of the machine.

Examples of machines built by other than the selling manufacturer were certain models of Seeburg orchestrions. The pianos for these were apparently made under the Seybold Piano name by the E. P. Johnson Company of Elgin, Illinois. Certain Automatic Musical Company machines used Bollerman pianos, and the Link Piano Company used instruments manufactured by the Haddorff Piano Company of Rockford, Illinois.

Note also that the Berry-Wood Auto-Orchestras used a full 88-note scale, a feature quite uncommon in the coin-operated field.

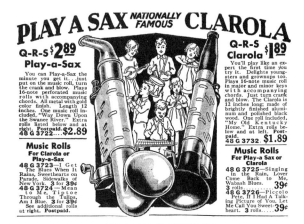

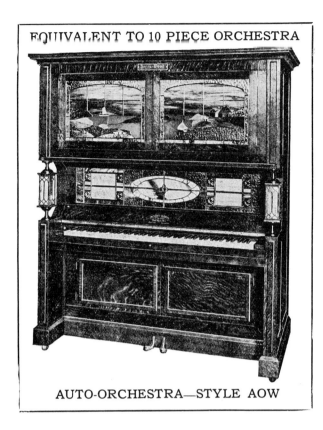

EQUIVALENT TO 10 PIECE ORCHESTRA

AUTO-ORCHESTRA—STYLE AOW

BERRY-WOOD PIANO PLAYER CO.—Incorporated. Main offices and factory, Southwest Boulevard and Twentieth street, Kansas City, Mo. Eastern offices and factory, 348-50 Canal Place, New York. Make "Berry-Wood" Automatic Coin Operated Pianos and Auto-Orchestrions. Style "C" 88-note endless music roll player. Style "E" 88-note rewind music roll player. Style "F" 88-note rewind music roll player with flute or violin pipes. Their 88-note Auto-Orchestras "A-O-L" and "A-O-H" were put on the market early in 1911 and contain full scale 88-note piano, violin pipes, flute pipes, bass drum, snare drum, cymbal and triangle. These Auto-Orchestras have an unusual feature, the complete 88-note scale, and are remarkably powerful and musically attractive instruments. In 1912 this company placed another style Auto-Orchestra on the market, Style A-O-W. This style represents a thirteen-piece orchestra and contains flute pipes, violin pipes, bells, xylophone, bass drum, snare drum, snare drum on rim, tympani, mandolin, castanets, tambourine, cymbal and crash cymbal. This instrument is particularly adapted for use in moving picture houses, as the different orchestra features speak either singly or in unison, which brings into play the various instruments. The factories of this company are under direct supervision of Fred. W. Wood, an expert on player-piano construction, who has secured forty-five patents on various devices used in these players, and the above enumerated instruments are products of his extensive experience covering a period of many years. The instruments made by this company are noted for their extreme simplicity of construction and durability, and nothing but the finest grades of material are used. The company enjoys the distinction of using strictly high-grade pianos. The officers of this company are Fred. W. Wood, president; E. D. Carney, vice-president, and J. F. Campbell, secretary and treasurer. In high commercial and financial standing.

AUTOMATIC MUSICAL INSTRUMENTS

THE TONOPHONE

Full Size Automatic Piano with Nickel-in-Slot
Attachment

The Tonophone was Awarded a Gold Medal at the
Pan-American Exposition, Buffalo

Where the New Wurlitzer Caliola is Built
THE RUDOLPH WURLITZER MFG. CO.
NORTH TONAWANDA, NEW YORK

Wurlitzer Violin—Flute Pianino

The regular Pianino (44 note Electric Piano with Mandolin attachment and without keyboard), combined with 21 Violin Pipes and 21 Flute Pipes.

This instrument is equipped with long frame roll, which will play 6 or 12-tune rolls.

Height, 5 feet. Width, 3 ft. Depth, 2 ft., 1 in. Shipping weight, 700 lbs.

Wurlitzer Pianino

The standard 44-note Electric Piano with Mandolin attachment and without keyboard. Equal in tone to that of any full scale Piano. This instrument is equipped with the long-tune roll frame playing a 6 or 12 tune roll; a feature that makes it remarkable.

Height, 4 ft. 5 in. Width, 2 ft. 10½ in. Depth, 2 ft. 7¾ in. Shipping weight, 500 lbs.

While most historians agree that Seeburg was an important concern in the coin-operated piano field, the mighty house of Wurlitzer certainly played the lead. And in terms of all music, the latter was much larger in that it has always handled all types of musical instruments. Rudolph Wurlitzer, founder of the company, was born in Schoeneck, Germany, in 1831, and came to America at the age of 22 with no money and no knowledge of the English language. After a succession of odd jobs, he found employment in Cincinnati, Ohio, with a bank which allowed him the privilege of sleeping in a loft over the office, and paid him $8 per week.

Nearby was a musical instrument retailer, and young Rudolph was amazed not only at the inadequacy of the man's stock, but at the high prices resulting from the many middlemen between the European manufacturers of the articles and the final buyer. Tak-

ing $700 which he had saved, he sent to family connections back in his German home town the money together with instructions on musical instruments to be purchased and sent to him, which he then promptly resold to American dealers at greatly reduced prices over what they had been paying previously. The Wurlitzer business had been founded.

He was joined in the early 1860's by his brother, Anton, and in 1872 the partnership of Wurlitzer and Bro. was formed. The Rudolph Wurlitzer Company was incorporated in 1890, and Rudolph continued as President until 1912. In that year he became chairman of the board, and the eldest son, Howard, took over the reins of the company, with Rudolph H. as vice-president and Farny R. as treasurer. Rudolph Wurlitzer, senior, died January 14, 1914.

Automatic instruments were included in the firm's line early in its history. The 1879 catalog, for example,

Wurlitzer Electric Piano—Style S

The latest style of Wurlitzer Electric Piano with beautiful art glass front, all the musical and mechanical improvements and the general case design is the most attractive ever put out. The art glass designs vary. Automatic mandolin attachment.

This instrument is equipped with a long roll frame. which will play either 1, 5, 10 or 15-tune rolls.

Height, 4 ft. 10 in. Width, 5 ft. 2 in. Depth, 2 ft. 4 in. Shipping weight, 1,050 lbs.

Interior of the
Wurlitzer Electric Piano—Style IX.
Showing the New Direct Drive Mechanism and Roll Changer

Dustproof Action Case

The action case of all Wurlitzer Instruments is absolutely dustproof. The tracker bar is divided and a metal screen placed in between the two sections. This catches every particle of dust and foreign matter and prevents it from entering the pouches.

On other instruments dust and foreign matter is drawn into the action case and must of necessity collect under the pouch, holding the valve open and collapsing its pneumatic. The result of this is that the action is made sluggish and finally put out of commission altogether.

Tempo Regulator

A Tempo, or time Regulator that actually does regulate the time of the music. By simply turning a small knob to the right or the left the music is made to play faster or more slowly as desired.

Metal Tracker Bar Adjusting Screw

By simply turning a screw to the right or left the tracker bar may be moved in either direction as desired in order to make the music track perfectly over the tracker bar. This causes the music to play correctly, and insures it against the effect of dampness or atmospheric changes which may cause it to shrink or expand.

Interchangeable Parts

All parts of the Wurlitzer Automatic Musical Instruments from the small set screws to the complete mechanism are interchangeable. All repair parts are carried in stock at each of our branches and can be secured promptly.

Metal Tracker Bar

All Wurlitzer Instruments are equipped with the perfect Wurlitzer all metal tracker bar. The holes in the tracker bar always keep their original shape and size and correspond perfectly to the holes in the music rolls.

Direct Drive

The *Direct Drive* does away with the belts and pulleys. It simplifies the mechanical construction of the Piano and reduces the necessary number of parts. It has eliminated all Automatic Piano trouble.

Wurlitzer Electric Piano—Styles IX and I

Wurlitzer Style IX Piano

The latest style of Wurlitzer Electric Piano with beautiful art glass front, all the musical and mechanical improvements and the general case design is the most attractive ever put out. The art glass designs vary. Automatic mandolin attachment.

This instrument is equipped with Automatic Roll Changer playing six five-tune rolls.

Wurlitzer Style I Piano

Same design as IX, equipped with long roll tracker frame will play either, 1, 5, 10 or 15-tune rolls.

Height, 4ft. 10 in. Width, 5 ft. 2 in. Depth, 2 ft. 4 in. Shipping weight 1,050 lbs.

WURLITZER

NET PRICE LIST OF

AUTOMATIC INSTRUMENTS

EFFFCTIVE MAY 15th, 1920.

This list cancels all former price lists.

Style	Catalogue Page No.	Price
Pianino	7	$ 600.00
Violin-Flute (Pianino)	8	800.00
S	9	950.00
I	11	1150.00
IX	12	1250.00
AX	14	1550.00
DX	15	1750.00
BX	16	2000.00
CX	17	2200.00
Solo Violin Piano		2100.00

F. O. B. Factory

The Wurlitzer Automatic Music Roll Changer

Makes it possible for a Wurlitzer Instrument to play as many as 30 different selections without change or attention.

Another Special Feature of the Roll Changer being that the customer may select the roll of his choice and play any character of music.

**Classical,   Opera,   Songs
Dances, or the National Airs**

There are 6 different rolls playing five tunes each, and all 6 rolls are inserted at one time.

The entire set of rolls may be played through, one after the other, without any attention whatsoever or individual rolls may be selected. This means a musical program of an hour and a half to three hours' duration, without repetition and without bother.

The Wurlitzer Automatic Roll Changer has been pronounced a marvel of mechanical ingenuity and effectiveness. We have been at work on it for many years, knowing that when perfected it would revolutionize the automatic musical instrument business and place the Wurlitzer instruments so far beyond other makes that all comparisons would cease.

There is nothing to compare with the Wurlitzer Music Roll Changer, and there can never be anything at all like it, for every feature and part is fully covered by patents that have been taken out both in the United States and foreign countries.

Spools for rolls are adjustable insuring perfect tracking.

Wurlitzer Orchestra Pianos—Styles DX and D

Wurlitzer Style DX Piano

Equipped with Wurlitzer Patent Automatic Roll Changer, playing six five-tune rolls. A new style that has all of the exclusive Wurlitzer mechanical improvements. For beauty of design and tonal quality it is unexcelled. The art glass designs vary somewhat.
Instrumentation:
Piano with Mandolin Attachment, 38 Violin Pipes (21 First Violin and 17 Viola), 38 Flute Pipes.

Wurlitzer Style D Piano

Same as Style DX, but equipped with long roll tracker frame, playing 1, 5, 10 or 15-tune rolls.
Height, 4 ft. 11 in. Width, 5 ft. 3 in. Depth, 3 ft. Shipping weight, 1,250 lbs.

listed reed organs with pin cylinders producing six or eight tunes, pipe organs in mahogany cabinets playing 27 tunes, the Automatic Pianista (presumably a Forneaux machine imported from France), playing 4½ octaves. The first piano was introduced to the line in the late 1890's, with the association of the Wurlitzer Company and Eugene DeKleist, a barrel organ manufacturer located in North Tonawanda, New York.

DeKleist was born in Dusseldorf in 1867, and in his early years was associated with the London offices of Limonaire Freres of Paris, manufacturers of merry-go-round organs and music cylinders. Here in 1892 he met William Herschell, a Scot from Dundee, brother of George and Allen Herschell of the Armitage Herschell Company of North Tonawanda, builders of merry-go-rounds and other amusement park devices. As a result of this visit, DeKleist visited the North Tonawanda Company and then decided to live permanently in the United States. In 1893 he started the North Tonawanda Barrel Organ Works and was so successful that by 1897 he had this business more or less monopolized in America.

In that year he traveled to Cincinnati to try to interest Howard Wurlitzer in a distributorship proposition for his machines, but instead Wurlitzer encouraged him to devote his attention to perfecting a barrel-operated coin piano, which eventually was marketed in 1899 under the name Wurlitzer Tonophone.

The Tonophone was an immediate success, and in 1904 the Pian-orchestras (ranging in price from $1,500 to $10,000) were introduced to the line. By 1908 the merchandising of these machines, together with the carousel and band organs, had become such a profitable activity for Wurlitzer that the assets of DeKleist were purchased, leaving the latter a wealthy man. In his remaining years he served for a time as mayor of North Tonawanda but eventually returned to his native Europe, where he died in 1913.

Throughout the years, Wurlitzer introduced the widest variety of coin-operated and automatic music machines of any manufacturer in the field. An 82-page catalog of 1910 listed 50 machines, including the

Wurlitzer Flute or Violin Piano
Styles AX and A

Wurlitzer Style AX Piano

Equipped with the Wurlitzer Patent Automatic Roll Changer, playing six five-tune rolls. A high class piano combined with mandolin attachment and violin or flute effects.

Wurlitzer Style A Piano

Same as style AX, but equipped with long roll tracker frame, playing 1, 5, 10 or 15-tune rolls.

Height, 4 ft. 10 in. Width, 5 ft. 2 in. Depth, 2 ft. 8 in. Shipping weight, 1,200 lbs.

Wurlitzer Solo Violin Piano
Coin Operating Attachment

The Solo Violin Piano combines practically a full eighty-eight-note piano with a scale of Violin Pipes, having a range of fifty-one notes. This combination provides for all the expression and accent necessary to play the best classical music.

This instrument is equipped with the Wurlitzer Patented Automatic Roll-Changer. The music is arranged to play the Violin as solo, and the Piano as accompaniment. Write for special catalog.

Height, 4 ft. 10½ in. Width, 5 ft. 1¼ in. Depth, 3¾ ft. Shipping weight, 1250 lbs.

Wurlitzer Electric Piano—Autograph Style

The Wurlitzer Autograph Piano renders an absolutely true reproduction of the individual interpretations personally played by many of the world's renowned artists. The Autograph Piano is a distinct departure from any instrument ever manufactured for use in supplying musical entertainment in public places, especially designed to play the most difficult classical compositions COMPLETE. This Piano is to the PUBLIC PLACE of business, what the REPRODUCING PLAYER GRAND PIANO is to the PRIVATE HOME.

This instrument is equipped with the Wurlitzer Patented Automatic Roll-Changer.
Height, 4 ft. 9 in. Width, 5 ft. 1 in. Depth, 2 ft. 4¾ in. Shipping Weight, 1050 lbs.

Rare WurliTzer race-horse piano.

The "Wurlitzer Harp

CIRCA 1906.

WE DESIRE to announce that after eight years of constant labor, the "Wurlitzer Harp" is now ready for the market, and we will assure you that it is a wonderful attraction from both a musical and mechanical standpoint. This is the latest addition to our line of Automatic Musical Instruments, and is by far the most refined of all musical attractions. The harp is in full view, being covered by a large plate glass, thus affording your customers the opportunity of watching the fingers (almost human) pick the strings. The soft, sweet music of the Wurlitzer Harp makes it especially desirable for places where an electric piano can not be used on account of the music being too loud.

Being operated by a nickel-in-slot arrangement, it is not only a great attraction, but a money-maker of no small proportion.

DESCRIPTION

Case, handsome quarter-sawed oak, with carved panels. Height, 6 feet 6 inches; width, 3 feet; depth, 2 feet. The perforated music rolls are only 8½ inches wide, and contain six tunes each. The harp is fitted with an automatic rewinding device, which, when the end of roll is reached, automatically re-winds itself in thirty seconds. A dial, with numbers from 1 to 6, always indicates the number of the tune that is being played. An electric light on the inside of harp, just above the strings, proves an attractive feature. Another feature of no small importance, is the fact that six nickels can be inserted at one time and you will receive six tunes without any further attention.

Price, $750.00 Including One Roll of Music

Extra Rolls, $7.50 Each.
List of Tunes Upon Request.

These Harps are Furnished with Either
Direct or Alternating Current Motor.

SOLD FOR CASH OR ON THE EASY PAYMENT PLAN

A Refined Musical Attraction, with Nickel-in-Slot Attachment
and Operated by Electricity

Automatic Harp, the 44-note Pianino, the Mandolin Quartette and Mandolin Sextette, Violin Piano, Violin-flute piano, as well as a large variety of Pian-orchestras, which were automatic pianos instrumented with oboe, flute, and violin pipes, drums, cymbals, and other traps, to simulate actual human orchestras.

The Wurlitzer Automatic Roll Changer was introduced about this time. It is a highly complex mechanical device containing six music rolls on a ferris-wheel arrangement, incorporated on certain models and permitting them to play up to 30 selections without repetition, but unfortunately also without opportunity for selection of individual numbers.

The Wurlitzer Automatic Harp business got its start when Howard Wurlitzer visited a cafe in Cincinnati and saw one operating. The proprietor told

him that it was manufactured by one J. W. Whitlock of Rising Sun, Indiana, a small town on the Ohio River.

Mr. Wurlitzer visited Whitlock, with the result that the latter contracted to build 1,000 of the machines for sale under the Wurlitzer name. A second contract followed for an additional 1,000, but only about 400 of these were delivered when they lost favor on the market, and no more were manufactured.

The Whitlock Company arranged over two hundred popular tunes for playing on the harp. The music which emanates from these interesting machines is quite guitar-like, although it seems likely that with appropriate musical arranging, they could indeed with numerous arpeggios sound very much like the real thing.

Style LX

WURLITZER Orchestra Piano—Style LX

This instrument combines a Piano with Mandolin attachment, 38 Violin Pipes (21 First Violin and 17 Viola), 38 Flute Pipes, Set of Orchestra Bells, Bass and Snare Drums and Triangle. The different musical sections can be cut off at will. The art glass designs vary somewhat. Equipped with WURLITZER Patented Automatic Roll-Changer playing six five-tune rolls.

Height, 7 ft. 9 in.   Width, 5 ft. 4 in.   Depth, 2 ft. 5 in.   Shipping weight, 1,500 lbs.

1903

Self Playing Xylophone

With or Without Slot Attachment.   Operated by Endless Perforated Music Roll.

THE amount of money fed into slot machines is something astonishing. Those dealers who are fully awake to that fact are taking their profits weekly and daily on musical coin operated instruments. Among the very best of these the XYLOPHONE stands out as a money earner.
    Write AT ONCE for terms and territory.   What you are going to do next month is not bringing you any money to-day.
    Address, Regina Music Box Co., New York or Chicago, who control certain sections for us, or direct to the manufacturers

Automatic Musical Company,
BINGHAMTON, N. Y.

An early entry into the coin-operated music field was the Automatic Musical Company of Binghamton, New York. This firm was started by two brothers named Harris, and most of their efforts consisted of making adaptations of player mechanisms to pianos built by other manufacturers. They did, however, do considerable experimentation in other fields as well and their Automatic Xylophone, produced in 1903, undoubtedly was the forerunner of the marimbaphones and xylophones installed in pianos produced by most other manufacturers in later years.

At one time they were a distributor for the Encore Automatic Banjo, a machine now considered to be a very rare prize by collectors of automatic music equipment. By 1908 they had succeeded in producing a violin-playing machine, and thus joined the select fraternity of concerns able to perfect such a complex device.

But evidently the Harrises were better gadgeteers than they were businessmen, for around 1910 they had fallen into debt so badly that a committee of creditors was formed to help bail them out, and thus try to save their investments in the Binghamton concern. This committee selected Mr. E. A. Link, who had been associated with the Schaff Piano Company of Huntington, Indiana, to take over operational control of the company. This he did, and evidently he saw a good future for the concern because by 1913 he assumed full control of the enterprise, and the name was changed to the LINK Piano Company. From then until 1929, the concern made various types of automatic pianos and pipe organs which were sold all over the United States.

While it never was a large concern as compared to Seeburg and Wurlitzer, nevertheless the shop force of around 75 men managed to build a goodly number of machines over the years and today they are commonly found in the collections in all parts of the country.

The pipe organs were produced mainly for the mortuary and theatre trade, although some were made for private homes as well. The theatre organs were marketed under the name "Link C. Sharpe Minor Unit Organ," in cooperation with one of the best-known theatre organists of the day, Mr. C. Sharpe Minor, who was associated with Grauman's Chinese theatre in Hollywood, California. Some of these organs were paper-roll operated, and were arranged in such a manner that the movie projectionist could select the type of music appropriate to the particular scene on the silver screen, merely by pushing the proper button on a control panel next to his work-station. What a simple way to achieve struggle-music for fight scenes, sob-music for heart rending situations, and hurry-music for forest fires and broken dams! A simple way, indeed, for replacing the piano player normally seated in the orchestra pit, thus adding to the profits of the organization . . . what the movie projectionist's union had to say about this early automation is not recorded!

The LINK company was one of the automatic piano manufacturers to survive the demise of that type of entertainment, but only because it entered other fields of endeavor. Mr. Edwin A. Link, son of the founder, was more interested in airplanes than he was in his father's products, and being of an inventive mind he made a sort of airplane cockpit, mounted it on large bellows, and through the use of various player-piano components instrumented the device so that it actually simulated, right on the ground, conditions of aircraft flight.

This device was not financially successful for quite some time, but the gathering war clouds prior to World War II created a need to train thousands and thousands of pilots in a hurry. The LINK aviation trainer was for this purpose an invaluable tool, with the result that a great many of them were built during the war years and the company was expanded to several thousand workers in order to meet this production demand. After the war the company re-engineered its products and created highly complex electronically operated flight simulators, many of which cost around a million dollars. But anyone interested in player pianos can only feel at home with the original LINK "Blue Boxes," because they are in reality about half airplane and half player piano.

From a technical standpoint, the most interesting feature of the LINK pianos is their method of handling the paper music. The endless tune-sheet as such was first patented by Hobart in 1908, but the few makes of pianos which utilized his system (notably certain

Flight is simulated when student, enclosed under canopy, uses instruments to maneuver the Link on its swivel mount. Needle on instructor's desk records the Link's action.

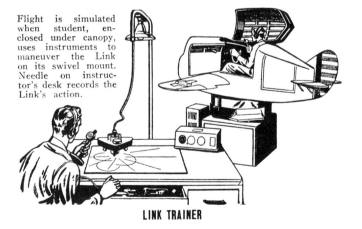

LINK TRAINER

Style 2
The Link Coin-Operated Electric Piano
Art Glass and Case Design Subject to Change Without Notice

What It Does For You

1. Yields from 20 per cent. to 100 per cent on your investment.
2. Attracts people to your place of business, entertains them while they are there, is continually earning money for you and eventually more than pays for itself.
3. Keeps people from leaving too quickly. Every experienced storekeeper knows that the most fatal thing for business is to permit his store to appear unpatronized.
4. Enhances appearance of store interior. Its beautiful colored glass panel and handsome case finish enrich appearance of your fixtures.
5. It earns money. Costs practically nothing to keep up and is always on the job collecting profitable nickels.

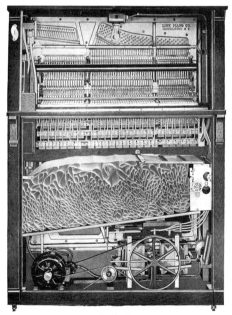

Style 2
Showing Motor and Interior Construction
Piano and Mandolin

Peerless and Electrova models) had the paper feeding vertically from a storage box. LINK, on the other hand, fed the paper horizontally into a storage section, as can be seen from the accompanying pictures. Early models of LINK pianos had a chain-driven feeding device to assist the apparent impossible mess of paper to feed from one end of the box to the other. According to the late George Thayer, the man who did most of the technical development of the machines, one day in a piano being tested at the plant a shear pin broke in the drive mechanism for this unit and it was noted that the music would feed perfectly well of its own accord! Thereafter, the chain-driving device was left out although the bottom board of the music storage box was sloped slightly downward at one end to give the paper some guidance.

Points of Excellence

1. Simplicity of construction. All parts are interchangeable and built of the very best material.
2. ENDLESS music roll containing 15 selections.
3. Every pneumatic in the instrument is individual.
4. Does not tear edges of music roll. Has adjustable metal duct bridge.
5. Has magazine slot registering one to twenty coins.
6. It is the finest built automatic piano in the world.
7. No intermission between end and beginning of roll as is common in rewind instruments. This is a very essential point where the piano is to be used for a continuous performance.
8. Plays last piece on roll at same tempo as the first piece.
9. All attachments may be cut off, so instrument will play piano only.

Size, 49 inches wide; 24 inches deep; 66 inches high

Style 2 -- B

*Piano, Mandolin, Snare Drum, Triangle, Tom-Tom,
Tambourine and Chinese Wood Drum*

Easy to Maintain Given a small bit of your floor space the Link requires but little attention from you to be about its work of gathering nickels. The dropping of each coin starts the motor. The motor starts the vacuum pump and the roll. Each piece is ready for the next customer when the preceding piece stops. A little oiling and dusting keeps it even tempered and industrious.

Small Investment Required In even poorly located stores the Link proves an excellent investment. An average of $50.00 a month is a very common thing, $50.00 a week is not extraordinary.

Terms can be arranged so that the instrument not only pays for itself, but you are actually making money on it while paying for it. On request we shall be glad to furnish you with names of Link owners in your vicinity, and let them tell you what

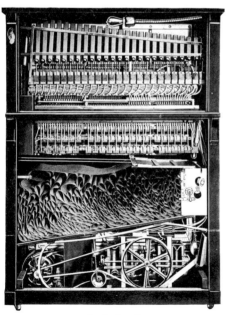

Style 2 -- E

Piano -- Mandolin -- Marimbaphone

No Rewinding No Pauses The Link is played by an endless music roll on which are fifteen pieces of popular dance music. As patrons drop nickels these pieces are played in rotation. No adjustment, no rewinding, is necessary. The same selection is not repeated for half an hour. Each roll contains enough music so that it need not be changed as often as on other makes of instruments.

15 Popular Pieces on Each Endless Roll Each nickel dropped in a Link brings full value of snappy music, accurately timed, perfectly accented, "full of pep," contagious with entertainment. Only pieces that have proved themselves hits in New York and Chicago are cut into Link rolls and fifteen on one endless roll. Each piece invites the listener to hear the next. Each adds life and high spirits to the store—and profits to the bank roll.

OUTSIDE VIEW
Style A, AX, B, C, D, E

Height, 6 ft. 4 in.; width, 5 ft. 6 in.; depth, 2 ft. 8 in.
Case design subject to change.
Art Glass Front, (design subject to change.)
Case, Oak, Mission Finish, or Two Tone Walnut.

A MAGNET FOR NICKELS THAT ARE
99% PROFIT

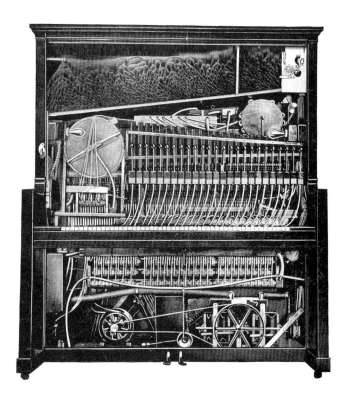

Style A-X—Piano, Mandolin, Marimbaphone, Snare Drum, Triangle,
Tom-tom, Tambourine, Chinese Wood Drum

IF DOLLARS ARE HARD TO GET
GO AFTER PROFITABLE NICKELS

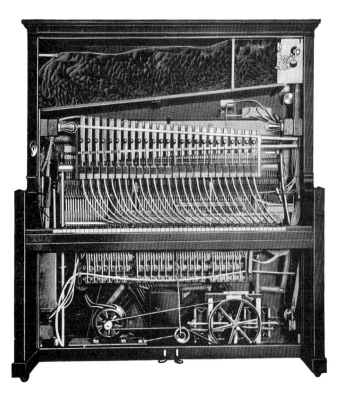

Style E—Piano, Mandolin, Marimbaphone

NO REWINDING — NO PAUSES
10 TO 15 POPULAR PIECES ON EACH
ENDLESS ROLL

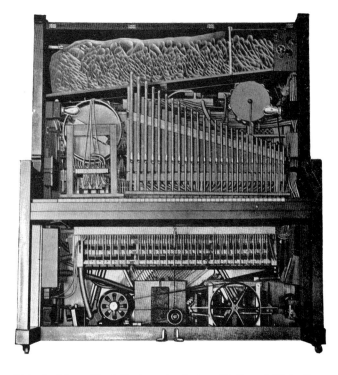

Style A—Piano, Mandolin, two sets of pipes, Violin and Flute, Snare
Drum, Triangle, Tom-tom, Tambourine,
Chinese Wood Drum

EASY TO MAINTAIN
SMALL INVESTMENT REQUIRED

The Link Case DeLuxe

Obtainable in Styles A, AX, B, C, D, E

LINK PIANO COMPANY, Binghamton, N. Y.

While this type of music arrangement was very dependable and resulted in little wear on the paper, changing a roll in one of these machines was not a task to be taken lightly! Of course, the big advantage of the continuous loop of music is that no re-roll device need be provided, resulting in considerable simplification of apparatus. One unfortunate aspect of the LINK music situation is that this company made all of its own music, usable only on its make of machines, with the result that in later years it has become exceedingly scarce.

When the company finally left the piano and organ business, after the financial crash in 1929, what piano roll business that remained was taken over by one Ray Deo, who had been employed in the music cutting room of the factory. Quite a number of LINK rolls were thereupon sold under the name Deo Music Roll Company. However, even the limited market for these soon evaporated and the late Mr. Deo in 1956 told the writer that eventually he sold the perforator for junk and burned the two or three thousand remaining music rolls for firewood.

STYLE SPECIFICATIONS

Style A—Piano with mandolin, two sets pipes, violin and flute, snare drum, triangle, tom-tom, tambourine and Chinese wood drum.

Style A-X—Piano with mandolin, marimbaphone, snare drum, triangle, tom-tom, tambourine, Chinese wood drum.

Style B—Piano with mandolin, snare drum, triangle, tom-tom, tambourine and Chinese wood drum.

Style C—Piano with mandolin and flute pipes.

Style D—Piano with mandolin, flute and violin pipes.

Style EX—Piano with mandolin and marimbaphone.

In all styles the different attachments are controlled by the music roll and play at the proper time in each selection.

All attachments may be cut off so instrument will play piano only.

WHAT IT DOES FOR YOU

It gets the money.

It costs you nothing, as it pays for itself and soon becomes a source of revenue.

It gives you no trouble whatever.

Every day without an Automatic Instrument means that you're letting good dollars get away from you.

POINTS OF EXCELLENCE

1. Simplicity of construction. All parts are interchangeable and built of the very best material.
2. ENDLESS music roll containing ten to fifteen selections.
3. Every pneumatic in the instrument is individual.
4. Does not tear edges of music roll. Has adjustable metal duct bridge.
5. Has magazine slot registering one to twenty coins.
6. Simplified Expression Devices. Control not only usual expression, but permit accenting of any single note or phrase to any degree.
7. No Intermission between end and beginning of roll as is common in rewind instruments. This is a very essential point where the piano is to be used for a continuous performance.
8. Plays last piece on roll at same tempo as the first piece.

Mr. Edwin Link, pictured above at his home in 1965, holds the false keyboard which was used many years previously in the Link Piano and Organ factory to tune cabinet-style pianos such as the model 2-B at his right.

A type of automatic piano found early in the history of these machines was the 44-note cabinet style. Just what logic dictates this particular number of notes is not clear, unless it just happens that since 44 is half of 88, which is the normal piano scale, some genius figured that perhaps half a piano is better than none at all. Examples of machines using this scale are the Mills Automatic Pianova (made by the Pianova Company of New York and also sold as an Electrova), the Wurlitzer Pianino, certain models of the Peerless line, the North Tonawanda Pianolin, and also the Mills Violano-Virtuoso, of which more later.

Undoubtedly the standardization of roll manufacture which was agreed on at the great Buffalo, New York, convention in 1908 did much to forstall further development of the 44-note piano as a type, because no standardization was ever carried out for this scale. Each 44-note piano used rolls which would fit it, and no other make.

A great disadvantage of any scale of less than 88 notes is that most music is composed with the assumption that all these notes will be available when the music is played, so that when these are scored for use with a machine having a lesser number, the arranger is often obliged to all but mutilate the work to make it fit. This probably also explains why much of the music for these small machines is not well known — it had to be written around their limited capabilities, and therefore never achieved any degree of popularity — except perhaps in a negative sense to the saloon keepers who had to hear the same stuff, day in and day out!

This group of rare, early 44-note pianos represents, in spite of their deplorable condition, the sort of "find"

Mills Automatic Pianova
This is the Kind You Want for an Arcade

May be operated either with or without slot attachment or arranged to play continuously, using the endless perforated music roll, containing five selections each.

———

For a medium priced musical attraction we highly recommend the Pianova as a thoroughly satisfactory instrument.

———

DIRECTIONS WHEN ORDERING

If direct current, state current and volts. If alternating current, state current, volts and cycles.

This information you can obtain from the Company that supplies your light.

———

Height, - 65¾ ins.
Width, - 35½ ins.
Depth, - 24 ins.
Weight, 618 pounds boxed.
Weight, 488 pounds unboxed.

that all collectors dream of making! They were located in 1957 in a barn in downtown Providence, Rhode Island, by the writer who lost no time in acquiring them. There were 45 in all, and they formed the basis of the Roehl piano collection — many were sold and swapped for other machines, and some were kept. A few years later quite a number had been restored to their original condition by various owners. All the machines had been put in storage at the advent of prohibition by a piano mover who bought out a "route" of machines to get what money they contained. In the thirty or so years of storage in an unheated, unattended and often damp barn they became badly deteriorated, but not so much so that many hours of work by a number of people weren't gladly spent in an effort to hear them once again!

Like home players, there was no shortage of makes of coin-operated machines built in the United States. This list of names is not necessarily complete, but it probably includes almost all of the makes.

American	Link
Anderson	Marquette
Ariston	Midget Orchestra
Armstrong	Mills
Autoelectrola	Monarch
Berry-Wood	National
Billings	Nelson Wiggen
Capitol	Netzow
Carleton	North Tonawanda
Casino	Originators
Chicago Electric	Operators
Coinola	Pianotainer
Colonial	Pianova
Concertrola	Presburg
Cote	Price & Teeple
Cremona	Rand
Decker Bros.	Reed
Eberhardt	Regina
Electra	Reichard
Electratone	Schaeffer
Electrova	Schultz
Englehardt	Seeburg
Empress	Seltzer
Evans	Standard
Haines	Starr
Howard	Tangley
Ideal	Victor
Jewett	Violophone
Kibby	Waltham
King	Watson
Kreiter	Western Electric
Lehr	Wm. A. Johnson
	Wurlitzer

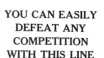
Early in the 1920's, two of J. P. Seeburg's associates, Oscar Nelson and Peter Wiggen, left the great master of the coin piano business and struck out for themselves, forming the Nelson-Wiggen Company. There were only a few years remaining in which the industry was prosperous, and they made good use of them because their products became known far and wide.

It is probably fair to say that they were better gadgeteers than musicians, for their instruments represent some of the most complicated instrumentation ever put into pneumatically controlled pianos. The particular piano on the opposite page which the lady is inspecting is considered by some authorities to be about the ultimate in the science of cramming lots of musical doodads into practically no space! Originally located in Philadelphia, this piano was eventually "found" and added to the collection of the late

Richard Shattuck of Eldred, Pennsylvania. When the picture was taken it was on display at the Musical Museum at Deansboro, New York; eventually it was sold to and became part of the William Allen collection in Santa Ana, California.

This machine contains the piano, a mandolin attachment, bass drum, snare drum, cymbal, tympani effect, tambourine, castanets, Indian block, xylophone, and triangle — all in a space no larger than an ordinary upright piano!

Probably because both Seeburg and Wurlitzer had been successful in making small pipe organs in combination with pianos for the mortuary trade, Nelson-Wiggen brought out their selector duplex organ shown on the following page. The outstanding feature of this particular model was the duplex characteristic of the music rolls. The music was cut into the paper in such a manner that when the roll progressed in a forward direction the organ would play from one set of holes, then play from the other set as the roll was rewinding! This gave the obvious advantage of permitting no interruptions to occur. After all, what more horrible thought than that of the pallbearers having to mark time in carrying the remains of the deceased from the sanctuary, while waiting for an organ of some less progressive manufacturer to rewind a music roll in complete silence! Nelson and Wiggen had turned a neat trick in meeting this eventuality.

NELSON-WIGGEN

Selector Duplex Organ

A small Automatic Organ suitable for Chapels, Lodge Halls and Moving Picture Houses. Contains 8 foot organ bass, 4 foot flute and 4 foot Quintadena. Full Size Piano and Specially arranged organ roll with ten pieces, playing without rewind.

Write for Catalog

NELSON-WIGGEN PIANO CO.
The Better Automatic
1731-1745 Belmont Ave.
CHICAGO

The Western Electric Piano Company (not to be confused with the telephone manufacturing concern) was a real late comer to the Automatic Piano field, entering it in 1924. The President of the company was A. F. Larson, previously associated with the piano company of his own name, and other officers were R. I. Wilcox and B. C. Waters. As noted in the advertisements, this company featured the "Selectra" on certain of its models, and this was one of the most unusual features in the business in that it permitted the patron to select the tune he wanted to hear from among the ten available on the roll, instead of having merely to hear the next one in succession, as was the case with practically all other makes.

A very clever gear-driven device, it was necessary for the operator to play entirely through the music roll any time a new one was inserted and make appropriate adjustments to coincide with the ending of

---

MUSICAL AUTOMATICS

Have you looked in vain in the past for a real musical automatic? If so, your search is at an end.

Our line comprising nine distinct and different styles is offered for those better piano merchants who wish to represent and sell a *musical automatic*.

STYLE 4X
Walnut, Mahogany, Mission Oak, Silver Grey Oak

Our instruments contain many exclusive features in construction and orchestration. Case designs are particularly high class.

One of our big features is soft music—any automatic can play loud; ours play soft. Real music.

Write for full information

NELSON-WIGGEN PIANO CO.

"The Better Automatic"

1731-45 Belmont Avenue   CHICAGO

MAKE 1925 BUSIER

You can do this with

The Finest

Selectra Model "S"

AUTOMATIC ELECTRIC PIANOS and **Orchestrions**

This Great Line Has Many Exclusive Features Including the Wonderful

SELECTRA

Which Enables You to Select Tunes at Will from the 10-Tune Standard Music Rolls

The Finest

Is Highest Quality and Sells at a Sensible Price

Get the Agency and make sure of a busy 1925.

Selectra Model "B"

Mascot Model "C"

WESTERN ELECTRIC PIANO CO.

429 West Superior St.
CHICAGO

BUSY TIMES AT WESTERN ELECTRIC PIANO CO.

Full Production Going on with Overtime Work to Catch Up on Rush of Orders—Meanwhile Moving to New, Enlarged Factory Progresses Apace

B. C. Waters

CHICAGO, June 8.

AT the plant of the Western Electric Piano Co., makers of "The Finest" line of automatic pianos and orchestrions, 429 West Superior Street, there is much activity at present carrying out plans for the removal of the company to the much larger quarters at 900-912 Blackhawk Street, announcement of which was recently made in THE MUSIC TRADES. The new plant will give the company more than double its present floor space and will be one of the most modern of its kind in the country in point of equipment, arrangement of departments and all the things that spell perfection in modern industrial housing.

"While our growth has been rapid," said B. C. Waters, secretary and general manager of the company, "it has been expected by us. We knew when we started in business that we had a product of highest quality and we also felt that we had exclusive features that could not but find popularity with the dealer and the ultimate purchaser. The success which has come to us proves that we did not over-estimate matters. Every month since our inception has shown a gain over its predecessor and the present year has been exceptionally busy. Our line has been taken on by dealers in all parts of the country and months ago we realized that our quarters were inadequate.

"In spite of the fact that we have been running at capacity and working overtime, we have been away behind in orders for months. We expect in our new location to soon catch up on business and to be in a position to take care of orders promptly."

One of the features that has made The Finest line talked about is the "Selectra." This is a device by which the operator of an instrument can select at will any tune on the ordinary ten-tune roll. Instead of taking the numbers in rotation, he can make his choice, touch a button and the tune he wants is played instanter.

Many other novelties have been introduced, and in the near future the company will make some important announcements along this line. All are designed to create more interest in the automatic instrument on the part of the public, and that they will do so the testimony of dealers who have been "let in" on some of the new ideas attests.

The new ideas are worked out by the officers of the company. A. F. Larson, president, is one of the best known manufacturers of automatics in the country. He has devoted his life to this work and in addition to knowing every detail of the business has an inventive turn that is remarkable. R. I. Wilcox, vice-president, is also widely known for his inventive genius, and Mr. Waters, although he is devoted especially to the selling of instruments, is a practical man of wide experience and is the father of many ideas embodied in the product.

The company expects to be entirely settled in its new quarters by the end of the month.

each tune. More often than not, the result was that the patron heard the end of one tune and the beginning of the next — as one might expect, since it was usually up to the bartender of the establishment to keep the music changed periodically.

Probably the best known product of this company was the so-called "Derby" model, really a gambling device in disguise. It is a small electric piano, with a small race-track circle about a foot in diameter behind the front glass. Miniature horses mounted on a merry-go-round arrangement spin around the circle as long as the music plays; when it stops they continue to spin until their inertia is spent, and the horse nearest the post is declared the winner.

SELECTRA MODEL S. PIANO AND MANDOLIN—SELECTION CONTROLLED

Western Electric Piano Company
429 West Superior Street
CHICAGO, ILL.

ART AND BEVEL GLASS PANELS

PLAYS ANY SELECTION FROM
THE TEN TUNE MUSIC ROLL

Height 57¼ Inches
Width 62½ Inches
Depth 30 Inches

THE FINEST AND MOST MODERN AUTOMATIC ELECTRIC PIANO

STYLE "X"—PIANO, MANDOLIN AND XYLOPHONE

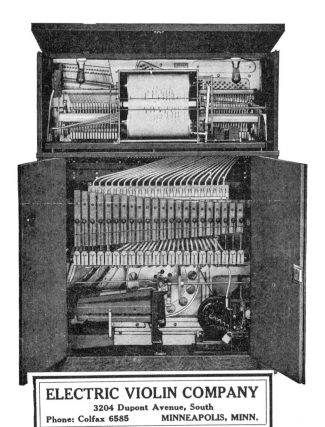

Western Electric Piano Company
429 West Superior Street
CHICAGO, ILL.

Height 62 Inches
Width 46½ Inches
Depth 22½ Inches

THE MOST HIGHLY DEVELOPED MECHANICAL CONSTRUCTION

MASCOT, MODEL C

Western Electric Piano Company
429 W. Superior Street
CHICAGO, U. S. A.

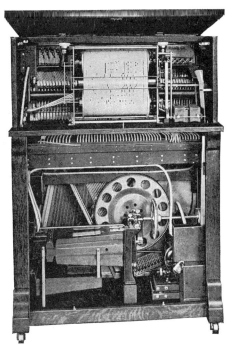

PIANO AND MANDOLIN

Height 51½ Inches
Width 37 Inches
Depth 23 Inches

THE FINEST SMALL KEYLESS PIANO

SELECTRA MODEL B.   PIANO, MANDOLIN AND XYLOPHONE

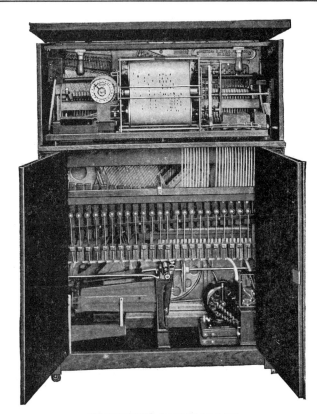

SELECTION CONTROLLED

Height 62 Inches
Width 46½ Inches
Depth 22½ Inches

THE FINEST

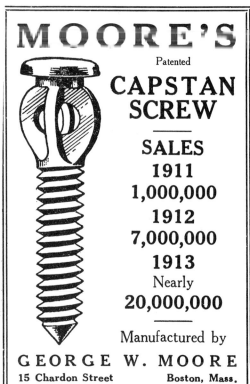

The outstanding product sold under the National name is their job which permits selection of individual numbers. It has a ferris wheel arrangement for supporting the music rolls, and eight separate coin slots. Insertion of a coin into a particular slot brings the proper piece of music into position for playing. Unquestionably, in its day this was a tremendous advance from a technical standpoint. Western Electric's Selectra, which accomplished the same thing from a single roll, did not appear until several years later.

This particular machine is on display at Knott's Berry Farm at Buena Park, California, and this and one other picture in this book were provided for this work through the courtesy of Mr. Walter Knott — founder and owner of the farm. Of course it is not now really a farm at all, but rather a world-famous restoration of a ghost town of the old West.

This early version of the National piano appeared in 1911; of special interest is its feature of having a metal action. While various metal actions came into vogue in other makes of players in later years, practically all of the early coin machines had mechanisms constructed of maple, spruce, and gumwood.

PIANOTAINER

OAK OR MAHOGANY
Width 39 in.   Height 55 in.   Depth 21 in.

The Pianotainer (evidently a combination of the words "piano" and "entertainer") certainly saw very limited production because they are exceedingly rare today. Very possibly its promoters tried too hard to feature the fantastically low price of three for $1,000, and fell into the trap of not providing enough "room" for salesmen and distributors to earn a reasonable commission in selling it — with the inevitable result of few, if any, sales forthcoming.

Cremona—Theatre Orchestra, Solo Style M3

Most connoisseurs of the mechanical piano consider the Cremona, manufactured by Chicago's Marquette Piano Company, to be just about the Rolls-Royce of the field. While a good many of the machines on the market were shabbily constructed, to say nothing of being poorly designed in the first place, no such complaints could be registered concerning the products of this company. As an example of the careful attention to promotion of longevity in the use of the instruments, note that the bellows were lined with "newborn calfskin"!

Like many other concerns in the mechanical piano field, The Marquette Company had its fingers in the theatre-piano pie. The style M3 illustrated above was over sixteen feet in width, from the extreme edge of the box to the left of the piano containing various drums and traps, to the right edge of the other external box which contained sets of organ pipes. Unlike the *Link* theatre machine illustrated earlier, the operator of the Cremona had to be content with whatever music was next on the roll — he had no opportunity to select struggle music, sob music, or hurry tunes by the mere press of a button!

Note, however, that this machine has two music rolls. One roll plays while the other one rewinds, in order to permit uninterrupted selections during the starring of the favorite matinee idol of the day! This was a feature quite commonly used in instruments of this type, as well as on merry-go-round organs and mortuary organs in order to minimize the disruptive influence of periodic silence.

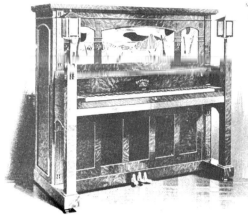

MARQUETTE PLAYER PIANO STYLE A
Foot power. Hand power.

MARQUETTE PIANO CO.

Manufacturers of

Marquette Player Pianos

Marquette Player Actions

and the "Cremona"

Offices 808-810 Republic Bldg.

Factory: Sangamon St. and 14th Place

CHICAGO

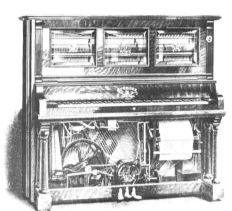

CREMONA ELECTRIC PIANO, COIN OPERATED
Style A, Art Cremona

The Cremona Piano

A revelation in electric pianos, coin operated. A magnet for crowds, a magnet for nickels, and a great side line for regular piano and player piano dealers.

This company created many of the most desirable features of the electric piano in its present development. For a list of our prices see our new illustrated catalogue—just off the press.

It is positively convincing.

CREMONA No. 3
With lower panel removed, showing perfect accessibility of motor and mechanism, and easy, instantaneous insertion of music rolls.

Cremona—Style A Art

The original lines of this Art style appeal to lovers of the beautiful and meet the approval of the most exacting. The piano may be played automatically or by hand when desired. An attractive instrument for ice cream parlors and similar locations.

CASE—Arts and Crafts case, built from original exclusive designs by our own designers. Regularly furnished in mission oak finish. Mahogany finish if desired. Illuminated art glass panels and hanging lamps. Rolling fallboard with continuous hinge. Empire top.

CONSTRUCTION—Piano is full 7½ octaves. New improved overstrung scale—International pitch. Three stringed unisons. Double copper wound bass. New type double repeating action with patent brass flanges. Ivory keys. Imported felt hammers.

FEATURES—

Mandolin Attachment—Which may be cut in or out manually or automatically, or may be set for continuous playing.

Modulant—The latest improved automatic expression device; varies the tonal expression from very loud to very soft without impairing the perfect rendering of the music.

Distant Control—When desired can be equipped for operation from a distance, either by push button or wall boxes.

Magazine Slot—For coin operation. Instrument is furnished with or without as desired. Slide to take nickel, dime, quarter or other coin, as ordered. From one to twenty coins can be registered at a time. Our coin slide eliminates defective and odd size coins and steel slugs.

Multiple Tune Music Rolls—Plays standard music rolls of ten, fifteen or twenty pieces.

Bellows—Cremona Slow Speed Bellows. New-born calfskin lining. Stationary center-board. Phosphor bronze bearings.

Coin Boxes—Iron Coin Boxes with substantial locks are used.

Motor—Special type quiet running piano motor—voltage and current as desired.

DIMENSIONS—Height 57 inches; Width 64½ inches; Depth 28½ inches.

WEIGHT—Boxed for shipment 1,040 pounds.

THE MARQUETTE PIANO CO.   CHICAGO

Cremona—Orchestral K

A late development in the Cremona Orchestral is the Style K. Altogether a wonderful instrument full of remarkable musical results. Built especially for high class trade desiring a superior instrument.

CASE—A new and original Grecian design, made of the finest quarter sawed oak. Regularly furnished in mission oak; other finishes to order. Beautiful art glass panels in top frame. Two brass trimmed art lamps. Design subject to change without notice.

CONSTRUCTION—Piano is full 7½ octaves. New improved overstrung scale. Three string unisons, double copper wound bass. New type repeating action with patent brass flanges. Ivory keys. Imported felt hammers.

INSTRUMENTATION—Three sets of pipes for effects of flute, piccolo and violin, piano, mandolin, triangle, tambourine and castanets.

FEATURES—

Modulant—The latest improved automatic expression device; varies the tonal expression from very loud to very soft without impairing the perfect rendering of the music.

Expression Shutters—Automatically controlled.

Distant Control—When desired can be equipped for operation from a distance, either by push button or wall boxes.

Piano Mute—Operated by knob on side of piano.

Tempulator—A new device by which the time of the music when played automatically can be varied to suit the nature of the piece or to secure the fine time variation required for the modern dances.

Magazine Slot—For coin operation. Instrument is furnished with or without slot as desired. Slide to take nickel or other coin, as ordered. From one to twenty coins can be registered at a time. Our coin slide eliminates defective and odd size coins and steel slugs.

Multiple Tune Music Rolls—Plays 88-note specially orchestrated music rolls.

Coin Boxes—Iron Coin Boxes with substantial locks are used.

Motor—Special type quiet running piano motor—voltage and current as desired.

DIMENSIONS—Height 67½ inches; Depth 30½ inches; Width 64 inches.

WEIGHT—Boxed for shipment about 1,295 pounds.

THE MARQUETTE PIANO CO.   CHICAGO

The REGINA Company of Rahway, New Jersey
was best known for its wide variety of music boxes,
all of which played metal discs in place of the pinned
cylinders common to the European type of box. One
of their many styles of music box is shown below.
Less common are the Regina pianos, one of which is
at the left. The Sublima piano is definitely a mandolin-
like affair from the standpoint of its tone; metallic
hammers with a repeating strike give an unusual tinkly
quality to its output. As the ad indicates, these machines were available with either spring-wound or
electric motors, the former presumably being used
in places lighted with gas instead of electricity. Some
of these machines were also marketed under the name
"Wurlitzer Tremolo Piano."

Regina also distributed the more common type
players for home use, and had a line of conventional
coin-operated pianos as well. One of their most unusual pieces was an orchestrion of sorts, called the
"Automatic Concerto", wherein the piano notes and
the various drums and traps were actually operated
from a slowly rotating metal disc 32 inches in diameter. The disc had projections punched into it, in
exactly the same manner as the smaller music boxes
as shown in the Christmas scene.

Regina "Electric Broom" vacuum cleaners are made
today in the Rahway, New Jersey factory where
abounds a rich history of automatic music dating back
to the 1880's.

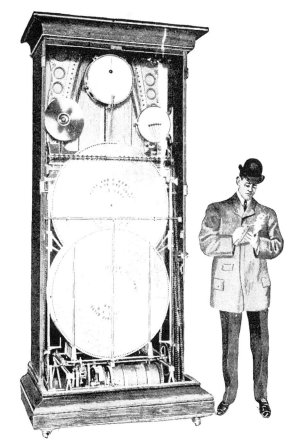

The Regina Automatic Concerto. Open.

THE ELECTROVA AS A MONEY MAGNET

WE MUST tell you something about the wide and diversified fields in which the Electrova daily proves its ability as a money magnet.

First of all, it is a business proposition pure and simple. You will find that it will attract custom to your place of business— custom which you have not heretofore had.

If you are the proprietor of a cafe, the Electrova Piano will adorn and brighten your place. But the most important fact is that it will get the money. The splendid cash returns should certainly induce you to investigate what can easily be shown to be a profitable investment. We do not mention the increased percentage of bar receipts; our reference is solely to the actual amount of money that will find its way into the slot and down to the cash box.

And bear in mind that this money is all velvet.

In the lobby of a hotel— well, in the lobby of a hotel in Salt Lake City, the receipts in the cash box of an Electrova has shown a record of $126.85 during the month of October, 1911. This should look good to you if you are the proprietor of a hotel.

And billiard parlors prove a fertile field in which to garner the nickels—twenty of them make a dollar, you know. If you conduct a billiard parlor, it should not tax your credulity to believe that an Electrova, playing as it does, lively and inspiriting music, would prove a large source of revenue from your patrons. And again, let us remind you that this is extra money and you do not have to work for it.

It has been shown that for use in dancing academies the Electrova easily puts the piano player out of business. All pianists do not play dance music in time. But the Electrova always plays in time, and it has always been a prime favorite with dancing academies. And the Electrova never becomes tired; it is always ready to play.

The up-to-date drug store, the cigar store, the candy store, and ice-cream parlor, all have a splendid opportunity to increase their profits. Indeed, it is hardly necessary to designate what kind of business (if the business is done with the general public) that the Electrova will not help and permanently strengthen. And in this connection bear in mind that the instrument will in a short space of time yield enough in actual cash receipts to pay for its initial cost—and the initial cost is the only cost. The Electrova, as we have before stated, does not get out of order. We could not afford to place it on the market if it did. Hundreds of letters have come to us wholly unsolicited, in which the writers state that the Electrova has never given them a moment's trouble, but, on the contrary, has proven an unqualified financial success.

Style "66"—Art Style.   Expression Player

THE above engraving shows style "66" closed, and ready for playing by hand, by coin in the slot or continuously by electrical connection.

The case is a masterpiece of cabinet-making, is finished in mission oak, has beautifully colored leaded glass panels; two beautiful lamps mounted on posts at each side of the case, which illuminate while the instrument is playing.

Equipped with motor to operate on standard local current, automatic expression device; magazine slot, automatic mandolin attachment, Tempo regulator, and tone modulator. Plays 88-note rewind roll music, 10 tunes on a roll. Can also be furnished with Flute or Violin attachment at a small additional cost.

Height, 4 ft. 9 in., Length, 5 ft. 5¼ in., Depth, 2 ft. 6 in.

IN ORDERING, please send us the following information: Is the Electric installation in your city a direct or alternating current? If it is a direct current, what is the voltage? If an alternating current, give the number of alternations and voltage. It is necessary that this information should be accurately furnished.

COIN Operated Electro-Pneumatic Pianos have come to stay. Their merit has been demonstrated by the exacting test of time. It is needless to discuss this phase of the question—it is only necessary to determine which coin operated instrument is the most durable and less likely to get out of order.

We believe that we can clearly show that the Electrova ranks first. Simplicity of construction is the basis of our claim; perfect performance the result. We invite comparison, and this we would not do unless we were confident that the Electrova would prove its superiority on every point.

In addition to the automatic operation of the Electrova it is in every respect a perfect piano, and possesses a full deep and rich tone; $7\frac{1}{3}$ octaves, ivory keys, full bell-metal plate, over-strung bass, and in point of design and detail in finish, the instrument will satisfy the most exacting.

The Electrova Company of New York City was an early concern in the coin-piano field, with the model illustrated being marketed around 1912. A number of these machines were acquired by the writer in the collection shown on an earlier page, and it is also interesting to note that Electrova's style 44 was exactly the same as the Mills Automatic Pianova. It seems likely that this model was made by neither company, and that the Pianova Company of New York actually was the manufacturer.

1913.

TRADE MARK REG. U.S. PAT. OFF.

Coinola Midget Orchestrion has proven to be the most successful keyless instrument ever manufactured. It is equipped with the same "trouble proof" rewind mechanism and twenty coin magazines as the keyboard styles, and is a large "money getter." A handsome case design—quarter sawed oak veneered in rich mission finish. Beautiful art glass panel as show on cut.

INTERIOR MIDGET PIANO STYLE A

INTERIOR MIDGET ORCHESTRION STYLE X

INTERIOR MIDGET ORCHESTRION S STYLE'S X, F AND V.

EXTERIOR COINOLA MIDGET
HEIGHT 5 FT. 4" WIDTH 3 FT. 10½" DEPTH 2 FT. 2½"

Midget A plays piano and mandolin using regular 65 standardized music.

Midget Orchestrion X plays piano, mandolin and two octaves of solo Xylophones with vibrating pneumatics, using solo O music roll.

Midget Orchestrion F. plays piano, mandolin and two octaves of rich mellow solo flute pipes, using solo O music roll.

Midget Orchestrion V. plays piano, mandolin and two octaves of solo violin pipes, using solo O music roll.

Midget Orchestrion K. plays piano, mandolin and two octaves of solo flute and violin pipes, using solo O music roll.

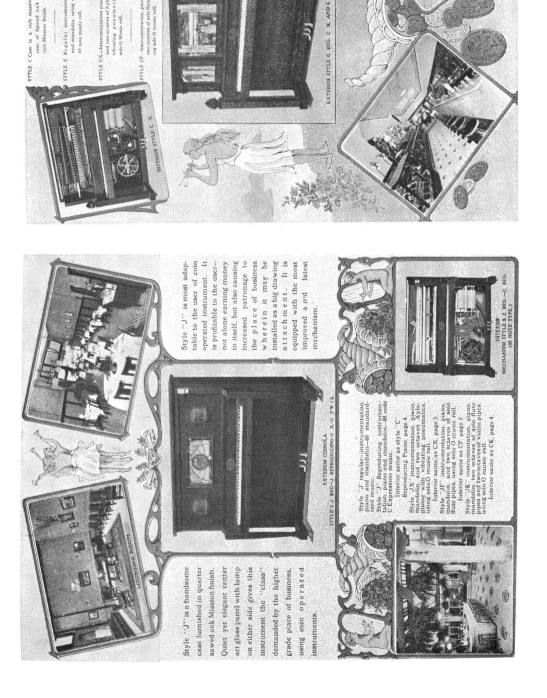

Of all the coin-operated pianos and orchestrions sought by collectors in the mid-Twentieth century, probably no machines are more greatly desired than the Coinola, manufactured by the Operators Piano Company of Chicago. This concern, started in 1904 and incorporated in 1909, grew to such an extent that it had to move several times around the city of Chicago to find space in which manufacturing might be carried on. Under the guidance of L. M. Severson, the president and general manager, a number of different lines were produced, and according to a trade journal of the day, "the product is noted for its durability and is known as 'Trouble proof.'" (Editor's note: We'd like to see a coin-operated piano that is trouble-proof!)

and most of the others. Most historians who go for this sort of thing are in complete agreement that when it comes to a coin-operated piano, there is nothing quite like the music made by the Coinola Style X, Style CO, or better yet, the SO.

The following catalog pages are reproduced from an edition of the early 1920's, although this concern was actually in business as late as 1931.

The reason for the interest on the part of collectors, however, is mainly because the orchestrions put out by this company used the style "O" music roll. The arrangement of the perforations in this style of roll was such as to permit a great deal more music to be cut into them than was the case of rolls used by Seeburg, Nelson-Wiggen, Western Electric, Link,

EXTERIOR STYLE S. O.

INTERIOR STYLE S. O.

Style "SO"—an orchestrion of beauty, character and stability. Instrumentation—piano, mandolin, two octaves orchestra Xylophone bars, two octaves of flute pipes, two octaves of violin pipes, bass and snare drums, cymbal, Indian block, triangle, tympani, tambourine, and 15 in. Chinese crash cymbal, equipped with an automatic swell for expression.

This instrument with its richly figured red gum case will stand out as an individual commanding notice yet which fits in and harmonizes with its surroundings to produce that true spirit of refined elegance which characterizes artistic fame.

Height 7 ft.
Width 5 ′ 3 in.
Depth 2 ′ 6 in.

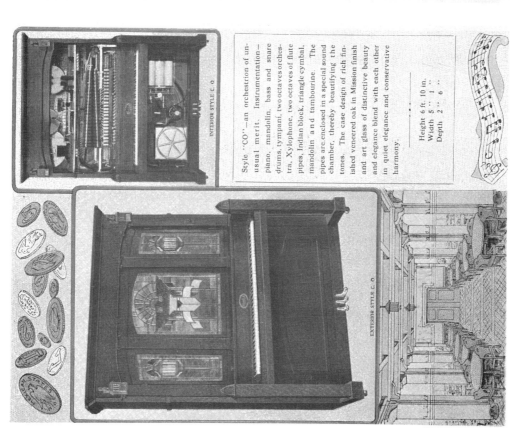

EXTERIOR STYLE C. O.

INTERIOR STYLE C. O.

Style "CO"—an orchestrion of unusual merit. Instrumentation—piano, mandolin, bass and snare drums, tympani, two octaves orchestra, Xylophone, two octaves of flute pipes, Indian block, triangle cymbal, mandolin and tambourine. The pipes are enclosed in a special sound chamber, thereby beautifying the tones. The case design of rich finished veneered oak in Mission finish and art glass of distinctive beauty and elegance blend with each other in quiet elegance and conservative harmony.

Height 6 ft. 10 in.
Width 5 ′ 1 ′′
Depth 2 ′ 6 ′′

COINOLA CABINET PLAYER

A new product of the ingenious mind of Louis M. Severson, president of the Operators' Piano Company, 1911-1913 North Clybourn avenue, Chicago, is a cabinet player that fits any piano. The cabinet player rests on the key blocks with its mechanical fingers striking the regular keys. It is simply another step forward in conjunction with the Coinola player mechanism.

The Style C-1 Coinola Cabinet Player, as shown here, is quadruple veneered in mahogany or in figured oak Mission finish. Its construction is so it can be put on or taken off at a moment's notice. The music roll plays ten pieces. It is equipped with magazine slot holding twenty nickels. Its mechanism, like all other Coinola instruments, is compact, accessible and absolutely durable.

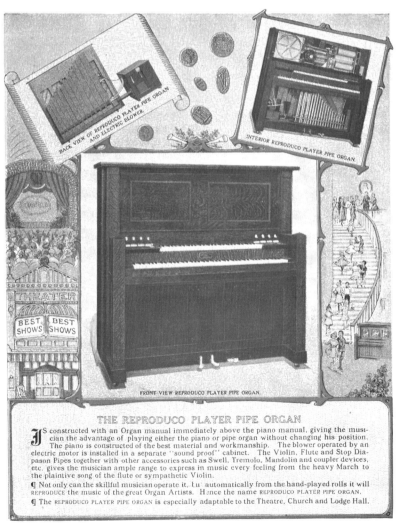

BACK VIEW OF REPRODUCO PLAYER PIPE ORGAN AND ELECTRIC BLOWER.

INTERIOR REPRODUCO PLAYER PIPE ORGAN.

FRONT VIEW REPRODUCO PLAYER PIPE ORGAN.

THE REPRODUCO PLAYER PIPE ORGAN

IS constructed with an Organ manual immediately above the piano manual, giving the musician the advantage of playing either the piano or pipe organ without changing his position. The piano is constructed of the best material and workmanship. The blower operated by an electric motor is installed in a separate "sound proof" cabinet. The Violin, Flute and Stop Diapason Pipes together with other accessories such as Swell, Tremolo, Mandolin and coupler devices, etc. gives the musician ample range to express in music every feeling from the heavy March to the plaintive song of the flute or sympathetic Violin.

¶ Not only can the skillful musician operate it, but automatically from the hand-played rolls it will REPRODUCE the music of the great Organ Artists. Hence the name REPRODUCO PLAYER PIPE ORGAN.

¶ The REPRODUCO PLAYER PIPE ORGAN is especially adaptable to the Theatre, Church and Lodge Hall.

The Old Piano Roll Blues

The Player-Piano's Thanksgiving

The man who sells pianos has traditionally had a big disadvantage in comparison with the sellers of most other types of household merchandise. Those who sell automobiles to the consuming public may be sure that the customer will eventually want a new one and will probably return, and even those who sell furniture have a certain recurrence in their clientele. Appliances wear out and people come back to the dealer for new machines and devices. But not so with pianos, because it is rare indeed that any family ever buys more than one in a generation.

The advent of the player was therefore a tremendous boon to the retail end of the piano industry, because it gave the dealer the opportunity to keep on selling merchandise — in the form of rolls — to those who had purchased player pianos from him. Of course he had always sold sheet-music in the past, but buyers were limited to those who could play. Now, everyone —musically skilled or not — became a potential customer. The older folks who weren't too "lamed-up" with arthritic ankle and knee joints to pump the pedals were hot prospects for the old standard numbers like "In the Sweet Bye and Bye" and "Silver Threads Among the Gold." If they were inflicted with the infirmities of advanced age they were even better prospects for a job of electrifying their old piano, or maybe even purchase of a new electric one.

The teen-age and young adult set, naturally enough, bought all the latest popular and hit tunes, all the

way from "Come, Josephine in My Flying Machine"
(1910) and "Alexander's Ragtime Band" (1911) to
"After You've Gone" (1918) and "If I Could Be
with You (One Hour Tonight)" (1926). During
World War I, the big rush was on for all the patriotic
airs. "Goodby Broadway, Hello France" was probably
never equaled in its capacity as a one-step to make
the most of pure mechanical interpretation of piano
music, and enthusiasts of schmaltzy numbers never
fail to recall the heart-rending strains of "Rose of No
Man's Land." Of course as soon as the war was over,
every player owner needed the latest release of "How
Ya Gonna Keep 'Em Down on the Farm—(After
They've Seen Paree)?"

As if the market for sales to oldsters, adults, and
teen-agers wasn't enough, the dealers were able to do
business with the toddler set as well. Every major
roll company had its repertoire of numbers based on
the Mother Goose Rhymes!

And not only was the dealer able to peddle rolls
on the basis of age groups and individual musical taste,
but he could approach the customer on the basis of his
nationality, political beliefs, or the organizations to
which he belonged.

Every roll company worth mentioning had Jewish
rolls, Greek rolls, Italian rolls, Polish rolls, and for all
we know, perhaps some enterprising manufacturer
even made rolls with words printed in Hottentot
language along the edge of the paper. There were
long-forgotten marches composed and perforated to

the honor of our various Presidents, and it is probably small comfort to rock-ribbed Republican students of player piano history to have to admit that one of the finest marches ever put on a paper roll was the "Franklin D. Roosevelt March," composed at the time of his original nomination for the Presidency by the Democratic party. But perhaps Republicans can be consoled by the fact that the march dedicated to Calvin Coolidge probably sold a lot more copies.

In addition to music perforated for various fraternal and religious organizations like the Knights of Pythias, the Knights of Columbus, the Elks, the Masons, the Mystic Shrine, and heaven-knows-what-all, there was at least one little-known roll — a march — dedicated to the glory of the infamous Ku Klux Klan!

And of course the dealers whose moral principles were perhaps not as high as most could turn a fast buck by selling the inevitable "party rolls" with suggestive verses which hit the market in the '20's. From time to time the executives of the major roll companies felt obliged to assure the public, through the trade press, that they deplored this practice and that *their* concerns would certainly never stoop so low. It seems incredible that the often-laughed-about purveyors of "feelthy peectures" had their counterparts in peddlers of "feelthy piano rolls," but odd as it seems, it happened.

Q R S Music Co. Launches Campaign Against Filth in Popular Songs with Vigorous Circular Letter

Letters Received from Dealers in All Parts of Nation Indicate Large Portion of Trade Stands with Music Roll Manufacturing Company on This Campaign—North Dakota Dealer Writes Sizzling Letter—U. S. Censorship of All Songs Suggested

CHICAGO, Nov. 30.

THE crusade launched by the Q R S Music Co. against indecent songs is meeting with the indorsement of the trade at large, judging from the hundreds of letters the company has received in reply to a letter it mailed out a few days ago. The letter, inspired by a song which was finding considerable vogue, read:

"We think it's demoralizing and vicious. How do you feel about it?

"We are inclosing a few excerpts of a new song, just published.

"Suggestive songs for grown-ups are bad enough, but when it comes to corrupting the minds of children we draw the line. We don't want profits from such a source.

"If there be some dealers who must have this roll, it will have to come from some roll manufacturer who is willing to help still further debase the morals of the music industry. It will not be available in any roll made by the Q R S Music Co."

Children would naturally be interested in such a song or roll, the circular intimates, and adds: "But let's help to keep their minds clean as long as possible. Are you with us? What do you say?"

During this week the letters in reply have been arriving from dealers in all parts of the country and these letters indorse the stand of the Q R S Co. in strong fashion.

Michigan Dealer Approves

Here is a typical reply, from a Michigan dealer:

"The stand you are taking to refuse to sell rotten songs is very fine. If music publishers would refuse to publish the trash that is printed and music dealers would refuse to sell the stuff, we think the industry would be doing the general public a wholesome service."

J. A. Poppler, president of the Poppler Piano Co., Grand Forks, N. D., writes a letter that sizzles with opposition to the filth song and gives permission to publish his stand. He says in part:

"Your company asks if we are for you in your attitude of refusing to cut this filth on rolls. Say, man! we have condemned and fought this stuff for ten years, as has any clean-minded official of any piano store in the trade.

"The hisses of an incensed public have forced theater managers all over the country to abolish suggestiveness from the stage and the manufacturers and the Music Merchants Association can strangle these morons in our midst today.

"I am no prude nor Puritan, nor do I think many of us could be so designated, but I get as hot under the collar as do you when we get sample copies of stuff like this and realize that the postal authorities allow it to go through the mails and find its way to the homes of decent Americans.

"I hate to think what would happen to one of those fleas if a Western man ever caught him spilling any of his suggestiveness to a girl out here, regardless of whether any ties of friendship or relationship existed."

Mr. Poppler berates the publishers who produce songs that are questionable, and says what has particularly galled him is "that these scum have the power, through their ill-gotten gold, to force upon the music merchant through a nationally advertised campaign their low-down putrid belchings."

"Keep up the good work. You will lose nothing and gain much, eventually, by holding your standards high, by recognizing and conforming to the clean and manly ideals of the great majority of United States citizens."

Many Letters Received

The pile of letters received by the Q R S Co., of which the two quoted are good examples, are the strongest possible indorsement of their stand for decent music. This is not the first shot fired by the company in the interest of the clean and wholesome and against the off-color songs. A number of songs that attained considerable popularity never appeared in the Q R S lists because they were condemned as soon as they reached the eyes of the heads of the company. In one instance a number was cut and ready for circulation when its contents were reviewed and orders were given to destroy the entire batch.

"We are not purists, or anything like that," said E. J. Delfraisse, advertising manager of the Q R S Music Co., to a representative of THE MUSIC TRADES, "but we do believe in decency and insist upon making our money in a decent way. This is not, of course, the first of the indecent songs. There have been a lot of them from time to time, but in recent days the output of the salacious has taken on a rawness never before dared. Our product is designed for use in the homes of the country and other countries. The fact that numbers are released by reputable companies makes the buying public easily decide that they must be all right. It is not until they are played that the filth strikes the one who has purchased the number. It stands to reason that such a number, finding its way into decent homes, is bound to have a bad effect—to hurt the sales of player-pianos and phonographs.

"One of the dealers who wrote commending our stand suggested a United States censor to pass on all songs prepared for publication. This is not a bad idea if it can be carried out.

"Some of the letters indorsing our stand were signed not only by the heads of the music house but by the clerks, and attention was called that some of the young ladies in the phonograph record and music roll departments are often embarrassed by both the names of the songs asked for and the text of the numbers.

"We are going to keep up the fight and feel sure that with the feeling of resentment against filth songs that is developing in the country it will not be difficult. We have received commendation from such houses as the Victor, the Brunswick, the Vocalstyle Music Co. and from various newspapers."

In its campaign the Q R S Music Co. recently wrote the Music Industries Chamber of Commerce asking that it use its influence to bring the dealers to realize the necessity of keeping the popular music cleaner. The letter pointed out that the chamber could do a world of good if it would get the dealers and manufacturers with whom it is associated in every line of music to sign a pledge not to purchase, to sell or in any way exploit any salacious or suggestive so-called popular songs. It was pointed out that if the market is not there the composers and publishers will soon quit merchandising that type of song.

The crusade is not in any sense against jazz music, but is emphatically against the smutty words that many of the jazz tunes carry.

While they might be condemned in some quarters today, one of the finest series of party rolls ever put out was the Home Minstrel Series, made by the Vocalstyle Music Company. Each roll (there were eight in the series) was a complete minstrel show. Not only were the words to the songs printed along the edge of the paper so that the "company" could gather 'round the piano and join in the singing, but each roll came equipped with a special joke book from which the interlocutor and Mr. Bones could carry on a snappy line of banter. Following is Joke Number 6 from the "Vocalstyle Home Minstrel Series," roll No. 1:

Inter: Mr. Tambo do you drink gin?

Tambo: Do I drink gin? Why, say, Mr. Interlocutor, Do a swim duck?

Inter: Mr. Tambo, I am sorry to say that I grasp the significance of your reply. But your sentence was hardly correct from a grammatical standpoint.

Tambo: How so? How so?

Inter: Why you said "Does a swim duck" when you should have said "Does a duck swim?"

Tambo: Well, now that you're so smart, can you all tell me why a white duck goes under the water sometimes?

Inter: Why, er — er. No; I must confess ignorance on the subject. "Why does a white duck sometimes go under the water, Mr. Tambo?

Tambo: Why, for divers reasons, Mr. Interlocutor.

Inter: Very clever, Mr. Tambo. Very clever.

Tambo: Yes! and I'll bet you don't know why that same duck comes out on the shore either.

Inter: Well, I may as well ask "Why does this self-same white duck come out on the shore?"

Tambo: Why, for sun-dry purposes, of course.

Joke Number 7.

etcetera, etcetera.

NEW VOCALSTYLE MINSTREL ROLL

No. 6 of Series Issued by Vocalstyle Music Co. Which Have Had Splendid Success—Window Card to Exploit Them Now Furnished the Dealer and Bringing Results

The Vocalstyle Music Co., Cincinnati, O., has issued a new "Minstrel" roll, which is No. 6 of the series, in which the operator of the player-piano acts as interlocutor and has his "com-

New Vocalstyle Window Card

pany" divided in a semi-circle around the player. Contained in the box with each of these rolls are six leaflets giving the full instructions regarding conducting a minstrel show with the Vocalstyle roll. All the jokes to be used in the performance are printed on this leaflet.

In the accompanying illustration there is shown a reproduction of a window card which has been prepared by the Vocalstyle Co. for the dealer's use in advertising these records.

The sixth and last roll of this series is contained in the March bulletin, which has been compiled and issued in a new and attractive form and contains several of the very latest popular selections. The minstrel series was arranged and composed by A. E. MacElroy, advertising manager of the company, and A. B. Furlong, sales representative.

157

As was noted earlier, the fact that one could operate a player piano without really having to learn very much did little to further the cause of good music. In recognition of this, there were published instruction rolls of one sort or another, designed specifically to teach a person how to play the player piano properly. The best known of these was a set of four rolls put out by the Gulbransen Company, accompanied by a booklet written by a Mr. John Martin, "Player-pianist Extraordinary," wherein he explains the various movements to be applied to the expression levers and to the pedals to achieve true musical results.

According to Mr. Martin: "I have been asked hundreds of times if it were not necessary to understand music to play a player well. I always answer in the negative. Some of the very best playerpianists cannot read a note of music, yet they revel in the concertos as though their life had been spent in music. . . .

"If you like music, that is all that's necessary, and just to the extent of your appreciation of music will you play your Player well. . . .

"The Player, as I see it, simply works the keys or furnishes the technique, the thing it takes so many, many hard years of practice to accomplish on the *other style of Piano*." (Italics ours. Ed)

Indeed, the trade press was continually admonishing piano dealers to sell players on the basis of what fine music could be extracted from them, but evidently few salesmen ever took the time or went to the trouble to learn these finer techniques. This of course was not a problem in connection with reproducing pianos as a type, but even here there were many purchasers who bought on the basis of "getting a player they wouldn't have to pump."

Another market which some concerns tried to exploit was that concerning actual teaching of how to play the piano the old-fashioned way, by hand. For instance, the set of six "Educator" rolls put out by the QRS Company contained 132 lessons and sold for $11.50, and while unquestionably there was considerable thought put into the design of these, this writer has yet to know anyone who actually learned to play through this means.

The Hallet and Davis people in 1926 brought out a famous set of instruction rolls for use with their Angelus reproducing piano, under the guidance of the great concert pianist, Leopold Godowsky, who short years earlier had formally introduced the Ampico to the public in a recital at the Biltmore Hotel in New York. The promoters of these instructions were careful to point out that they were in no way to be construed as replacing the teacher, but merely

forestall any criticism on the part of people who depended on this type of work for their daily living.

There were well over 50 companies established in the roll manufacturing business in the country at one time or another between the turn of the century and the end of the 'twenties, and a complete run-down on their individual histories would make another book the size of this one. But some of this information is worth noting here. These outfits are arranged alphabetically and not necessarily in their order of size or importance.

Altoona. This company was organized in 1919, to manufacture Victory, Superba, and Master music rolls, with factories at Altoona and Lansdale, Pennsylvania. According to the *Purchaser's Guide to the Music Industries, 1920,* "the firm holds long lease on six buildings at Seventh Avenue and Thirty-Fifth Street, New York City, upon which a sixteen-story building will be erected for the exclusive use of recording and manufacturing music rolls." This grandiose scheme evidently never came off, for rolls made by this company never hit the market in any great quantities.

Atlas Player Roll Company. This concern held forth in Newark, New Jersey, and according to their advertising "the product embodies a number of revolutionary features, such as great variety of musical effects in recording, tuneful and original interludes, modulations and changes of key, thereby holding the interest of the hearer throughout the length of the roll. Popular song numbers include not less than three choruses in each roll."

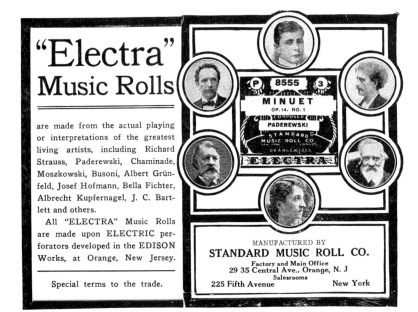

The Background
of
A BUSY ROLL DEPARTMENT

COLUMBIA WORD ROLLS

JULY—Advance

	Title	Played by:	
612	Choo Choo Blues	Clarence Johnson	Blues
613	Faded Love Letters	Nell Morrison	Waltz
614	A Kiss in the Dark	Nell Morrison	Ballad
615	I Never Miss the Sunshine	Florence Sanger	Fox Trot
616	Keep Off My Shoes	James Blythe	Fox Trot
617	That Red Head Gal	Florence Sanger	Fox Trot
618	Wolverine Blues	James Blythe	Blues
619	Tell Me Gypsy	Wayne Love	Fox Trot
620	Gulf Coast Blues	James Blythe	Blues
621	Every Step Brings Me Closer to By Lovin' Honey Lamb	Florence Sanger	Fox Trot
623	Look for the Silver Lining	Wayne Love	Fox Trot
624	Dreamy Melody	Nell Morrison	Waltz
625	In June	Wayne Love	Fox Trot
627	Snake's Hips	Paul Jones	Fox Trot
628	I Love Me	Florence Sanger	One Step
629	I Dream of a Castle in Spain	Wayne Love	Fox Trot
631	Yes! We Have No Bananas	Gladys Baywill	Fox Trot
632	Pappa Better Watch Your Step	Paul Jones	Fox Trot

To Retail at

Why Pay More? # 75c **None Better.**

Made of the best materials obtainable.

Will please your trade and double your sales.

Quality and price make Columbia rolls the dealer's best profit producer in a roll department.

A trial order will convince you.

Columbia Music Roll Co.
22 S. Peoria St.
CHICAGO   ILL.

The Billings Player Roll Company of Milwaukee, which was established in 1921, manufactured the "staffnote" player roll which boasted the unique feature of having the melody notes printed in regular music staff form along the edge of the paper, thus making it simple for the playerpianist to follow along by hand if he so desired. This firm was founded by Fred C. Billings, for years a prominent figure in the player industry.

Bennett & White, Inc., manufactured the Artempo rolls for home players in Newark, New Jersey, having started business in 1913.

Clark Orchestra Roll Company. This concern specialized in the manufacture of rolls for coin-operated pianos, and very quickly after its establishment in 1920 became the leader in its field. Ernest G. Clark, the President and Treasurer, was one of the pioneers in the early history of the Q.R.S. Music Roll Company, and he remained with that concern until his own firm was established. He was a brother of Melville Clark, mentioned elsewhere in this book. The factory at DeKalb, Illinois, was equipped with much machinery which had been developed by Mr. Clark, and it certainly was put to excellent use . . . no other concern ever put out such a fine variety of high quality nickelodeon music as did this one, and it is probably fair to say that coin-operated piano music, as it is known by the collectors today, is pretty much judged by the rolls put out by this company.

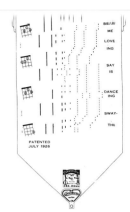

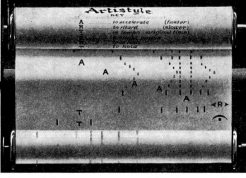
ROLL CATALOG IS GUIDE TO RIGHT NUMBERS FOR MOVIES

Automatic Music Roll Co. Issues Catalog of Music Rolls for Use on Seeburg "Celesta" Pipe Organ

CHICAGO, Nov. 2.—Ignorance of motion picture theater operators can no longer be accepted as an excuse for the playing of Chaminade's "Scarf Dance" as the musical accompaniment for a two reel "slapstick" comedy. The Automatic Music Roll Co. has just issued a catalog of music rolls for use on the Seeburg "Celesta" de luxe player pipe organ and other Seeburg pipe organ orchestras as a guide to the owners of motion picture houses in selecting the most suitable music for the various types of films.

"For your consideration and to assist you in obtaining the best results from your Seeburg Celesta de luxe player pipe organ and other Seeburg pipe organ orchestras we offer the following suggestions," says the foreword of the new catalog. "For feature pictures and storm scenes, use rolls that are listed as dramatic and heavy dramatic. For cowboy, Indian, news reels, intermissions and comedies, use marches, hurry music, light dramatic and popular rolls. For sentimental scenes, popular ballads and light dramatic."

The catalog says that "wonderful results can be obtained by the regulation of the tempo lever" on the Seeburg instruments. A chart of the proper regulation is given, which recommends a slow speed for heavy dramatic or tragic rolls, a medium speed for light dramatic, medium to slow for ballads, medium to fast for comedy rolls and fast for storm scenes. Marches should be timed to the time of the action depicted on the screen, the chart says.

Over sixty rolls are listed. The first eight are dramatic rolls and include such selections as Huerter's "Melodie," the "Mill by the Sea" by Adams, Winne's the "Twilight Hour," Frommel's "Chant D'Amour" and DeLeath's "Coronado Land," which compose the first roll listed. Sixteen light dramatic rolls are next listed. A good example of the type of music that is recorded in these rolls is contained in the roll numbered "MSR—781." This roll is composed of three of Friml's compositions, the "Valse Parisienne," "Mignonette" and "La Danse des Demoiselles," and also Zamenick's "In a Canoe" and Spear's "Summer Thoughts."

Verdi's "Overture to La Traviata" and Raff's "Cavatina" are the two selections which have been recorded for the first of the heavy dramatic rolls, of which there are two. These rolls are followed by classical dramatic, hurry music, overtures, organ dramatics, solos for the violin and flute, marches and one steps, comedy, "Gems," light operatic, light comedy, light comedy waltz rolls, comic opera, ballads, popular ballads, rolls composed of popular selections, waltzes, "Old Favorites," plaintive dramatic, southern melodies, oriental themes and chapel and sacred music.

Columbia Music Roll Company of Chicago put out rolls under the Columbia name, but evidently this concern was short-lived.

The *Connorized Music Company* of New York was one of the leaders in the field. In 1911 we find them boasting of a new line of rolls — "a Special Concert Edition consisting of specially musically artistic arrangements for musically cultured people." In 1913 they refer to their latest achievement — "The Connorized Concert Phrased Roll, a hand-played roll which has already won favor among musically cultured people for artistic superiority." All of these were, of course, perforated into "Connorized" paper, which, it was claimed, would neither shrink nor swell in any climate. By 1920 the company had a branch in St. Louis, Missouri, to take advantage of expanding midwestern markets. By 1925 they were really reaching out for markets, and claimed to have the largest selection of Italian songs and dances issued by any player roll company. Their catalogs of Polish, Bohemian, Lithuanian, Slavische, Hungarian, Jewish, Spanish, etc., were said by them to be the most complete on the market.

The *DeLuxe Reproducing Roll Corporation* was a branch of the Auto-Pneumatic action company, which produced the Welte-Mignon (Licensee) reproducing piano action for sale to independent piano manufacturers. It was, obviously, concerned with the manufacture of music to fit this particular action and as such recorded the artistic efforts of many of the great musicians of the twenties. It was located in the same buildings in New York City as the Auto-Pneumatic organization.

"New" and "News" Are Same Thing in Orchestra Rolls, Says Former Reporter, Now a Dealer

"People Won't Read Yesterday's Newspaper, Why Should They Hear Last Month's Rolls"? His View — Acting on This Principle, He Changes Rolls Often and Counts Up Many Shekels—Also Runs Music Appropriate to Season

DE KALB, ILL., Nov. 1, 1926

EDITORIAL policies employed in the operation of a string of automatic pianos by a former newspaper man have led to singular success, according to an article in a recent issue of the "Coin-Slot," official publication of the Clark Orchestra Roll Co.

"One of our good dealers from Indiana, a former newspaper man, is now operator of a string of automatic pianos," says the "Coin-Slot." "His experience in editorial work has taught him the value of news and he has carried this idea into his automatic roll business with marked success.

"In talking with him recently, a 'Coin-Slot' reporter asked him just how he increased the income from his players so greatly. Instead of the ordinary earnings, his string of instruments is coining him money 'hand over fist.'

"'In the first place,' he said, 'I see that every single piano on my string has a new roll each week. We wouldn't think of trying to interest newspaper readers in an edition that was many hours old. How, then, can we expect the public to pay their good money to listen to music they have been listening to for more than a week?

"'And another thing,' he added, 'why not make use of news, in the case of music rolls, just as in the case of newspapers? The publishers have learned that whatever is timely sells them more papers. Let Decoration Day come along and feature stories about the holiday are printed. In the same way, Labor Day, Thanksgiving, Christmas and all the rest of our national events are played up and interesting features presented to the readers. Result—bigger profits for the publisher.

"'How does that apply to music rolls? Well, simply this way. When the Fourth of July is due I see that my players have good snappy march rolls ready for the public. At Christmas time, I make use of music appropriate for the occasion, and so on the year round.

In other words, I offer the public music that they're thinking about and when they find that my pianos give them the melodies they want they don't lose any time in paying their money into the coin-slot.'

"This Indiana dealer has hit the nail on the head. What pays him will pay you and we're glad to pass along this idea for what good it may be to you. Our monthly catalogs carry a complete list of music appropriate to almost any occasion. There should be little trouble in selecting music that will have news value and boost the 'circulation' of your coin-slot."

On the cover of the "Coin-Slot" appears a reproduction of a photograph showing seventeen of the employees at the large factory of the Clark company. The caption says that reason for harmony in Clark orchestra rolls is harmony in the factory, and these seventeen reasons are presented.

This Music-Roll is my interpretation. It was recorded by me for the Duo-Art and I hereby authorize its use with that instrument.

Genevieve Pitot

TEMPO 70

AUTHORS ROLL No. 102855

"BONNIE SWEET BESSIE" J. L. Gilbert
Arranged and Played by Genevieve Pitot

THERE is a tender sentiment, reminiscent of the folk songs of Scotland, in "Bonnie Sweet Bessie". Its melody is simple yet beautiful and appealing. The story told in its words might have come down from some old ballad, a tale of "true love that ne'er goes unrequited." Here too is the sentiment, tinged with sadness, that characterizes the old folk love. "Bonnie Sweet Bessie" was written many years ago but it still retains its freshness and charm; it is still loved and sung just as it was by past generations.

A highland laddie there lived o'er the way,
A laddie both noble, and gallant and gay,
Who loved a lassie as noble as he,
A bonnie sweet lassie, the maid o' Dundee;
This lassie had lands, but the laddie had nane,
And yet to her it was all the same,
For dearly she loved him, and said she knew,
This laddie, dear laddie, was gude and true.

Ere years or even months had fled,
This laddie and lassie were happily wed,
Nae better wifey e'er lived on the lea,
Than "bonnie sweet Bessie, the maid o' Dundee."
A happier hame nae man ever had,
Than this which held twa hearts so glad,
And ne'er did Bessie have cause to rue,
Her wedding this laddie, sae gude and true.

But sorrow came to her heart one day,
Her dear darlin' was taken away,
Then oh, how sad and lone was she,
Poor "bonnie sweet Bessie, the maid o' Dundee."
And when in the ground her darlin' they laid,
Her heart then broke, and the fervently prayed,
"O God in heaven, let me go too,
And be wi' my laddie, sae gude and true."

— TEMPO 70 —

DUO-ART
The AEOLIAN COMPANY

September 26, 1925

A NEW type of Duo-Art music roll, the first of which will be released in October, is announced by the Aeolian Co., New York. Under the title of "Authors' Roll," a limited number of records of this series will appear from time to time in the Duo-Art catalog.

The author's rolls will be a series of well known songs in which the contribution of the author is given special attention. On the end of each roll will appear the words of the song, with editorial text describing the piece, its musical significance and the reasons for its popularity.

The first release, to appear in the October Duo-Art list, will be the well known Scotch ballad "Bonnie Sweet Bessie" by J. L. Gilbert, arranged and played by the young American pianist Genevieve Pitot. The three verses of the song are given in their entirety on the roll end. The text points out the kinship of the song to the old Scotch folk tunes in simplicity and beauty of melody and story context.

"The Duo-Art author's rolls are the first of their kind ever to be published," says an Aeolian official, "and should find an immediate and wide popularity with the roll-buying public. They fill a need long felt with this type of ballad—that of making the listener better acquainted with the mood and meaning of the song so that he may have a clearer understanding and keener appreciation of it."

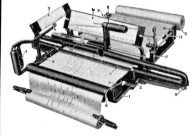
Duo-Art. The rolls for this make of reproducing piano were, of course, made by the Aeolian Company. The *Ampico* rolls were also put out by the concern which made those pianos incorporating that action, and an interesting article describing their production appears elsewhere, as reprinted by permission of the *Scientific American* magazine.

After the Aeolian factories suffered reverses in the 'thirties and the concern was combined with the American Piano Company, certain manufacturing economies were introduced with the result that the very late Duo-Art rolls are printed with Ampico labels. Certain musical arrangements were cut for both types of reproducing pianos, and it is interesting to be able to play these on two pianos, side by side, as a means of judging the interpretive capabilities of the two systems of musical reproduction.

The Globe Company of Philadelphia manufactured a lot of rolls under its own name in the early 'twenties, but it eventually became part of the Standard Music Roll Company of Orange, New Jersey, which then applied the Globe name to its line of less expensive rolls.

Gulbransen. For the most part, the manufacturers of pianos left the highly specialized art of player roll manufacturing to firms expert in this field, but this company was an exception to the rule. The Gulbransen Music Roll Corporation of Chicago was incorporated at a really late date — 1926 — to make "new improved music rolls true to hand playing minus mechanical effects."

The *Imperial Player Roll Company* of Chicago was founded around 1915, and one of its officers was Thomas E. Kavanaugh who later became general manager of the National Music Roll Manufacturers Association, also of Chicago. This concern was controlled by the Cable Company, which explains why, in addition to the regular lines of Imperial Hand Played Records and Imperial "Songrecords," it was the sole licensed manufacturer of Solo Carola Record Rolls. The piano which used these is pictured in this book.

As might have been expected, at least one concern set up in business to make rolls for composers unable to see the big outfits perforate their music. This was the *Individual Player Roll Company* of Jersey City, and according to Mr. Anthony Galasso, the manager, their business was "Recording player rolls for song writers, composers, and dealers under their own special labels."

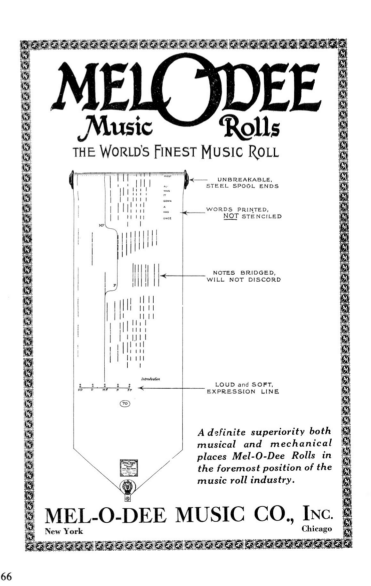

The *International Player Roll Company* manufactured rolls under that name starting in 1919. The trade
literature of the day credits the firm with an outstanding product known as the "International Concert

Series," in which were featured "all of the better class
of operatic, medleys, and classical numbers." Eventually the firm joined the QRS Company.

The *I.X.L. Company* of Philadelphia produced
I.X.L rolls, but there is little reason for listing them —
other than to note the catchy name — because they
apparently never produced any great quantity of
music.

Mel-O-Dee. The Mel-O-Dee Music Roll Company
was one of the largest, undoubtedly because it was
a subsidiary of the Aeolian Company. The factory
at Meriden, Connecticut, was complete with its own

box-making department, machine shop, and printing
establishment, and was modern in every respect. We
are told, in their literature, that "The Mel-O-Dee
Music Company ranks as one of the largest manufacturers of music rolls in the world today (1923).
It is the pioneer in the music roll history and has enjoyed unparalleled advantage in being closely associated with the development of the player-piano itself
through its position as one of the allied and subsidiary
corporations of the Aeolian, Weber Piano and Pianola
Company. The pre-eminence of Melodee music rolls is
the result of definite superiority, both musical and
mechanical. From a musical standpoint, the skill and
vast experience of those responsible for the artistic
arrangements of Melodee music rolls make possible
remarkable results obtainable with these rolls, upon
all makes of player pianos. . . .

". . . The products of this company, which are internationally known, embrace: The Melodee Song-
Roll, played with the words of the song printed on
the roll; the Melodee Hand-played, being a faithful

What Do You Think of This Ad?

It appears in four colors on the Outside Back Cover of the October Cosmopolitan.

Over Four Million People will see this opening Ad of our Fall Campaign and will read and remember — Q. R. S. Player Rolls are better.

QRS PLAYER ROLLS are Better

"Listen In"

The Lady: "Hello—is this the music dealer!"
The Dealer: "Yes, indeed—what can I do for you?"
The Lady: "Can I buy some music rolls now and pay for them at the end of the month?"
The Dealer: "Certainly. Glad to accommodate you."
The Lady: "Then you may send me 'Sad Hawaiian Sea'—No. 2288."
The Dealer: "That's one of the best of the new numbers."
The Lady: "And don't forget—I want Q·R·S Player Rolls because they are better."

Why don't you 'phone your music dealer—?

See How Much Easier Your Player Pedals with Q R S Rolls

All player pianos operate by air.

The air is admitted to the mechanism through perforations in the player piano roll.

Consequently whether or not your player pedals easily depends largely upon the kind of player roll you use.

It's worth spending a few moments trying out. Go to any music dealer and purchase a Q R S Player Roll. Take it home and try it.

Q·R·S PLAYER ROLLS

will make your instrument pedal easier and open your eyes to new musical possibilities in your player piano.

For the Q R S Player Roll possesses human interest, produces human music and is better although it costs you no more.

Eighty per cent of the music dealers of America are cheerfully accepting a smaller profit on this roll because they realize that the satisfaction coming from more natural, artistic player music will eventually sell more rolls and player pianos too.

There is a real scientific reason why Q R S Player Rolls make pedalling easier. This reason is fully set forth in a folder sent gladly at your request.

Q R S COMPANY

CHICAGO   NEW YORK   SAN FRANCISCO

We Suggest the following New Word Roll Numbers for Your Roll Library

511 A Little Birch Canoe, Waltz Ballad   .85
630 You Don't Know, Ballad Fox Trot   .90
750 Tell Me, Ballad Fox Trot   .90
655 After All, Fox Trot   .90
643 Lonesome, That's All, Ballad   .90
349 Mammy's Lullaby, Waltz   .80

AUGUST WAS GOOD MONTH FOR MUSIC ROLLS IN MILWAUKEE

Rolls of Songs Recently in Demand in Sheet Music and Record Form Especially Popular

MILWAUKEE, Sept. 1.—Music rolls have been very good during the month of August, due principally to an increased demand for players reported in several stores. The demand is largely for rolls of popular songs which recently have been active in sheet music and records.

Gimbel Bros. state that the roll business has shown an increase over last year. This department handles Q R S, Imperial and U. S. Music Co.'s rolls. Adam Schroeter, manager of the piano and music roll departments, states that a group of about ten rolls has been showing marked activity during the past few weeks. Such popular numbers as "Yearning," "Ah-Ha,"

"Collegiate," "Midnight Waltz," "Susie" and "Who Takes Care of the Caretaker's Daughter?" are included among those popular numbers which have been reordered several times to meet the constant demand.

The Milwaukee Piano Manufacturing Co., retailer of the Waltham line, have been featuring Q R S foreign word rolls with considerable success, according to Charles L. Nodine, manager. A special window display has been used to call attention to the foreign numbers, and many people who were unaware that they could get these rolls have appreciated the suggestion carried in the display. Groups of rolls were placed in the window, with a card attached to each group indicating the language. German, Italian, Lithuanian, Russian, Bohemian, Hungarian, Polish and Slovenian rolls were included in this display.

The Milwaukee Piano Manufacturing Co. has found a ready market for the Harry Snodgrass rolls, which always are in demand. The more recent numbers of "Under the Old Apple Tree," "Down by the Old Mill Stream" and the third of that group have taken very well. Other popular rolls include "By the Light of the Stars" and "Yearning," the newer number "Susie," and the old favorite, "Ah-Ha."

169

QRS INTERESTS PURCHASE U. S. MUSIC CO.

Roll Companies Consolidated Under One Head—Seeburg Celesta Proving Valuable in South— Theater Installs Schiller Grands—Other News

T. M. Pletcher, Head of the Q R S Music Co.

November 6, 1926

KEEN interest was aroused in the trade this week over the announcement by T. M. Pletcher, president of the Q R S Music Co., that his company had purchased the United States Music Co., one of the largest and best known makers of music rolls in the country. The amount paid is said to be about half a million dollars, and the Q R S Co. acquires the good will, patents, machinery, inventory, etc., and the U. S. line will be added to the regular line of Q R S music rolls.

"We have no desire to hog the music roll business," said Mr. Pletcher to a representative of THE MUSIC TRADES, just after the deal had been closed, "but we feel that we are improving the service to the trade by this important move. It is an advantage to the dealer to get all his requirements in any line from one source and the addition of a seventy-five cent roll puts us in a position to serve him in this way. One can readily see the annoyance a drug store or a hardware store or a grocery store, for example, would have if it were necessary for it to buy its various commodities from different houses. This has been made easy for such stores by the jobber who handles everything in each line and one order brings all requirements.

"By the new arrangement we will be able to serve the trade with a complete line of music rolls as follows: Q R S rolls at $1; U. S. rolls at 75 cents, and, after Jan. 1, Imperial at 50 cents.

"There need be no worry about what Q R S will do, because our policy of liberal treatment and fairness has been established for twenty-five years. Service is the one thing we are anxious to give, and this move places us in a position to give much better service.

"It is our intention to continue to manufacture and market the U. S. roll and to maintain its standard of quality as a 75 cent roll, and since we will market it as one of our regular line of rolls the dealer can expect our customary service. We will continue to make the Q R S roll. We will continue to nationally advertise Q R S rolls extensively."

Arthur A. Friestedt, president of the United States Music Co., will come to the Q R S Co. in an advisory capacity, and George L. Ames, vice-president and sales manager of the U. S., will become sales manager of the Q R S music roll business. No change will be made in the present officers of the Q R S Co.

The Q R S Co. is one of the largest manufacturers of music rolls in the world. It maintains factories in Chicago, New York, San Francisco, Toronto, Canada; Sydney, Australia, and Utrecht, Holland. The plant of the United States Music Co. will be maintained as well as the organization. The purchaser takes over the entire U. S. catalog of masters, patents, machinery and the entire stock of inventory, both finished rolls and raw material. The U. S. Co. has an output of over 2,000,000 rolls a year and the Q R S Co. sales last year totaled 6,700,000 rolls.

The purchase was made without issuing any additional stock of the Q R S Co. Because of the added volume, with very little additional expense, it is estimated that under normal conditions the deal should add a quarter of a million dollars to the Q R S Co.'s annual profits. The stock of the Q R S is listed on the Chicago Exchange and its recent advances have been the occasion for comment from the financial writers of the press. A little over a year ago the Q R S Co. started to manufacture radio tubes under the trade mark "Q R S Redtops," and it is estimated that it will do a million dollars in tubes this year. The company earned the last fiscal year between five and six dollars per share on the Q R S roll business alone.

Arthur A. Friestedt, who has been a strong factor in the roll business for years, decided some time ago to liquidate the U. S. Music Co. in order that he might take life a little easier. He told his plan to Mr. Pletcher, and negotiations, which terminated recently, were opened.

Southern California Music Co. Q R S Roll Department Is One of Largest in America

Two Views of Southern California Music Co. Q R S Roll Department

LOS ANGELES, Sept. 21, 1925

ONE of the largest music roll departments in the country is the Q R S department of the Southern California Music Co. of this city. It is not only spacious, but is unusually attractive and very conveniently arranged.

In addition to the general department there are demonstration rooms, where the customer may rest in comfort while hearing the rolls played. This department is in charge of Miss Florence Beebe, who for many years was head of the roll department of May & Co., Cleveland. She is one of the best posted music roll saleswomen in the United States.

Herewith are shown views of the Q R S department.

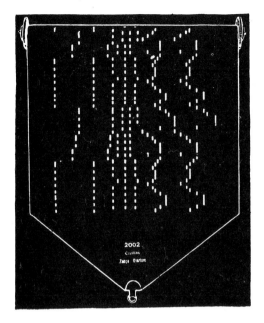
reproduction of the pianist who originally recorded the composition, also the Melodee Mathematically arranged roll, taken from the score either with or without embellishments, depending on the character of the composition."

The *Mel-O-Art Player Roll Manufacturing Company,* on the other hand, was a firm located in Baltimore, Maryland, which made a specialty of old-time tunes and blues.

The *National Music Roll Company* was a division of the Englehardt-Seybold Company and had factories at St. Johnsville, New York. In addition to making all the rolls for the Peerless automatic pianos, photo-orchestras, and orchestrions, their output of regular 88-note piano rolls for home use came under three titles: Master records, Auto-Inscribed, and Hand-played. The Master records were exact reproductions of the original composition; the Auto-Inscribed were described as ". . . . a temporized roll in the individuality of the arranger," and of course, the hand-played rolls were hand reproductions of the artist. The literature goes on further to point out (in 1914, when this company was going strong) that "one of the remarkable special features of their equipment is that each music-perforating machine is in direct rhythm, thereby insuring perfect reproduction of a music roll." (Whatever *that* means —Ed.)

One of the best known names in the trade was the *Pianostyle* label, put out by the company of the same name. This concern was organized in Brooklyn, New York, in 1913, and was in business throughout the period of popularity of the player piano. The work force of about 100 people made rolls not only for the domestic trade, but also for a considerable export trade to South America and Europe which the company had succeeded in cultivating over the years. Like many others, it eventually joined the QRS Company.

But of all the concerns which engaged in the manufacture and sale of player piano rolls, undoubtedly the one worthy of the greatest recognition is the organization which since 1900 has produced, and continues to produce, rolls under the *QRS* label.

This company had its beginnings as a part of the Melville Clark Piano Company in Chicago and De-Kalb, Illinois, around 1900. By 1920 the company had succeeded so well in marketing its product that it had become by far the largest concern of its type in the world, and unquestionably the inertia gathered in this drive did much to help it stay in business long after all the others had fallen by the wayside.

The origin of the name "QRS" is obscure. One early piece of advertising uses the phrase "Quality Real Service", and it's certainly possible that the firm's founders had this in mind. Another theory, told the writer by a music arranger who worked for the company in the 1919-1923 era, suggested that the roll-making department was originally of such minor importance in the Melville Clark piano factory that it didn't even rate a separate slot in the company mail-distribution box.

Any mail to be sent to it was therefore put into the "Q" slot, since there were no employees whose names started with that letter. Soon the mail for this part of the business expanded such that the mail clerk started using the "R" slot, and eventually had to slop over into the "S" box. Folks around the plant then started referring to the cutting room as the "QRS" department, and the name stuck. It's as logical an explanation as any other we've heard!

In the late 'teens the music roll operation was separated from the piano part of the business, with the QRS name being officially assigned to that new entity. The Clark Orchestra Roll Company continued to make coin-piano rolls at that location, and eventually the DeKalb factories became part of the great WurliTzer empire where to this day hundreds of pianos are built daily.

Throughout the years of its existence, the company secured the services of all the leading pianists in the field of popular music, and many in the classical field, as well. Names like Lee S. Roberts, Felix Arndt, Pete Wendling, Victor Arden, Phil Ohman, Russell Robinson, James P. Johnson, J. Lawrence Cook, Zez Confrey, Fats Waller, and Max Kortlander are familiar ones to all devotees of the piano music in America; they are just a few of the greats whose efforts have been preserved forever through QRS roll cuttings.

While the peak of popularity of the player piano itself occurred in 1923, the roll business peaked in 1926, and during this year QRS produced and sold almost ten million rolls! Of course a factor which aided in this total was the acquisition of around twenty-five of the smaller concerns during the 'twenties — such noted names as Vocalstyle, U. S., Imperial, Pianostyle, International, and Angelus were among the firms absorbed. In fact, there may have been questions raised among the trade by all these purchases of other firms, because in November of 1926, shortly after QRS had acquired the United States Music Company for around half a million dollars, the QRS President, Mr. T. M. Pletcher, felt obliged to explain to the trade press that "We have no desire to hog the

QUICK WORK ON ROLL

"The Miami Storm," New Waltz Song, Is Ready for Sale Twenty-four Hours After Arrival

Twenty-four hours after Max Kortlander, recording manager for the Q R S Music Co. received the Triangle song hit, "The Miami Storm," he had word rolls all made up and ready for shipment. This is the first time that anything like this has been accomplished in the music roll industry.

Joe Davis, head of the Triangle Music Co., feels sure he will have a sensational sheet music, record and roll seller in this new publication, which was written by Carson J. Robison.

music roll business, but we feel that we are improving the service to the trade by this important move."

When the market for rolls and players was foreseen to start dropping, officials of the company looked for other fields in which to keep busy their hundreds of employees in factories in New York; Chicago; San Francisco; Toronto, Canada; Sydney, Australia; and Utrecht, Holland. One result was a venture into the radio tube market, and for a time considerable business was done in the manufacture and sale of "QRS Redtop" tubes. Another venture was into motion picture cameras and projectors, in association with the DeVry Company, and still another was in the neon sign business.

Max Kortlander, one of the staff artists during the 1920's, evidently had more foresight than most people as to the future of the piano roll business, as he saw fit to purchase the remains of QRS after the stock

Max Kortlander

market tumbled and the roll-making business had dropped to only a fraction of its former glory. He renamed the business the IMPERIAL INDUSTRIAL CORPORATION, apparently reasoning that with

such a name, should piano-roll manufacturing disappear altogether, in fact with an impressive-sounding title they could go into almost any line or work and sound more or less legitimate! The business was moved to New York City, where it remained for some 30 years.

In an interview in 1961, the author asked Mr. Kortlander how he had managed to keep such a business alive. He stated that one thing that helped, even though their market was pretty limited, was giving the public what it wanted. He said that when the public wanted ballads, that's what they turned out. When they wanted rock-and-roll, that's what they got! There's more to business than this, of course, but it never ceases to amaze the writer how many unsuccessful would-be business men never want to realize that the customer is King!

A most friendly and genial man, Mr. Kortlander supervised the operation of a plant with about eighteen employees in 1961, at a time when the business was on the upswing. When asked about the ups and downs of the business through the years, he explained that the business went down until World War II, when for some as yet unexplained reason, the demand for rolls became so great that the company simply couldn't produce enough of them. After the war the demand slackened again, and 1952 was the real all-time low point of production with perhaps fewer than 200,000 rolls being made.

Max Kortlander died suddenly on October 11, 1961, at the age of 71, shortly before the first printing of this book was released. For a few years after his death the company was run by his brother, Herman Kortlander and his widow, Gertrude Kortlander, who continues as a consultant to the present corporation.

In April of 1966, Mr. Ramsi P. Tick, a piano roll collector, lawyer, and former manager of the Buffalo Philharmonic Orchestra formed a new corporation (Q-R-S- Music Rolls, Inc.) which acquired the assets of the Imperial Industrial Company. As president of the new corporation, one of Mr. Tick's first decisions was to move the company from its decaying surroundings in the Bronx to his hometown, Buffalo, New York. (He was born there November 12, 1924).

As the second edition of this book is written, the company is enjoying considerable prosperity, with perhaps half-a-million piano rolls being produced yearly.

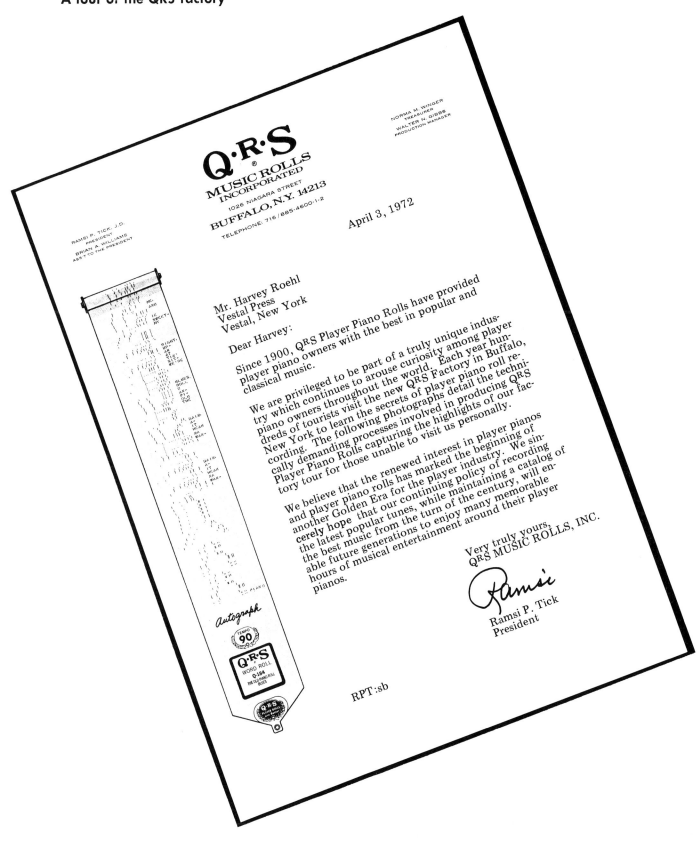

Q·R·S
MUSIC ROLLS
INCORPORATED
1026 NIAGARA STREET
BUFFALO, N.Y. 14213
TELEPHONE: 716/885-4600-1-2

NORMA M. WINGER
TREASURER
WALTER N. GIBBS
PRODUCTION MANAGER

RAMSI P. TICK, J.D.
PRESIDENT
BRIAN A. WILLIAMS
ASS'T TO THE PRESIDENT

April 3, 1972

Mr. Harvey Roehl
Vestal Press
Vestal, New York

Dear Harvey:

Since 1900, QRS Player Piano Rolls have provided player piano owners with the best in popular and classical music.

We are privileged to be part of a truly unique industry which continues to arouse curiosity among player piano owners throughout the world. Each year hundreds of tourists visit the new QRS Factory in Buffalo, New York to learn the secrets of player piano roll recording. The following photographs detail the technically demanding processes involved in producing QRS Player Piano Rolls capturing the highlights of our factory tour for those unable to visit us personally.

We believe that the renewed interest in player pianos and player piano rolls has marked the beginning of another Golden Era for the player industry. We sincerely hope that our continuing policy of recording the latest popular tunes, while maintaining a catalog of the best music from the turn of the century, will enable future generations to enjoy many memorable hours of musical entertainment around their player pianos.

Very truly yours,
QRS MUSIC ROLLS, INC.

Ramsi P. Tick
President

RPT:sb

174

Ramsi P. Tick, President, QRS Music Rolls, Inc.

Rudy Martin, staff arranger and recording artist at the Recording Piano. Master roll at right of picture. Four to eight hours are required to master a standard three-minute long roll.

Close-up of "stops" above keyboard. Pulling out a "stop" holds down a key to free artists' hands to play other notes. Use of "stops" enables one artist to create a four hand arrangement.

Close-up of master roll as it is being cut on the Recording Piano.

Rudy Martin checks final master roll using a "keyboard" ruler.

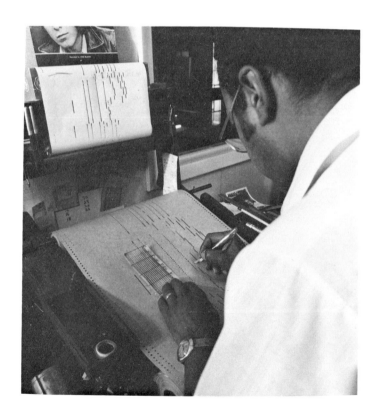

Rudy Martin cuts in an extra note with an X-acto knife. Perforated square of master paper is used as a scale to measure the length of any note on the master roll.

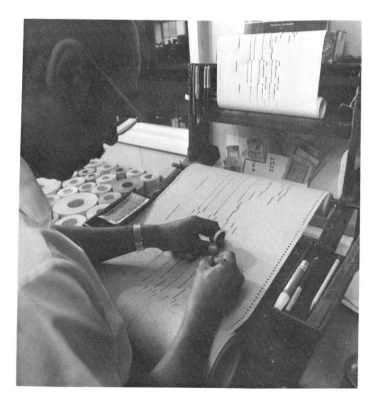

Final editing process. Rudy Martin tapes over any extraneous notes. Total editing process may take up to eight hours depending on the complexity of the arrangement.

(Above) After editing, the master roll is copied to make a perfect production master. Rudy Martin watches tracking of original master during duplication.

(Below) Original master passes over tracker bar above. Duplicate master with all errors corrected is perforated below. Corrected master is then sent into production.

(Above) Production perforator. Largest perforator has four channels of paper with tracking head for master roll in the center. Each channel of paper contains 16 sheets of paper. This perforator can therefore make 64 copies of a master roll in ten minutes. Notice rolls of paper on racks behind each channel. Paper is overwidth and trimmed as it passes through the cutting head (see strips of paper to the right of machine).

(Above) Danny Papa tracks master roll during run of 64 copies of a best-selling song.

(Right) Close-up of master roll passing over tracker bar of 4-cut perforator.

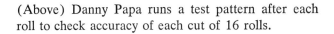

(Above) Danny Papa runs a test pattern after each roll to check accuracy of each cut of 16 rolls.

(Right, above) Tony Paul operates a 2-cut perforator. This perforator makes 32 copies of the master roll. It is used for slower selling standard songs.

(Right, below) Ken Maracle operates Recordo perforator. This perforator makes 32 copies of the master roll. It is equipped with extra punches in the cutting head for the purpose of making Recordo and other expression rolls.

(Below) Ken Maracle cuts off stack of 16 finished rolls to be placed on finishing table for labeling and tabbing.

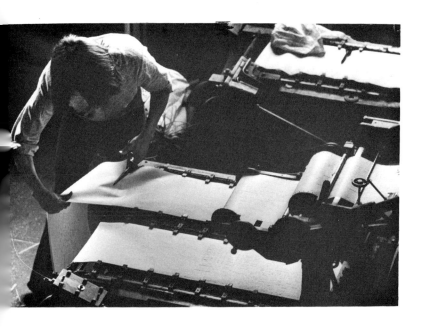

(Left, top) Hand stamping title and tempo on each roll. Stack of 16 rolls is then moved forward to be cut to a point by blades of paper cutter to the right in the picture.

(Left, center) Clare Tatko inspects tab ends cut from strips of gummed paper tape on original machine adapted from shoe-making equipment sometime near the turn of the century.

(Left, lower) Sally Wehrmeyer applying tab ends. Tabs are moistened and affixed to the point of each roll.

(Right) Rudy Martin makes a "layout roll" from first production run of a new song "American Pie." Roll is marked for song lyrics. A dark line is drawn next to each note that requires a syllable. Roll is then used to make word stencil. Layout is then stored for reference to the master roll.

(Below) Doug Roe cuts word stencil letter by letter on teflon-coated fiberglass cloth. Layout roll at left in picture is used to determine spacing between syllables.

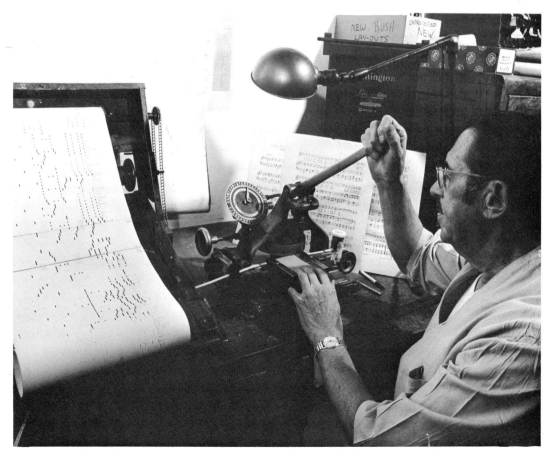

(Left and center, above) Sequence shot of song lyrics being stenciled onto roll. Roll passes through stencilling machine in two or three seconds. Song lyrics can be seen along the right edge of the stopped roll.

(Above, right) Vera Sardes spooling roll.

(Below) Spooled rolls are placed on trays to await boxing and labeling. Alice Tatko and Clare Tatko label and box rolls.

Jo Ann Castle, who was with the Lawrence Welk show for 10 years, recorded 10 tunes at the QRS factory on March 16, 1972. These were done with a "marking" machine, which was used in the first 30 years of the company's history to produce "hand-played" rolls. In the picture above we see Miss Castle with Brian Williams, assistant to Mr. Tick, as he checks the equipment and the paper. Below, Miss Castle is actually recording "The Shiek of Araby"; the device at the lower left is marking on a long sheet of paper the actual notes as they are struck by the artist.

No story on the making of 88-note piano rolls would be complete without proper recognition of J. Lawrence Cook, considered by many to be the "Dean" of American roll arrangers. Mr. Cook started in this activity in 1921, and his first arrangement sold commercially is "Dying With The Blues", shown here as it appeared on the end of the roll box. In the intervening years he arranged literally thousands of music rolls, and as the second edition of this book is prepared, he is still at it. The picture of him at the arranging piano was taken in 1961 at the QRS factory when it was located in New York City.

The author considers J. Lawrence Cook's long suit his ability at clever modulations from key to key within a given selection; music roll enthusiasts who consider themselves students of perforated arranging are encouraged to study his works to see if this isn't so! One would gain the impression by listening to his works that he particularly enjoys little musical "tricks" and "jokes" . . . for example, he'll often change from one key to another, to another and still another between sections of a selection and the listener begins to wonder where he's going to end—and all of a sudden he's right back in the same key he started with! The subtleties of these musical movements are such that one frequently doesn't realize that frequently he's been led right around Robin Hood's barn, right back to the starting place.

The vast majority of the music rolls cut during the 1930's and 1940's are the work of J. Lawrence Cook, and anyone who has followed this type of music in that period has to be familiar with his works simply through the sheer weight of numbers!

The *Recordo Player Roll Company* of Chicago is best known today in terms of the music it put out for use with expression pianos. In the early twenties it took over the Imperial Music Roll Company noted earlier in this chapter, and shortly thereafter was absorbed by the QRS Company, as also noted.

The *Republic Player Roll Corporation* of New York City enjoyed the distinction of being associated with Kohler Industries, which in turn controlled a number of factors in the player industry. Its advertising was particularly unusual in that most of it consisted of amusing drawings of dancing player rolls, or some type of animated scene.

Rythmodik was the name of the affiliate of the American Piano Company which made their line of regular 88-note rolls for home players, and the factory was located in Belleville, New Jersey, with recording studios being in New York City. Just in what ways

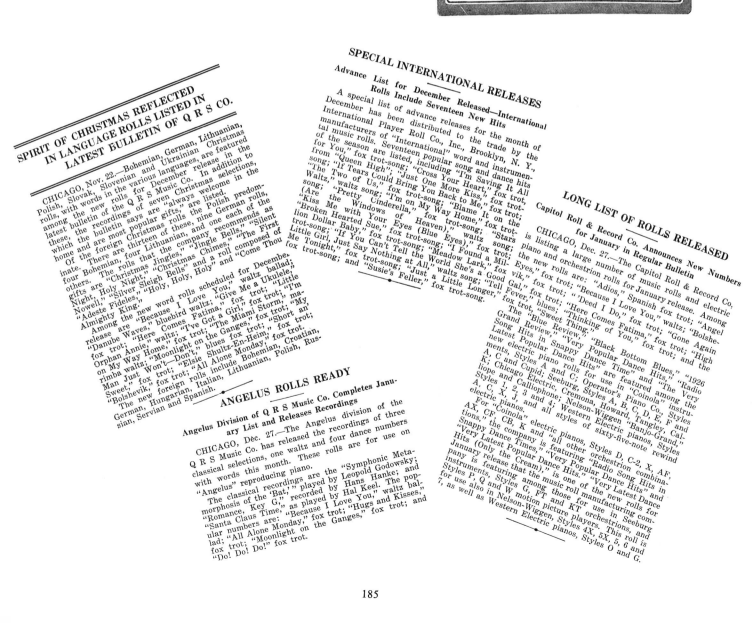

these rolls differ from rolls made by other manufacturers is not clear, but the company made great claims for their ability to make the ordinary player piano sound more like a reproducing piano would be expected to play. As stated in a leading trade journal ". . . (these rolls) contain not only every variation in tempo, but to an astonishing degree they reproduce without any assistance whatever on the part of the operator, the actual tonal effects, notably the singing tone, which the artist produced on the recording piano when the record was made. Beauty in piano playing depends very largely upon the quality of tone the performer is able to obtain from the instrument, and in reproducing this quality through Rythmodik records the player piano seems endowed with the very soul of the recorded artist. . . . with them anyone can, without previous knowledge or experience, obtain immediately a brilliant and musical effect. Buttons and levers need never be used unless one wishes to substitute his own reading for that of the artist who made the record. This is always possible, and those who derive pleasure from personal interpretation may still do so, but with far more beautiful results, for they are no longer handicapped by the mechanical and perfunctory touch inseparable from the ordinary roll, but instead will be guiding, as it were, a pair of skillful and sensitive hands."

The *Standard Music Roll Company* of Orange, New Jersey, was another leader in the field. One of their best known products was the ARTo Word roll which it was claimed "would teach you to sing." It was stated by the manufacturer that "one distinct characteristic of the roll is that the first letter of each word clearly shows the note upon which the word is to be sung. Thus, voice modulation is possible before the note is struck and thus the word can be sung at exactly the correct time and not a half-beat behind the music." It was also pointed out that "all ARTo rolls are contained in beautiful sepia art boxes, suitable for use in any drawing room."

A later development of this company was the Standard Play-A-Roll, and while just how it differed from any other type of roll is not explained, one advertisement of this company points out that *"Every* Play-A-Roll must meet a musical standard equal to a first-class performance by the best exponent of modern piano playing. This is something really new in player roll production."

The *United States Music Company* started in business around 1906, and throughout the period of player popularity aggressively merchandised rolls under the U. S. label. Among other innovations introduced by the

DIVISION POINT NEEDS STANDARDIZATION

Vocalstyle Music Co., in Official Publication, Warns Manufacturers That Unless Hammer Rail Division Point Is Standardized, Industry Faces Ruin

CINCINNATI, OHIO, Oct. 5.

RUIN of the expression electric player-piano industry, unless the manufacturers adopt a standard dividing point in the hammer rail in order to obtain the proper pianistic effect from music rolls played upon expression instruments, is predicted in an article appearing in the latest issue of "Vocalstyle Notes," official publication of the Vocalstyle Music Co.

"It is evident that the piano manufacturers, who are dividing at variance with the standard observed by roll manufacturers, are going to receive a lot of adverse criticism from dealers and purchasers of expression instruments," says the publication. "In looking over the many different pianos that were displayed at the New York conventions, it was found that the manufacturers of expression players had not observed any set rule with regard to the division point in the hammer rail. Some divided between E and F. Some at other places.

"The manufacturers of player rolls have always observed a standard division point, between C-sharp and D, the logical division point. These rolls played on pianos divided at other points would not give the proper pianistic effects. In an effort to have the piano interests observe the same standard observed by the roll makers, the Vocalstyle Music Co. sent a letter to all manufacturers of reproducing player-pianos, pointing out the advantages of getting together on this point.

"In order that the dealers may be posted on this campaign we are quoting our letter:

"'Most of you will recall that some years ago a convention was called at Buffalo to consider the advisability of standardizing the tracker bar on player-pianos. At one stroke this convention, held in 1908, wiped out all the confusion that imperiled the future of the player-piano industry with the adoption of the standard 88-note tracker bar.

"'With the advent of the electric expression player we find ourselves again embarrassed with a difference in construction that is proving a handicap to manufacturers, dealers and music roll manufacturers alike. This condition, while not so serious, happily may be easily overcome. With the popularity of the expression player growing daily it behooves us to get together on this matter before it is too late.

"'We have reference to the division in the hammer rail. At present there are three manufacturers of expression rolls. All have standardized so that the division comes between No. C and D. The dealer who demonstrates an expression player divided between E and F will find it impossible to get the proper pianistic effects using this combination, and naturally will fail to make the sale. This state of affairs multiplied indefinitely will spell ruin to the industry. On the other hand, with hammer rail divided to correspond with the rolls the expression players will sell themselves. We will all benefit financially while we are advancing the cause of music generally.

"'This subject was discussed at some length at the New York Convention in June. Manufacturers and dealers were unanimously of the opinion that if this matter was called to the attention of the manufacturers they would be very glad to standardize the hammer rail.

"'It will be a great pleasure to do whatever we can to help this movement on to a successful and speedy conclusion. Please command us whenever we can be of any service to you.

"'In conclusion let us recall a slogan that is as apt today as it was when it was originated: "The player-piano is only as good as the roll it plays." The truth of this statement was never more forcibly demonstrated than it has been in connection with the reproducing rolls. You have a good instrument. You'll get the best results from it through the use of the best rolls you can get.

"'We want you to see for yourself what marvelous effects are possible when your piano appears to the best advantage. You don't half suspect how fine your player really is. And these rolls, remember, play on any standard 88-note player.

"'Would you like to have one with our compliments? Then just fill out the requisition and send in to us.

"'Yours very truly,
"'THE VOCALSTYLE MUSIC CO.,
"'A. B. Furlong, Jr.'

"Piano tuners throughout the country are being advised of the movement started by Vocalstyle, and are being asked to co-operate with us in bringing about the standardization that will help dealers sell these pianos and keep their buyers satisfied after the sale is made.

"If the piano you are handling is not divided between C sharp and D you should write the factory, asking them to change. It's for your good and theirs.

"Up to the time of going to press we have received a letter from the Lester Piano Co., Philadelphia, stating that they had instructed their superintendent to change to this standard division point."

PLATE 4

1. MASTER ROLL.
2. HANDLE FOR ADJUSTING MASTER ROLL.
3. MASTER ROLL DRUM.
4. FEED RATCHET FOR MASTER ROLL.
5. RATCHET ARM AND PAWL.
6. GEAR FOR REWINDING MASTER ROLL.
7. TAKE-UP SPOOL FOR MASTER ROLL.
8. TRACKER BAR AND PNEUMATICS.
9. PAPER GUIDE.
10. SEPARATOR GUIDE RODS AND BALL BEARING PAPER RACK.
11. AIR PUMP.
12. AIR TANK.
13. PAPER FEED CONNECTING ARM.
14. CHANGE FEED ROCKER ARM.
15. FEED RATCHET ARM AND PAWL.
16. FEED RATCHET.
17. PAPER FEED MECHANISM.
18. PAPER FEED BEARING BRACKETS.
19. AIR ESCAPEMENT VALVE.
20. MOTOR—ONE HORSE POWER.

Acme Music Roll Perforator

PATENTS PENDING

"DIXIE" IS SIXTY-SIX YEARS OLD *1924*

American Folk Song Classic Was Written by Daniel D. Emmett, New York Minstrel, Who Died in Poverty After Amassing and Spending a Fortune

"DIXIE," the battle song of the Confederacy, celebrated its sixty-sixth birthday recently.

Although generally associated with the South, this American classic was not written by a southerner. The song itself and its author, Daniel Decatur Emmett, were born in New York City. It is the product of a single day's work under pressure and was written as a "walk around," or closing march, for a minstrel troupe playing in Mechanics' Hall in 1859, which then stood at Broadway and Park Place.

Jerry Bryant, one of the owners of the minstrel troupe, decided the finale of the show was weak and asked Emmett, who was a member of the company, to write a "hurrah walk around, something to make a noise with, and bring it here for rehearsal Monday morning."

That was Saturday. Emmett spent Sunday in his dingy hotel room in Barclay Street grinding out the words and lyrics of "Dixie," and submitted the song to Bryant the next day.

When it was sung for the first time Monday night it won twenty curtain calls. Within a week everybody was whistling it. Emmett was paid $500 for the copyright, a huge sum for those days, and a New York publisher brought out the hit in sheet music form for the holiday season. Its fame and popularity continued to grow and it became a national favorite.

Emmett wrote many other songs, but none of them ever caught the public's fancy like "Dixie." He made a fortune and frittered it away. In 1891 he was found playing a violin in a New Orleans dive.

Members of the theatrical profession raised a fund and bought a home for him in Mount Vernon, Ohio, where he eked out a bare existence by chopping wood. The Actors' Fund of America furnished him a comfortable living until his death in 1904 at the age of eighty-eight.

How to Make the Reproducing Library Pay

Miss Marian Reed, Manager of the Ampico Library, Homer L. Kitt Co., Washington, D. C., Relates Personal Experiences in Building Up and Maintaining a Profitable Roll Department

Written Exclusively for THE MUSIC TRADES
By MARIAN REED, Manager, Ampico Library, Homer L. Kitt Co., Washington

EVERY house that handles a reproducing piano is obliged to assume the burden of an adequate library of records as a complement to its reproducing piano department. In the majority of cases this department is a losing proposition and a source of irritation instead of the actual inspiration of which it is capable when functioning properly.

The manufacturers, realizing the tremendous value of the library, have competed with each other to secure the finest artists and build up a catalog which will meet with the approval of the most exacting musical critic. They have never failed to emphasize to their representatives the importance of this department.

It is being constantly reiterated and must always be remembered that in selling reproducing pianos, one sells first MUSIC. This seems difficult for the average piano salesman to understand. He has spent much time in the past talking "action," "case," and other trivialities and now is suddenly awake to the fact that he knows nothing about the new subject. In most cases the salesman is content to learn the names of two or three selections and with "Liebestraum" and Prelude in C sharp minor tucked under his arm, feels thoroughly competent to meet the world, the flesh and the devil and when he gathers himself together after the encounter, seems no nearer guessing the reason for his defeat.

If the old player-piano methods of salesmanship are obsolete, so too are the player roll department methods. Just any young person with pleasing personality who can read the names and numbers on the boxes is not enough for the reproducing library.

GOOD music must be sold. The reproducing piano, by eliminating the distraction of a personality, is training the music lover to listen. The librarian's task is to tactfully call attention to the beauties of the composition. The librarian need not necessarily be a trained musician, but must be a music lover with intelligence, catholicity of taste and an unflagging determination to learn.

Let me give an incident to illustrate. A customer had three successive packages of records sent to his home for selection and returned all three with almost no selection having been made. This was a challenge to the librarian, who decided the customer must be sold before leaving the library. The customer purchased a large order of the best selections in the library, not one of which was finer than those sent to the home on approval. Why did the customer buy in the studio and not keep the records sent to the home? Simply because a little hint disclosing the inner beauties of the composition was needed to put it over. The more one knows about an article the more one enjoys it.

How, then, Mr. Librarian, must you prepare yourself, if you wish to put the department on a paying basis, increase sales units and indirectly assist in selling more instruments?

First—KNOW YOUR GOODS.

Know it from many angles. Play a selection until you can recognize the melody, then play it some more and listen for new chord combinations, humorous or dramatic passages or unusual technical difficulties. Play it again and decide as to its emotional appeal and which of your customers would like such a selection; then make a note of your decision.

Miss Marian Reed

Read the life of the composer and make a note of at least two interesting, dramatic or humorous incidents and use them in your selling. The more incidents remembered, the more interesting the salesman. Learn all you can about the artist playing for you. Make him real to your customer.

Know the names of several other compositions of similar appeal. Remember to obliterate as far as possible your personal taste and learn to hear something of interest in every composition. Never let a composition be too big, too highbrow for you. Play it, study it and learn to find its hidden beauties. Remember, the blind cannot lead the blind. Learn to use the information without being pedantic.

Second—KNOW YOUR CUSTOMER.

The librarian should have a complete record of each customer, the kind of instrument owned, all records purchased and, if possible, all records tried and rejected. Glance over this record when the customer visits the studio. It will furnish inspiration for new suggestions. Never be content to sell continuously the same kind of selection to a customer. The wider the range of selection in a customer's library, the greater the opportunities for selling.

Don't make the mistake of thinking that a customer's range of taste is limited to "Old Black Joe" if he mentions he likes old melodies. He probably doesn't know his own capacity for musical enjoyment. A customer visited our library and flatly announced he liked nothing but popular music, but went home with Hungarian Rhapsodies, a Chopin Polonaise and other delightful selections under his arm. A liking for pronounced rhythm does not mean that the fox trot is the only dish to serve.

Never be afraid to try out a few selections on the customer. Study him as he listens. At the least hint of boredom shut off the record, but play it as long as attention holds. Become an expert emotion reader. The more sensitive you are to the customer's reactions the larger your sale units will be.

So much for the customer in the studio. But what about the customer who should be buying music frequently and does not? This is indeed a serious problem. The librarian's first task is to discover the causes of indifference, and in the writer's numerous investigations the following reasons seem to be predominant:

1. Instrument not functioning properly.
2. Instrument purchased as a piece of furniture only or to "keep up with the Joneses."
3. Customer oversold.
4. Owner has musicians in family and enthusiasm for instrument as a source of entertainment not keen.
5. Owner has many other interests and pleasures and needs to have his attention repeatedly focussed on his instrument.

A PERSONAL call on the customer followed by the service man will go a long way toward taking care of the first cause.

The second case can be slightly remedied by an appeal to social activities. Show the aspiring hostess how to use the instrument as a unique entertainment feature.

Only increased prosperity can help the third.

The fourth case is a real calamity. The instrument being used as an occasional accessory will never function as it was meant to function, namely, bring the best music into the home of the silent piano. One makes only occasional sales to such customers.

The fifth case is a real challenge to our ingenuity and sales ability and results of a most interesting nature have been obtained by the writer's "direct to customer" appeal. Never depend on the monthly bulletin alone to do the work. While interesting and of great value, it needs the backing of the persistent sales effort of the librarian. Be careful not to overwork the telephone. Use Uncle Sam. We never tire of the postman and the little two cent stamp can be a very useful servant. All brochures and letters should be worked out with the customers to whom they are sent definitely in mind. Decide to sell a definite record to a definite customer or group of customers, or select records whose titles will start a train of thought in the mind of the customer. It is the reaction to the suggestion which counts. Keep away from the commercial. Always be dignified and remember to maintain variety. The element of surprise helps to awaken interest. In other words, use your brains.

When the customer calls at the studio let him find a librarian courteous, well informed and, above all, filled with enthusiasm for the beautiful music at his disposal and his delight in an opportunity to share it with the customer.

Never be anxious to sell. Listen to the selection as it is played, enjoy it yourself and the customer will catch the spirit too. Avoid conversation during the playing of a selection. Provide a comfortable chair for the customer and remember that "atmosphere" is no small factor in the selling game.

Just a word in closing about the department itself. Eliminate the old roll department atmosphere. Provide a room with a grand piano, soft lights, comfortable chairs and a rug or two, one or two well chosen pictures and any accessories which suggest refinement and culture. Remember in selling music one deals with the arts. There is no customer so dull as not to respond to the subtle suggestion of the aesthetic. Your salesroom can be a compliment or an insult to your customer.

1922

The triumph of the U. S. Exchange Plan, is a tribute to the rare combination of U. S. Player Roll superiority with the most successful merchandising plan ever conceived.

"There'll always be a U. S. Exchange Plan—no matter the price of rolls."

UNITED STATES MUSIC COMPANY

2934-2938 W. Lake St.	122 Fifth Avenue
Chicago	New York

Sell More Rolls—You'll Sell More Players

company, rubber spools were of prime importance. Just what advantage rubber gave over the metal or Bakelite spool ends used by most manufacturers is apparent only if one assumes that the customer was expected to drop the spool as often as he played it! This concern had its main headquarters and factory in Chicago, but also had a branch in New York City; QRS acquired it in 1926.

A number of rolls with the *Universal* label turn up today in every collection. The concern that made these was a subsidiary of the Aeolian Corporation, and around 1920 its name was changed from Universal to Mel-O-Dee, a firm discussed earlier in this chapter.

The Vocalstyle Music Company of Cincinnati, Ohio, laid claim to being the pioneer manufacturer of rolls upon which appeared the words for songs, having produced such a roll as early as 1908. According to one trade paper ". . . to the inventors and manufacturers of Vocalstyle alone is due the distinction and credit of adding to the literature of the player-piano the immense wealth of vocal music without which the instrument would lose much of its charm, educational influence and popularity in the home."

A further paragraph goes on to state that "by means of Vocalstyle expression marks the ambitious seeker of voice perfection may avail himself of the guidance of the world's greatest singers. Schumann-Heink, David Hispham, Evan Williams, Alma Gluck, and many other vocal celebrities have indicated their method of song interpretation exclusively for Vocalstyle song rolls."

That this company was adept at trying to corner every phase of the player roll market can be appreciated by noting that in addition to the usual line of music, they put out a number of special series of rolls. In addition to the already-noted Home Minstrel Series, there was a Children's Game Series, a Nursery Rhymes and Slumber Songs for Children series, a group of Vodvil-style Rolls, as well as the Riley Recitation Rolls (evidently based around James Whitcomb Riley's poetry), and numerous others. Vocalstyle eventually was acquired by QRS.

The Coin-Slot

VOL. 1   DECEMBER NUMBER, 1925   NO. 7

POPULARITY CONTEST ENDS WITH
EARL G. ALDEN AS WINNER OF PRIZE

It's over! The big music popularity contest, which created tremendous interest in all parts of the country, terminated November 15th and from the mass of ballots the judges have picked as winner the name of Earl G. Alden, Waukegan, Illinois, who has received a certificate good for ten dollars in merchandise from the Clark Orchestra Roll Company.

Each contest held has created more and greater interest and this time the judges had a hard time to tally the votes and select the winning entrant. If you don't believe the trade knows good music sit in on the counting of the next contest. And doesn't that suggest too, that the public, whose nickels you attempt to win with your automatic pianos, is just as critical of quality and newness in the music rolls?

To those who don't know Earl Alden let us tell you he's a hustling, energetic music man. He has long discovered that automatic pianos and rolls offer a lucrative business to the active music dealer. His piano and roll sales tell a convincing story of his faith in the automatic game. And listen, folks, much of Earl's success lies in his use of the latest rolls, as he'll frankly admit if you question him.

And now if you want to see a group of ten of the country's biggest sellers, look over the program listed here as the "Big Ten Conference Winner". Whatever the formation, however muddy your field or unpromising the weather, this "Big Ten" will put a "touchdown in income on YOUR automatic player.

CLARK ORCHESTRA ROLLS

(For 65-note Rewind Electric Pianos)

628
THE "BIG TEN" CONFERENCE WINNER

1 Collegiate, One-step
2 Oh, How I Miss You To-night, Waltz
3 Yes Sir, That's My Baby, Fox trot
4 Ukulele Lady, Fox trot
5 Midnight Waltz
6 By the Light Of the Stars, Fox trot
7 Moonlight and Roses Bring Mem'ries Of You, Fox trot
8 Brown Eyes—Why Are You Blue? One-step
9 Sometime, Waltz
10 I'm Knee Deep In Daisies, Fox trot

THE PRIZE-WINNING ROLL—A SURE-FIRE MONEY MAKER

WORTH IT

"Why was it you tipped that boy so handsomely when he gave you your coat?"

"Look at the coat he gave me."

HE WAS

"You looked foolish the night you proposed to me," reminded Mrs. Spatt.

"I could never deceive you, could I, darling?" he husband agreed.

Father—My son, I'm afraid I'll never see you in heaven.

Son—Whatcha been doin, now, Pop?

CLARK ROLLS MUST PASS TWO INSPECTIONS

Ernest G. Clark, President, De Kalb Manufacturing Firm, Insists That Rolls Be Perfect Regardless of Production Cost, Says "Coin-Slot"—How Inspections Are Made

DE KALB, ILL., June 7.—Music rolls manufactured for electric pianos by the Clark Orchestra Roll Co. here are required to pass two inspections to insure perfection before they are packed for shipment. This is to prevent rolls being sold in which there may be an occasional extra note or omissions as the result of slight inequalities in the operation of the perforating machine, according to the latest issue of the "Coin-Slot," official publication of the Clark company, which says that the invariable rule of Ernest G. Clark, president, is that the rolls must be perfect regardless of production cost.

"As the cutting of music is taken from the machine the top sheet is rolled up separately and brought to a special inspection table," the "Coin-Slot" says. "The rest of the cutting is stored in a handy rack.

"First of all the inspector pulls out of an adjacent bin a 'first piece,' really an original sheet, the exact counterpart of the cutting just completed. This sheet, however, has been carefully scanned and tested on a player-piano by one of the music roll editors and it is mechanically and musically perfect. With this original laid out on the table and the top sheet from the cutting placed over it, the inspector can easily and quickly compare the two, detecting 'extra' notes and marking in omissions called for by the master.

"These latter are then punched in by hand in the whole cutting after the top sheet has been replaced with its mates. The original is now filed and the cutting carried to the spooling table for another careful inspection. Mr. Clark insists on perfection and he has found that in the spooling operation there is a wonderful opportunity to catch flaws which might otherwise escape detection.

"With the cutting extended on the spooling table, the girl operator places in the spooling machine one of the heavy cardboard cores on which Clark orchestra rolls are wound. The core is held in place by metal flanges which are rotated by gears as the handle is turned. With one end of the music sheet securely fastened to the core, the girl spooler slowly winds the paper onto the drum, closely inspecting the sheet as it passes before her eyes. As the winding process proceeds the paper passes underneath a tracked bar which applies a suction to the paper, removing dirt and lint which might otherwise cause trouble by clogging the tracker bar of the automatic piano.

"When the roll is spooled the flanges are taken out, the cloth fastener and label applied to the front end of the sheet and the finished roll slipped into its box, previously labeled."

"DANCE OF GNOMES" TOPS LIST

Most Popular Ampico Rolls in Portland, Ore., Also Include "Say It Again" and Others

PORTLAND, ORE., June 8.—The most popular Ampico rolls of the May list, according to Rodney Johnson, manager of the roll department of the G. F. Johnson Piano Co., are: "Dance of Gnomes" (Liszt), played by Brailowsky; minuet, "Suite Bergamosque" (Debussy), played by Robert Schmitz, and the Grieg "Norwegian Folk Song," played by John Tasker Howard.

"Mother, My Dear" (Treharne), played by Mortimer Browning, proved the most popular number for a Mother's Day gift. Popular numbers holding first place were "Say It Again," "Everything's Gonna Be All Right," "I Never Knew How Wonderful You Were," "Sympathy" and "Drifting and Dreaming," both played by Vincent Lopez.

THE COIN SLOT

Vol. 1   December, 1923   No. 7

Devoted to increasing profits from electric pianos. Published monthly by Clark Orchestra Roll Company, DeKalb, Illinois, and distributed exclusively to dealers.

Pianola and Empress orchestrions, as well as all orchestrion combinations are served by this style "O" CLARK ORCHESTRA ROLL.

ALMOST ONE PIANO A DAY IS JUSTER'S RECORD

Twenty automatic pianos in thirty days is the record made by Mr. Juster of Green Bay, Wisconsin, who is successfully selling Western Electric coin pianos throughout the northwest.

The secret of Mr. Juster's success is hard work and a good piano. The record he is making can be equalled by any other energetic dealer who has faith in himself and realizes the size of the automatic field.

"There isn't any other article in the world," declared Mr. Juster to a Coin Slot representative, "that will pay for itself like the automatic player. An auto is an expense. So is any other merchandise you can name. But an automatic piano will actually pay its own way in a short time."

He asked especially that no names be mentioned in reporting the interview but it is a matter of record that some of his piano buyers have earned as high as $250.00 in a month while the payments may run only $50.00. But no matter what the piano earns, he pointed out, the purchaser will always have the monthly payments materially reduced thru the earnings of the instrument.

Asked what one thing was most important in the sale of automatics, Mr.

Juster replied that new music was the main requirement and he so arranges his sale prices as to cover a year's service in tunings and repairs, with a change of music EACH WEEK.

Mr. Juster has touched upon two points eternally emphasized by the Clark Orchestra Roll Company: the fact that automatics are EASY to sell because they pay their way and the importance of late rolls. Music dealers who have never sold automatic pianos have yet to experience the thrill of a sale devoid of the resistance encountered in selling a player piano which is simply an outright expense with no means of returning the investment except in enjoyment.

When music dealers generally come to realize that automatics are a valuable and money-making line to sell, the few dealers who already know that fact will find it harder sailing. Perhaps the initiated few would prefer to "let the ignorant ones sleep on", as one dealer expressed himself.

We wonder where the music publishers find names for all of their compositions. There must be some alliance with the person or persons who name Pullman cars. Perhaps it would be possible to combine their efforts and use the same names on both cars and music.

Black Romeo: "Did you get those flowers I sent you, honey?"

Black Flapper: "Nothin' else but."

Black Romeo: "Did you like those flowers I sent you, honey?"

Black Flapper: "Nothing else but, Romeo."

Black Romeo: "Did you wear the flowers, honey?"

Black Flapper: "Nothin' else but."

Black Romeo: "Is that so, honey, what did you pin 'em on?"

It's a lucky thing for the few music dealers who know the money which can be made with automatics that the rest of the trade isn't wise. There are rumors of a Society For The Supression Of Knowledge Of The Money To Be Made With Automatics. Applications are now being received by the secretary, Earl G. Alden.

Buy a new roll of music every week.

AS A TYPIST, MR. OBERG FOUND A THRILL TO KEY

Punch! Punch! Punch! The song of the shirt has nothing on the music made by Phil Oberg as he typewrites the latest jazz or heart-throb ballads onto the slowly moving master with this ingenious punching machine.

Phil didn't undergo a course in pugilism before taking up his work with the Clark Orchestra Roll Company. Although he is known as a master puncher —his work is musical and not fistic. Long years of experience in this important task have given him the knack of anticipating the right punch to deliver a "knock-out" when the music is finally played on the automatic piano.

Before Mr. Oberg receives the master for punching, it leaves the recording machine as a roll of paper with a lot of short and long pencil lines spattered on, apparently without regard to order or purpose. The uninitiated would say a youngster had been permitted too free a use of the lead pencil but to Mr. Oberg's experienced eye every line means a certain note on the

piano and it is possible to read the melody from the master just as the musician plays from the printed score.

The master is fed through the punch machine by cog wheels which engage holes in the edge of the paper. The progress of the sheet is controlled with mathematical exactitude by Mr. Oberg who operates the drive wheel with one hand while the other hand operates the punches.

Not unlike a typewriter, the punch machine consists of banks of keys. Each key controls a punch and enables the operator quickly and accurately to perforate the proper note.

Odd as it may seem, Mr. Oberg punches only the beginning and end of the long notes and observers are tempted to point out his oversight. But there is a reason for the omission. It is far

quicker and just as effective, to connect the first and last perforations of each note by the cut of a sharp knife. And this is just what is done by girls who complete Mr. Oberg's work on the punch machine. And when the master finally leaves the perforating department it is an actual music roll although hardly adaptable to the ordinary player piano because of its greater width. It is, however, tested and played on special pianos which enables the editor to catch mistakes and to check harmonies.

But how does the master make the finished roll, you ask? How can hundreds of rolls be produced from the one master?

Wait. Next month's Coin Slot will reveal the wonderful process by which the masters are duplicated.

An automatic piano that is not producing for its owner is nothing more than a piece of furniture. Why not pass a law compelling all automatics to go to work?

Said an automatic piano owner the other day, "I burn up all my old music rolls after they've served a month. If I kept them I would be tempted to keep them playing and I know that that would immediately stop the income because the public won't play to hear old tunes." He's not so far wrong either. The only way to keep children from over-eating candy is to keep the candy out of their sight.

IN A CLASS BY OURSELVES

Did you ever realize that the Clark Orchestra Roll Company is the only exclusive manufacturer of automatic music rolls. All other coin-operated music roll producers are also manufacturers of automatic pianos or players. Perhaps that explains the superiority of Clark Orchestra Rolls over music produced by firms with divided interests. With us music rolls are our sole interest, not a means for selling more pianos.

Fiddle Boxes

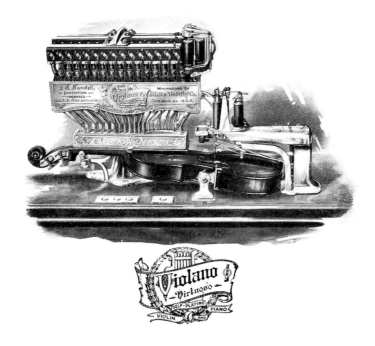

There is something about the violin that has always captured the imagination and fancy of inventors of mechanical music devices, and there have been many attempts to submit that instrument to operation through gadgetry rather than by human effort. Of these attempts, four are worthy of note here, and of these only two reached the market-place in anything like what might be considered quantity production.

The two machines of minor importance are, first, Professor Wauters' device, as described in a 1907 issue of *Scientific American Magazine,* and secondly, the Violinista which appeared in France in the middle 'twenties.

The machine developed by Professor Wauters was actually done by him for the Binghamton Automatic Musical Company in his salaried capacity of what we would now call a development engineer. He was responsible for perfection of roll-perforating machinery in addition to development work on various mechanical aspects of the pianos put out by the concern.

Little is known of his efforts other than what is printed in the article at the right, and it is unlikely that any of these machines are in existence today. As to its operating principles, it seems likely that the overall configuration of the machine may well have been influenced by the then-popular Automatic Banjo

AN AUTOMATIC VIOLIN PLAYER.
BY GEORGE GILBERT.

In view of the present popularity of the piano player, and the marvelous perfection this instrument has attained in reproducing the work of the best musicians, it is very evident that it will be only a question of time before other musical instruments must similarly surrender to mechanical control. The latest development along this line is a machine which will play violins and kindred instruments. As may well be imagined, the violin offers difficulties which are peculiar to itself, and we are not surprised to learn that the violin player illustrated herewith is the culmination of seven years of continuous labor and experiment.

The instrument requires no alteration in the violin itself, and any violin may be placed in the player and removed without injury. The parts are pneumatically controlled in a manner similar to that of the ordinary piano player. A perforated music sheet selects the notes which are to be sounded. This sheet travels over a "tracker board," provided with the usual ducts in which an exhaust is maintained. There are two ducts for each note, and as these are uncovered by perforations in the music sheet, the air rushing into one of the ducts acts through the medium of the usual valves and pneumatics to press a finger down on one of the violin strings at the proper point on the finger board, while the air in the other duct puts into operation the bowing mechanism of this string. The bowing is done by means of four crystal disks, one for each string. In the accompanying drawing the details of the bowing mechanism are shown. Fig. 1 illustrates a section taken through the body of the violin *A*. The strings are indicated at *B*. The disks *C*, with which the bowing is done, are an inch in diameter and ⅛ of an inch in thickness. They are mounted in the ends of levers *D*, which are connected to the pneumatics *E*. When one of the bow ducts is uncovered, it operates a valve, which connects its respective pneumatic *E* with the exhaust chamber of the machine. The pneumatic is thus deflated, swinging the lever *D* to which it is connected, and bringing the disk *C* on this lever into contact with the selected string *B*. The disk *C* is rotated at high speed by means of a belt, which is guided along the lever *D*, as best shown in Fig. 2, and runs over a pulley *F* at the opposite end of the lever. When the lever *D* is swung into operative position by the pneumatic *E*, the pulley *F* is brought into contact with a driving pulley *G*, and is set in motion by a frictional contact therewith. This motion is communicated to the disk *C*, which operates on the violin string. The speed of revolution may run up as high as 2,000 revolutions per minute. The rate at which the disks revolve determines the loudness of the tones. A device is provided for applying rosin to the disks. This consists of a small cup attached to a spring arm and containing rosin, which bears against the revolving disks.

The fingers of the violin player are sixty-five in number, although more can be added if desired, to reach the extreme high range of the *A* and *E* strings. There is a finger for each note. The model shown employs fingers reaching the seventh position. In front of each string is stretched a rubber band, upon which the ends of the fingers strike, thus producing a touch like that of the human finger, and making it possible to imitate the "slide." The tremolo is produced by a set of four hammers, which are actuated by electric vibrators of the type used in call bells. When a hammer vibrates against a string, next to the bridge, the tremolo effect is produced on that string. All the strings may have this effect, or one, as the character of the music demands.

Directly over the violin are four small pitch pipes, which are blown, on pressing a button, by causing air to pass through the pipes, each of which gives the tone of one of the strings, *G*, *D*, *A*, or *E*. The operator then tunes the violin in unison with the pitch pipes.

Violinists know that it is hard to keep a violin in tune. But few appreciate that this is due to the sweat of the player's fingers, which makes the strings stretch. Strings on instruments placed in the violin player do not need much tuning. Silk *E* strings have been found to last two months, and have stayed in tune two weeks without attention.

The tempo is varied by means of a friction pinion which is moved radially on the face of a large driving wheel. This device for varying the tempo enables the simulation of rubato passages when it is operated by a skilled musician.

Instruments of the violin family have four strings, each with a range of two octaves. The violin player enables each string to be treated, at will, as a separate violin, as each bow is controlled by a separate mechanism. In the model shown, the higher portions of the *G* and *D* strings are not utilized, but they can be by supplying extra fingers. Notes on a violin are found sometimes on each of the four strings. For instance, the *G* above the treble staff may be struck on all the strings; so that if a trill were being performed on that note on one string, an arpeggio passage containing the

Front View of the Automatic Violin Player.

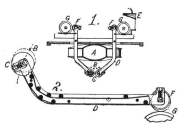

Details of the Bowing Mechanism.

Side View of the Player Casing Opened to Show Ducts.

same note could be produced on the other strings. Of course, no human player could do that. It is possible for the player to render a solo part, with a cello accompaniment on the bass strings, or a solo with two accompanying violin parts, all on one violin. The possibilities for combinations of orchestral effect, therefore, are seen to be many.

Harmonics are produced by the application of just enough pressure to a finger to make it rest lightly in the string sounded, thus imitating the action of the human finger. Trills are produced with striking clearness by providing a series of small perforations in the music roll. The same principle applied to the bow pneumatics produces springing bow and flying staccato.

In making the first music rolls for the player, the inventor, Prof. Wauters, of Binghamton, N. Y., had many technical details to solve. Instruments having fixed strings or tones are played on the tempered scale. But violins play on the untempered chromatic scale, and therefore it was necessary for Prof. Wauters to lay the groundwork for producing music rolls for instruments of that character.

A view of the "Violonista" with cabinet open to show interior mechanism

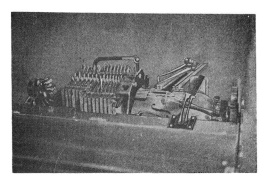

Top of the instrument, showing the position of the violin and the bow

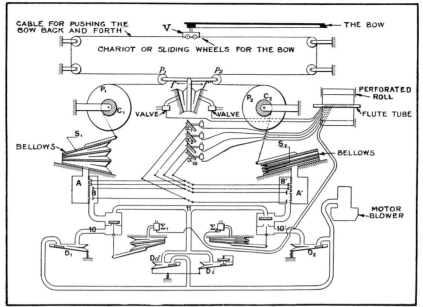

How the "Violonista" is operated. The small chariot, V, to which the bow is attached, moves back and forth over the violin strings, being actuated by the cables passing over pulleys P_1 and P_2. These are attached to the bellows, S_1 and S_2, through wheels C_1 and C_2. The air necessary for operation is fed to the bellows through the regulators D_1 and D_2. Besides the latter and the electric blower, there are other auxiliary bellows and valves Dd, Di, E_1 and E_2. These regulate the pressure in the air reservoirs A. B., A_1 and B_1. The smaller bellows, a_1, a_2 and a_{10} control the action of the perforated music roll which in turn controls the operation of the artificial fingers and the bow

A Violin Played by Mechanical Hands

One of the intriguing problems that has held the attention of mechanical engineers for at least the last three centuries is the production of a device that will play a violin without the aid of human hands. The photographs and diagram above illustrate the latest and most successful attempt but because of the intricacy of the proposition, it is interesting to review the work that has been done heretofore. In 1627 in his "Traité de l'hormonie Universelle," Father Marsenne mentions a device of German origin which was called the "Harpsichord" and which was purported to produce mechanically the sounds of a violin. The apparatus, however, was very crude and the best record that we have of an instrument of this kind that was really successful is that of the "Virtuosa" which was perfected in America in 1908. In this device, the fingering of the strings was accomplished by means of keys that were actuated by electro magnets. The strings were set in vibration by one or more whirling disks that were brought in contact with them as required for the rendering of a musical piece. This instrument was quite a success musically but from a mechanical standpoint, it had several weak points. Not the least of these was its short life. Now we have the "Violonista," perfected by two Frenchmen, Emile d'Aubry and Gabriel Bareau. The musical score for the Violonista is perforated on a roll of paper in much the same manner as that for a player-piano. The perforations control the flow of air and consequently the actions of the mechanical fingers and the bow. The positions of the parts are shown in the photographs. The violin proper is mounted on a series of hinges. The mechanical fingering and the bowing is said to be nearly perfect.

---

which this firm helped to market.

If this machine was not successful, it is probably safe to assume that an important reason was the apparent lack of a string-tightening device to keep the violin in tune, independent of changes in weather and humidity — this in spite of what Mr. Gilbert says about perspiration being the real cause of violin-tuning troubles!

Evidently the editors of the *Scientific American* kept a sharp eye out for developments in the mechanically-played violin field, for the story on the Violinista is from the December 1926 issue of that paper. Little is known in this country of the efforts of d'Aubry and Bareau, the two Frenchmen who perfected this device, other than what is reprinted here.

It is likely that if they ever received any benefits from their work, they must have been largely in the realm of personal satisfaction rather than monetary because by 1926 the interest in this type of apparatus had pretty well waned. As has been shown earlier, the market for this sort of thing, at least in the United States, disappeared after 1929.

Actually, the write-up is somewhat incorrect as it appeared in the original magazine. The references to the "Virtuosa" as having been perfected in 1908 and of rather short life, are quite inconsistent with the facts, as we shall see. Undoubtedly the writer of the article looked through some old issues of his paper and came up with the story from the May 30, 1908 copy on an early Mills model, and neglected to examine the facts pertaining to the outstanding success of later Mills machines in the American market.

A PLAYER-VIOLIN

THE FACT that a mechanical violin player has been devised, together with a description of the principle on which it is working has been announced already in these columns. We are now able to give a more detailed account of the instrument, together with illustrations of it, from an article contributed by A. Troller to *La Nature* (Paris, June 8). Every one, says Mr. Troller, knows the mechanical piano, whose latest form reproduces faithfully even the interpretation of a talented artist. Its performances are surely worthy of being called wonderful. But what word, asks our writer, shall we find for this new instrument, which associates the violin and the piano?

VIOLINA; FULL VIEW.

The violin, if we are to believe those who play it, is the most difficult of musical instruments—that which requires from the player the finest ear, the most skilful manipulation, and the [illegible] How can it be that these qualities may be obtained from a mechanism—no matter how complex and ingenious? Mr. Troller answers.

"The results given by the 'Violina,' which is the instrument's name, are really surprizing; an ample and varied tone, perfect modulation, without leaps or shocks, and all the accustomed effects of the violin.

"We are not prepared to say that to hear the 'Violina' is the same as to listen to a virtuoso; the emotions that it evokes are not, and can not be, so deep; but they are still of a high artistic quality, and it is to be hoped that the mechanical violin may rid us forthwith of all our mediocre performers.

"The mechanical piano, as is well known, depends essentially on the following arrangement—a roll of paper, properly perforated, turns before the openings of a series of tubes, connected with a reservoir of slightly comprest air. The air that is allowed to pass through the perforations in the paper enters the tubes, which conduct it to what are practically so many little comprest-air motors, actuating the hammers of the piano. . . . . . .

"In the 'Violina' the mechanical principle is the same—pneumatic control of all the movable organs, regulated by means

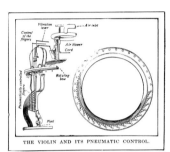

THE VIOLIN AND ITS PNEUMATIC CONTROL.

of a roll of perforated paper. But there can be no question . . . of causing the strings of the violin to vibrate by means of an ordinary bow. The solution found by the inventors of the 'Violina' is of remarkable originality; it constitutes the essential

novelty of the instrument. The bow of the 'Violina' is formed, as our figure shows, of numerous fibers stretched on a movable horizontal circle. As it would be difficult to set simultaneously in vibration the strings of a single violin, it was decided to use a group of three violins, each having only one active string.

"The circular bow turns, and its speed, sometimes retarded, sometimes accelerated, is controlled by one of the little comprest-air motors of which we have spoken. Ordinary violins, whose stems are hinged on pivots, are prest against the turning bow, and the pressure of contact corresponds to the intensity of the sound that is to be obtained. Movable fingers, actuated also by pneumatic means, depress the string at the desired moment, so as to give the tone its proper pitch. . . . . .

"How are the perforated rolls prepared that control the movements of the three violins? They are executed with minute care by workmen who are at the same time musicians of the first rank. Here must be noted a sensible inferiority of the 'Violina' to the latest model of automatic piano. The latter may reproduce the performance of a master, the perforation being done automatically by the playing of the artist. It is not the same with the 'Violina.' It would hardly be possible for a violinist in manipulating his bow to actuate a perforating mechanism and so prepare rolls adapted to the instrument.

"However this may be, the automatic piano and violin combined offer us a most agreeable duet and an infinitely varied repertory. The instrument reflects the greatest credit on the mechanical skill of its inventors, five Austrians whose names deserve to be recorded here—Messrs. Bajde, Karl and Ernst Henning, Froensdorf, and Hupfeld."—*Translation made for* THE LITERARY DIGEST.

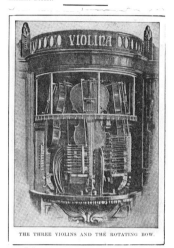

THE THREE VIOLINS AND THE ROTATING BOW.

The first of the violin players to be produced in any quantity was the Hupfeld Phonoliszt-Violina, as described in the accompanying article from *The Literary Digest* in 1912. Of course the term "quantity" is apt to be misleading, for while this machine was a true production item, it is believed that by 1961 there were only about six machines remaining in the United States.

The Phonoliszt-Violina is an entirely pneumatically operated device, and the rather cumbersome appartus used to make it operate resulted in three violins having to be used, rather than just one. Each violin only has one active string, with the result that in spite of its size and bulk, the machine is not as loud as one might expect.

Instead of the usual arrangement of a bow being brought into contact with a violin string, reference to the drawing below shows that in this machine it was done the other way. The inverted violins are hinged at their scrolls, and the rotary bow encircles them. At the proper instant, the appropriate violin is moved outward to contact the bow and thus produce the sound. The bow is constructed of some 3,000 horsehairs each about a foot in length, and each forming a chord between two pins on the bow frame. This large number of hairs thus forms in effect a new inner circle, to which each string is therefore tangent.

These machines were imported to America by E. Bocker of New York City from the German Hupfeld organization which built them as well as many other types of automatic instruments. Note in their ad (reproduced on this page) the reference to their new Phonoliszt-Violina with *six* violins!

All of the work of those responsible for the preceding three machines is as naught however compared with the magnificent efforts of an obscure Swedish immigrant to America by the name of Henry Konrad Sandell. He came to this country in the late eighteen-eighties at the age of 10, and without any subsequent higher formal education of any sort, proceeded thereafter to make a mark in the field of automatic instruments probably not matched by any other person.

According to *Billboard* magazine, by the time he was 18 Sandell was chief electrician for the Adams Westlake Company, and by the age of 21 had made his first applications for patents on a coin-operated mechanically-played violin. By the time he was 70, he had secured over 300 patents of various sorts on violin-playing machines and many other gadgets as well. It appears that he was not one to capitalize on his efforts; he always worked as a salaried employee and it is unlikely that he gained any great amount of money from his developments.

He was employed for 20 years following 1904 by the Mills Novelty Company, which provided the manufacturing and the distribution facility for his inventive genius. Mills was engaged in the manufacture and sale of all sorts of coin-operated penny-arcade and gambling machines, and at a time when the amusement park craze was at its height in America, the devices that Sandell could come up with were ideally suited to expand their line.

Notwithstanding what *Billboard* says, the first reference this writer has been able to find about Sandell's early violin machine was in a March 1906 issue of *Street Railway Journal,* in a section devoted to advising street-car company managements of the newest attractions which they should consider for installation in their amusement parks. In the mid-twentieth century when trolley cars have all but disappeared from the American scene (except for a few hold-outs like Boston) it is not generally remembered that the traction companies were responsible for establishing most of the amusement parks which graced the outskirts of

---

MAY 30, 1908.   **Scientific American**

A NEW AUTOMATIC VIOLIN PLAYER.
BY THE ENGLISH CORRESPONDENT OF THE SCIENTIFIC AMERICAN.

One of the most novel and ingenious automatic musical instruments devised within recent years is now on exhibition in England. This is the Mills automatic violin player, which, as may be seen from the accompanying illustration, is a delicately constructed and remarkably designed automatic violin, in which the fingers of the player are supplanted by mechanical agency. The instrument is the result of several years' experiment and scientific research, and although played by electro-mechanical agency, the rendering of the music is so delicate that it is difficult to distinguish it from that of a master hand. The sweetness is remarkable, as are also the harmony and volume of tone.

The instrument, as may be seen from the accompanying illustration, comprises the ordinary type of violin, complete in every detail, with the usual strings and facilities for tuning. The instrument is held firmly at the neck, to secure the same position as if held under the chin, while the opposite end is held by a solid support. Above the strings is mounted an intricate and elaborate mechanism, with lever rods, which act as fingers, and by depression upon the strings in the correct positions give the required notes. The bow, or rather series of bows, since there are many in order to secure full chord effects, is represented by a number of revolving disks, which in their rotating passage strike the strings as they are depressed upon them according to requirements, and in conjunction with the mechanical fingers sound the required notes. There is a complete absence of harshness, such as might naturally be expected in a mechanically-operated instrument, while the diminuendo and crescendo effects are faithfully reproduced. The mechanism is operated by a small but powerful electric motor driven by batteries; the control is effected by means of an ingenious arrangement of electro-magnets. The whole of the mechanism is in motion at one and the same time, each composite part performing its allotted function in accordance with the musical score, at the correct moment.

Every person familiar with the instrument is fully acquainted with the difficulties attending its mastery, and the many musical impressions peculiar to violin playing. Yet all such, as staccato, legato, pizzicato, arpeggio, shake, trill, thirds, fourths, octaves, tenths, portamento, are marvelously produced. It renders with complete accuracy and striking execution the most difficult classical passages as readily as the more simple popular airs.

Moreover, it exceeds the capabilities of the human player. Duets and even quartets are given with as

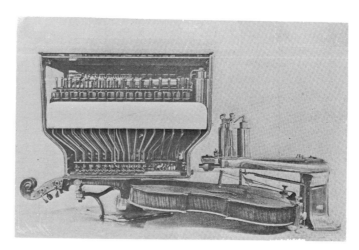

AN AUTOMATIC MACHINE FOR PLAYING THE VIOLIN

much facility and delicacy as solos, it merely being a matter of coupling up the mechanical actions. In this manner a single instrument can render the full effects of a stringed orchestra, while moreover, in order to complete its possibilities, it will play its own accompaniments to solos, and very often the four strings are brought into requisition at the same time.

The automatic player has been investigated by many of the leading violinists, who have listened to its renditions of the most intricate and difficult music, and have pronounced them to be musically perfect, while time, melody, harmony, and expression are produced with such distinctive skill as to testify to the precision of the mechanical arrangements. The invention has aroused the greatest interest in England and Europe, since it is to the violin what the pianola is to the piano, and demonstrates to a striking extent the musical qualities of the instrument when developed to its fullest extremity.

Many Coin Machine Inventions Pioneered by Henry K. Sandell

CHICAGO, Oct. 25.—The life of Henry K. Sandell, currently 70 and adding new achievements yearly as he goes about his duties as A. B. T.'s designing engineer, virtually parallels the history and amazing growth of the coin machine business.

Born in Sweden, Sandell moved to Chicago when 10 years old. Altho during these many years he has patented upward of 300 devices and innovations, many of which required the use of higher mathematics, Sandell never has had any formal education.

When 18 years old, Sandell, then chief electrician for the Adams Westlake Company, applied for his first patent which concerned a mechanical movement to overcome dead centers in machinery. Three years later he was to patent his coin-operated violin, which was to bring him everlasting fame. Operated much the way player pianos produce their automatic music, a model of this coin violin is now on permanent display at famed Smithsonian Institute, in the nation's capital, and with it is the up to date life story of Sandell.

The idea behind the automatic violin was based on Sandell's invention of automatic equipment for producing perforated paper holes. It is listed as one of the 10 best inventions to come out of the 1910-'20 era, a period noted for world-changing inventions. When the late Teddy Roosevelt visited the Seattle World Exposition in the early 1900's he ranked Sandell's violin with such worthy contributions to the world as the reaper, color photography and the steam turbine.

Once With Mills

Sandell has been with A. B. T. for the past five years. This, however, was not the only time he was ever connected with a firm making coin machines. In 1904 and for the following 20 years he supervised manufacture for Mills Novelty Company, now known as Mills Industries, Inc., and somehow found time to invent and patent new devices concerning electricity, radio and even television.

Strangely enough, despite the many citations and awards Sandell has received during his full life, the one incident that impressed him most was when Cornell University invited both himself and the late Herbert S. Mills, founder of Mills Novelty, to exhibit his automatic cello at a concert on the Cornell campus, February 12, 1912. Sandell says that the reason that the event stands out so clearly is that Mills was thrilled to know that Sandell, noted for his quiet, unassuming ways, was finally getting the acclaim that Mills believed should have been established long before.

In the intervening years between joining A. B. T. and leaving Mills, Sandell was unaffiliated with the business world, living in semi retirement and going ahead with many new experiments. Sandell says that it also was the only time that he could find time to look for a wife. For at the tender age of 53 he got married and is now the proud father of Yvonne, 12, and Konrad, 10.

Still Producing

Well known for his work on the A. B. T. auto clerk, introduced to the coin machine world at the end of last year, Sandell's most recent patent was taken out in favor of a high efficiency, reversible, shaded pole motor.

But whether Sandell is describing his patents on FM transmitters and receivers, electric lights, motors or his developments in metalurgy he frowns upon the use of the word genius or any other praise in connection with his work. He says simply that any accomplishments that have come his way are the result of a devotion to work and his strong religious beliefs.

Henry K. Sandell

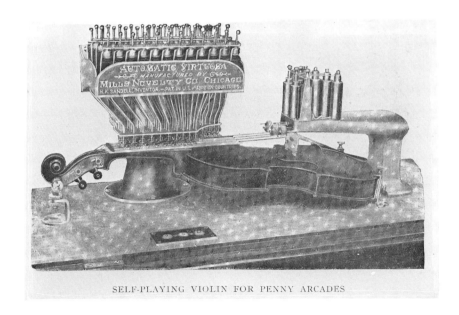

SELF-PLAYING VIOLIN FOR PENNY ARCADES

the cities of our country. They were built at the end of the car lines primarily as revenue-generating devices, and were for the most part wonderfully successful until the public began acquiring automobiles and didn't have to depend on the old Osopeachy Traction Company or the East Overshoe City Railway for transportation. At any rate, the editors of the *Journal* seemed to think that Mills' new coin-operated Violin-player, called the "Automatic Virtuosa," was a right fine idea.

And they must have been right, for between then and 1929, when production was finally discontinued, literally thousands of these machines were built. The actual total number is not clear, but it appears to have been around four or five thousand. While it seems incredible to most people that a mechanically operated violin could ever make anything approaching acceptable sounding music, the fact is that if these machines are properly adjusted they can be made to produce magnificent results. Unfortunately, few of the scores of machines still in existence can make this claim, and this writer would exhort those who think poorly of Mills machines not to come to any final conclusions about their capabilities until they have made a real effort to hear one that has been properly set up for operation and properly tuned and regulated.

The Mills Company, headed by Herbert S. Mills, took advantage of every opportunity to claim distinction for its violin player, and its grand chance came when it was invited to exhibit the device at the Alaska-Yukon-Pacific Exposition in Seattle in 1909 by the Patent Office of the United States Government. According to the official report submitted by President Taft to the Congress, pertaining to the exhibit hall of the U. S. Government,

". . . the Patent Office collected and presented an exhibit of great attractiveness, consisting of a few of the more important of the later inventions which are susceptible to exhibition under the conditions that were met in the Government building.

". . . As a fitting representative of the large and growing class of automatic musical instruments, the combined violin and piano produced by the Mills Novelty Company of Chicago was chosen, and without question it proved to be our best drawing card. Its beauty of tone and delicacy of shading were a revelation to those expecting mechanical efforts from mechanical instruments; and the ingenuity of its construction was invariably a matter of comment by the comparatively few whom it was possible to allow to examine its inner workings."

Such did President Taft report. And the honor of being selected for this exhibit was one that the Mills Company played right to the hilt, for in every machine produced by it after this was proudly proclaimed on a large and prominent sign

"DESIGNATED BY THE U.S. GOVERNMENT AS ONE OF THE EIGHT GREATEST INVENTIONS OF THE DECADE."

The early Mills violin-players operated only the violin, as in the case of the machine at the right, but all those produced after 1912 combined the violin with a 44-note piano action and the instrument was referred to as the "Violano-Virtuoso." It seems probable that the violin-piano combination must also have been available as early as 1909, because Taft's report on the exposition was in that year.

Most machines existing today have a patent date of June 1912 cast into the piano plate in a prominent place, and three of the drawings submitted by Sandell in support of these claims are reproduced here. The complete patent write-ups are most interesting to read, and while they are too lengthy to print in this book, they can be secured from the United States Patent Office for a small fee by anyone who really wants to dig into the subject.

The construction of the piano part of the Violano-Virtuoso is most interesting, in that Sandell designed it with the longest strings in the center and the shortest at the outside. This is a perfectly feasible arrangement when the piano is not to be played from a keyboard, and it results in an even balance of forces on each side of the plate. This, in turn, presumably aids in

Mills Automatic Virtuosa

Coin Controlled

A VIOLIN with automatic fingers to manipulate the strings, revolving discs to represent the bow, controlled by an ingenious arrangement of electro-magnets, and a small motor, all in motion and performing each their function at the proper moment and producing music that would be a credit to an accomplished musician—a violin turned into a thing of life—an automaton working with the precision of human hands controlled by brain, muscle and nerve.

The average coin-controlled musical machine is usually sadly out of tune, and its loud, harsh - sounding notes grate upon the ear of those musically inclined the least, not to mention the effect upon the trained ear of the accomplished musician. These serious objections have been carefully studied from a scientific standpoint, with the result that all of them have been eliminated. The resulting music is of a nature to be most pleasing to the ear, not too loud to be annoying in a public place, but soft and sweet, with volume enough to be heard from a reasonable distance. (For further particulars, address "Violin Dept").

Size, 5 feet 11 inches high; 3 feet wide ; 21 inches deep.
Shipping weight, 420 lbs.
Boxed for foreign shipment: Dimensions, 76x41x26 inches. Weight, 520 pounds.

This Machine Will Make Money For You

ARCADES, parks and pleasure resorts will find the Mills Virtuosa the most novel and attractive automatic machine introduced since the beginning of coin-controlled machines, and for this reason it will be well patronized and will pay for itself in a very short time.

Every hotel, cafe and refreshment parlor should have the Mills Virtuosa, because it will royally entertain customers with the latest music at no expense to the house, and besides will yield a large and steady income. It takes the place of an orchestra and makes money for you instead of causing you to spend it for salaries.

Drug and cigar stores, dry goods houses, and, in fact, almost any kind of store can draw additional trade by having the Mills Virtuosa, not to say anything about the money it will take in.

Operators will find the Mills Virtuosa the most interesting machine they have ever handled, because it is the easiest placed in good locations and because of the large amount of money it will take in. The novelty never wears out, because the music can be changed as often as desired.

Vaudeville Theatres will find the Mills Automatic Virtuosa a star act as a musical novelty.

The Mills Automatic Virtuosa is a big money maker wherever people are to be found.

For the home the Mills Automatic Virtuosa will furnish the most refined music, rendering not only the popular airs, but the most difficult and most exquisite music at any time simply by pressing a button. For the entertainment of the family and friends it is simply unequalled.

The superior finish and attractive design throughout make the Mills Automatic Virtuosa an ornament to the most luxuriously appointed home or the most elaborately furnished place of business.

VIOLANO-VIRTUOSO

Self Playing Violin With Piano Accompaniment

AGES of description could not do justice to this truly magnificent instrument which the U. S. Government has signally honored and designated as one of the *greatest scientific inventions* of the age.

The Violano-Virtuoso *combines in itself two of the world's most beautiful instruments—the violin and piano.* Either may at will be played alone. Together their tones blend in sweetest harmony giving practically all the effects of a splendid stringed orchestra.

Musicians rave over its music, which is indeed rendered with the wonderful inflection, technique and dramatic force of the greatest Maestros.

The World's Greatest Musical Attraction

No composition is too difficult for the Violano-Virtuoso. Classical, operatic, and popular music are all equally well played. There is no disagreeable suggestion of the mechanical. Every note is clear, full and true. The faults common to other automatic players are all successfully eliminated. It is without doubt the *musical masterpiece of the day.*

The Violano-Virtuoso may best be defined as a violin with piano accompaniment. The violin is played by a finger-like arrangement of electro magnets operated by a small motor. These violins are built specially for us by our own expert violin makers from the most carefully selected woods. With proper usage they should increase in value with each succeeding year.

The case of the instrument is artistically designed in the graceful classical style now so highly favored and comes in your choice of several rare woods. The ordinary electric lighting current supplies the necessary motive power and by simply touching a button the instrument may be started and stopped at will.

The music rolls used in the Violano-Virtuoso rewind automatically and are made of very tough specially prepared paper, the edges being mechanically trimmed as they are perforated insuring accuracy and perfect harmony.

For hotel and restaurant men, theatrical managers, proprietors of arcades, skating rinks, etc., the Violano-Virtuoso fills a long existing need. The novelty and almost human playing of the instrument attracts widespread attention. Furthermore it most satisfactorily takes the place of an expensive orchestra at a great saving in cost. The exquisite quality of its music finds favor with the most fastidious patrons. The Violano-Virtuoso proves therefore a most profitable investment. Full particulars and a beautiful illustrated art catalogue will be sent free to anyone on request.

Endorsed by the World's Greatest Musicians

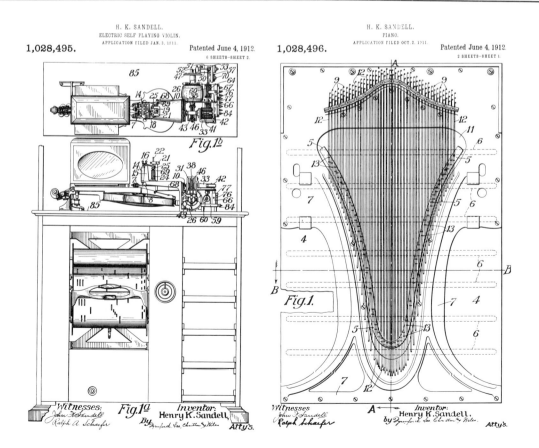

202

H. K. SANDELL.
ELECTRIC SELF PLAYING VIOLIN.
APPLICATION FILED JAN. 3, 1911.

1,028,495.

Patented June 4, 1912.
6 SHEETS—SHEET 1.

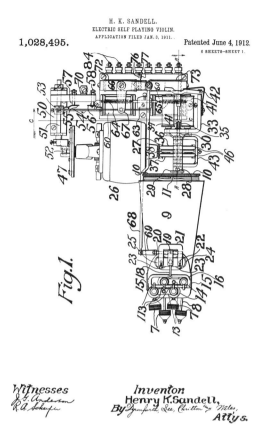

Fig.1.

Witnesses
J. J. Anderson
R. A. Schafer

Inventor
Henry K. Sandell,
By Denforth, Lee, Chritton and Wiles,
Attys.

Our "Baby Grand" Model Violano-Virtuoso here pictured is a trifle smaller than the "Concert Grand" shown on another page.

Manufactured by Mills Novelty Co.
Chicago, Ill.

VIOLANO VIRTUOSO

BOSTON CAFE
Aberdeen, S. Dak.

keeping itself in tune longer than with unbalanced construction as is found in a conventional piano. The only time the owner of a Violano-Virtuoso can expect trouble with this set-up is when he asks his piano tuner to tune it! Needless to say, the average technician who works on conventional pianos can quickly be driven stark, raving mad in trying to get one of these rigs to proper pitch unless he has the special chart provided by the manufacturer to assist in such circumstances.

Throughout the years, various different models of the Violano appeared, the best-known of which is the two-violin DeLuxe model, commonly referred to as the "Double Mills." This machine uses the same music rolls as the single models, so no new notes are played over what the one-violin jobs will do. However, since it is virtually impossible to keep two violin strings in exact pitch with each other, the result is not only one of increased volume, but a sort of apparent harmony as well.

MILLS MELODY VIOLINS

The Newest and Most Wonderful of Theatre Instruments

The mastery of the violin, first accomplished in the Mills Violano-Virtuoso, reaches its ideal culmination in Mills Melody Violins. By means of this wonder instrument it is now possible to play any number of violins—from one to a hundred—from a keyboard, in the way in which a piano or organ are ordinarily played.

The musician sits at the console, touches the keys, and plays the violins. He can draw out of the instruments any amount, any variety of real violin music. He can play all four strings at once, hold notes for any length of time, and perform a score of other feats that even the most skillful musician cannot do.

By means of Mills Melody Violins, one musician can take over the work of the first and second violin sections of a big orchestra.

For the moving picture house or legitimate theatre, this is the perfect instrument to be used in conjunction with organ or piano. It affords an endless variety of orchestral music and is a great entertaining feature for audiences.

Made in special models and finishes.

Manufactured by Mills Novelty Co. Chicago, Ill.　　VIOLANO VIRTUOSO　　BROADWAY CONFECTIONERY Fargo, N. D.

Complete Orchestra For Dancing

These drums, combined with either DeLuxe or Grand Model Violano, make a complete dance orchestra.

With DeLuxe Violano—makes six piece complete orchestra; two first Violins, two second Violins, Piano and Drums, including Base Drum, Snare Drum, Chinese Tom-Tom, Wood Clapper and Cymbals.

With Grand Model Violano—makes four piece complete orchestra; first violin, second violin, Piano and Drums as above described.

Drums and Violano played from single music roll Brings you latest dance music—new dance rolls obtainable every month.

Complete orchestra twenty-four hours a day. Ideal for any place where there is dancing.

Attracts young people. Increases business. Big extra cash profits—owners reporting intake of $75.00 to $200.00 per month.

Drums can be attached to any Violano carrying serial No. above 1200.

Mail the post card for additional information.

In order to make the music of piano and violin a little more schmaltzy, a "Violano Orchestra" was developed — basically a box containing a bass drum, snare drum, Chinese tom-tom, wood clapper and cymbals — which could be wired into the Violano to give a rhythm accompaniment for dancing.

For theatre work, the Mills Melody Violin was introduced. This was essentially a group of violin units, operated not from a paper roll but from a keyboard similar to that of a piano. According to the literature "By means of this wonder instrument it is now possible to play any number of violins — from one to a hundred — from a keyboard, in the way in which a piano or organ are ordinarily played."

And apparently in order to compete with relatively low-priced electric pianos, Mills introduced the Magnetic Expression Piano to sell for $800. This machine

The Violano-Virtuoso with Two Violins

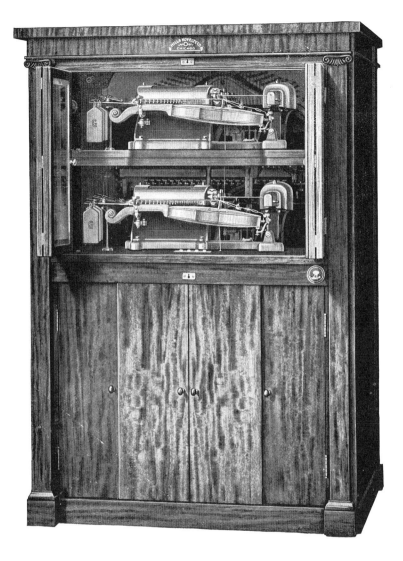

De Luxe Model Violano-Virtuoso

An Automatic Electric Piano of 44 Notes and Two Violins.
Price—$3,000.
Terms:—$450 cash with order, balance of $2,550 in 25 equal installments of $102 each (with interest) due each month after receipt of instrument.

Specifications: Shipping weight—1350 lbs.
Dimensions—5 ft. 9 in. high; 4 ft. 1 in. wide; 2 ft. 10¾ in. deep.
Finishes: Red Mahogany, Brown Mahogany, Oak (dull or polished).

Concert Grand Model Violano-Virtuoso

One Violin: 44 Note Piano.
Price—$2,500.
Terms: $375.00 cash with order, balance of $2,125 in 25 equal installments of $85 each (with interest) due each month after receipt of instrument.
Specifications: Shipping weight— 1250 lbs. Dimensions—5 ft. 5 in. high; 4 ft. 1 in. wide; 2 ft. 9 in. deep.
Finishes: Red Mahogany, Brown Mahogany, Oak (dull or polished).

See last page for Terms to Theaters.

Wall Boxes   VIOLANO

The Violano Wall Box

Made of durable, lasting sheet metal. Internal mechanism is so simple in construction that it eliminates all possibilities of wall boxes needing attention after they are once installed. Furnished in black enamel, white mahogany, oak and walnut finish. Any electrician can install them.

Increased Profits for Violano Owners

Violano owners everywhere have found that wall boxes greatly increase earnings from the Violano. When patrons have to walk more than a few steps to insert the coin to play the Violano it is inconvenient and requires special effort on their part to play the Violano.

With wall boxes, however, they can remain comfortably seated and are not required to interrupt their conversation or eating in order to pay for their Violano music.

Install A Wall Box in Every Booth or at Every Table

We suggest that you install a Mills Wall Box in every convenient location throughout your place of business. Give your patrons an opportunity to easily insert the coin necessary to play the Violano. These wall boxes are such huge profit-makers that they quickly pay for themselves and vastly increase the amount of money taken in by the Violano.

Wall Boxes Cost $10.00 Each

The price of these wall boxes is $10.00, and they are furnished in any finish desired.

An investment of $50.00, $75.00, or $100.00 in wall boxes will so greatly increase the money taken in by the Violano that in most instances the wall boxes pay for themselves during the first month.

Take advantage of this Violano companion profit-maker. Order wall boxes at once. Install just as many of them as you can find convenient locations in your place of business. They are huge profit-makers—render your patrons real service and quickly pay for themselves.

Easy to Install Without Marring Fixtures

Any electrician or person familiar with installing of electric wiring can easily and quickly install the Mills Wall Boxes in any location desired.

See Back Page for Easy Payment Plan

MILLS NOVELTY COMPANY, 4100 Fullerton Avenue, Chicago

Easy Payment Plan

Wall Boxes earn "BIG" profits—often doubling and trebling the usual Violano earnings.

To make it easy for you to install Wall Boxes at every table and in every convenient space in your place of business, we now offer you an opportunity to buy them on the following easy payment plan.

On orders for up to ten Wall Boxes, our terms are $10.00 with order and $10.00 per month until paid for.

When more than ten Wall Boxes are ordered, you pay $1.00 per Wall Box with order and $1.00 per Wall Box every month until paid for.

If you order 15 Wall Boxes you pay $15.00 with order and $15.00 per month until paid for.

If you order 20 Wall Boxes, you pay $20.00 with order and $20.00 per month until paid for.

This makes it easy for you to install a liberal number of Wall Boxes. We suggest that you order all the Wall Boxes you can find room for. They are big money-makers—and the more you install—the bigger will be your Violano profits.

**Mills Novelty Company
4100 Fullerton Avenue
Chicago**

MILLS NEW ELECTRIC PIANO

This new piano represents one of the greatest developments in the automatic piano field. There is no other piano that is in any way like it. It is built and operates in a way entirely different from all other instruments.

The Mills Eletric Piano is the only piano on the market today that is directly operated by electricity—it has no pneumatic apparatus whatever. It is a sixty-five note piano of the same magnetic action as the piano part of the Violano-Virtuoso, described in another part of this catalog.

It has a wonderfully superior tone, resembling that found in the most expensive home pianos costing thousands of dollars. Its graduation of expression over its entire range is so perfect, that when the music is heard in another room or any place where the instrument itself is not visible, it cannot be distinguished from that of an accomplished artist playing in person.

Because of the remarkable simplicity of construction, and the absence of a thousand complicated parts found in all other automatic pianos, this piano should give twenty years of steady service to its owner. It is the ideal instrument for the merchant who has a better class store, but who does not desire an instrument quite as expensive as the Violano.

Standard and special finishes in oak and mahogany.

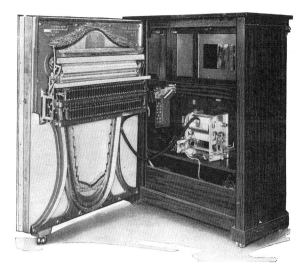

Note Simplicity of Mechanism and Operation

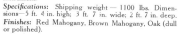

operated on the same general principles as the piano part of the Violano, but had a range of sixty-five notes instead of only forty-four. From this development it was only logical that the next step would be an orchestrion of sorts, and this was achieved through the Mills Piano Orchestra. This machine was essentially a combination of the Magnetic Expression Piano and the trapwork from the Violano Orchestra Box.

Undoubtedly the most important single development in the history of the Mills Violano-Virtuoso from the the standpoint of making it a commercial success was the idea of holding the violin strings taut by means of adjustable weights, rather than by use of the usual type of tuning pin that is common on the violin. The use of the weight on the string causes the tension to be uniform regardless of variation in humidity, and thus the string stays in tune for an indefinite period. This feature was of great value in a machine operated in commercial establishments, for it meant that the proprietor did not have to spend a lot of time fooling with the thing to keep it sounding properly.

Mills Piano Orchestra

Piano and Drums in single cabinet.

A combination of Magnetic Expression Piano and Violano Drums.

Ten dance selections on every music roll.

Recommended for moderate sized Road Houses.

Restaurants, etc., where there is dancing. Sure to be popular with the public.

Price is exceptionally low for this piano orchestra.

Earnings reported $50.00 to $100.00 a month.

Mail the post card for additional information.

See page 35 for larger view

Violano-Virtuoso
Home Model

The Automatic Model is Illustrated on Page 36

While rumor has it that Henry K. Sandell, this great yet obscure mechanical and electrical genius, finally went out of his mind and spent his last days in a mental institution, the fact is that he lived a very full and productive life in quite a normal frame of mind. He died in Chicago, where he had spent his life in America, on 29 January 1948 at the age of 70. Practically everyone who has studied the field of mechanically produced music agrees that Sandell's contribution to the industry was one of true greatness, and that America is richer for his having passed our way.

The basic price of the Mills Violano-Virtuoso was $2,000, in a day when a dollar was worth a dollar. When one considers how money has depreciated since the days when this machine was sold, to say nothing of the complex tax structures existing today that these early proprietors were not concerned with, the prices paid for the machines by the saloon and restaurant keepers were quite fantastic. Yet they were often surprisingly good investments.

One of the owners (a Greek, naturally) of the old Boston Candy Kitchen in Binghamton, New York, told

Where the Mills Violano Is Manufactured

THE Mills Building is located on the N. E. Corner of Jackson Blvd., and Green St., Chicago, five minutes away from Chicago's Loop District. All eight floors and basement of this building—a total floor space of over 200,000 square feet—are used in the manufacture of Mills products.

The Violano-Virtuoso as perfected by Sandell is an extremely complex piece of machinery, and a constant source of amazement to those who are familiar with them, yet oddly enough they are quite trouble-free and often will actually operate for many months and years without giving any service difficulties. Evidently the Mills Company assumed that complexity might be raised as an issue of sales resistance by potential customers, so they were careful in their literature to make it sound as if the machine was really a simple device. In one sales catalog we read:

"How Much Service Does the Violano Require?"

"Because of its extreme simplicity of construction and operation, it is very rare that any trouble is had with the Violano, provided the owner gives it a little care. The Violano-Virtuoso is built to keep in perfect working condition all the time. . . ."

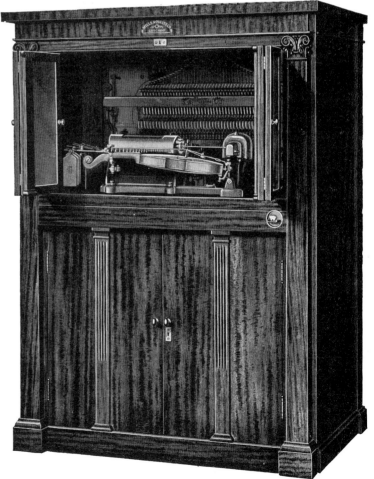

A Front View of our "Concert Grand" Model Violano-Virtuoso—Note that it takes up less space than a piano.

the writer that he and his brothers put in a "Double Mills" at a cost of over $3,000, yet the machine paid for itself within a year, strictly from nickels put in by customers wanting to hear this new marvel of the age. The store — essentially an ice cream parlor — had all the advantages. It was in a prime downtown location near a trolley stop, and in those days before air-conditioning a favorite way to cool off on hot summer days was to hail the open Binghamton Traction Company car, catch all the breezes on the 5c trip to the center of town, sit with your best girl on opposite sides of the marble-topped table, lean forward in the bent-wire chair and partake of a cooling strawberry frappe. One frappe, of course, with two straws, consumed while listening to the Violano produce the heart-rending strains of "Daddy, You've Been a Mother to Me" or perhaps "A Pretty Girl Is Like a Melody" at 5c per tune). As one fellow puts it, "In those days, that was really 'livin' it up.' "

But such performances repeated day after day bought these machines and returned a handsome profit once they were paid for. The same gentleman who told of the Booton Kitchen said that one of the best investments they ever made was to put in wall boxes at the booths. When the machine was new, it was so popular that people would put money in the boxes without regard to what money others had already dropped in. In fact, he told of one special roll of Irish tunes that came out close to St. Patrick's day in a particular year, a roll that had eight short tunes on it in place of the usual five. The local folks of the Auld Sod liked it so well that they kept the machine hot all day long, and at closing time at night the proprietors had to shut the machine off and empty the wall boxes of their money or the machine might *still* be playing!

Of course as the novelty wore off no such financial intake continued, and in later years the machine did well to take in ten cents in a week. It was finally removed from the premises in 1928 and put in a storage warehouse, and eventually appears to have suffered the fate of many of these fine music-makers — that of being destroyed in a fire.

THE production of the Mills Violano starts with the receipt of the raw materials. Materials and supplies are bought from the largest and best factories in the country. All materials are given first inspection and check-up when received. There are 64 different kinds of raw castings alone used on the Violano.

Receiving Raw Materials

THE feeder makes and breaks all electrical contacts for the electromagnets, which in turn strike the hammers that sound the notes. The feeder production starts from bare frame and each new part added and tested. It must be absolutely noiseless in operation and "worn in" by a rigid test of ten days' continuous running.

Assembling the Feeder, "The Brain of the Instrument"

A question often asked by Violano enthusiasts is that of how the music rolls were cut, and this picture provides the answer. The piano score was played from a master piano by a musician, and the violin score was taken from a keyboard similar to that of a piano. The latter machine was provided with a violin-player, so the operator would know what he was cutting into the the master roll. The man seated at the violin keyboard is believed to be Henry K. Sandell.

Most of the Mills Violano rolls were of the popular tunes of the day, but a number of foreign rolls were cut as well and occasionally a special roll of operatic music was produced. For the most part, the piano was scored to act as an accompaniment to the violin, but on certain very rare rolls the piano takes the melody and the violin does the other. And on even rarer scores, the piano plays hardly at all — these were known as "Violin Solo" rolls.

The standard pattern for the usual run-of-the-mill music roll was two fox-trots, a waltz, and two more fox-trots. Occasionally an all-waltz roll would be produced, and connoisseurs of the Violano generally concede that it is with these that the instrument really can be made to perform to perfection.

IN their studio on the sixth floor the musicians play in the music for the music rolls. In the background, man at the left is playing the violin (notice real violin on console above him) and man at the right the piano. The artist's playing is reproduced exactly as played.

Musicians "Playing In" the Music

THE violin fingerhead is here assembled and inspected. Fingers are lined up to gauges with minutely accurate measurements, as not the slightest variation can be permitted. The fingerhead is then played steadily for fifteen hours and inspected again.

Replacing 5 Human Fingers with 64 Mechanical Ones

ES being glued and all joints htly clamped into place. ases are fly finished; doors, hinges, etc., carefully set. r passage through factory re protected by the latest ve devices to prevent acci- narring or scratching.

Cabinets Getting "Dressed Up"

Toning and Finishing Tops and Backs

carver shaves and scrapes the rough shed back down to the proper thick- y hand. All the while he compares the the wood with the proper tone on the at his side. Then he matches the tone top and back to see that they are in harmony.

THE piano back is mounted on the swinging door of the instrument where it can be worked on most conveniently. The action is now tested to make sure it performs faultlessly, and the piano is tuned. Simplicity of construction is the remarkable feature of this piano.

Action Finishing and Tuning

THESE automatic music cutting machines are for quantity production, as each machine is capable of copying twenty masters at one time, taking but a few minutes to complete the job. It is because of this up-to-date machinery that we can produce the hits as quickly as they come out.

Roll Making Machines Busily At Work

Recording Machine Cuts Rolls As Played

THIS is the only machine in the world which makes the roll while the artist plays. The instant he strikes a note that note is cut right into the paper; when he has finished playing his selection, the whole roll is also finished.

Big Supplies of Rolls Always On Hand

EVERY roll and every selection on each roll is numbered and so classified that a customer's order can be shipped immediately. Our Music Catalogue lists the Popular, Classical, and Special Rolls we carry in stock. Each roll is made so perfect and strong that with careful handling it can play for years.

AFTER being completely finished, inspected, and finally O.K.'d, the Violano is sent to the shipping room to be packed and made ready for shipment. All parts are carefully protected and covered so that the instrument cannot be damaged in the slightest way in transit.

"Ready for Its Destination"

The True Nickelodeon Pianos

Scene from a typical theatre, with a Fotoplayer located in the orchestra pit.

Once in a while historical matters have a way of getting mixed up, and so it is with the term "Nickelodeon." Today one frequently hears a coin-operated piano referred to as "that old nickelodeon", but this is a term which was never applied when these machines were in vogue—it is strictly a latter-day usage, possibly as a result of the popular tune "Put Another Nickel In".

The late Ben M. Hall in his fascinating documentary of the American movie palace and its precessors, "The Best Remaining Seats", has this to say about the matter:

"In 1903, Harry, Jack, Albert and Sam Warner opened a ninety-six-seat store show called the Pioneer in Newcastle, Pa. . . . the Mark brothers, Mitchell and Moe, were busy with their Edisonia Hall in Buffalo . . . David Grauman and his bushy-haired young son, Sid, were showing movies to small but enthusiastic crowds in a converted store, named the Unique, in San Francisco . . . and John P. Harris, manager of a *musee* and curio hall in McKeesport, Pa., decided to exhibit "living pictures" on an 8 A.M.-to-midnight policy to enthusiastic locals. Harris minted a brand-new name for his movie show; he merged his admission price with the Greek word for theatre and came up with "Nickel-Odeon."

"By 1905 nearly any city worth five cents had one or more nickelodeons (alas, Harris's inspired name had become generic with the speed of a pratfall), and legions of Bijoux, Gems, and Cameos were arching their twinkling tungsten facades all across the land."

These early pioneers recognized early in the game that they had to do more than just show movies, and that some music to go along with the scenes on the silent silver screen would do much to assist in enjoyment by their patrons. Pianos were pressed into service, with some local chap or lady doing their best to provide some sort of accompaniment to the show by means of his or her artistry. Eventually a whole musical world of its own developed around techniques for doing this type of work, and of course as theatres really began to amount to something, orchestras and pipe organs were brought into the picture.

But our purpose here is to see what developments took place around the piano in these nickelodeons. Naturally enough, player pianos were brought into action, for their basic development was well-along by the time movies began to amount to something. And somewhere along the line geniuses in mechanical things began to adapt sound effect gadgets to assist the operators in their attempts to capture the appropriate mood for whatever happened to be appearing at the moment. Just who gets the credit

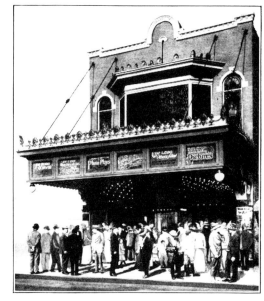

AMERICAN THEATRE, MILWAUKEE, WIS.

The American—Theatre Beautiful
THIRD AND WELLS STREETS
MILWAUKEE, WIS.

Jan. 12, 1916.

J. P. Seeburg Piano Co.
209 S. State St., Chicago.

Gentlemen:-The Style "M" Seeburg Motion Picture Orchestra purchased from you has been in use for fourteen hours daily for the past twenty months and has given excellent satisfaction.

When I purchased this instrument I did so because I considered it the best the market afforded, and I have had no occasion to regret it. It would not take me long to decide if I should have occasion to buy another, as I found it an excellent investment from an economical standpoint in reducing my music expenses very materially, and at the same time fulfilling every requirement.

Yours very truly,

J. B. Olinger

Seeburg Pipe-Organ Orchestra, Style "T" (Double Roll)

quipped with two manuals, organ and piano, also two music rolls for self-playing. These music rolls are hand played—
88-note piano roll and a hand interpreted, orchestrated roll, by means of which the entire instrumentation is played
tomatically, and reproduces the playing of some of the world's best known pianists and organists.

he lower roll is either an orchestrated or an organ roll. It will select its own instrumenta-
on and contains from three to ten pieces. The top roll is a standard player roll. With
ese two rolls perfect results can be obtained. Player rolls can be bought at any music
ore in any locality. Various instrumentation can be obtained by means of player roll.
r the average size theater this pipe organ and orchestra has been a great success.

he Seeburg self-playing **SOLO** feature is a wonderful achievement and places SEEBURG
struments in a class by themselves.

he air is supplied by the latest patent blower which can be placed in any convenient
cation. Double veneered hardwood case finished in Mission Oak.

eight 5 feet 3 inches. Width 3 feet 3 inches. Length 13 feet 2 inches.

eight boxed for shipment about 2000 pounds.

INSTRUMENTATION, "T"	
Organ-Piano	Octave Coupler
Violin	Castanets
Flute	Tom Tom Effect
Bass 8'	Fire Gong
'Cello	Steamboat Whistle
Xylophone	Thunder Effect
Tremolo	Wind Siren
Organ Swell	Baby Cry
Piano 88 Notes	Bird Whistle
Bass Drum	{ Telephone Bell
Snare Drum	{ Door Bell
Cymbal	Horse Trot
Crash Cymbal	Triangle
Tympani Effect	

*An almost unlimited variety of effects may
be obtained from key-board, such as: Cuckoo,
Scotch Bag-pipe Effect, etc.*

*"SEEBURG value quickly seen
as music changes with the screen"*

for these developments are lost in the mists of antiquity; all we know today is that some remarkable
gadgets were developed in the 25 years following
Harris's Nickelodeon and the perfection of sound
movies in the late 1920's.

By whatever name these instruments were known,
it's fair to suggest that these were the true "Nickelodeon Pianos". Each manufacturer developed his own
particular monogram, of course, with WurliTzer featuring the "Motion Picture Theatre Orchestra" and
"One-Man Orchestras", Seeburg pushing its "Pipe
Organ Orchestra", American Photo Player Company

having the "Fotoplayer", and so on. In the course of
development, most of these sprung up with ranks of
organ pipes in addition to the drums, traps, and other
sound effects which were attached to the pianos, so
many of them were indeed sort of half-pipe-organ and
half piano. From the standpoint of classification today,
the whole breed are known as "Photoplayers."

Photoplayers of any type are rare today, because
they were apt to be cumbersome and heavy, and when
the theatres went to sound movies there was no further
need for them. Movie houses exist on cash income,
not sentiment, so it's apparent that most of them were

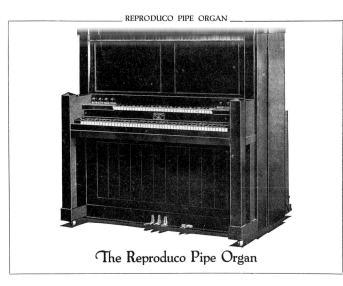

The Reproduco Pipe Organ

REPRODUCOS
— IN —
SAENGER HOUSES

Saenger's are now
Operating

42

REPRODUCO'S

Rapides Theatre, Alexandria, La.

Saenger Theatre, Pine Bluff, Ark.
Saenger Amusement Co.
Incorporated
New Orleans, La.

The Saenger Amusement Co. own and control several hundred theaters, reaching from Florida to Texas. In larger houses they use the Reproduco as a relief Instrument.

Operators' Piano Co., Chicago, Ill.   4-16-25
Gentlemen:
     It gives us great pleasure to recommend the **Reproduco** not only in the workmanship but also in the satisfaction it gives to our **Patrons**. Summed up in a few words, we are highly pleased.
          Saenger Amusement Co.,   E. M. Clarke.

Interior Duplex Reproduco

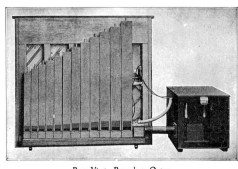

Rear View—Reproduco Organ

Specifications

1 8 foot Tone Diapason (12)
2 8 foot Tone Flute (49)
3 8 foot Quintadena (metal, 37)
4 Piano Manual 7 1-3 Octaves
5 Organ Manual 61 notes, Mechanical Registers
6 Tremolo
7 Diapason Stop
8 Flute Stop
9 Quintadena Stop
10 Mandolin Stop Accessories
11 Coupler
12 Electric Blower and Motor for Organ
13 Electric Motor for Vacuum
14 Complete Coinola rewind mechanism
15 Mandolin
16 Blower Chest and Cabinet
17 Catch-All Vacuum Cleaning Device

"BEN HUR"

We have had a number of requests for advice as to what rolls are best suited to this film.

We would suggest to owners of Reproduco's that you use roll 35 for general purposes and 49 for the battle scenes and chariot race. Roll 39 is also appropriate for general use.

"THE BIG PARADE"

This is a rather hard Picture to que but you should get very good results with the use of roll 46 for general purposes, using roll 50 for the comic situations. If you are the owner of a Duplex Reproduco you can cover the picture very satisfactorily by alternating between rolls 46 and 50

"BEAU GESTE"

This is a picture you can very easily adapt your rolls to.

We suggest using roll 13 for the first part, roll 46 for the Barrack Life and roll 49 for the war scenes in Africa.

PLANTATION MELODIES

N.O.S. 103   Plantation Echoes
Section 1—Old Black Joe; My Old Kentucky Home; Swanee River; Hard Times Come No More; Massa's in the Cold, Cold Ground.
Section 11—Bohemian Girl Melodies.

WESTERN SCENES

N.O.S. 49   Western Dramatic Music
[Mostly Speedy]

Dance of the Furies from Orpheus—Storm Hurry (Kempinski)—Greed, Op. 30 (Kempinski)—Descriptive Agitato (Kempinski)—Attack (Schertzinger)—Foreboding (Casini)—Furious Enemies (Damaur)—Excitement (Breil)—The Massacre (Schertzinger)—The Duel (Schertzinger)—Danger's Threat, Op. 47 (Kempinski).

COMEDY ROLL

N.O.S. 75   Comedy Special—Rags
Cute and Pretty—Harry Fox Rag—Come On Along—Pahjamah—Rockin' The Boat—Baltimore Blues—Pretty Polly—Cry Baby.

N.O.S. 50 Comedy (Speedy) Feature Roll
Dizzy Fingers—Smoky Mokes—Grand Concert Rag—Peace and Plenty Rag—At a Georgia Campmeeting—Silver Bell—Solita—Chatterbox Rag—Black and White Rag—Dixie Darlings—Midnight Fire Alarm—Meteor Rag—Peerless Rider March.

NEWS REELS

N.O.S. 23 Snappy Marches for News Reels etc.
1. General Pershing—2. The Pitt Panther—3. March Triumphal—4. National Emblem—5. The Invincible Eagle—6. Old Faithful—7. The Iron Division—8. Blaze Away—9. Miss Liberty—10. Spirit of Independence—11. The Potomac—12. Soldiers of the Sea.

GRAND THEATRE, ATLANTA, GA.

FORSYTH THEATRE
JAKE WELLS, MANAGER
ATLANTA. GA.

May 26th, 1915.

J. P. Seeburg Piano Co,
209 S. State St., Chicago.

Gentlemen:-

We have been experiencing all
sorts of trouble with the music
problem; and not until you induced
us to purchase a Seeburg did we
have any peace with music matters.

We simply turn on the current
in the morning and shut it off
at night and the instrument does
the rest. We have used an
operator a few weeks, but we find
that we get as much satisfaction
from the automatic operation. }!

We are not having any trouble
with fitting music to the pictures,
for the assortment of rolls you
furnished with the instrument, is
greater than the library of any
orchestra we have used in connection with pictures.

Very truly yours

N L Pardoza

Manager The Grand

smashed for junk when their usefulness ended. And
many of them were simply worn-out, if we can judge
by comments made to the writer some years back by
Oswald Wurdeman of Minneapolis who used to work
in the trade of maintaining them.

Mr. Wurdeman spoke of the aggravations of these
jobs: Most places of this character were open from
early in the morning to late at night, which meant that
essential maintenance had to be done in the wee morning hours; if a major job had to be accomplished, at
least enough of the machine had to be put back
together to that it could "limp along" and make at least
feeble sounds the next day. Theatres tend to be dark,
and what with candy and popcorn being consumed
and scattered about the premises, vermin are attracted,
and what better place for rat nests than inside the
chests and cabinets of these instruments? And since
these machines were frequently operated not by human
players, but merely had their electric drive motors
turned on early in the morning and left to bang away
all day long to provide heaven-only-what-knows type
of accompaniment from whatever music rolls happened to be on the spool-frame at the moment, the wear-
and-tear made maintenance doubly difficult. Sometimes whole piano actions had to be replaced, for example!

Schemes for bringing in the sound effects varied
among manufacturers. Fotoplayers were built using
leather cords, the handles of which would be yanked
by the human operator to sound the Chinese crash
cymbal, blow the locomotive whistle, enact the
crockery-smash, or what-have-you. These pianos
always played regular 88-note piano rolls without any
automatic instrumentation, so a real person always
had to be on hand to supervise their operation.
WurliTzer adapted Pian-orchestra rolls for their machines and since these carry the automatic registration
of stops and some effects in the form of extra perforations in the paper, they could be operated automatically if the theatre manager so desired and felt his
patrons would not object if the music emanting there-
from seldom, if ever, bore any relationship to any
particular scene. In addition, a series of toe studs were
available so that a human operator, if there was one,
could enthrall his audience with extra sounds without
having to remove his hands from the keyboard.

Seeburg had several models which could play both
a regular 88-note piano roll and a large orchestrated
one. Link made their machines with four rolls, each
ready for instant play, whenever the operator in the
movie booth saw fit to switch from one mood to
another.

It's probably safe to suggest that even though entire
libraries of music rolls specially arranged to suit the
moods and scenes of the movies were available to
operators, it's likely that most patrons of the nickelodeons were as apt to hear Chaminade's "Scarf Dance"
as accompaniment to a slapstick comedy as they they
were "Alexander's Ragtime Band" to a solemn funeral
scene. Movies were new in those days, they were a
novelty, and if they weren't as sophisticated as they
are today, who could care?

Interior of the "Ideal" Moving Picture Orchestra
Style "G"

FOTOPLAYER STYLE 25

THE FOTOPLAYER is a beautiful product of fine material and workmanship and is built to withstand the gruelling tests of a motion picture theater.

SPECIFICATIONS FOR FOTOPLAYER—Style No. 25

Length 14 ft. 4 in.   Width 2 ft. 4 in.   Height 5 ft.
Piano extends 14 inches.
High Grade Player Piano with double tracker device.
Piano muffler—Tremolo.

PIPES FOR ORCHESTRAL EFFECTS:

Violin	Flute	Violoncello

Set of Orchestral Bells (31)

TRAPS AND SOUND EFFECTS:

Bass Drum	Steamboat Whistle or
Cymbal	Locomotive Whistle
Snare Drum	Castanets
Chinese Crash Cymbal	Pistol Crack
Tom-Tom (Chinese)	Sleigh Bells
Tympani or Thunder	Klaxon
Wind Siren	Bird Whistle
Tambourine	Cathedral Chime
Door Bell or	
Telephone Bell	

Finished Stickley Oak, Swell Shutters, Suitable Bench, Lighting Fixtures over double tracker. Combination Blower Plant equipped with motor of sufficient capacity.

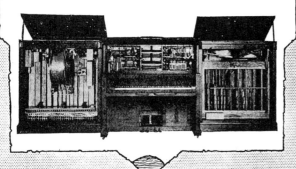

THE FOTOPLAYER is a marvel of technical construction producing the most beautiful organ, piano and orchestral effects.

The FOTOPLAYER music is human and a real satisfaction to critical taste and an enjoyment to the little ones.

The FOTOPLAYER may be used for vaudeville purposes. The entire instrument can be played manually—the pedal attachment permitting the pianist to play the drums and cymbals.

The FOTOPLAYER is designed to withstand the wear of continuous use. Permanent construction is made possible by superior workmanship, material and finish.

Perfect tonal qualities produce a human and artistic performance.

The double tracker device, permitting the operation by roll, is an economic advantage.

Hundreds of satisfied exhibitors pay eloquent tribute to the merits of the FOTOPLAYER.

A style to "fit your pit."

Write for further features.

The American Photo Player Company

VAN NUYS, CALIFORNIA, FACTORY

The Lyon and Healy Company of Chicago operated a training school for Fotoplayer operators. Note the leather cords which the player operates to play the various sound effects.

Scene from the American Photo Player Company in California.

An obviously-posed picture of girls tubing Fotoplayers. Note the two-tiered spool box for playing two different moods of music, and the individual roll-drive motors.

NOVEMBER 1918

CATALOGUE OF PICTUROLLS

INDEXED
AS TO
DRAMATIC
AND
EMOTIONAL
CHARACTER

Sherman, Clay & Co.

San Francisco   Oakland
Sacramento   Stockton
Fresno   San Jose
CALIFORNIA

OCTOBER—NOVEMBER

PICTUROLL BULLETIN

No.	Title	Composer	Price
101	**Golden Hours** (Reverie)	Johnson	.95

A very sweet SENTIMENTAL number which can be used to great advantage with almost any picture.

| 102 | **Indian Love Song** | Homer Grunn | .95 |

Wonderful number for DESERT scenes — suggests DISTANCE, STILLNESS, DESOLATION, as well as Indian Love.

| 103 | **Passepied** | Delibes | .95 |

This is simply a little gem and is splendid for scenes and dances of South Sea Island natives, or other native scenes of similar character. It is also a snappy bright neutral.

| 104 | **Visions** | Buse | .95 |

From the Berg Series. A beautiful PATHETIC number which has a strong heart pull.

| 105 | **Howdy—A Yankee "Pep" Step** | | .90 |

"Ted" said the words—"Josh" jingled the tune.
RUBE STUFF is hard to find. This nex FOX number is FRESH and sure 'nuff RUBE. You'll like it all right.

| 106 | **Twilight Dreams** | Ellis | .90 |

An excellent Ballad with a PLAINTIVE melody, particularly adapted to use with pictures

| 107 | **Battle of Ypres** | Borch | .95 |

A splendid BATTLE number. Fine for MOBS, great excitement and scenes of this character.

| 108 | **Eccentric Misterioso** | Kay | .95 |

A dandy Misterioso when played slow and soft. Played at full tempo, it is full of COMEDY. A very unusual type.

| 109 | **In the Village** | Godard | .95 |

(From Scenes Poetiques Suite)
Descriptive of MERRIMENT. JOY. BIG HAPPY CROWDS. Full of CHATTER, etc. It's a peach. You oughta have it. You gotta have it.

* Organ arrangement—not suitable for player piano.

ADD 5% WAR TAX

No.	Title	Composer	Price
107	Battle of Ypres	Gaston Borch	.95

A splendid battle number, fitting also mobs, riots, etc. Classified as—
Agitato—Battle.
Dramatic—Fast.
Hurry—Military.

108 Eccentric Misterioso........Kay .95
A dandy Misterioso when played slow and soft. At full tempo it is full of comedy. Classified as—
Mysterious—Sneaky (Played Slow).
Mysterious—Weird (Played Slow).
Comedy—General (Played Fast).

109 In the Village........Godard .95
(From Scenes Poetiques Suite)
Descriptive of merriment, joy, big, happy crowds. Classified as—
Hurry—Merry.
Intermezzo—Joyful.
Neutral—Bright.

110 Kathleen, Valse Intermezzo........Berg .95
This waltz is especially fine for pictures. Not too "dancy." Classified as—
Neutral—Waltz.

111 A Love Theme........Kay 1.15
A beautiful, intense love theme. Classified as—
Love Theme—Strong.
Sentimental—Strong.

2 Caravan........Bainbridge-Crist .95
(Egyptian Impressions)
Creates the real Oriental atmosphere. Classified as—
Foreign—Oriental.

Dance Fantastique........Reynard .95
A bright, joyful Intermezzo,—fine for a "spell-breaker." Classified as—
Intermezzo—Bright.
Intermezzo—Joyful.
Intermezzo—Lively.
Neutral—Bright.

ather of Victory........L. Ganne .9
(Le Pere de la Victoire)
big, wonderful, thrilling, military march. ssified as—
Foreign—French.
arch.

No.	Title	Composer	Price

83 The Lady Picking Mulberries........Edgar S. Kelley .95
This is pure Japanese atmosphere. Classified as—
Foreign—Chinese.
Foreign—Japanese.

84 I'm Giving You to Uncle Sam........Schertzinger .85
A stirring military march. Classified as—
March.
Patriotic.

85 Withered Flowers........Kiefert .90
(Intermezzo Pathetic)
A beautiful roll for sympathetic, light, sad scenes. Classified as—
Pathetic—Light.
Pathetic—Sweet.
Sentimental—Light.

86 Andante Mysterioso, No. 15........M. L. Lake .90
A most effective number for light, subdued, mysterious scenes. Classified as—
Dramatic—Light.
Mysterious—Light.

87 Grotesque or Clown Music........J. S. Zamecnik .80
A "sure-fire" Comedy roll. Classified as—
Comedy—General.

88 The Fighting Allies........M. L. Lake 1.25
A GRAND SELECTION, INTRODUCING THE NATIONAL AIRS OF SERBIA, RUSSIA, ITALY, BELGIUM, ENGLAND, FRANCE, and the UNITED STATES OF AMERICA IN THE ORDER OF THEIR ENTRANCE INTO THE WAR.
While conceived as one continuous selection, each and every one of the NATIONAL AIRS can be effectively rendered separately. Classified as—
Foreign—Belgian.
Foreign—French.
Foreign—Italian.
Foreign—Russian.
Foreign—Serbian.
Patriotic.

89 Slimy Viper........Gaston Borch .95
A mysterious, treacherous atmosphere creator. Classified as—
Dramatic—Heavy.
Mysterious—Heavy.
Mysterious—Sneaky.

No.	Title	Composer	Price

57 "General" Excitement (Presto No. 5)........M. L. Lake .95
The name tells it. Sword fights, duels, etc. Classified as—
Agitato—Fight.
Agitato—Light.
Dramatic—Fast.

58 "General" Agitated (Agitato No. 6)........M. L. Lake .95
A fast, dramatic, exciting number. Classified as—
Agitato—Fight.
Agitato—Light.
Hurry—Dramatic.
Dramatic—Fast.

59 "General" Mysterious (Misterioso No. 13)........M. L. Lake .95
Great with murder, stealth and gruesome scenes. Classified as—
Mysterious—Gruesome.
Mysterious—Light.
Mysterious—Sneaky.
Mysterious—Weird.

60 "General" Sneak (Pizzicato No. 14)........M. L. Lake .95
A light, weird, hair-raising, mysterious number. Classified as—
Comedy—Sneaky.
Mysterious—Light.
Mysterious—Sneaky.
Mysterious—Weird.

61 Fire, Fire, Fire (Allegro No. 10)........M. L. Lake .95
Nuff Sed. Classified as—
Characteristic—Western.
Hurry—Chase.
Hurry—Western.

62 A Reel Race (Allegro No. 10)........M. L. Lake .95
As indicated. Races and railroad scenes especially. Classified as—
Hurry—Chase.
Hurry—Railroad.

*63 Scenic Filler (Secret Greetings)........A. von Fielitz .85
Fine for scenic pictures, water scenes, loving memories, etc. Classified as—
Pathetic—Narrative.
Sentimental—Strong.

No.	Title	Composer	Price

20 Elegie, Melodie........Massenet .90
For bereavement, hopelessness, desolation, what is more fitting than this masterpiece? Wonderful organ solo effects—Classified as—
Pathetic—Deep.
Pathetic—Slow.

*21 Norway Waltz........Eddie Horton .75
Exceptionally fine waltz for use on organs. Classified as—
Neutral—Waltz.

22 War—Battle Music........Adapted from Beethoven .80
All that the name implies. Classified as—
Agitato—Battle.
Agitato—Storm.

23 Hurry! Hurry! No. 7........Adapted from Rubinstein .90
This will make fires, riots, strikes, mobs, etc., register 100%. Classified as—
Agitato—Light.
Hurry—Dramatic.

25 I Am a Bold Policeman........Jack Russell .75
Great for sneaky stuff in comedy. Classified as—
Comedy—Sneaky.
Mysterious—Comic.

26 Action Furioso........Eddie Horton .75
Thrill stuff from start to finish. Classified as—
Agitato—Fight.
Agitato—Low.
Tension—Dramatic.

27 Drunk, Soused, Spree........ .85
This never fails to bring a laugh when played with "Jag" action. Classified as—
Comedy—Jag.

8 Agitato No. 11........Adapted from Liszt .90
Another one—all thrills. Classified as—
Agitato—Joyful.
Hurry—Merry.

Sentiment—A Reverie........E. B. Sawtelle .90
A plaintive, old-fashioned love theme. Classified as—
Love Theme—Old Fashioned.
Pathetic—Light.
Sentimental—Plaintive.
Sentimental—Strong.

No.	Title	Composer	Price

9 Agitato No. 9........Adapted from Grieg .85
Great for fights, quarrels, approaching disaster, fear. Classified as—
Agitato—Fight.
Agitato—Light.
Hurry—Dramatic.
Tension—Dramatic.

12 Sorrow, Sadness, Desolation........E. B. Sawtelle .85
This will bring the tears with scenes of deep pathos. Classified as—
Dramatic—Light.
Pathetic—Low.
Pathetic—Strong.

13 A Little Sob Music........Dixie Johnson .75
Another strong number for sob scenes. Classified as—
Characteristic—Church (Played Slow)
Pathetic—Light.
Sentimental—Plaintive.

*14 Love Scene Music........E. E. McCargar .75
An appealing melody, slightly pathetic. Classified as—
Love Theme—Quiet (PP—Slow).
Love Theme—Strong.
Pathetic—Narrative.
Sentimental—Light.

15 Sob Sister........E. B. Sawtelle .90
A quiet love theme, strongly sentimental. Classified as—
Love Theme—Quiet.
Pathetic—Slow.
Pathetic—Sweet.
Sentimental—Strong.

16 "Reuben and Rachel"........Gooch .75
Country—Jay music, pure and simple. Classified as—
Comedy—Rube.

17 Mushy Music........Jack Russell .85
Adds fifty per cent to tender-moment scenes. Classified as—
Love Theme—Quiet.
Love Theme—High.
Pathetic—Light.
Sentimental—Strong.

*18 Molly Darling........Hays .80
An appealing, old-fashioned love theme. Classified as—
Love Theme—Old Fashioned.
Sentimental—Light.

19 Battle Hymn of the Republic........Steffe .85
An exceptional arrangement of "John Brown's Body." Classified as—
Patriotic.

223

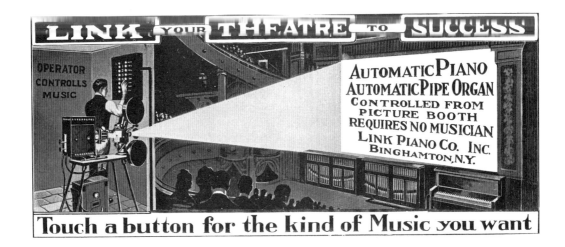

The LINK Company made much of the fact that the motion picture operator could serve a double duty, thereby saving the cost of a musician and still providing an element of relationship between screen moods and the type of music played. As the ad says, "OPERATOR CONTROLLS MUSIC." This particular ad appeared on the face of a desk blotter!

Music control Switch-box. Can be used in any part of theatre. Touch a button for the kind of music you want.

STYLE M P Jr.
MISSION FINISH

Height 4 ft. 9 in.; Depth 2 ft. 6 in.; Length 12 ft. 6 in.

Music Roll Cabinet

Inside Music Roll Cabinet

STYLE M P Jr.

SELF PLAYING PIANO FOR MOVING PICTURE THEATRES

This instrument is the size of an ordinary piano with cabinet containing the music rolls setting along side, making the total length 12 feet, 6 inches.

In the music roll cabinet are four rolls of music, each roll containing from eight to fifteen selections. The music is like an endless belt so that it does not have to rewind, thereby eliminating all rewind annoyances. The music on each roll is all of the same character, for instance,—one roll may be all sob music, one roll all popular songs and dances, one roll all marches and on the other roll would be characteristic music such as national airs, chase or pursuit, Indian war dances, battle scenes, Oriental scenes, funeral and ceremonial scenes and military scenes. In addition to the buttons that control the changing of the rolls there are buttons that control the soft and loud expression. The music is controlled by push buttons placed in the operator's booth or any part of the theatre.

If the scene is a sad one and you want sob music, all you have to do is to touch a button for the roll containing sob music. When the scene changes to a heavy dramatic picture, push the button controlling the dramatic music and the change is made instantly. On the other rolls you can keep music of light, airy character for your news weeklies and comedies.

The idea is that in the morning you are to select the music which is appropriate for the picture you are going to run just the same as a conductor of an orchestra would select his music for his musicians. Place the different rolls in the instrument and you are then ready to play your show and do not have to change the music rolls again until you change your picture.

Every shade of expression, tempo and modulation is cut into the roll so that the results obtained are so absolutely perfect that if you were sitting in the room adjoining the one in which the instrument is being played, you would imagine you were listening to a piano being played by a first-class musician.

THE RIGHT MUSIC AT THE RIGHT TIME

is the most vital for the success of the picture house, for without it the proper effect of the picture is nullified, which means eventual loss of patronage. With the LINK PLAYER the musical program is directly under the control of the picture operator and at his will the music changes instantly by pushing a button even to the stopping of playing one selection at any note and the beginning of another of different tempo the next second. It is thus possible at all times to have melody to correspond and be consistent with each picture shown. It plays with all the expression and technic of a high-class artist and must be heard to be appreciated.

This instrument is not equipped with a lot of pedals and hand levers to operate, therefore it does not require a thoroughly competent musician to follow the picture.

INSTANTANEOUS CHANGES

from one selection of music to another with change in tempo at the instant the scenes are shifted on the screen are the most important factors for the successful display of a film. In this the ordinary piano player is deficient and the effects desired are oftentimes spoiled. The ordinary automatic piano is almost worse than useless for the picture theatre on account of lack of music control.

CLUBS, PRIVATE HOMES AND BALL ROOMS

It is an ideal instrument for private entertainment and dancing as you have music suitable for all the latest dances, also classical and popular songs at your command by simply pushing a button. You select the kind of music you wish, be it a one-step, waltz, fox trot, etc. It is not necessary for you to change your music rolls to play these different classes of music as you have them on the instrument at all times.

"The Soul of the Film"

SEEBURG
Twin-Roll
Reproducing
Pipe Organ

The Seeburg twin-roll "reproducing pipe organ" is very rare, although a number of similar machines known as the Seeburg "Celeste" were made using a single music roll.

A variation on the Photoplayer theme is the mortuary organ. This one, made by WurliTzer, has one keyboard for the piano and another for the organ pipes fitted inside the piano case. A music-roll can be used to play it.

This early WurliTzer photoplayer appears to be a forerunner of the electronic "Side Man" produced by them two generations later. It appears to contain only bass and snare drums.

"D" DUPLEX ORCHESTRA

FOR THEATRE OF 150 SEATS

THIS is an ideal instrument for very small house where drums might be too loud. It is a high-grade piano with mandolin attachment. Built for hard continuous professional concert work. Has violin and flute pipes, yet takes up no more space than good sized upright piano. It has a double interchangeable 10-tune roll as shown on next page.

This is a full scale keyboard piano that can be played by hand without the use of electricity, just like the ordinary piano. It has a wonderful tone, an easy playing action and great depth and brilliancy of power. It is an instrument built by us particularly for professional work—built to stand the wear and tear that instruments get in public places.

DUPLEX ORCHESTRA STYLE "G"

SUITABLE FOR HOUSE WITH SEATING CAPACITY OF 200

AN orchestral effect of four pieces (piano with mandolin attachment, flute, violin and drums), with mechanical requirements of expert motion picture trap drummer, (triangle) castanets, horse trot, tom-tom, fire gong and electric bell).

The Duplex Roll mechanism that is described on another page gives you continuous music. There are two long rolls of ten tunes each making a loading of twenty different tunes at one time.

Now this piano can be played by hand, just like the ordinary piano, without turning on the electricity. If, however, you wish to bring the novelty effects into play, you can do so by pushing a button and turning on the electric motor and stopping the motion of the roll by pushing another button. Then the pianist can, by pushing different buttons and touching the pedals, bring in the different pipes and combinations to play in connection with the piano, and strike the drums and the novelty effects, etc., by touching the extra pedals shown in the illustration.

This piano also is a high-grade professional Wurlitzer make, built for constant use.

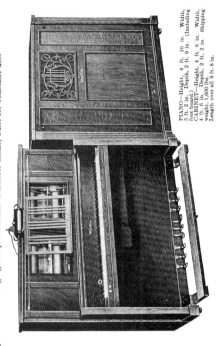

PIANO—Height, 4 ft. 10 in. Width, 5 ft. 2 in. Depth, 2 ft. 9 in. (Including foot board.)
CABINET—Height, 4 ft. 6 in. Width, 4 ft. 6 in. Depth, 2 ft. 2 in. Shipping weight, 1,000 lbs.
Length over all 9 ft. 8 in.

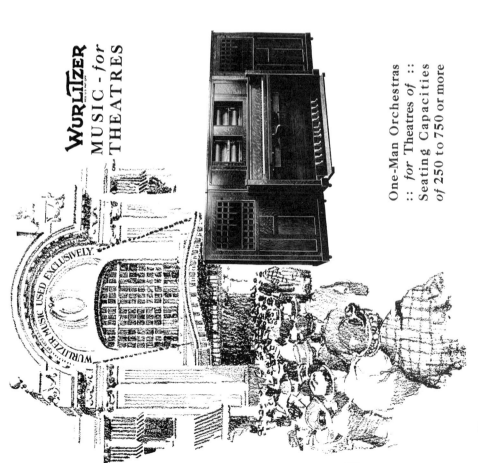

WURLITZER
MUSIC - for THEATRES

WURLITZER MUSIC USED EXCLUSIVELY.

One-Man Orchestras :: for Theatres of :: Seating Capacities of 250 to 750 or more

Where the Wurlitzer Motion Picture Theatre Orchestras are made.

North Tonawanda, New York

DUPLEX ORCHESTRA STYLE "O"

SUITABLE FOR HOUSE WITH SEATING CAPACITY OF 250

Played by Hand or with Rolls

A MORE elaborate orchestral effect than the G Model. Automatic features are the same. Instrument produces more effects and greater volume. The piano department is a high-grade professional concert instrument. The organ proper produces the same effect as an orchestra of 4 pieces with snare and bass drums. It has 10 Motion Picture effects.

The style "O" instrument as described above is a little more elaborate in its orchestral effects than the style "G". The automatic features are just the same, that is, it is equipped with the Duplex Roll mechanism. You notice, however, the difference in the layout of the case. There are two small cabinets built that fit on each side of the piano, making the instrument a little more symmetrical in appearance than the style "G". It also is equipped as follows: Namely the flute pipes, violin pipes, then the bass drum, snare drum, castanets, horse trot, tom-tom, fire gong, electric door bell, kettle drum and bird whistle. In addition to this, it has an extra set of heavy bass pipes that give this instrument a little more foundation of tone. There is one octave of bass pipes added to the regular scale of the flute pipes, giving a depth of tone making this instrument a little more attractive than the style "G".

It is also equipped with the Duplex Roll mechanism, and if you will note carefully the description of this on another page, you will find how you could use one of these instruments by having the button controlling the operation of the rolls placed in the front part of the theatre or up in the operating booth. One button would turn on the electricity and start the instrument to play, a second button would change from one roll to the other; simply a touch of the button and the change is made instantly, and a third button would turn off the electricity and stop the instrument. We wonder if anything could be more ideal.

ORCHESTRA STYLE "YO"

PLAYED WITH STANDARD CUT 88-NOTE PIANO ROLLS

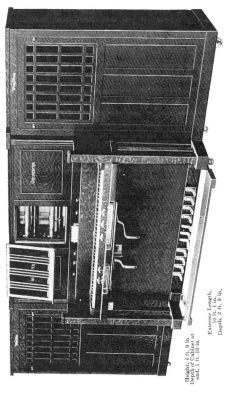

Height, 1 ft. 9 in.
Depth of Cabinet at end, 1 ft. 10 in.

Extreme Length, 10 ft. 1 in.
Depth, 2 ft. 9 in.

TWO rolls of music in instrument at one time enable the player to change from one piece to another as the picture progresses. As one roll plays, the silent roll can be run forward or back. Styles "U" and "K" as pictured on the following pages can be equipped with this standard piano roll playing device and are sold under our factory numbers as "YU" and "YK".

The "YO" Orchestra shown above is an instrument containing the same instrumentation as the style "O". This arrangement, however, with the roll mechanism is quite a bit different and it is made for those people who like to add their own individuality to the playing of the pictures and who prefer to make their own interpretation.

This instrument is equipped with the Duplex Roll Mechanism which plays the ordinary roll that is used upon the house or home piano, an 88-note roll that is not in any way at all self-registering. All that this roll does is to strike the proper note just like it does on your player piano. It is necessary for you to sit at the keyboard of this instrument and manipulate the different stops and the different effects. The roll itself takes care of the most difficult or the most simple compositions for you. Your own individuality then goes into the handling of this instrument, just as though you were the leader of an orchestra, because by the manipulation of these different stops, controls, etc., you can control the expression of the instrument.

Rolls, of course, are very inexpensive for an instrument of this kind. You can purchase them any place where music rolls are for sale, as they use the same roll as used upon the regular home player piano. The manipulation of the same is simple, it is durable and it can also be played by hand, the player bringing into use the different effects and the pipes in connection with the piano keyboard as he can on the style "G" and style "O".

Air motors are required with this instrument to operate the music roll, and an outside blowing attachment stands in behind the instrument. This also could be placed at a distance away from the instrument if you so preferred.

The style "U" and the style "K", as shown on the following pages, can also be equipped with this standard piano roll playing device, and are then sold and known as our factory numbers "YU" and "YK".

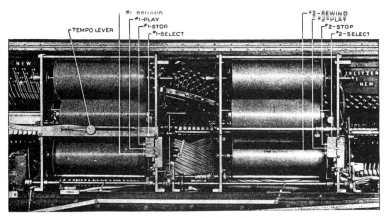

Double-Roll System for "D," "G" and "O" Orchestras

THE Wurlitzer Duplex Roll System as illustrated above is an exclusive Wurlitzer feature, one that enables you to play your pictures quite intelligently from the paper roll. First of all, this roll mechanism gives you continuous music, for just as soon as one roll gets through playing, the other roll starts to play and the silent roll rewinds, getting into position to play again.

You can change from one roll to another by a simple push of the button.

Now a more simplified way to handle this proposition would be to equip the instrument with a roll of good music on one side and some Jazz music on the other. Then if the Jazz roll is playing and is not at all in keeping with the scene in the picture, a simple touch of the button will stop the Jazz roll instantly and the other roll will start to play. Then if you desire to return to Jazz roll at any time, a simple touch of the button and the Jazz roll will start to play and the better roll will stop. This is all done instantly; there is no wait in the music after the touch of the button is made.

This double-roll system enables you to have continuous music as well as music suitable for the different scenes in the picture without the expense of a musician. A button in the projection booth makes it possible for the operator to change from Jazz to soft classic music instantly with the changing scene on the screen. Each one of the rolls contains from 5 to 10 selections.

This enables you to cover an entire performance without repeating a musical number. There are no belts or wheel mechanisms to get out of order in these instruments. It is nearly fool proof and hundreds of them have been in constant operation for years without giving one bit of trouble. This is one of the exclusive Wurlitzer features found in no other instrument.

Net Price List
of
Wurlitzer Motion Picture
Theatre Orchestra

March 1st, 1920

The Rudolph Wurlitzer Co.
New York   Cincinnati   Chicago

WURLITZER

—NET PRICE LIST—
of
Wurlitzer Motion Picture
Theatre Orchestras

EFFECTIVE MAY 15th, 1920

This List Cancels all former Price List.

Style	Price
"D" Duplex Roll.........	$ 1800.00
"G" Duplex Roll	2200.00
"O" Duplex Roll	2600.00
"U" Duplex Roll	4250.00
"K" Duplex Roll	6100.00

F. O. B. Factory

WURLITZER

The following are the prices
for the

Style	Price
Y O	$ 2800.00
Y U	4250.00
Y K	6100.00

Equipped with the 88 Note Duplex Roll System

F. O. B. Factory

The Rudolph Wurlitzer Co.
New York   Cincinnati   Chicago

The Melodies Linger On

Automatic music machines are fun. What better evidence than this happy group, listening to a Coinola orchestrion in the home of Frank and Hope Rider of Wabash, Indiana? Reginald Waylett (with pipe) of Edenbridge, Kent, England and Mr. Rider are on the left; Don Parker of Churubusco, Indiana and Eddie Freyer of Flemington, New Jersey, are at right. The instrument is semi-original; the orchestrion effects have been added to a lesser instrument.

Fortunately for those who consider the development of the mechanical piano a real part of the important heritage of modern man, a number of interested collectors in America and Europe have made real efforts to preserve the few remaining machines and the music rolls which operate them. Some of these collections are in public places where they may be played and enjoyed by all; others are in the homes of private individuals who have them mainly for the entertainment and enjoyment of themselves and their friends.

As is the case with most fields of endeavor, specialization tends to set in with collectors. There are those whose interest centers entirely about reproducing pianos, and maybe even those of a particular make to the exclusion of others. There are those who find fascination with the nickel-grabbing coin machines. Still others content themselves with collecting a particular type of music roll for the 88-note home piano, such as rag-time, operatic, classical, or perhaps those of interest to a particular ethnic group. Others are mainly concerned with band or fair organs, which of course aren't pianos at all, but certainly can be considered distant cousins of them. Then there are music box collectors, but curiously enough these folks and piano collectors seem to be a different breed, although there naturally is some carry-over from one field to another. Of course it may be that since pianos are as heavy, clumsy, and space-consuming as they are, most collectors feel they have to stick to one aspect of the art and do their best with it rather than to try to have a comprehensive grouping of machines, even though they might inwardly aspire to such a goal.

Lack of space is, of course, a real problem. There are those who really have plenty of space, but whose wives simply feel that kitchens, bedrooms, and living spaces must be devoted to more practical considerations in family life than the restoration of orchestrions, band organs, and the like, and that the basement and the garage are the only suitable places for them. But collectors' wives are generally an understanding lot, mainly because they know that when hubby is embroiled in the innards of one of these fantastic music-makers of a by-gone day, he's apt to be right where they can keep an eye on him!

The pictures in this chapter represent a number of collections known to be outstanding, and they give a fairly good cross-section of the restorative work that has been done in this field. Of course there are scores of fine groupings of machines across America and Europe, and no slight is intended to those which are not included. In organizing this section of the book, an attempt has been made to show as many different types of machines as possible, with a minimum of repetition of specific models.

Visitors to the Musical Museum at Deansboro, New York, are greeted by a fine show of various types of automatic musical artifacts, as we see on the opposite page. Arthur Sanders is showing a Horton Autophone to some young guests and their mother, while his wife Elsie looks on. They'll be treated to a brief discussion of such goodies as a Tel-Ektra (at left on the counter), a Poughkeepsie-built Welte-Mignon grand piano, an original German Welte reproducing piano (upright, in rear), a Regina 15½" automatic changer music box, and a variety of small music boxes. Of special interest are some of the bird-music boxes, of which the one featuring several small birds in a nest is an outstanding example. This museum is a favorite with vacationers in the Central part of New York State, and many parents like to bring their children for they can actually play many of the exhibits themselves. The large display room above features WurliTzer, Nelson-Wiggen, North Tonawanda, Coinola, Link, Peerless, and Seeburg instruments, looking from left to right!

Photo credits here go to the Syracuse, New York Herald-American. Over the years the Deansboro Museum has been featured in many news articles, if for no other reason than it has been in business for so many years. Now operated by two generations of the Hardie Sanders family, its visitor list numbers in the hundreds of thousands.

This interesting collection has sparked the interest of many persons in the fascinating field of automatic musical instruments, and has led to the development of many other collections throughout America. Unlike many public collections which are located near the hub-bub of busy cities, Deansboro's main tourist attraction is a feature of a sleepy little town a good bit off the beaten path. Which makes it all the more worth-while to visit!

When Arthur Bronson, Jr. and his son tire of the hard work of raising beef cattle on their Dundee, Michigan, farm, they relax by working on the collection of automatic musical instruments which provide a common ground for fun by man and boy. To house their collection adequately, they have erected a fine spacious building, a corner of which you see here. The big machine is a WurliTzer style 47 Pian -Orchestra, a magnificent instrument of obviously massive proportions. Note that it has *two* wonder lights, on either side of a peacock, whose moving tail which is illuminated with colored lights casts reflections throughout the room by means of surrounding mirrors! In addition to the small cabinet piano at the right are a Coinola Reproduco and a Coinola Style C-2, to add to the joyous melodies produced by music boxes scattered around the floor.

The State of Montana, America's "Big Sky" country, had as its second territorial capital the place called "Virginia City". It came into being as a result of a gold strike by Bill Fairweather in the early 1860's, and it quickly became a promising mining town in the best tradition of the Western movie! Complete with numerous stagecoach robberies and shoot-outs and vigilantes, its rich history makes a fascinating story of the opening of the American West to the White man's "civilization." The vast amounts of gold mined in nearby Alder Gulch helped immeasurably to finance the Union cause during the American civil war.

After the gold ran out, Virginia City became but a shell of its former self, and such surrounding gold towns as Nevada City (a mile West) all but disappeared. In the 1950's, however, Montana State Senator Charles Bovey and his wife took an interest in restoring the place to resemble its former self, and they have spent countless amounts of money and energy during the intervening years to do just that. Today it is an outstanding tourist attraction, and is an important forefunner of many similar projects throughout the country.

The Boveys and those who have worked with them have made every effort to re-create the place much as it must have been, with a minimum of commercial pizzaz to mar their efforts. The many stores and shops are a true picture of a fascinating past.

Scattered here and there in the two towns, Virginia and Nevada cities, are restored mechanical pianos and other antiques to entertain and amuse the visitor. While not strictly from the same time period as the hey-day of the area, they relate beautifully to the general sense of antiquity which abounds.

The gentleman above, shown doing some nerve surgery on a Mills Violano-Virtuoso, is Oswald Wurdeman of Minneapolis, Minnesota. Ozzie's father was a Mills distributor throughout several mid-western States, and Ozzie grew up in the business of servicing all types of electric pianos and related devices. For a number of years, he and his son Tom have spent their summers maintaining the music machines in the Virginia City complex, to the delight of the many thousands of tourists who visit each season. Below and at the right are photographs taken in the famous "Bale of Hay" saloon, a spot which maintains the authentic flavor of the old West. The curved-case Violano-Virtuoso is a rare early model, much sought-after by connoisseurs of mechanical music devices, and it serves to tickle the ears of patrons of the peep-show machines next to it while they have their sights tickled by the bawdy scenes therein!

235

The beautiful art-glass front panel on the Seeburg Style J orchestrion on the opposite page, showing America's Capitol in Washington, D.C., is a favorite of visitors to Virginia City's Bale of Hay saloon. Note especially the side panels of the instrument, which house art glass lamps at the upper front. Mounted on the top of this musical jewel is a Deagan Una-Fon, a set of electrically-operated bells which were widely used for bally-hoo purposes for parades and carnivals half-a-century ago.

At left, above, are a Regina Sublima, a Seeburg L, and a Cremona "A" roll piano featuring the famous trademark of singing canaries on the bevelled-glass front panels, all being listened to attentively by the Victor Dog. These are in the music hall at Nevada City, as is the large Gavioli fair organ in the second picture. The music hall is a log building, built from remains of structures demolished at Yellowstone National Park, some 80 miles distant, and hauled all the way by Charley Bovey and his men to provide the unique setting seen here. The unusual North Tonawanda "Midget Orchestra" immediately below is no longer to be seen in this Montana location, and examples of this type are exceedingly rare today.

The bottom pictures on this page depict other machines in the "Bale of Hay;" the left one being a Reproduco piano-pipe-organ of an early type converted to play type OS and NOS music rolls, and the other being a Cremona Orchestral J instrument which contains a full set of traps and novelty effects.

An outstanding piece in the collection of Larry Givens, Wexford, Pennsylvania, is this magnificent Welte brass-horn orchestrion. It stands twelve feet high and is played by large pinned wood cylinders much in the manner of a Swiss music-box, with the energy provided by falling weights—similar to what keeps a grandfather clock running. The cylinders are about four feet long; the projections on them open valves and move levers to cause pipes to play and drums to rattle. They are mounted on a sort of track, and are changed by removing them through the side of the case.

Below, left, we see a very rare reed organ operated by hand-cranked paper rolls, sitting next to a dandy Seeburg KT Special orchestrion.

The instrument at the lower right is not really a steam calliope, but rather one operated by air. This is the Air-Calio—"The New Calliope with an Extra Punch"—manufactured by the North Tonawanda Musical Instrument Works mentioned earlier. This outfit would be a real asset to anyone's collection, and its dulcet tones are made to be heard either through keyboard operation or by paper rolls. Says the sales literature of this device: ". . . Special voicing of pipes, pitched to play with the band and lower bass tones than any calliope made, makes the instrument smooth, of pleasing tones and great volume, without being offensive."

Reading clockwise, the instruments shown here in the Givens collection are a LINK 2EX coin-piano with xylophone, a WurliTzer Style 125 Military Band organ, an Aeolian Orchestrelle, an Encore Automatic banjo, and a 2-violin Mills Violano Virtuoso.

The Orchestrelle is a large pedal-operated reed organ, produced in a variety of models by the Aeolian Company around the turn of the Century, and of course it is paper-roll operated. Because they have many banks of reeds and various controlling stops, they are capable of quite elaborate orchestral effects when played by a clever operator. Large quantities of these machines were sold in Great Britain.

The Encore banjo is considered a real prize for any collection, and this one is a jewel, restored to perfection. This one was 'rescued' from a restaurant in New York State's Catskill Mountain region, where it had stood unused in a back corner for many years. These machines were built by the American Automatic Banjo Company and most were leased on 'routes' much as is done by present-day coin-phonograph operators, rather than having them available for cash sale. Most were made for coin-slot play, but some were set up for home operation without the money feature.

The two-violin Mills machine is also considered to be a 'find' for any enthusiast for these types of devices, and the one shown here has always been maintained in fine operating order as have most of Mr. Givens' collectibles. Housed in a fine large building erected especially for the purpose, this collection must be rated as truly outstanding.

As the second edition of this book was under preparation, this collection was sold to a dealer, who in turn sold the instruments to other enthusiasts for their continuing enjoyment of the musical outpourings from the innards of these glorious devices.

At top, left, is an exterior view of the establishment, with one of Al's antique cars present. Immediately below is part of one wall, featuring a Seeburg Models KT and G at the left. The upper right pictures a Seeburg horse-race piano at the left, and a LINK flute-piano at the right.

Visitors to the Nickelodeon Tavern are treated to seeing many fine antiquities besides automatic instruments; Al has filled the place with peep shows, mutoscopes, and all sorts of paraphernalia designed to bring back fond memories to anyone old enough to have been able to recognize such things prior to the 1929 market crash and the great depression which followed. A disasterous fire ruined many of this man's holdings some years back, but sufficient artifacts remain to make a visit to this joyous spot something to be remembered for years afterward.

The happy bartender above is Al Svoboda, owner of Svoboda's Nickelodeon Tavern at 24th and Butler, Chicago Heights, Illinois. This famous spot has been a favorite with residents of the area for many years, and Al's many "connections" in the Chicago area—a center of piano manufacturing activity in the 1920's—have helped him build an extensive accumulation of coin-operated instruments.

240

Dr. and Mrs. George Coade of Carlsbad, California, faced up to the problem of housing automatic instruments by having this 800 square foot building with twelve foot ceiling constructed solely for this purpose. Not only do they take a great deal of pride in showing the collection to friends active in the hobby, but they entertain many community groups from time to time and they also have used special "showings" as a means of benefitting various civic music organizations.

The six instruments shown in the picture below and the following two pages were photographed especially for PLAYER PIANO TREASURY by Dan Adams, and he has depicted them in fine fashion. From left to right, below, we see the Philipps Paganini Violin Piano marketed by WurliTzer, and three Seeburgs—the G orchestrion, the KT Special orchestrion, and the Style KT, popularly known as the "Seeburg Eagle."

The Philipps Paganini features a reproducing piano together with several ranks of beautifully-voiced violin and string pipes, all of which is intended to simulate as closely as possible the playing of human musicians. WurliTzer imported these machines from Europe, and promoted them actively in the United States, but since sales never reached significant numbers they are today indeed rare.

In one of their advertising brochures WurliTzer extolls the virtues of this particular instrument, declaring that it is so realistic in its performance that it ". . . will take the most critical audience by storm!" Records do not reveal if any such degree of overwhelming acclaim ever actually was made by any early group of listeners, but there is no doubt that they are certainly pleasant machines to which to listen. The builders obviously paid a great deal of attention to the voicing of the pipes, and connoisseurs of pipe organs are generally amazed when they hear the beautiful "string" tones produced by the "Paganini" instrument.

The Seeburg "G" is a favorite of all automatic music collectors, and it's a large instrument even though dwarfed by the Paganini. Note the "flaming torch" art glass lamps on each side of the front; the designers of this particular case really outdid themselves for a taste of victorian magnificence.

The "KT Special" was not marketed until 1925, very late in the automatic piano game, so its production quantities were limited. It's considerd a real "find" today, because it contains a full complement of trapwork to add to the music of the basic piano, yet its small size will permit entry into homes which have normal ceiling heights. This particular instrument never actually saw commercial service, and as such is certainly almost unique in its class.

The Seeburg "Eagle" is a six-instrument machine, featuring piano, xylophone, mandolin attachment, tambourine, triangle, and castanet. At least one is known to have been built with a snare drum included.

There is little doubt that the Weber "Maesto" orchestrion is the most life-like of anything in its class of instrument ever perfected by man. This was, indeed, the aim of its German designers, and the fact that they succeeded in this effort can be attested by the many connoisseurs of automatic music machines who agree that there is simply nothing else that can equal it.

Fortunately for the owners, some recent music is available for it. Art Reblitz, a professional musician, has arranged latter-day tunes for the machine and it's a great treat to hear it belt out such numbers as "Thoroughly Modern Millie" which the originally-available music rolls predate by several decades.

Covering almost the entire rear wall of the "piano house", this machine generally startles those who hear it for the first time, in its true-to-life renditions as well as for its overall magnificence. Only a handful of these models are left anywhere in the World today, which is reason enough for its owner to display a pleased smile as he carefully fondles one of the priceless music rolls which store the data required to make it spring to life for the entertainment of all within earshot.

Unlike the more typical orchestrion which turns various instruments and ranks of pipes off and on from time to time, the Maesto makes full use of the musical potential of doing this more frequently. In his excellent new arrangement of "Crazy Words, Crazy Tune", Art Reblitz features 32 register changes in the first four measures of music! At least one music roll in the collection was pronounced by a knowledgable music expert to create a performance almost exactly as the Paul Whiteman band sounded.

One of the greatest joys of collecting is sharing the beauty of ones possessions, and George and Susie Coade make a particular effort to permit others to gain a fuller appreciation of the fantastic music machines of a past day.

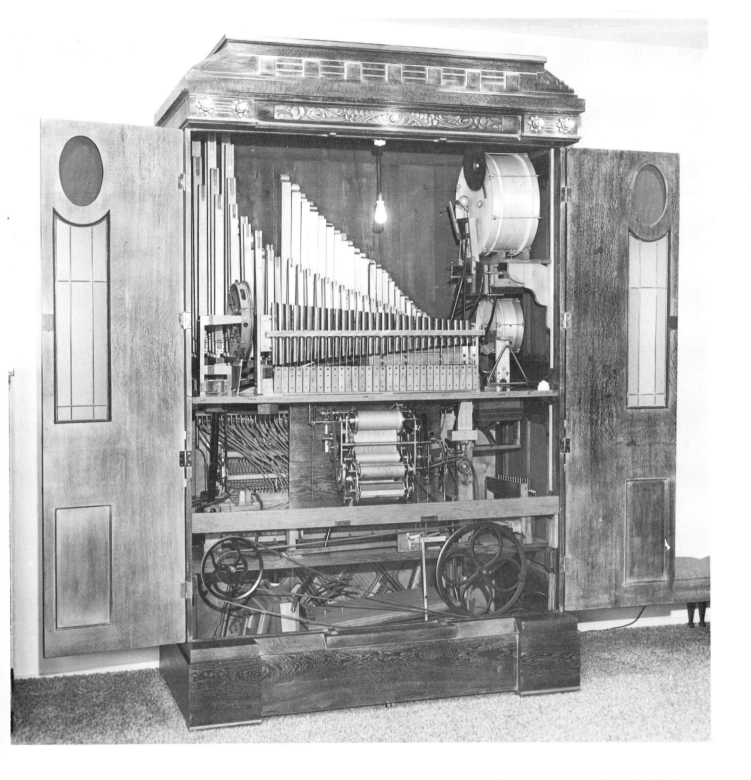

This beautifully-restored WurliTzer Style 30A Mandolin Pianorchestra was rescued some years ago from the Martin Hotel at Skaneateles Falls, New York, in a condition which can best be described as an almost hopeless wreck. It changed hands several times following this "rescue" by Larry Givens of Pittsburgh, Pennsylvania, but complete restoration was not done until it was acquired by Terry Hathaway of Sante Fe Springs, California. So well-done is the rework of the entire instrument that it hardly seems possible that it could have been that good the day it left the factory, yet Mr. Hathaway spared no effort to make the restoration as completely "original" as possible.

In its 10-foot high 6½ foot wide case it holds a piano with mandolin attachment, 30 piccolo pipes, 19 viola pipes, 30 violincello pipes, 30 violin pipes, 37 flute pipes, bass and snare drums, chimes (13 bars), xylophone (30 bars), kettle drum and cymbal, triangle, castanet, and tambourine.

As stated in the original WurliTzer advertising: "This style is built with the Automatic Roll Changing Device, but may be had without it, if desired. By means of this wonderful device a program running from an hour and a half to two hours may be given without the necessity of changing the music rolls or giving the instrument any attention whatever."

The collection amassed by Harvey and Marion Roehl of Vestal, New York, is intended to be a representative one, with examples of almost every type of automatic instrument once common throughout the land. Located in three rooms attached to their home, and occupying 1800 square feet, are some 25 major machines and a sprinkling of lesser ones.

At right is a rare 57-key Gavioli fair organ, awaiting restoration. The author of this book is shown admiring the three-motion bandmaster—a fine example of the wood-carver's art who will, when rebuilt, carry a baton in his right hand for keeping time to the music, move his right hand periodically, and move his head from side to side.

The picture below shows, from left to right, a Seeburg KT Special orchestrion, a North Tonawanda Pianolin (one of 20 similar machines found in a hoard of 45 in a Providence, Rhode Island barn in 1957), a WurliTzer 146-A band organ from the En-Joie park merry-go-round in Endicott, New York, and a Model 192 North Tonawanda Military Band Organ.

The KT Special saw service in a Chicago saloon, while the Pianolin (a 44-note instrument with 44 pipes) is believed to have been part of an "operator's" route in a cafe in New Haven, Connecticut. The background of the brass-horn machine is not known, but chances are it served many years in either a roller-skating rink or some other part of an amusement park for which instruments of this kind were ideally suited in terms of their decibel output!

A dilemma faces the owners of this collection, as it does most others, in that much of the real joy comes from rebuilding the instruments, piece by piece, to their factory-original condition . . . yet with a grouping of any quantity of them, there simply aren't enough days and years in a normal lifetime to complete the job. To say nothing of the fact that one's standards of workmanship tend to go up, with consequent slowing down of work, and more total time being required to do the job as it should be done!

Pianos at right are a LINK Flute-piano, a Cremona G, and Seeburg E. The Link saw service for many years in Hillsgrove, Rhode Island, and was purchased from a convent, of all places. The Cremona G, with its gorgeous golden-oak finish, is believed to have served patrons of a Smithville Flats, New York, tavern. The Seeburg saw tavern service in Champlain, New York, near the Canadian border south of Montreal.

Below, left, is a WurliTzer BX Orchestrion built in 1914, according to extant archival records of the WurliTzer Corporation, and at the right is the well-known Seeburg G orchestrion. Note the art glass in the door at the right edge of the picture; this was destined for use in a Peerless orchestrion, but apparently was never put to that use for it was found together with several other panels in a crate some years back by Arthur Sanders of Deansboro, New York.

Note also the movie projector between the two orchestrions. This is used to show "old-tyme films" on the screen on the opposite wall of the room, to be accompanied by the American Fotoplayer shown in subsequent pictures. Fortunately, in recent years reprints of many silent movie classics have become readily available for home use, and the merry antics of Laurel and Hardy, Charley Chaplin, Buster Keaton and many others have stirred much mirth within the confines of this music room!

The American Fotoplayer depicted here dates from around 1921, and was completely rebuilt by its its present owner. Its side chests were found in their original crates (apparently, when the instrument was taken out of service the boxes were still on hand) and the markings on them indicate that it was first shipped from its Van Nuys, California factory, to the Grand Theatre in Ephrata, Pennsylvania.

The pull-cords in front of the operator control such sound effects as sleigh bells, locomotive whistle, tom-tom, bass drum, cymbal, chinese crash cymbal, pistol shot, wind, bird whistle, and trolley gong. Other effects available include thunder, tambourine, casta-nets, horses' hooves, doorbell, and snare drum—all of which may be operated in conjunction with the piano, a complete set of orchestra chimes, bass pipes, flute pipes, and violin pipes. The operators of these gadgets back in the silent movie days must have been busy persons indeed!

The scene from the Laurel and Hardy movie at left is from their award-winning "The Music Box". The antics of these two comedy geniuses as they attempt to deliver a crated player piano up an enor-mous flight of stairs generally create gales of laughter from any audience, and the novelty effects thrown in from the Fotoplayer serve only to enhance the efforts of these wizards of mirth whose greatness is perhaps only recently begun to be truly appreciated.

Still another movie-house instrument is the Reproduco, built by the Operators' Piano Company of Chicago. This model is devoid of trapwork, but features three ranks of organ pipes. It was installed in a theatre in Derry, Pennsylvania in 1927, and was used for only two years when the advent of sound movies eliminated the need for it.

The machine at right is a Wilcox and White "Symphony" player reed organ, built around 1893, and first advertised as a "self playing orchestra." With three full sets of reeds in a case of Circassian Walnut, it adds a real air of dignity to the music hall in which it resides.

The reproducing pianos below are a Marshall and Wendell Ampico "B" at the left, and a Bauer Welte-Licensee on the right—the first dating from 1931 and the second from 1924. Resting between them is a Sterling "cabinet" or "Push-up" type of piano player, dating from the turn of the Twentieth Century.

Not shown in this picture, but residing at the opposite end of the same room is a Steinway Model XR Duo-Art. Thus in one small space one is permitted to listen to the three major reproducing systems which were marketed in America half-a-century earlier, and to make comparisons as to the capabilities of each to reproduce the actual artistry of a human pianist.

The "Tom Thumb" 61-note piano at the left was introduced by Kohler and Campbell Industries around 1926, and early advertising suggests that this was done to take advantage of the fact that people were tending to move to apartments and smaller living quarters of all types. Judging by the extreme rarity of these instruments today, one might conclude that the marketing efforts along these lines were not spectacularly successful. This particular piano is fitted with an expression mechanism, designed to play "Recordo" music rolls.

No pianos here in the picture below, but miscellaneous music-makers to add a further touch of nostalgia to the collection. The antique National cash register dispenses nickels which operate such items as the WurliTzer Automatic Harp at the left, and the Regina Hexaphone cylinder-record player immediately adjacent. A dandy 15½ inch Regina music box and an Edison Home Phonograph round out this section of the lower level of the music hall housing the Roehl hoard of goodies from a by-gone day. What fun it is to watch visitors of the younger generation as they suddenly realize that not everything worth-while on this Earth has been perfected in the last five years!

One of the greatest attractions in America's Mid West is the National Cowboy Hall of Fame at Oklahoma City. While it is not clear just what relationship these expert horsemen who work hard at maintaining a supply of beefsteak always in preparation for America's tables have to do with electric pianos, it's certain that many a hard-earned nickel has been dropped in the slot of such an instrument by the cowboy patron of the nearest saloon.

One of the problems facing the organizers of any public collection of such instruments is that of permitting listeners to hear them properly. If more than one play at once in a large room, the result is pure cacaphony . . . but if large numbers are to be permitted to hear, something has to be done. Stan Whitehurst, the Curator of the Silver Dollar Musical Museum, has seen to it that each machine sits in its own small cubicle, such that only those patrons in its immediate vicinity can hear it while other visitors can enjoy different machines only a few feet away in blissful ignorance of one they might have played only a few moments before. Naturally, this also helps keep coins flowing into the drop-slots of lots of machines, simultaneously, a necessity if heavy overhead and maintenance costs are to be covered.

The gorgeous buildings below are an appropriate setting for honors due these folk-heroes of the American scene, whose devotion to hard work and long hours is partially compensated by the chance to spend their lives out-of-doors among beauties of nature unequalled anywhere in the World.

Douglas Berryman, Director of the West Cornwall Museum of Mechanical Music, hastened to re-arrange the instruments at the left in order to have them included in this book, but since the museum was undergoing decoration at the time, only the machines themselves are pictured. In the upper picture, left to right, we see a Debain Piano Mechanique which uses music in the form of "planchettes"—some of which are seen on top. They amount to pieces of wood, with pegs arranged on them so cause the notes to sound as they are fed through a reading arrangement, much as cardboard book music is fed through a street organ.

Next is a Heilbrunn Sohne expression piano, then a Bluthner instrument capable of playing either 65 or 88 note music rolls, with a Weber P.E.D.A. (stands for Pedal or Electric Duo-Art) grand. The little organ is a Royal orginette.

The other pictures feature a Broadwood 65 note player with an Apollo push-up in front of it, a Rud-Ibach Duo-Art, and the aforementioned Weber. Note the box underneath the keybed for housing the folding pedals. This type of instrument is fairly common in England, but is seldom seen in the U.S.A.

This collection is open to the public, and the address is Goldsithney, Penzance, Cornwall, England.

Just before the book finally went to press, Mr. Berryman rushed to the Vestal Press this picture of still another grouping of instruments. Notable among them are the Phonoliszt-Violina at the left rear, and the interesting street piano in the center. Such street pianos operate by means of a pinned barrel, much in the manner of a Swiss music box, said barrel being turned by means of a hand crank by the man who pushes it up and down streets while at the same time asking for money for the entertainment provided thereby. Note the dandy little bell-playing lady at the lower left; she's a figurine from the front of some magnificent fairground organ from a past day.

When John Maxwell of La Mesa, California, received the word from his physician that he'd better do something about his high-blood pressure and other assorted physical maladies, it became apparent that he would have to make arrangements to get his mind off his normal work as a manufacturer of architectural woodwork—at least for part of each day.

He managed somehow to get interested in mechanical pianos as a sideline hobby, and the therapeutic value of relaxing with these interesting devices has done wonders for his state-of-mind and physical well-being! The nature of his full-time business has made it easy for him to construct one of the most beautiful music-rooms imaginable, and it's the envy of all collectors who are permitted to see it. Its Victorian decor blends beautifully with the instruments of the early part of the Twentieth Century, the Tiffany lampshades, and other assorted goodies that delight the hearts of antique fanciers.

Instruments from the factories of Seeburg, Regina, Cremona, Nelson-Wiggen, WurliTzer, and Schoenhut adorn this set of rooms, with a Cigar-Store Indian looking on carefully as if to suggest that inside part of this home surely there must be a place where John and Audrey are prepared to dispense the finest of the tabaconnists art!

Like most collectors of mechanical music or anything else, the owners are not satisfied to stop with what they have, and are always seeking more musical attractions. A large variety of other machines—band organs, calliopes, reproducing pianos, and the like—provide both entertainment and a means toward relaxation from a day's chores to the delight of all within listening distance of them in this beautiful Southern California residence.

Arcadia, California, is the home of the Jerry Doring collection, and like many others Jerry has been obliged to erect a special building to hold it all. Below we see a rare Peerless Arcadian Style "O" with extraordinarily beautiful art glass, next to a Cremona Orchestral "K" with the Victor dog "Nipper" poised to hear every note . . . not only of these two machines, but the adjoining WurliTzer Automatic Harp as well.

At left, Jerry works on an early Weber Otera orchestrion built in 1905. The top picture on the opposite page, left to right, features a Hupfeld Helios Keyboard Style IA, with a full complement of orchestral instruments inside. Adjoining it is an early Weber "Euterpe" orchestrion, operating entirely on air pressure, with no vacuum being involved. The Polyphon "Savoyard" Automaton features a young man who turns a crank while the music box inside plays, in the manner of an organ grinder making the rounds of the streets in Sunny Italy a century ago!

The lower picture opposite features once-again the omnipresent Seeburg Model G orchestrion, paired with its major competitor of an earlier business scene, the WurliTzer Style "C". Note the beautiful pipes in the art glass, the Aeolian harp at the center, and the rotating "Fascinator" or "Wonder Light" at the top of the instrument.

United Business Interiors of 1200 South Olive Street, Los Angeles, California, has as a part of its business activity what's known as the Heritage Museum, featuring a nice quantity of automatic music machines of all types—with a heavy emphasis on phonographs.

The three large instruments above are a WurliTzer Style 125 Military Band Organ, a Link 2E cabinet-style piano with xylophone and mandolin attachment, and a Seeburg "A" roll piano of doubtless early origin. A variety of small music-makers round out this scene of early-day Americana, although of course the Kalliope disc music box is of German manufacture.

On the opposite page we see the ubiquitous Mills Violano-Virtuoso flanked by a variety of early phonographs, notable among which is the coin-operated arcade model at the extreme right. The earliest versions of this had "listening tubes" for patrons of the establishment; this one was advanced technically to the point of having a horn so that many could listen at one time!

The large variety of phonographs in the other picture surrounding the Regina Music Box with its automatic disc-changer, make it apparent that a visit to this public establishment which is maintained by Gary Taplin should be a point of every automatic music enthusiast who finds himself in downtown Los Angeles. While it cannot be said that Southern California has a monopoly on fine collections of automatic musical instruments, it is a fact that a goodly percentage of the beautifully-restored examples of these types of devices have found their way to this part of the United States. Whether this is due to the general economic climate of the area, or the interest generated by such attractions as Disneyland and Knott's Berry Farm, or simply the stimulus of Hollywood is not clear . . . but the reasons matter not; the fact that these historic treasures are being preserved is what is important.

Frank Holland is the chap responsible for the development of the British Piano Museum at 368 High Street, Brentford, Middlesex, England—in the greater London area—and his hard work and perseverance have produced the fine grouping of instruments shown in the picture below. With the able assistance of Dora Brasher, he sees to it that all visitors are thoroughly indoctrinated in the history and lore of automatic pianos and related instruments during whatever time they choose to spend viewing the collection which, at the time these pictures were taken, was housed in an old church building.

From left to right, we see the Welte Philharmonic Reproducing Pipe Organ with 471 pipes in 10 ranks, two manuals, 27 note pedal klavier, all operated by a 120-note paper music roll,

Next to it is a Welte reproducing piano, using the "original" music rolls produced in Germany. Then an Imhof and Mukle Orchestrion, circa 1900, featuring piano, mandolin attachment, bass drum and cymbal, kettle drum, clarinet, piccolo, violin and bells, and with two fair organ figures added.

A Welte orchestrion, circa 1890, Serial No. 455, model 2/3, with bass drum and cymbal, kettle drum, triangle, and 3 ranks of pipes, next to which is an Aeolian Orchestrelle Model F.

Then we see a Weber "Brabo," with its massive piano, xylophone, and violin pipes (in corner with the mirrors) with an EMG Gramophone next. At the back of the room are the violin machines, featuring an American-built 2-violin Mills Violano-Virtuoso together with a single-violin model, and then a Hupfeld Phonoliszt-Violina with 3 violins and single roll unit.

In the front row, starting back at the left, we see a WurliTzer roll-changer unit from America, a Piano Melodico by Racca of Bologna operated by 73-note folding book music, and a Steinway-Welte grand— green paper model—once the property of the King's Physician.

The next grand piano is one of Mr. Holland's choice pieces. It's a Steinway Duo-Art grand which was once the property of the Princess Beatrice, the younger daughter of Queen Victoria.

Next is still another similar instrument, followed by an Erard-Ampico Model A grand, and then a Ronisch-Hupfeld Triphonola grand. In the foreground we see an Edison phonograph of 1908 with 5 'stethoscope' listening tubes, a Regina 19" musical box, a Musical Cabinetto from Boston, Massachusetts, and a reed organ which we are advised was by the American Orguinette Company, which was the forerunner of the giant Aeolian Corporation.

In the picture at the right, Mr. Holland delivers a lecture on the history of the instruments in the British Piano Museum to a group of visitors from the Musical Box Society International, as they stopped off during a tour of Europe in the Summer of 1971.

Still another attraction for musical-minded tourists is the collection owned by Paul Corin in the Cornwall region of England. The full address is St. Keyne Mill, St. Keyne Station, Liskeard, Cornwall, England, and its in the midst of one of the United Kingdom's most attractive and quaint areas. In the picture above a massive German Steinway-Welte reproducing piano is flanked by a magnificent Mortier dance-hall organ (note the accordian built into the facade), a Hooghuys fair organ, and a Welte orchestrion. Mr. Corin is very proud of the fact that this collection has been featured on numerous color television programs, both for popular consumption and for the educational networks—in England, the European Continent, and Australia as well. The rustic countryside of Cornwall is a splendid place for these historic treasures to be preserved, among buildings and sites whose background parallels the development of anglo-saxon civilization.

Stone Mountain, Georgia, at the foot of the famed granite monolith on which is carved Gutzon Borglum's famous monument to the Confederacy, is lucky to have Tom Protsman's museum to help entertain its many visitors. With the able assistance of John Bagley, they have assembled and restored a nice group of automatic instruments. Center picture, left to right: A 43-note Tangley air calliope, a 69-key Mortier dance-hall organ, and a very old WurliTzer Model 125 band organ. John reports having found a ticket "King Brothers Circus" (El Paso, Texas) dated 1904 in it! Lower picture: A Coinola "X" built in 1927 (and a real favorite of all enthusiasts for electric pianos), a Seeburg "Eagle" Model K, A Seeburg "G" orchestrion built in 1913, and a rare Seeburg Model "C" featuring a xylophone tucked inside.

Most operators of public museums find it desirable to remove the art-glass panels from the front of their exhibit pieces because the public enjoys seeing the "innards". From a purely economic point of view, a given instrument which is coin-operated will invariably take in several times as much money as one whose inner workings are hidden. Knowledgable owners will of course take good care of these beautiful examples of the glass-worker's art, however, and readers are assured that Mr. Protsman has the panels from these machines in careful safekeeping.

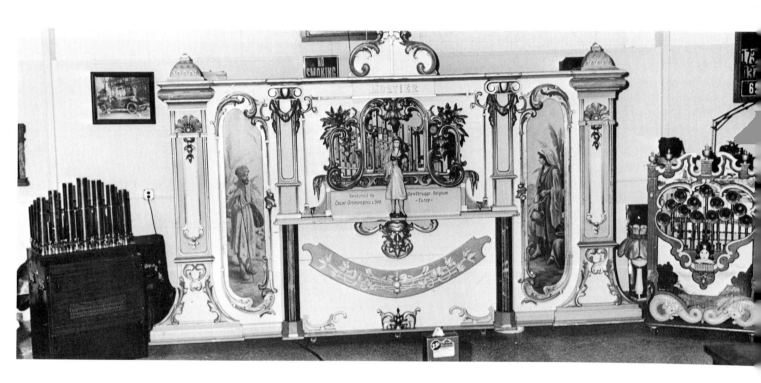

What a dandy display of musical merriment! Visitors to this Georgia house of goodies have a chance to hear a Cremona G, Seeburg E, Seeburg KT, a home-built orchestrion, a Nelson-Wiggen 4-X, a Polyphon disc-type music box, and a Pianolin in this room. Phonograph and art glass lamp-shade collectors can have their full share of enjoyment, too, what with several Coca-Cola and Tiffany lampshade and cylinder record players scattered about the premises. All these machines are of the Protsman collection.

When car fancier Walter Bellm of Highland, Illinois, tried to purchase an antique automobile from Bob and Herb Horn of Sarasota, Florida from their museum, they wouldn't sell. So Walt bought the whole place! At the time, music machines were a small part of the over-all activities there, but they so captivated Walt and his wife Ellen that they immediately took a great interest in them, and proceeded to scour the United States for fine examples which they might put on display. This was in the late 1960's.

The result is the mind-boggling array seen below and on the opposite page; a comprehensive collection of music makers which almost defies description! The activities surrounding the acquisition of this famous tourist attraction and the work on the collection were to absorb so much of the Bellm's time that they sold their trucking business in the Mid-West, in order to devote their full energies to the task and the pleasures and headaches that go with this type of activity.

Mr. Bellm is quite adamant in stating that for success as a place where tourists visit, one must not use the word "museum" as it connotes something in which most Americans tend to have little interest, and will therefore pass by. The Bellm collection is therefore known as an "attraction", a title applied to many commercial establishments in the business of entertaining tourists in the State of Florida.

Practically all the music machines on display are in good working order and, is if it isn't hard enough to believe what one sees on the usual tourist tour, there is in the warehouse another similar machine as "back-up" for almost every machine displayed! See if you can identify what you find in these pictures.

When Jerry Cohen of Studio City California visited Al Svoboda's Nickelodeon Tavern in Chicago Heights and was bitten by the "Automatic Music Bug" he really fell hard. Nothing would do but to build a collection of his own as soon as possible, and you see the outstanding results here.

Studio City is in the midst of what was once the movie capital of the World, which explains the presence of numerous posters from the era in which these machines were commonplace.

Jerry faced a unique problem in preparing to house this hoard. It seems that a local zoning ordinance prohibits construction of any out-building on a residential lot, with the exception that a swimming pool cabana is acceptable. But the ordinance doesn't state that the cabana can't be filled with music-makers instead of shower stalls, nor does it state any limits on size. We suspect that Jerry built the small pool merely to justify the more important poolside building!

The instrument on the opposite page with Mr. Cohen is a Weber Styria orchestrion; the picture below features a Link, a WurliTzer Violin-Piano, a Nelson Wiggen cabinet-style machine, and a Cremona Orchestral J. Above, left, is another view of the Link which careful observers may detect has a case not seen in Link literature. This is explained by the fact that when received by Jerry, the case was almost a total wreck so he had a duplicate built! Thus this piano is somewhat unique in the annals of Link history. The large machine at the right is a Hupfeld orchestrion, with a double tracker system permitting one roll to play while the other rewinds.

Mechanical music forms an important part of family life in the home of Dave and Mary Bowers in Beverly Hills, California. With a place large enough and with ceilings high enough to house practically anything but the largest fair organs, there is plenty—around to entertain the youngsters Wynn and Lee and have enough left over to please all the visitors who drop in. The beautiful Mason & Hamlin Ampico "B" reproducing piano above, shown entertaining Terry Hathaway in addition to the family, features a Louis XVI case and was built in 1930.

The Seeburg Style H below and at the right is one which for many years stood in the Cliff House in San Francisco. Its case has been professionally refinished and reworked to the point where it is doubtful if it looked as fine as this even when it left the factory some fifty years before this is written, and of course its art-glass is in magnificent shape.

The Weber Maesto, below and left, is seldom found in private homes because of its size, and one should perhaps say seldom found, period—because of their extreme rarity today. A similar one owned by Dr. George Coade is seen open, elsewhere in this chapter. This instrument is considered by many to be the oustanding example of the work of the orchestrion builders of a by-gone day, because it was built very late in the game, and every known device was incorporated to insure that it would resemble as closely as possible a human orchestra. To say that they succeeded well would be a gross understatement! Nothing can compare with the artistic renderings of the Maesto.

This very Seeburg "G" was the first instrument of its kind in the Bowers collection, and in a letter to the author he states ". . . I purchased it because I liked the sound of yours. For many years it entertained visitors to Valente's Tavern in Chicago, Illinois. Now it is in the guest room of our home in Beverly Hills. A copy of the same roll I first heard at your house—the one with "Japansy" as the second tune—is kept on it at all times so I can play it for visitors."

Mr. Bowers and Mr. Hathaway, pictured opposite, for several years ran a business in Santa Fe Springs, California, dealing in large quantities of just such automatic musical instruments as are pictured in this book.

Mr. Bowers is a prolific writer, and a frequent contributor to learned journals such as the Bulletin of the Musical Box Society, as well as being the author of several books in this and other fields. One of his notable contributions is the "Encyclopedia of Automatic Musical Instruments", a large seven-pound, 1,008-page tome dealing with almost everything there is to know about the history of this unusual aspect of human endeavor.

This magnificent WurliTzer Style 34A Mandolin Pianorchestra is owned by Terry Hathaway of Sante Fe Springs, California, and the opulence of its casework has been captured in a delightful manner by the expert camerawork of Dan Adams. Built by the European Philipps firm as their Model 11, it has 188 pipes, xylophone, piano with mandolin, chimes, bass and snare drums, kettle drum and cymbals, triangle, tambourine, and castanets. It's 10 feet 10 inches high, 9½ feet wide, 51 inches deep, and the catalog lists a shipping weight of a ton and a half!

The unlikely-looking pile of lumber and junk on the opposite page is actually a very fine style LX WurliTzer orchestrion, which Ed and Murray Clark of Clark's Trading Post, North Woodstock, New Hampshire, had to dismantle before it could be removed from the building in which they found it! Seldom do collectors have the good fortune to find an instrument in as nice condition as this one was, so it seems a shame that it had to be broken apart. But shortly after this picture was taken, it was glued back together, none the worse for the experience! Since then, it entertains hundreds of visitors every day during the Summer season at this outstanding White Mountain tourist attraction.

The rare Electrova at the left of the WurliTzer is part of the collection "found" by the writer in a Providence barn in 1957. After a fine restoration by Murray Clark, it now is just about as good as new.

The WurliTzer band organ on the back of the truck was also restored from junk, and now its raucous blasts entertain the tourists who stop at Clark's to witness their famous trained bear acts, see the outstanding kennel of Eskimo sled dogs, and to ride the train. Ed and Murray and their families have assembled a collection of one of each make of gear-driven steam logging locomotives built in the United States, and throughout the summer season, those who stop to see the bears perform are treated to a ride on this fine standard gauge railroad in an observation car towed behind one of these intriguing little pufferbellies.

The proud owner of the fine orchestrion above is Steve Radjenovich of Minneapolis, Minnesota, shown displaying a trophy awarded to him for his excellent exhibit at an antique show in that city. This machine is of European origin, and was originally built to play folding cardboard music. Mr. Radjenovich purchased it from the B.A.B. Organ Company of New York City, after this firm had converted it in such a manner as to be able to play paper music rolls as well as the cardboard.

Of particular interest is the volcano in the art glass on the front. When the machine is operating, an ingenious system of lighting behind the glass produces the effect of a continuous eruption of boiling lava and gases from the crater of the mountain!

The small band organ with which Steve is entertaining the children from the neighborhood of his Minnehaha Parkway home is one of the smaller WurliTzers. According to the WurliTzer catalog, this style is ". . . designed especially for Miniature Carouselles, Kiddie Swings, and other children's amusements. Just the size for a pit show . . ."

The collection of William Allen, Santa Ana, California. How many of these machines can you identify from the other pages in this book?

While collections have been built in recent years throughout the World, it seems as though California must hold some sort of record for such activity. A large number of machines have been located at Disneyland; three of them are shown here. Above, left, is a large WurliTzer Pianorchestra, while at the right is a Welte Orchestrion. Welte instruments are characteristically identified by the sunburst pattern of brass horns in the center section.

Electrova machines disappeared from the market in the teens, but officials of Disneyland managed to find one for display as shown at the left. This one is particularly interesting because of the attractive "folded" arrangement of the rank of flute pipes immediately behind the glass front.

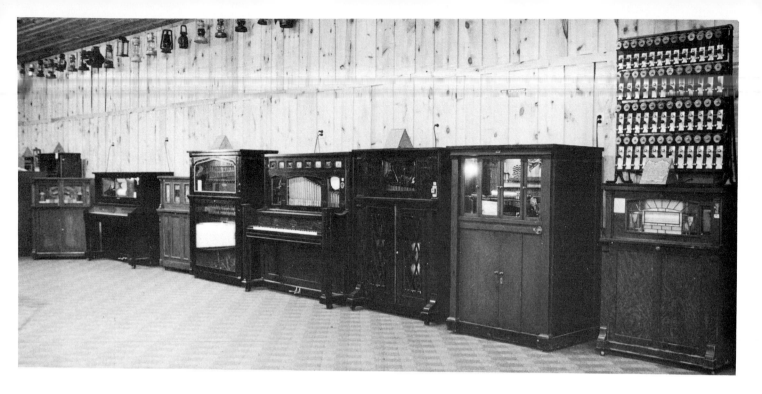

Manly, Iowa, is a tiny crossroads community near the Minnesota border, north of Mason City, of the type that one would normally zip right through were it not for the fine group of machines assembled by Tom Fretty who operates a reclaimed freight outlet as his main business. With the aid of Tom Wurdeman of Minneapolis who has done much of the restoration work, the Frettys are enabled to entertain not only midwesterners but thousands of tourists from all over who have heard of this interesting collection and who are prepared to go a few miles off the Interstate Highway to enjoy it.

Seven American manufacturers are represented in the picture above, taken by Ron Andersen of North Mankato, Minnesota . . . Seeburg, Operators Piano Company, WurliTzer, Link, Cremona, Mills, and Western Electric—the latter being the one under the Deagen Una-Fon which is an electric musical-chime device. Since Western Electric Piano Company was secretly a part of Seeburg, which wanted to stir up a little competition for what the management considered lethargy on the part of many of its dealers, the count of seven is correct!

Below is still another line-up of instruments with emphasis on European manufacture. Note the ever-present coin-slot, ready to accept quarters from those who wish to hear!

When Jake and Elizabeth DeBence were farming, they looked forward to an early retirement. When Jake turned 50, they sold their place and turned to a life of fun with automatic music! Today they have a museum of fascinating things from a by-gone day just south of Franklin, Pennsylvania; it's literally a barn jammed with all such goodies.

In the lower picture, at the right of a nice line-up of Tiffany lampshades, popcorn machines, and assorted electric pianos, is a Berry-Wood A-O-W like the one shown in color on the frontispiece of this book. At the upper right we see this instrument down to most of its bare essentials, undergoing a thorough restoration. If the curious musicians on our title page had had this opportunity, they wouldn't have been required to stand on their heads to see its innards!

At the right is a dandy Wellershaus fair organ. While maybe it doesn't seem appropriate to include such in a book about pianos, these automatic instruments certainly are a sort of relative if for no reason other than their common ability to process musical data in the form of punched holes in cards or paper.

Eureka Springs, Arkansas, is a community established on the sides of hills in the beautiful Ozark countryside of the northwest corner of this Southern state. Right on top of one of these small mountains is where Floyd and Martha Miles chose to set up their interesting collection of music-makers. While they are particularly interested in reed organs, there is nevertheless a large group of automatic pianos, worthy of a trip from quite a distance to see. The attractive building which houses them is a credit to this fine establishment of musical Americana has 5,000 square feet of floor space in which to exhibit the various aspects of the collection which includes a variety of non-musical items as well to entertain clock, button, and rock enthusiasts.

Below, Mr. Miles explains the operation of a fine Coinola-Style "X" orchestrion which features a complete "orchestra" in its lower section. This one has a set of metal bar bells, in place of the usually-found wooden xylophone directly behind the snare drum assembly seen at the lower right. These metal music-makers lend an air of distinction seldom found in any type of automatic piano; one might refer to this particular aspect of the instrument as an "automatic glockenspiel".

At the right, above, is a stunning array of small organs at the left, disc and cylinder type musical boxes at the center, and phonographs at the far wall.

The lower right page pictures a lineup of (from the right) a Coinola, a Mills Violano-Virtuoso, a Coinola X orchestrion, a Link, a Seeburg Mortuary organ, and a Cremona orchestrion. At the far end are a pair of piano players, as discussed in the first chapter of this volume.

The picture below shows a scene that is truly hard to believe unless one has witnessed it in person. But it's real, as the writer can testify, as he took the picture! Neal White of Troy, Ohio, stands engulfed in a sea of massive dance-hall organ facades of the European variety, in a building owned by him and Roy Haning. After having operated a highly-successful appliance business for a number of years, they retired to a life of fun with automatic instruments which they use not only for personal entertainment, but which they also buy and sell for business purposes. The orchestrion directly in front of Neal is a large one in itself, as such instruments go.

Page opposite, upper right, shows Roy in a happy mood over having just acquired a Nelson-Wiggen Banj-O-Grand, a rare find, while at left the partners are putting finishing restorative touches on a Coinola CO orchestrion owned by Bud Bronson of Dundee, Michigan. It is evident from the appearances of these two gentlemen that they throughly enjoy these musical endeavors!

When Bill Wasemann of Mansfield, Ohio looked a few years back for a reproducing piano to his liking, he just couldn't find one. So he proceeded to buy a brand-new seven-foot Steinway, construct a complete "pneumatic stack" from scratch to fit the instrument, and adapt various Ampico Model "B" components to fit within the confines of the case. (He had to settle for putting the vacuum pump in the adjacent garage).

As anyone familiar with these instruments can imagine, this was no small task, and it required a great deal of engineering know-how and skill. As Bill says, "When I went to cut the holes in the key-bed for the poppet wires, I didn't know whether I was creating a masterpiece or simply ruining a perfectly good Steinway!" The writer can attest to the fact that he did indeed create a masterpiece, as it's a glorious instrument to which to listen. Photos by the author.

Gay 90's Village

ON U. S. HIGHWAY 60 & 62 - SIKESTON, MISSOURI

One of Missouri's outstanding commercial tourist attractions is the Gay 90's Village at Sikeston, operated by Paul and Laura Eakins. They have been collecting and displaying their finds for a long time, and have achieved lots of nation-wide publicity—and justifiably so, one might add, for their restorations are always top-notch.

At the upper left is the two-violin Violano-Virtuoso, with the "Violano-Orchestra" box attachment which provides a rhythm accompaniment to the violin and piano. These are exceedingly rare; they require a special music roll.

Center, left, is a WurliTzer automatic harp undergoing restoration. Some 1400 of these were built in the 1905-10 period; only a handful remain today. Their music is much akin to that of a guitar, although with clever arrangements no doubt it could sound very much like a true harp.

Lower left, reading l to r we see a Seeburg KT Special, a Link, a single Violano-Virtuoso, and the completed harp. On the opposite page, starting at the top and going from left to right:

A Seeburg G, a WurliTzer Flute-Pianino, A Seeburg KT, and an exceedingly rare North Tonawanda "Sextrola" once owned by the writer. The latter has piano, mandolin, organ pipes of 2 kinds and a 12-note glockenspiel. The name suggests the bawdy-house market, but probably is intended to mean "six instruments."

Center picture: The Hupfeld Phonoliszt-Violina with three violins, an early WurliTzer band organ played from a wooden cylinder, a Style 148 WurliTzer military band organ which approximates a 7-to-10 piece band, and an early barber chair with a set of individualized shaving mugs.

At bottom, a WurliTzer orchestrion, a Tangley air-operated calliope, a rare 3-disc Symphonion music box, an Artizan pressure-operated band organ, and a fine small "monkey-organ" operated by a 7-tune pinned wooden cylinder.

While it's not really a collection in the normal sense of the word, the establishment operated by John Farnsworth at Marion Center, Pennsylvania certainly needs a place in this book because so many artistic treasures are salvaged there. It's really a rebuilding factory, where Mr. Farnsworth and a crew of skilled technicians and apprentices rebuild straight pianos and reproducing pianos to almost unbelievable states of perfection!

In the Victorian-styled showroom below we see two Steinway Duo-Arts in the foreground, and an Ivers and Pond straight grand at the center rear. At rear, center, is a beautifully-restored Aeolian Orchestrelle—an elaborate reed organ of a type promoted aggressively half a century ago.

The picture above shows John Farnsworth in his apartment, where a beautifully-cased very-early model Chickering Ampico lends its attractiveness to the Victorian decor which abounds throughout the living quarters and showrooms.

It's always a treat to know of the work by an outstanding technician, and Ron Wehmeir of Cincinnati is one of these. The Louis XV Ampico at the upper left, and the Steinway Duo-Art at the right together with the WurliTzer theatre pipe organ at whose bench he's seated, are outstanding examples of magnificent restoration work by this skilled man.

The Wehmeir home is beautifully decorated in the best Victorian tradition, which makes all the more pleasing the setting for these fine instruments.

2,000 miles to the West, on the banks of the St. Joe River in Idaho's Northern panhandle area of magnificent mountains and streams, is the Golden 20's Museum owned by John and Stella Ragan. When they retired from their lifetime pursuits in Wisconsin, they established this fine hunting and fishing camp near the town of St. Maries and proceeded to fill one building with instruments collected over a period of many years back East. What finer way to enjoy one's retirement years than with such an ideal set-up for outdoor life and indoor music?

View of the Mekanisk Museum at the corner of Vesterbrogade and Platanvej in the heart of Copenhagen.

The Mekanisk Musik Museum in Copenhagen, Denmark, opened in 1972 by Claes O. Friberg and Q. David Bowers, attracted World-Wide attention within weeks of its establishment.

Europeans, unlike Americans, tend to seek out such places for visits during holidays and vacations, apparently as a result of their inherent interest in the history of their region of the World. Since the influence of European technicians and inventors in the field of mechanical music is so outstanding, there is little doubt that this museum will be a continuing success in its efforts to relive the heritage of the past.

Located in downtown Copenhagen not far from the famed Tivoli Gardens, it's a natural spot for attracting visitors from far and wide.

Odds and Ends

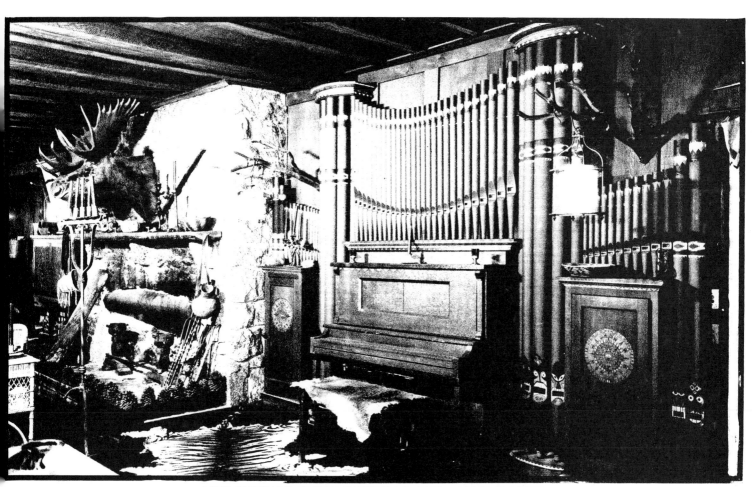

THE KING OF INSTRUMENTS IN THE WOOLLY WEST

Lover of the unusual, Cecil B. De Mille has a Wurlitzer in his mansionesque Paradise Ranch, Little Tejunga Canon, Los Angeles County, California. From the Sierra Madre Mountains, the Wurlitzer tone rolls forth, accompanied by glockenspiel, xylophone, cathedral chimes, harp, bells, kettle drums, and cymbals.

This book is supposed to be on the history of the mechanical piano, and for the most part it is. But in the process of gathering material for a scrapbook style of presentation, a lot of things turn up which, while they don't necessarily fit into an historical development, just seem too interesting to leave out. Some of these things in this assortment of odds and ends of course are directly concerned with player pianos, but are mainly of interest to the person who finds a certain fascination in the intricate mechanical details.

Other things shown here, like the ad for whiskey at $3.20 for four quarts, express charges paid, are merely to bring back thoughts of the "good old days." On second thought, maybe it's just as well that it isn't that cheap anymore!

And then the few pictures of calliopes and band organs are thrown in to whet the appetites of those collectors who are particularly interested in this sort of thing. There's another reason, too. Books are printed in multiples of sixteen pages, and stuff like this helps make sure that the publisher gets something in black and white on all the pages he has to pay for whether he uses them or not!

Direct from Distiller
to Consumer

$3.20 EXPRESS PAID.

Saving Middlemen's Profits,
Preventing Possibility of Adulteration.

We are distillers with a wide reputation of 30 years standing. Our whole enormous product is sold to consumers direct. We sell direct so that our whiskey may be pure when it reaches you. For medicinal purposes adulterated whiskey is dangerous. For sideboard purposes it is abominable, yet it is almost impossible to get pure whiskey from dealers. We have tens of thousands of customers who never buy elsewhere. A customer who once tries our whiskey is a customer always. We want more of them, and we make the following offer to get them:

We will send four full quart bottles of **Hayner's Seven Year Old Double Copper Distilled Rye for $3.20, Express Prepaid.** We ship in plain packages— no marks to indicate contents (which will avoid possible comment). When you get it and test it, if it isn't satisfactory return it at our expense and we will return your $3.20. Such whiskey can not be purchased elsewhere for less than $5.00.

We are the only distillers selling to consumers direct. Others who claim to be are dealers, buying and selling. Our whiskey has our reputation behind it.

References—Dun or Bradstreet or any bank or business house in Dayton.

HAYNER DISTILLING CO., 254 to 260 W. Fifth St., Dayton, O.

284

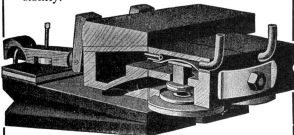

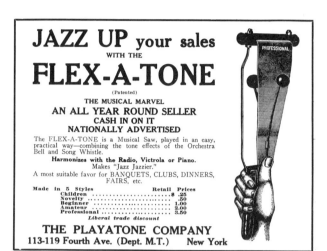
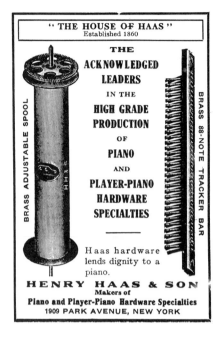

The picture above shows a grand piano fitted with the Aeolian Pianola attachment which was introduced to the market in 1950.

March 27, 1926

PANATROPE SAILS THROUGH SKY TO REACH CORSICANA QUICKLY

Reese & Sons, Texas Firm, Make Use of Newest Method of Transportation to Get Brunswick Instrument

CORSICANA, TEX., March 22.—When the first shipment of Panatropes arrived at the Dallas Brunswick branch, Reese & Sons of Corsicana became impatient to have one of the new instruments. Scorning the con-

Mr. Reese of Reese & Sons Congratulating Pilot Pedley on His Speed in Bringing a New Brunswick Panatrope from Dallas to Corsicana for Demonstration

ventional means of transportation, they arranged with Pilot Charles Pedley, popular aviator of that vicinity, to fly to Dallas and pick up the instrument.

In addition to the speed of delivery, the novelty of a musical instrument being delivered via air resulted in some front page publicity in Corsicana.

After getting away to so good a start in their promotional work on the Panatrope, Reese & Sons followed the lead with public demonstrations and other plans. Sales to date amply repaid this progressive dealer for the effort expended.

DIFFICULTIES OF PIANO TUNING IN FLORIDA

Amusing Experiences of a Tuner Among The Negro Clients—Rats and Mice Damage Pianos

By B. F. BIANCHI   November 27, 1926

PIANO tuning has its humorous side, especially among the Negroes of Florida, where rats and mice do a tremendous amount of damage to musical instruments. The following very interesting account of the life of a piano tuner in Florida appeared in the "Standard Player Monthly," house magazine of the Standard Pneumatic Action Co., New York. It is published herewith because the contents are certain to interest tuners in other States where conditions are markedly different from those in this section of the South.

The Florida Negroes live in little settlements by themselves a mile or so back from the towns and villages on little streets and alleys that are mostly stretches of sand without sidewalks or paving of any kind. Some of their houses are tumbledown shacks and some of them stand in neat yards and are well painted and preserved.

About nine out of ten of the Negro women are agents for some form of hair straightening treatment and have little signs above their front doors stating that they apply the "Poro" or some other systems. I don't know whether they make any money at it or not, but whenever one wants to find the "Lady" of the house and she doesn't answer a knock at the front door it is only necessary to go around the house to the backyard where the occupant can usually be found bending over a tub of clothes busily engaged in doing her "White folks washin'." I was amused one day when I went around back of a house to solicit a tuning to see a small colored urchin of about seven years of age doing a Charleston in a tub of dirty clothes. That was a happy way of getting the dirt out I suppose.

The Negroes have everything in the way of pianos from old squares to the nickel in the slot electrics. It is the height of their ambition to possess an electric piano as there is no work attached to them. Merely insert a roll and turn the button and the piano runs indefinitely. If they are too lazy to get up and insert a new roll it doesn't worry them, for as long as they have some music it doesn't make any difference what the quality. A few years ago they almost all had organs and a tuner had to know how to repair organs as well as to fix up balky sewing machines once in a while.

Rats and mice are very common in the Negro quarters and the Negroes as a rule don't seem to care much for cats, although about every family has a dirty mangy dog hanging around.

One day I started to tune a piano for a Negro and when I removed the front board, two mice ran out and ran around the room, chased very gleefully by a couple of kids who were hanging around watching operations. I sent one of them out to the store for some Rough on Rats which I put on some bread and left inside the piano and hope that it has disposed of the mice.

I asked an old colored woman one day if she would like to have her piano fixed up, and she said, "De rats done got my pianner all et up." I said, "Let's look at it" and on removing the bottom board saw an enormous rat hole in the bottom of the piano. Going out into the street I picked up an old auto license tag and bringing it in, nailed it over the hole in the piano and told the old lady that I guessed the rats couldn't get in that hole again. She was greatly pleased and paid me $3.00 without a murmur.

Damage by Mice, Costly

The mice usually have all the bridle straps inside the piano eaten off and a nice little nest at the side of the keys, filled with paper, rags, and chicken bones. One old woman told me the other day that a white gentleman charged her $36.00 last year to fix up her piano and all that I could see that he had done was to put in a home-made set of bridle straps, a job which isn't worth over $3.00 at the most.

Another woman told me that a man had guaranteed to tune her piano for $5.00, had gotten the money and fooled around the piano a few minutes and then had put all the chairs in the house up against the piano and warned her not to touch them until he came back, as it would "Sturb de tunin'"—"An' dat man never did come back."

Some of the local tuners have the pleasant custom of filling the interiors of the pianos with paris green, which is a green powder and lies all over the inside of the piano, and the next tuner who comes along is liable to get it in his eyes or in a cut or sore, and as it is a deadly poison it isn't very pleasant. I imagine it is put in to kill roaches or mice.

The one great trouble with Florida pianos is in sticking actions due to the damp climate. Press down a dozen keys in the extreme treble or bass and they don't come back. In cases of this sort we remove the action and go to the nearest filling station and get a quart of gasoline. The action is then taken into the yard and the gasoline poured all over it except for the hammers. After standing in the sun for an hour or so, the gasoline evaporates and the action dries and won't stick again for a year or so. We always get $2.00 extra for this job.

I was working on a player a while ago in which a row of the keys stuck and I couldn't seem to loosen them in any way. I knew it wasn't in the action, as it was loose throughout. I at last had to take the player action out and back of the player action and over and in between the keys was about a quart of rubber elastics, all rotted and hard. It seems that a couple of years ago there was a tuner working through that part of Florida and not knowing of the gasoline treatment for the sticking actions, had the

bright idea of pulling the hammers back with rubber elastics. They worked fine, until he got out of town and, of course, in time rotted away and fell down between the keys and clogged them up, making them much worse than they were originally. Unslaked lime is often used with good effect to keep the dampness out of pianos, being placed in the bottom of the piano in an open box and in the course of a year, will have absorbed so much moisture that it will have swelled to twice its bulk.

A colored woman whom I met a while ago, told me that she had "A 'lectric piano" and when I asked her how much she paid for it, she said, $900.00, so some of them have some very good instruments and taking it all in all, tuning among the colored folks is always interesting, and as the old song goes, "We don't make much money but we have a lot of fun."

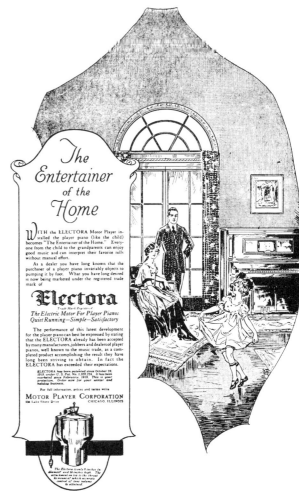
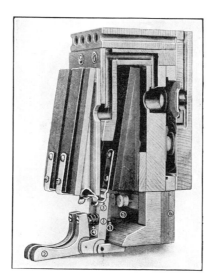

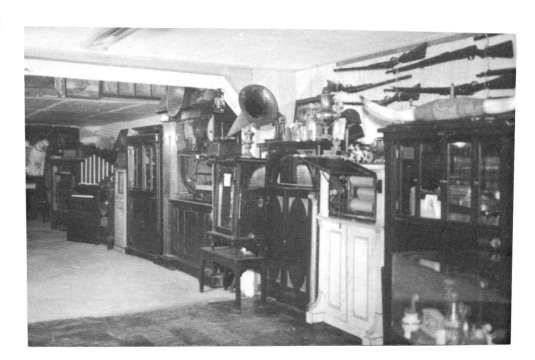

The Chuck Wagon Cafe and Musical Museum, operated by Bob and Gladys Nelson at Atoka, Oklahoma.

MUSIC ROLL MANUFACTURING FACILITY
HAROLD L. POWELL ASSOCIATES
North Hollywood, California 91601

Tracking master roll with Number 1 perforator and computer readout. Electrostatic cleaner left of console.

Side view of coring process pulling each roll from rack at the right. Paper rack, stock and trimmings are in the background.

Closeup of coring operation showing back of electronic computer master readout equipment.

Checking humidity and temperature at the paper rack. Electronic computer readout is at the right.

After copies are checked against master roll, any missing holes are put in with single hole punch. Note water cooled driver unit.

Labels, tempo and end tabs are added to Welte Piano Rolls.

Spool end is cemented into core of Duo-Art Music Rolls.

"A" style Nickelodeon Rolls being labeled.

An order being filled from Ampico stock.

Filling order in the "Welte Room." ➤

COUNT LEO TOLSTOI LISTENING TO THE WELTE-MIGNON AUTOGRAPH PIANO

289

THE ELECTRIC PIANO PLAYER.

ITS DEVELOPMENT AND CONSTRUCTION.

BY JOHN F. KELLY, PH.D.

THE wonderful results obtained by the great masters of the art of piano playing ordinarily serve to disguise from us the simplicity of the means employed. This mechanical simplicity at an early date directed the attention of mechanicians toward seeking a substitute for the pianist's fingers. When a piano key is struck its hammer is thrown against the corresponding string, from which it immediately rebounds part way, and in this intermediate position it is caught and held until the key is released. The depression of the key simultaneously lifts the damper from the string. Both hammer and damper are therefore clear of the string while it is sounding. Nothing can be done to the key before the hammer is thrown, or after it is thrown and before the damper is returned, that can at all alter the tone produced. In any given instrument the pianist controls manually only the velocity with which the hammer strikes the string, and the return of the damper. The ordinary pedals add no new feature; they merely add to the ease of control. The wonderful art of piano playing is therefore built up by varying two simple elements.

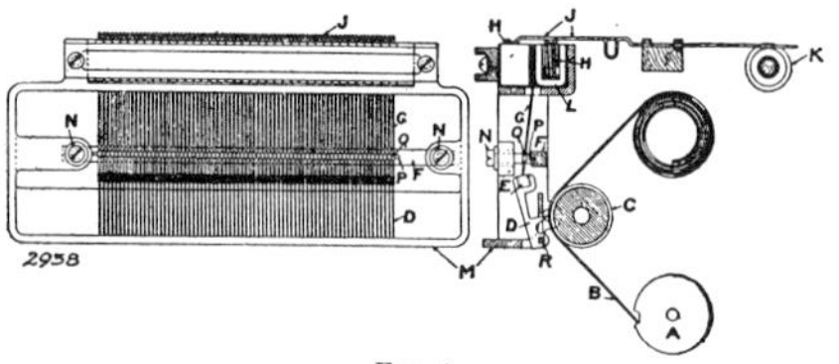

FIG. 1.

A, music-tape case; B, music tape; C, tracker roll; D, reading finger; E, ivory insulating block; F, contact bar; G, contact wire; H, resistance coil; J, comb wire; K, terminal; L, resistance coil frame; M, cradle casting; N, adjusting screws for contact bar; P, platinum strip and contact bar; Q, platinum bands on contact wires; R, swivel rod for reading fingers.

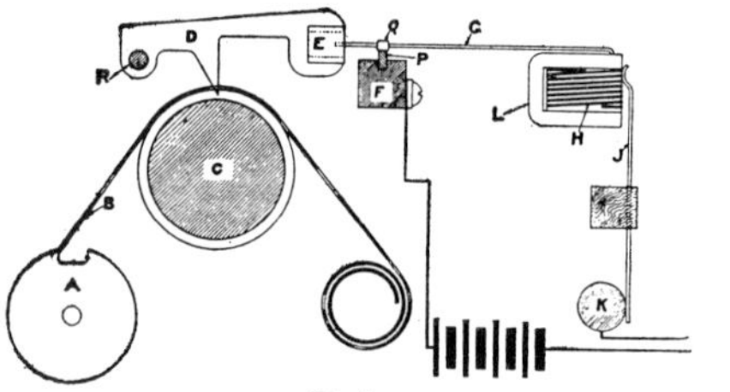

FIG. 3.

A, music-tape case; B, music tape; C, tracker roll; D, reading finger; E, ivory insulating block; F, contact bar; G, contact wire; H, resistance wire; J, comb wire; K, terminal; L, resistance coil frame; P, platinum strip in contact bar; Q, platinum band on contact wire; R, swivel rod for reading finger.

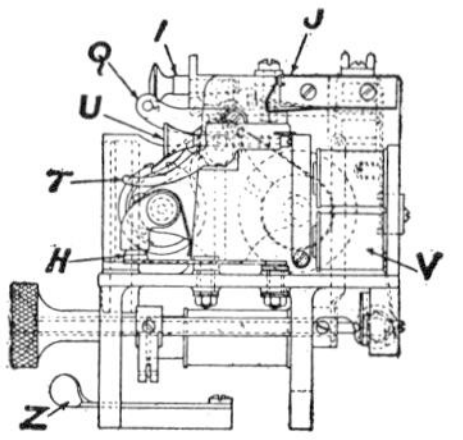

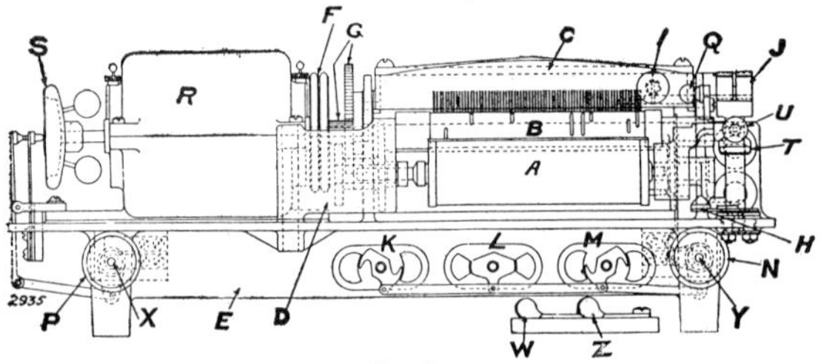

FIG. 2.

A, music-tape case; B, music tape; C, cradle; D, swinging carriage; E, base; F, rubber belt drive; G, gears; H, starting switch; I, expression cut-out knob; J, trip switch; K, forte expression magnet; L, medium forte expression magnet; M, piano expression magnet; N, expression handle; P, tempo handle; Q, carriage latch; R, motor; S, governor; T, lifting lever; U, trip button; V, trip magnet; W, bass subduing switch; X, sustaining pedal button; Y, soft pedal button; Z, treble subduing switch.

Froment appears to have attacked the problem as early as 1850, but the author has not been able to obtain any accurate account of this work. In 1861 a patent for an electric player was taken out in Würtemberg by Andre. In 1867 the celebrated mechanician Hipp exhibited an electrically operated piano which is worthy of some attention. It may be considered as the foundation of the work of the present day, and, indeed, in some respects it is in advance of much of the subsequent work. The Hipp apparatus consisted of two parts, a transmitter and a receiver. The latter consisted of a series of electro-magnets with armatures pivoted so as to swing toward and across the poles, and having the armatures connected by wooden rods with the jacks of the piano action. The transmitter employed a roll of perforated cardboard or cloth, similar apparently to the music rolls now so familiar, which was drawn by means of clockwork from one wooden roller to another. On its course it passed over a metallic roller and under a comb consisting of wires properly spaced and held in an insulating frame. The roller and the wires of the comb formed terminals of electric circuits including the magnets in the piano. The method of action is obvious. It is necessary to add that expression was controlled by the insertion of resistances in the common return. That he chose a type of magnet whose action could be modified in this manner is one of the evidences of Hipp's knowledge and careful work.

Another Swiss, Spiess, exhibited an electric player in Paris in the following year, 1868. So far as the description goes, this player seems to be substantially the same as Hipp's. We are more fortunate, however, in that we possess a contemporary statement as to the results obtained. The clearness and distinctness in rapid passages are the subject of special praise. It may be of interest to add that Hipp operated with ten Bunsen cells, and Spiess with thirty-six Daniell cells. To a considerable extent Hipp and Spiess must be regarded as being too far in advance of their time. The lack of a cheap supply of electric energy and the relatively small number of pianos in use would have precluded commercial success in any event.

At much about the same time as Hipp and Spiess, Prof. J. B. Webb and Mr. Oberlin Smith were at work on the problem in America. They sought to replace the perforated tape by one having the notes printed in metallic ink, and they tried also a conducting tape with the notes printed in insulating ink. Other work proved more attractive to both inventors, and they abandoned the piano player in an unfinished condition.

In the late seventies and early eighties William F. and Henry Schmoele of Philadelphia took out a number of patents relating to piano players. One of the patents described a music roll with the notes printed in metallic ink. The Schmoeles, who had on the whole a very clear idea of what a piano player ought to do, seem to have been deterred from the use of a straight electric action by the cost and unreliability of the supply of electricity at that time. They fell back on an electro-pneumatic action similar to that employed in playing organs from a distance, or, to compare their apparatus with what has now become more familiar, it resembled the present-day pneumatic action with the primary pneumatic replaced by an electric action.

At the Electrical Exposition of 1881 in Paris, Carpentier, the well-known instrument maker, exhibited a piano-playing apparatus which he called a repeating melograph. The name melograph had already been applied to an instrument exhibited in Vienna in 1873 designed to record piano playing. The complete Carpentier instrument was intended to cut a record of a composition played at the keyboard in the ordinary manner, and then to use this record as the music roll in the reproducer. In reproduction, which alone concerns us, Carpentier introduced a new idea. A shaft revolving at a fixed speed was placed under the keyboard. A number of brake shoes, corresponding to the keys to be operated and linked to them, were placed contiguous to the shaft, and pivoted so that a slight motion would apply them to it. When so applied the friction developed would pull down the piano keys w[illegible] force dependent on the speed of the shaft. The magnets controlled by the music roll, instead of operating the piano action, had only to throw the brake shoes against the rotating shaft. In this way it became possible to use smaller magnets and to economize in the use of electric energy, but unfortunately at the cost of losing control of expression.

Some dozen or more years later Carpentier's scheme was taken up by an American inventor, Mr. G. H. Davis, and embodied in a commercial machine. In the machine as now constructed Carpentier's cylindrical shaft has been replaced by one in the shape of the frustum of a cone with small apical angle. The chief improvement, however, is the addition of a hinged three-piece, soft-pedal bar, controlled by three levers. By means of this, expression may be imparted manually to music which, as controlled by the music sheet alone, would be perfectly flat.

Most inventors, however, have preferred to follow in the line marked out by Hipp. It has been shown that Hipp inserted resistance in the circuit with a view to varying the strength of the magnets, and so the intensity of the blow of the hammers. Although Du Moncel described Hipp as obtaining in this manner a satisfactory range from *forte* to *piano*, a little consideration will disclose an essential weakness in the scheme; any given resistance introduced into the main circuit will have an effect the greater the more magnets in circuit, a very undesirable result. Yet it was not until some thirty years later that it was shown that the true method is to insert a separate resistance in each branch circuit. Before condemning too severely the electrical inventors occupied with piano players for their slowness in discovering this point, it might be well to take into consideration that an analogous fault still exists in some of the pneumatic players of to-day.

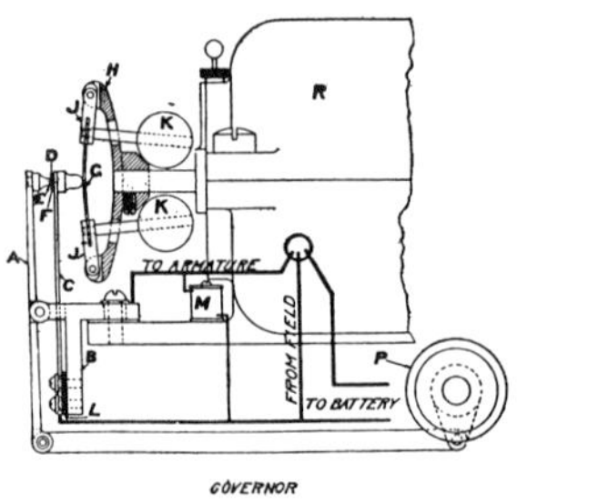

FIG. 4.

contact arm; B, governor bracket; C, follow spring; D, point of break; E, platinum point on contact arm; F, platinum point on follow spring; G, governor spring; H, governor disk; J, hinges for governor spring; K, governor balls; L, insulation block; M, shunt coil; P, tempo handle; R, motor.

In order, however, that insertion of resistance may give effective control of the magnetic pull, and hence of the touch on the piano keys, it is necessary that the magnets should be peculiarly constructed. It is necessary that the attractive force should be near its maximum when the armature first begins to pull on the piano action. When a magnet is employed in which the attraction on the armature rapidly increases as the armature moves toward the poles, it is practically impossible to control the movement by the control of the current. In such a case the current that is required to start the armature from its initial position suffices for a violent blow at the end of the path. Hipp perceived this, but it was overlooked by many of his successors.

Those who have had experience with pneumatic players know that one of the most serious difficulties with such instruments is the susceptibility of the paper music roll to atmospheric conditions. Naturally the same trouble is encountered when a paper roll is used in an electric player, and there are some new troubles. The fact that the paper is pulled between a wire comb and a rotating cylinder, instead of being drawn over a smooth tracker board, does not make for better tracking. And again, if the electric pressure be high, there is a tendency to burn the paper where it acts as a circuit breaker; while if it be low there may easily be uncertainty as to contacts.

In a series of patents running from 1901 to 1904 T. B. Powers, partly in collaboration with M. R. Jewell, has shown a player combination designed to overcome these difficulties. Powers's direct contributions are more important than those of any of his American predecessors, and he has also shown great talent in his utilization of the elements he took over from the prior act. His most important improvements are the substitution of thin metal tape for paper in the music roll, and the introduction of individual resistance coils in the branch circuits.

In 1905 the author acquired the Powers patents and organized the Telelectric Company to manufacture a player in accordance with them. Naturally in the course of manufacture many improvements in detail have been introduced, and some of great importance. It would be useless and wearisome to point all these out, but it will be of interest to describe the players now made, directing particular attention only to such changes as materially modify the musical results.

The apparatus in general plan recalls that of Hipp. The use of a metallic instead of a non-conducting roll has necessarily led, however, to a material change in the construction of the comb. In this instrument each of the elements of the comb consists of two parts—a reading finger proper, and insulated from this a wire acting as a contact maker. The contact is made with a separate contact bar instead of with the tracker roll as in the Hipp apparatus. These elements, and a corresponding set of small resistance coils, are, in the standard sixty-five-note apparatus, set in a special frame, which, from its being pivoted in front to allow of a rocking motion, is usually called the cradle. The cradle is shown in Fig. 1, and its relation to the rest of the machine in the general view, Fig. 2. In Fig. 3 the construction and relation of the reading finger *D*, with its contact wire *G*, to the contact bar *F* and the resistance coil *H* are clearly indicated. The ivory block *E* serves to insulate the reading finger from the wire. It will be clear also from this figure that the metal music tape *B*, when unperforated, will lift the reading finger *D*, and so break the connection between the contact wire and the bar *F*. The wire *J* is one of a set forming a second comb serving to maintain connection between the resistance coils and the cable terminal *K*. When the cradle is rocked upward the resistance coil is raised, and, as an inspection of the figure will show, resistance is introduced into each circuit. This rocking of the cradle may be effected either automatically by means of the magnets shown at *K*, *L*, and *M* in Fig. 2, or manually by means of the handle shown at *N* in the same figure.

The winding and unwinding of the tape constituting the music roll are accomplished by means of an electric motor *R* provided with a governor *S*, Fig. 2. The transmission from the motor to the winding and rewinding rolls is through a pair of rubber belts and a set of gear wheels. The lifting of the tracker roller into place by means of the lever *T*, Fig. 2, puts the winding gear in mesh, while the lowering of the same roller shifts to the rewinding gear. This shift may be effected by pressing the button *U*, but ordinarily it is effected automatically at the end of the selection by means of the trip magnet *V*, Fig. 2. At the end of the music tape an opening is cut which allows a special reading finger to close the circuit of this trip magnet, thus dropping the tracker roller and shifting the gear.

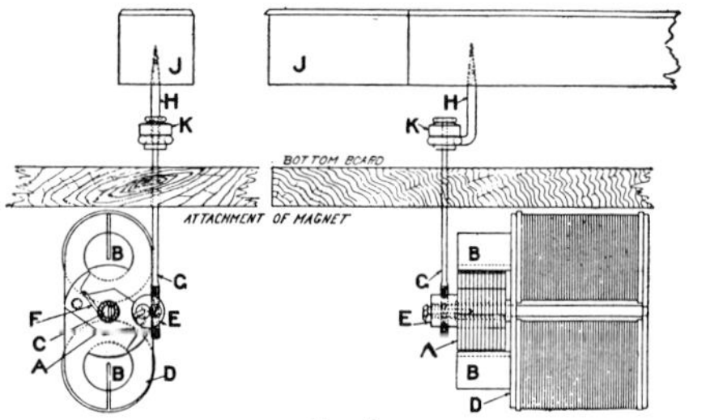

FIG. 5.

A, armature; B, poles; C, armature shaft; D, brass yoke; E, swivel; F, armature return spring; G, pull down wire; H, screw eye; J, piano key; K, rubber buffer.

* Paper read at a meeting of the Franklin Institute.

With this instrument a governor must be provided. Not only must this maintain a steady speed, but it must maintain steady any speed the operator may choose. The simple make-and-break ball governor shown in Fig. 4 accomplishes this remarkably well. [illegible] contact arm H by means of the handle P, Fig. 1. This simple and absolute control is of special value in accompaniments. Because of it, it becomes easy for any singer to accompany himself.

Fig. 5 shows two views of one of the actuating magnets and the means of attaching the armature to the piano key. It will be observed that the rotary armature is so shaped and set with reference to the poles as to insure a strong initial attraction, which, as before pointed out, is necessary in [illegible]er that the touch on the piano keys may be effectively controlled by varying the current in the magnet winding. A small screw eye is put into the key, the connection between this and the armature being made by means of a flexible steel wire. The eye of the screw carries a small rubber cushion to prevent any clicking from being developed by the wire striking against the screw. It will be observed that this method of connecting leaves the keys entirely free at all times, so that for instance, one may play a duet with the electric apparatus as a partner.

Magnets similar to the key magnets, but larger, are used [illegible]r operating the pedal bars. These magnets are controlled by perforations made at suitable points in the music tape, or they may be operated at will by the

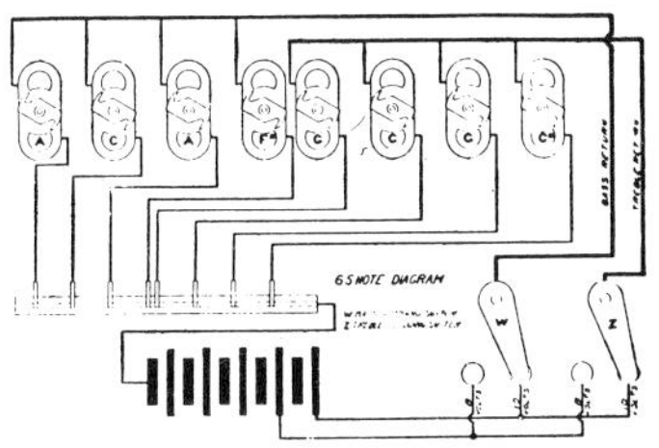

FIG. 6.

W, bass subduing switch; Z, treble subduing switch.

buttons *X* and *Y*, shown at the centers of the handles *P* and *N* in Fig. 2.

The music tape is a brass ribbon 5 inches wide and 0.003 inch thick. The perforations for the notes are arranged in a similar manner to those on the paper rolls, but on a much smaller scale. The brass is only one-third as long as the paper for the same music. That the same proportion is not exactly preserved in width is due to the fact that the brass tapes carry other perforations than those corresponding to the notes. Perforations, as stated already, are provided for controlling the action of the pedals, for varying the resistance in the circuit, and for shifting to the rewinding gear at the end of the selection.

The cutting of each selection is so arranged that the tempo of any selection will be normal for a fixed motor speed. This applies even to what may be called the normal variations from the standard tempo of the selection. Such variations are incorporated in the cutting. Variations in tempo to suit special tastes may be readily introduced by turning the handle *P*, Fig. 2, righ[illegible] [illegible] may be required.

Apart from the variation in tempo, the means of obtaining expression so far described consist in the variable touch on the piano keys obtained by the use of variable resistance and the use of the pedals.

It will be evident from this description, therefore, that two distinct purposes have been kept in view in the building of the Telelectric player. On the one hand the attempt has been to build a machine which, when left to itself, will reproduce with perfect accuracy the music as written by the composer and with the proper interpretation. From this standpoint the music rolls are cut, carefully avoiding all "adaptations" to make it easier for the player, and all the peculiarities of interpretation of this or that virtuoso. For steady use and to meet the general cultivated taste, standard

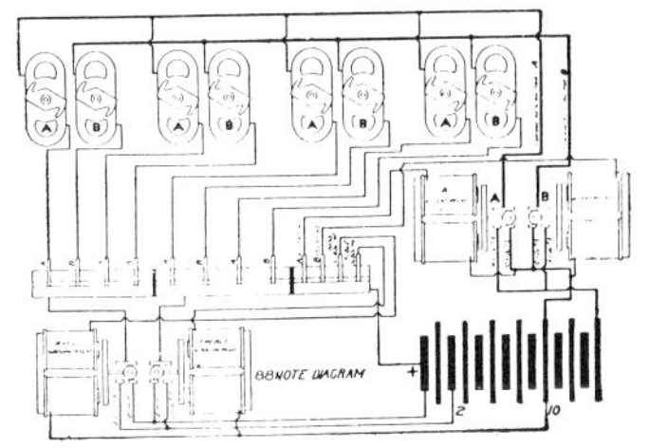

FIG. 7.

normal music is best, and music so cut forms the best basis for those who wish by manual control to obtain a personal interpretation. On the other hand, keeping in view this desire for a specialized or individualized interpretation, the instrument is provided with extremely simple means by which anyone with special tastes may vary the expression to suit himself.

Still further control of expression is of course desirable. In many cases a much improved effect is produced by playing bass and treble at different degrees of force. This is accomplished in a simple manner by dividing the magnets into two groups, so that two different electromotive forces may be simultaneously used. The electromotive forces may be varied by means of the switches *W* and *Z* in Figs. 2 and 6. This improvement is incorporated in all the sixty-five-note standard players. If the author were to use the language of the piano-player advertising agent, he would describe this change as causing the accenting of individual notes and as bringing out the melody. This language is far too strong, and, like all exaggerated language, it is not only harmful in its direct untruth but it leaves one without terms to describe further [illegible] Of course when the notes are thus divided into two groups all notes occurring simultaneously in either group are struck with equal force.

The musical advantage of a distinct individual accent is so great, however, that for two years the author has largely devoted his efforts to securing it, with the results that are shown in the eighty-eight-note player, Fig. 7. The simplest way to get an individual accent would be to practically duplicate the tape, using different electromotive forces on the parts. Imagine the music tape as made up of two parallel longitudinal bands, corresponding to a divided contact bar with a permanently maintained difference in potential. Imagine also the reading fingers, rheostats, and other accessories duplicated in each section, i. e., one wire from each section for each magnet and piano key. Then it will be clear that a note would be accented or not according to which section carried the corresponding perforation. Unfortunately the system calls for music rolls nearly twice the width required for non-accenting rolls, greatly increases the cost of the rolls, and is otherwise clumsy.

To keep the roll within reasonable dimensions, and at the same time obtain the requisite control over the force of the blow supplied to different keys, was the subject of much thought. The author became satisfied that some system of grouping the notes must be used, and worked out several plans for the control of the groups. These plans, with the exception of that now being introduced into practice, it is unnecessary to describe. As to the grouping, the first idea that presented itself was, instead of simply dividing the scale into bass and treble, to cut it up into numerous sections. It would thus be possible to confine the accent within a narrow section. Unfortunately, until the section is reduced to the compass of but a single note it is always possible that it may contain a note which it would be undesirable to acccent. Indeed, the narrower the section the more important it is that it should not contain a second accented note. The next idea that presented itself was to include in each group only notes of the same name: C's in one group, C-sharps in another, and so on to the end of the scale. This is very much more satisfactory. Even if two notes should happen to be [illegible] in one group, it would occur sometimes, so that both might catch the accent, as the two are consonant, the effect would be substantially that of accenting the single note. Indeed, with the old-fashioned player the accenting of a note can often be simulated by cutting its octave to sound with it. The author thought it desirable, however, to go further than this, and on this octave grouping he superimposed the division into bass and treble. In consequence of this double grouping it is possible to obtain four different strengths of blow on the piano keys simultaneously. This capability, added to the power of control over expression already described, ought to satisfy the most exacting requirements.

The arrangements for carrying out this method are clearly shown in the diagram, Fig. 7. The key-operating magnets are from one end of the circuit divided into two groups, and from the other end into twelve. The source of electromotive force has four terminals, ordinary 0, 2, 10, and 14 volts. Switches are so arranged that the wires leading to the magnets on the one side may be connected either to the 0 or the 2-volt terminal, and on the other to either the 10 or the 14. These changes are independent of each other. It is therefore possible to supply any magnet with 8, 10, 12, or 14 volts at will. The switches are operated by quick-acting electro-magnets, and these, in turn, are controlled either by special perforations in the music-roll, or at will by the operator through specially provided buttons. At the will of the operator, also, any one or more of the means of expression may be left music-roll-controlled while he manually controls the rest. He may pick out that portion of the expression in which he feels he can best express his individuality, leaving the rest of the machine, or he may take entire control and make the expression entirely his own.

A word as to the future. It would seem that the idea is still prevalent that a piano player must be necessarily inartistic. Logically, those who hold this idea should condemn the piano also, for piano playing is but mechanicalized harp playing. In all arts and crafts alike there is, and always will be, a place for hand work. Pioneer work falls to the hand, and in the arts especially there is a peculiar grace arising from the flexibility of the instrument. But power, [illegible] machine. The grace of the harp, and the fact that it allows of a more highly individualized playing, have in no wise prevented the more mechanical piano from becoming a hundred times more common, and the favorite instrument of great artists. And while, as in passing from the harp to the piano, so in passing from the simple piano to the piano and player, there may be in some respects a loss, it would seem that for this loss there is a more than equivalent compensation; in speaking of compensation the author has in mind not only that thousands are reached by the player who otherwise would be deprived of all good music, but also that to some extent there are direct artistic compensations. While the piano mechanism restricted the performer in some directions as compared with that of the harp, in others it opened out to him a wider field. And the player in turn will again widen the field. The composer will no longer have to think of the limitations of ten fingers on two hands. Consider what this may mean in transcriptions of orchestral music, or, if we have the daring, let us even dream of what it may mean in original piano music. There is another reason why our ultra-artistic piano lovers should take a more generous attitude toward the player. The growth of the piano trade, if it did not actually hinder the making of harps, at least did nothing to advance that art. The piano-playing business, on the other hand, tends to enormously increase the number of pianos in use, and each of these pianos should be recognized as the possible means of development of a future artist. And surely the struggling musician will be none the less likely to develop into an artist because he has at his disposal a machine which will make it possible for him to hear the great music of the world. As well might we say that it would be harmful to a young painter to be placed in possession of a set of photographs of the world's masterpieces in painting.

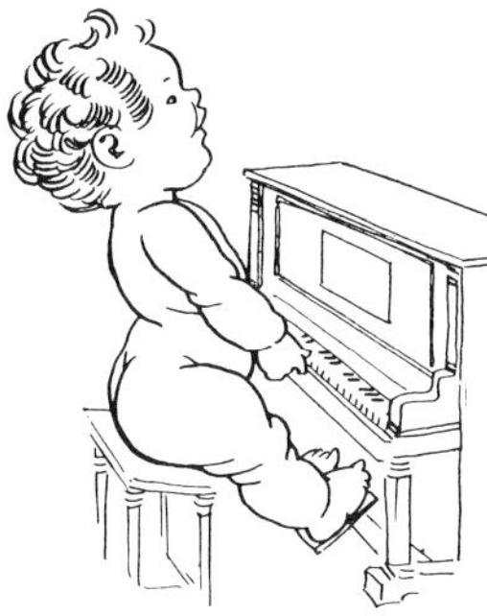

Ode to a Playerpiano

There's a joy that's found each day, with a Player
home to play,
You can scarcely find a greater recompense.
When from work you come home, weary, music always makes you cheery
And the pleasure to be gained is—well—
IMMENSE!

If that "straight" piano's soundless and your thirst for music boundless,
Why not make a change and get one that will PLAY.
Then—ah then, a home of gladness, where it once was silent sadness,
And you'll see th' old-time grouches fade away.

When the children's practice closes, Grandma wakens from her doses
Plays, herself, the old-time themes she loves so well,
Mother has *HER* sunshine hour—Father has a "Music Shower,"
Be it jazz or sentimental wedding bell.

There's no need to fret and pine (tho' you may not read a line)
Of the music that is written on the page.
For the roll brings syncopation, when you have that inclination,
It's the biggest joy-producer of the AGE.

Theo. T. Levy.

The New York House of the Regina Music Box Co.

THE establishment occupied by the Regina Music Box Co. at the junction of Broadway, Fifth avenue and 22nd street, is undoubtedly, one of the busiest centers in this great Metropolis. Located in the very heart of the shopping district, and attractive by reason of its admirably ar-

EXTERIOR OF THE REGINA WAREROOMS.

ranged display of instruments of various styles and prices, it catches the eye of passers by, and no matter what hour of the day the Regina warerooms are passed there is sure to be a goodly number of people outside and inside admiring the magnificent exhibit of music boxes. The cuts herewith furnish an excellent idea of the appearance of the exterior and interior of this vast establishment whose products are known the length and breath of the land.

The beginning of the holiday season finds a tremendous influx of retail business at the new Regina warerooms. On the main floor, where the largest and most costly instruments are on exhibition, recitals are constantly in progress. In the well-lighted basement, too, purchasers of smaller musical boxes are always to be seen.

Their expressions of pleasure and astonishment are frequent, and orders, ofttimes for orchestral instruments, are freely given. The Regina Corona, representing maximum results so far achieved, finds many purchasers.

The Review, during a visit to the warerooms on Monday, found opportunity for

a short talk with Mr. Tietz, of the Regina Music Box Co. Asked to state his views concerning present conditions and future prospects he said: "Results thus far obtained at these new warerooms prove conclusively the wisdom of the move made. The number of interested visitors is increasing from week to week, and the percentage of purchasers is gradually growing larger.

"The volume of business at the factory at present is simply tremendous. It is taxing all our resources. Our work throughout the States and foreign countries, as you know, is done through wholesale agents. Orders are pouring in from every one of these agents. You might naturally suppose that the call would be, to a great extent, on the smaller and less costly styles. It is not so. Thousands of the smaller boxes are now being sold for Christmas presents. They are always in demand, too, for birthday and wedding presents. But the largest and most elaborate are being ordered from all points, in addition to our orders here."

"Do you include the new 'Regina Corona' in your statement concerning large instruments, Mr. Tietz?"

"Yes. Of course, the intricacy of the mechanism makes it more costly, but that does not hinder its sale. At this moment there are more than 300 orders on our books for Coronas. They are all required—

urgently called for—to fill orders for Christmas presents. We shall do our best, but you can readily understand that the call is too heavy for a prompt response."

"What has been your experience, so far, Mr. Tietz, with the mechanism of the Corona—does it give much trouble?"

"I am glad to say not. Frankly, I was nervous about it at first, thinking that the efforts of purchasers to adjust the discs and so on would lead to complications, but events have proved that there's no need for anxiety. Out of the large number already made and sold, only three or four have been heard from, except in letters of enthusiastic praise. In each instance a simple re-adjustment was needed owing to careless following of instructions. The mechanism itself has proved to be absolutely reliable."

"Are you ready to speak concerning the Regina program for the coming year?"

"There is not much to tell at present in that connection, except that we have decided to introduce the Corona mechanism into the next smaller styles. Some examples will be ready early in 1899."

"Are you at liberty to make any statement concerning the output of Regina products during 1898?"

"It is too early, as yet, to say much under that heading. I can tell you, however, in a general way, that the business of the current year will not be far from the half-million dollar mark."

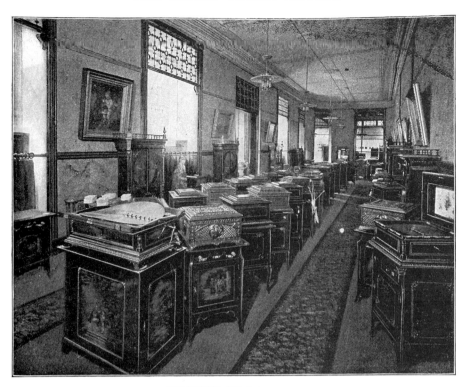

THE REGINA WAREROOMS.

REGINA CORONA, Nos. 8 and 8a, with Automatic Tune-changing Device.

No. 8, for Parlor use ; No. 8a, with Slot Attachment ; Long-running Movement ; two large Combs, with 172 Tongues, tuned in chromatic scale, embracing over seven octaves ; Case in Oak or Mahogany ; Dimensions, 72x39x24 inches ; Dimensions of Tune Sheets, 27 inches diameter.

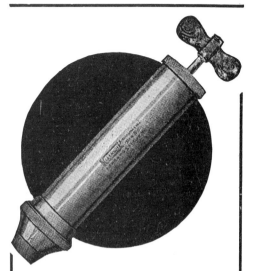

294

The DEAGAN UNA-FON

has brass band volume to attract the crowd
—and quality of tone to hold it

The DEAGAN UNA-FON is a sturdy, compact, portable musical instrument—easy to play, from electrical keyboard. It is fool-proof and trouble-proof, and is the only musical instrument made rugged enough to stand up under road use day after day.

USES—The Una-Fon is adapted for use in any enterprise which depends for its success on its power to attract and entertain the public. The following are only a few of the ways in which the Deagan Una-Fon is used: Street Advertising, Political Campaigns, Carnivals, Ballyhoos, Tent Shows, Pavilions, Skating Rinks, Merry-Go-Rounds, Amusement Parks, Cabarets, Parades, Lobby Concerts, Pit Attractions, Band and Orchestra Auxiliary, Land Sales, Auctions, Chautauquas, Lectures, Missions, Outings, Boats and Fairs.

TONE—In Clarion-like brilliancy, rousing and ringing quality the Una-Fon has no equal. It draws and holds the crowd. It couples volume and richness of tone with a peculiarly exhilarating quality that is irresistible.

VOLUME—In volume and carrying power the Una-Fon is without a peer—a feature that, in street work, makes it audible many blocks away. On the water its remarkably clear, brilliant tone carries great distances. Both sizes are now equipped with Octave Couplers.

TUNING—The Una-Fon is tuned minutely accurate and is the only instrument made that will remain in tune always. It is not affected by atmospheric conditions. It can be used in any weather, the actions being fully protected.

KEYBOARD—The electrical keyboard furnished with the Una-Fon is identical in appearance and arrangement of keys, with the keyboard of an organ or piano. It is attached to the Una-Fon with a ten foot flexible cable and Deagan patented terminal.

MAINTENANCE COST—With storage battery we furnish, the current cost is only two or three cents per hour. We can supply a motor generator for operating Una-Fon from regular lighting circuit alternating current, 60 cycle, 110 volts for $100.00 net. If Generator is wanted instead of Battery add $75.00 to price of Una-Fon. Cost of electric current about same as with battery. Weight of Generator 60 pounds.

J. C. Deagan *Inc.*
Established 1880

DEAGAN BUILDING
RAVENSWOOD AND BERTEAU AVES.
CHICAGO

No. 433 Deagan Una-Fon
33 Units. E to C. 2¾ Octaves Chromatic, with Octave Couplers. Complete with keyboard and storage battery. Ready to play when unboxed.
Price $375.00

No. 449 Deagan Una-Fon
49 Units. C to C. 4 Octaves Chromatic, with Octave Couplers. Complete with keyboard and storage battery. Ready to play when unboxed.
Price $500.00

OPERATION OF THE PNEUMATIC PLAYER ACTION

Refer to Illustration "D"

The first operation necessary in getting ready to play the pneumatic player action is to insert a music roll in the spool box, thus sealing all holes in the tracker bar so that no outside air may enter. If the instrument is electrically operated, we now turn on the switch starting the electric motor and the pneumatic pump is put into operation. The function of the pump is to reduce the pressure within the action and create what is termed a vacuum. With the tracker bar closed by the music roll, as at "BB", we have a vacuum in the action and tube right up to the tracker bar. There is a small bleed or vent which is set in a small channel connecting vacuum chamber "AA" to the tube leading to the tracker bar. This vent is about one-sixth the size of the hole in the tracker bar and it is very important in the operation of the pneumatic action.

At point "DD" is seen the valve down upon its seat and outside air passing over the top of the valve and down into striker pneumatic "EE".

Now to play a note on the piano, we must cause the striker pneumatic "EE" to collapse. This is done by a hole in the music roll exposing a hole in the tracker bar "B" which allows the outside air to rush into the tube leading down to the bleed and the underside of the thin leather pouch "C". Outside air is admitted in such quantity to the tube at point "B" that the small bleed at the front of low pressure chamber "A" cannot reduce it quickly, and the air pressure in the tube and under the thin leather pouch is raised nearer to the outside atmospheric pressure. We now have a low air pressure above it. As explained on page 11, atmosphere will always try to equalize itself in space, so the thin leather pouch "C" is now raised to a convex position by high pressure trying to equalize with the low pressure above. As the pouch assumes a convex shape, it raises the valve "D" to its top seat, thereby cutting off outside air to striker pneumatic "E". The air within pneumatic "E" is now connected to low pressure chamber "A" and it also rushes to equalize in pressure. This operation allows the outside air to get in its work on the movable leaf of striker pneumatic "E", causing it to raise and hit the piano action wippen and the hammer to hit the string.

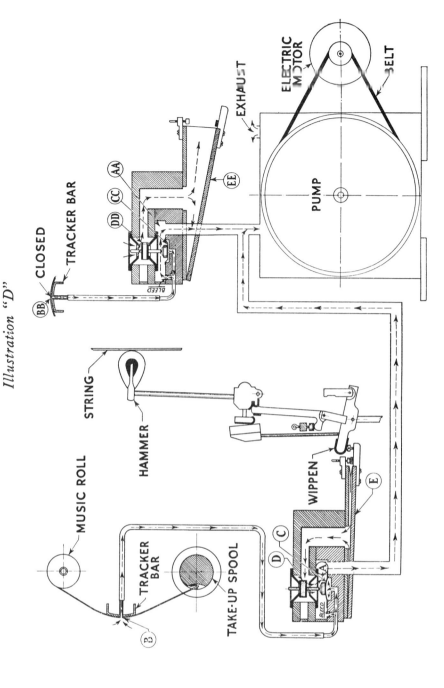

OPERATION OF PNEUMATIC PLAYER OPERATION

DIAGRAM OF PNEUMATIC PLAYER OPERATION

Illustration "D"

ELECTRIC MOTOR

BELT

EXHAUST

PUMP

TRACKER BAR

CLOSED

AA

CC

DD

EE

BB

BLEED

STRING

HAMMER

MUSIC ROLL

TRACKER BAR

TAKE-UP SPOOL

WIPPEN

B

D

C

E

A

BLEED

SIMPLEX Perfects a
Completely Assembled ACTION
Ready for Immediate Installing

NOTE—
The white circles show location of 8 attaching screws, 2 in each.

Musically, this new SIMPLEX Artistyle is a perfect Reproducer, enchanting to hear

THE music loving world has been waiting for this truly great invention. Now, by featuring and pushing it you can do MORE BUSINESS and make GREATER PROFITS! The leading and exclusive features of SIMPLEX ARTISTYLE are:

1. Completely assembled as a unit at the factory and *ready* to place in Piano.

2. Installation and Testing can be done 80% faster than the Foot Player type.

3. Only *8 screws* necessary in the fastening process.

4. There are 150 less pieces for the Installer to handle.

5. Does not require an expert to install and adjust.

6. Guarantees an Upright Reproducer at a price much below that of many Foot Players.

7. A Reproducer that is absolutely foolproof and trouble-proof.

8. The artistic, musical capabilities are unlimited.

Send for further illustrations and details to

SIMPLEX PLAYER ACTION CO., Worcester, Massachusetts
THEODORE F. BROWN, President

Top →
Tuning Pins →
West Plank →
Back Brace →
Iron Frame →
Steel Wire Strings →
Music Roll Bearing →
Felt Hammer →
Tracker Box Sliding Panel →
Automatic Tracking Device →
Tracker Ports or Openings →
Sustaining Pedal Valve Lever →
Take-up Spool →
Tracker Tubing →
Sustaining Pedal Lever →
Treble Soft Lever →
Bass Soft Lever →
Hinged Lever Cover →
Valve →
Vacuum Chest →
Adjustable Striking Pitman →
Key Lever →
Key Balance Rail →
Striking Pneumatic →
Pedal Opening Door →
Reservoir →
Feeder Bellows →
Foot Pedal →

298

An expectant and excited group of passengers hurried aboard a train in Worcester, Mass. on the afternoon of July 4, 1856. The train was a holiday excursion bound for Fitchburg, Mass. The excitement was unusual even for a holiday because the trip was to feature a demonstration of the American Steam Piano Company's steam calliope. The huge instrument was mounted on wheels and attached to the rear of the train. Passengers settled in their seats and waited eagerly for the first notes. At 3 o'clock a young girl pressed down a key, releasing a jet of steam that gushed forth through a whistle and resounded off the distant hills. It was the first note of "Old Dan Tucker," and on its signal, the train began its journey. Throughout the journey the steam calliope rendered traditional favorites, its booming voice echoing through the New England countryside. Farmers and shop workers dropped their tools and came running to hear. It was a successful excursion, and marked the birth of an instrument that has thrilled and entertained Americans of all ages.

But perhaps the most thrilled of all was the calliope's inventor, Joshua C. Stoddard. His invention was a success and the girl who played the calliope on the trip was his 7-year-old daughter, Jennie. But in a short time his invention became the source of unhappiness to him. His parents were ashamed of the machine their son had built because they considered it useless and Worcester soon banned its playing within the city limits because of excessive noise. In later years, although calliopes could he found throughout the U.S., Stoddard did not earn any money from them.

Joshua C. Stoddard was born on his father's farm in Pawlet, Vt., on August 26, 1814. His father sent him to Paw-let Academy for formal schooling and trained him in farming at home. Joshua became interested in bees that his father raised on the farm, and soon became an enthusiastic beekeeper, a vocation that he worked at all his life.

It was while working on his father's farm that young Stoddard heard a train whistle for the first time. Every time he heard a train approach he would listen attentively for the whistle. He soon noticed that different whistles produced different tones. To the inquisitive youth this was fascinating, and later served as the basis for his idea for a steam calliope.

Young Stoddard lived with his parents until January 23, 1845, when he married Lucy Maria Hersey and moved to Worcester. The Stoddards lived in Worcester for 40 years and had 6 children; 5 boys and a girl. Stoddard made his money from an apiary while devoting his spare time to various inventions. His first successful invention was the calliope, which he completed a few years after his marriage. The first instrument consisted of 15 whistles, of graduated sizes, attached in a row to the top of a small steam boiler. A long cylinder with pins of different shapes driven into it ran the length of the boiler. The pins were so arranged that when the cylinder revolved, they pressed the valves and blew the whistles in proper sequence. The different shapes enabled the operator to play notes of varying length. Later, Stod-dard replaced the cylinder with a keyboard version. Wires running from the keys to the valves enabled the operator to play the instrument like a piano.

The first showing of the calliope—a keyboard version—took place on July 4, 1855 on Worcester Common. While Stoddard stoked the wood fire to maintain the pressure, his daughter Jennie played such tunes as "Yankee Doodle" and "Columbia, the Gem of the Ocean." The showing was a success, and Stoddard had his instrument patented in October of the same year.

Stoddard founded the American Steam Piano Company with financial backing from Worcester industrialists. Although the calliope enjoyed enthusiastic reception from the public, Stoddard was inept in handling the business. Soon, one of the company's financial backers, Henry A. Deny, began to take control from Stoddard. Within 5 years after the founding of the company, Stoddard was removed and Deny became president. Deny not only headed the company, but claimed the invention as his own.

Under Deny, the company prospered. Steam calliopes became popular on river steamships, in fairs, parades, amusement parks and circuses all over the country. Air-operated models are still found in circuses today, besides having become standard equipment on carousels.

After he had lost control of his company, Stoddard returned to farming and beekeeping. Still inventive, he patented a successful hay rake in 1870 and a fire-escape in 1884. In 1901 he invented a fruit-paring machine, but it was not successful. He died on April 4, 1902 in Springfield, Mass, bereft of reward—save the satisfaction of accomplishment from his idea of making harmony in steam.

ESSO OILWAYS FOR SEPTEMBER 1956

Geo. D. Sweet Stock Company, Season 1927

Emphasizing the Theme in a Player Piano

THE first successful mechanical piano players had no sooner made their appearance than there was an immediate demand, at least on the part of those who [possessed the so-called musical ear], for some means of playing the solo, melody, or theme with a stronger emphasis than the accompaniment. Most of us who own or have owned piano players (and this is particularly true in cases where the operator had never learned to play by hand) will remember how the first delight at hearing a musical composition being played directly under one's own control, was quickly followed by a desire to subdue the accompaniment and bring out with clearer emphasis the theme or melody. The inability, in the early players, to emphasize the theme was due to the fact that a uniform tension was used for all the operating pneumatics throughout the scale.

There is probably no element in the player that has been made the subject of so much patient investigation and clever invention as that of theme or solo expression, and, during the past decade, some very ingenious devices have been tried out and placed upon the market with more or less gratifying results.

Broadly speaking, there are four classes of theme-expression devices. In one of the earliest of these, an attempt is made to emphasize the theme by dividing the scale into sections, in each of which the tension of the player-pneumatics is regulated by their own control valves. In this type, the operator endeavors to throw increased tension into that particular section or zone in which the theme notes occur. The obvious defect of the arrangement is that not only the theme notes in any particular section will be emphasized, but also such notes of the accompaniment as also happen to lie in that section.

Another type of player is provided with two separate sets of pneumatic actions, each operated by its own tracker-bar range; one being used for the melody and the other for the accompaniment notes. If this were carried out literally, there would be a call for a tracker-bar with 88 melody notes and 88 notes for the accompaniment; but the difficulty of having a bar and music roll of this length led to the adoption of a bar containing only about 120 apertures.

One of the best known and most successful melody playing pianos secures the desired effect by cutting the perforations in the music roll so that the accompaniment notes are struck first under the normal air tension, and then the air tension is increased in the slight interval before the melody note is struck. The admission of the high tension before the sounding of the melody note is done automatically by means of perforations on the edge of the music sheet.

It will be noticed in the three systems above mentioned that the emphasizing of the melody is accomplished through automatic means for increasing the air tension under which the melody notes are struck.

In the player piano illustrated in the accompanying drawings, the novel features of which have been patented by Mr. Paul Brown Klugh, of Chicago, Ill., the accentuation of the theme or solo is accomplished by controlling the length of stroke of the hammers. The way in which this is done will be understood by a study of the drawings in which the player mechanism is shown in a light tint and the solo mechanism in a darker tint.

The solo action is arranged in the upper portion of the piano case and extends throughout the full length of the hammer scale. Back of the hammers is arranged a series of adjustable hammer stops, there being a stop to each adjoining pair of hammers. The position of these stops, that is to say the distance between them and the piano strings, is governed by the action of the solo pneumatics P, P' and a series of springs A, A'. When the operator is pumping, the solo pneumatics are normally inflated, as shown at P, and the springs A and the hammer stops a are in the positions shown in the drawing. When a solo note is to be struck, the pneumatic is deflated, as shown at P'; the corresponding spring is sprung back into the position A' and the hammer stop to which spring is connected is thrown back into the position of full stroke, as shown at a'. The effect of this arrangement is that the hammers corresponding to the accompaniment notes travel, relatively, a short distance before they strike the strings, and the whole accompaniment is played with soft tonal effects; but the hammers which sound the theme or solo notes, traveling through a greater distance, strike their respective strings with greater force and with much louder resulting tone.

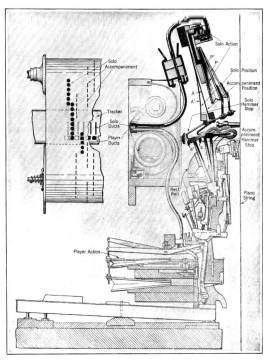

Mechanism for intensifying the theme in a player piano

The operation of the solo action is controlled automatically through the music sheet and tracker bar. The tracker bar is provided with the usual apertures, spaced to register with the note perforations of any standard music sheet. The tracker bar is also provided with apertures in the shape of narrow slots, one [above the end of each player aperture as shown]. The [large player ducts are apertures open into a series of] tubes which lead down to the player action, and the slotted solo ducts are connected to tubes which lead up to the solo action.

The music sheet differs from the standard music sheet by having note perforations which differ from each other, and as the sheet travels over the tracker bar certain note perforations (those for the accompaniment) register only with the large player ducts and others (those for the solo) being wider, register with both player and solo ducts.

Now as the music sheet travels over the tracker, each accompaniment perforation will pass to the side of the slotted solo apertures in the tracker and will pass over the regular player or accompaniment apertures, and each of the solo perforations will pass over both the slotted solo and the regular player or accompaniment apertures; but when the solo perforations pass over their respective solo apertures in the tracker, they will deflate their respective pneumatics, throwing the respective hammer stops back, and, by increasing the length of stroke of the hammers, will cause said solo notes to be struck with greater force and with resulting louder tonal effects.

Furthermore, in addition to this automatic selection and emphasizing of the solo, the tonal power of the notes may be varied by varying the vigor of the pumping and thus changing the air-pressure in the player action. Again the degree to which the solo notes are emphasized may be varied by varying relatively the short-stroke and long-stroke positions of the hammers.

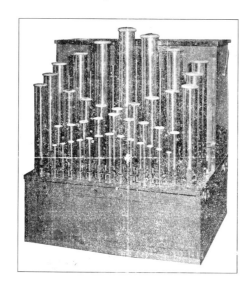

Automatic Military Band

With Motor Truck

Style No. 1110   82 Keys

18 Music Selections

For Circuses and Advertising Purposes

DESCRIPTION

Body, 13 ft. 8 in. long and 6 ft. 9 in. wide, inside.

Double doors in the rear, and ventilated top.

Ornamented with wood carvings and pillars and carvings on side and rear panels.

The end and side panels are hinged at the bottom, and lean outward 6 in. from the top, in order to allow the music to be heard and to protect the instrument during damp weather.

The side panels are easily removed during fair weather, leaving an opening on each side uncovering the front. To protect the instrument, in case of emergency, canvas roll curtains are placed at the top of the instrument ready to be drawn down in case of sudden rain.

The panels, rear doors and sides and also curtains are ornamented with oil paintings.

Permanent blind work in lower panels to allow ventilation, but exclude dampness.

Top of body is finished with scroll work, among which may be placed hexagon signs which revolve, showing 6 signs one every 30 seconds, on the rear end and both sides and lighted by electric lights.

The signs and the lights in signs are run by an electric motor which receives its power from a storage battery placed in strong boxes situated behind the instrument just inside rear doors, and covered with cushions, making them comfortable seats for attendants.

The chassis is a three-ton truck and has single tires in front and dual tires in the rear.

The chassis is supplied with a cab seat, a mica front curtain and side curtains, and regular standard equipment, including headlight with Presto tank, and is sold under regular guarantee of the motor truck company.

The wheels of the chassis are equipped with sunbursts which are covered with gold leaf, the same as are the carvings and columns on the body.

The body and chassis may be painted any color purchaser desires.

Signs and side panels of body lettered in gold.

Automatic Military Band—Continued

With Motor Truck

Description of Instrumentation

INSTRUMENTS, VISIBLE—8 heavy brass trombones; 23 brass trumpets; 18 brass clarionettes; 14 brass piccolos; 28 flageolets; 14 stopped pipes; 18 violin pipes; bass and snare drums and cymbal.

INSTRUMENTS, INSIDE—16 violoncellos; 11 violin pipes in accompaniment; 18 stopped pipes; 29 open pipes.

INSTRUMENTS, BOTTOM—8 contra basses; 37 stopped pipes.

STOPS—1 for trombones; 1 for trumpets; 1 for clarionettes; 1 for piccolos; 1 for violin pipes.

CASE—Quartered white oak, piano finish; mahogany, walnut or rosewood stain; richly and heavily carved, gilded engraved scroll work, or finished in white enamel paint and handsomely decorated in variety of colors.

82 notes, operated by endless perforated paper, in either single-piece or three-piece rolls. 18 single-piece rolls, or 6 three-piece rolls of music included in price of outfit.

In order to have the instrument the same on both sides, we have one side filled with mute instruments, but the openings inside the chassis are free, so that the music is heard on either side practically the same.

Price of this outfit furnished on application.

Patented, February 11, 1908; May 26, 1908; June 9, 1908.

Motors

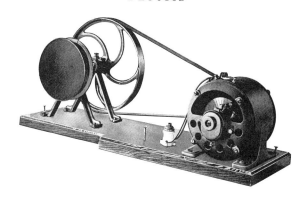

When desired, we furnish either Electric, Water or Gasoline Motor, or Gasoline Engine of different h. p. and types, fitted upon a platform with countershaft, pulleys, belting, oilcups, wiring and electric connections, or piping, etc., complete, ready for attaching at platform. Prices furnished upon application. For electric service, state whether you have direct of alternating current. If D. C., give the voltage. If A. C., give the voltage and cycles. For water service, state the pressure, size and length of pipe from the street to main.

A beautiful display of automatic musical wonders at the Musee de Musiques, operated by Baud Freres in L'Auberson, Switzerland, near the French border close to Geneva. A marvelous display of artifacts from the Swiss music box industry is part of this delightful exhibit.

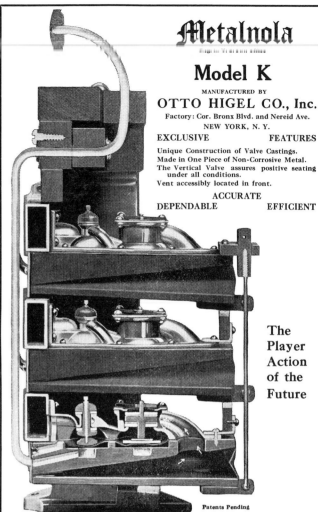

The Danquard Player Action School Completes Course in Memphis and Later Opens in Dallas

Group of Tuners and Piano Technicians at Memphis Session of Danquard
Player Action School

THE second visit of the Danquard School in its present southern itinerary was to the city of Memphis. There a number of tuners were found eager to take up the free course of instruction offered by the school in player and reproducer regulation and adjustment.

Most of the men who registered attended both afternoon and evening sessions, and studied hard for the three weeks the school was in the city.

The school was held in the Hotel Gayoso. Those who attended expressed themselves as deeply grateful to the Standard Pneumatic Action Co. and the Auto Pneumatic Action Co. for the opportunities afforded to learn more about foot power players and the Welte-Mignon (Licensee) reproducing action.

From Memphis the school moved to Little Rock, Ark., at the Hotel Marion.

On March 8 it opened in Dallas, Tex., at the Hotel Adolphus, and dealers in and about Texas sent their salesmen and tuners to the school.

"A good knowledge of player actions is a big asset to a good player-piano salesman," said a Dallas music merchant. "Player technicians, of course, find such knowledge absolutely essential."

The Law of Supply and Demand as related to a Musical Appetite

Some years ago, while travelling in the far West, I arrived in a small town in the state of Washington. It was suppertime and after registering at the only hotel in the town, I went into the dining room, sat down, and gave the waiter who was also, by the way, the proprietor, an order for roast beef.

"Sorry, Sir," said he "but we have no roast beef today. All we have is roast lamb and liver and bacon."

"But," said I, "what I wanted was roast beef. It's the only thing I seem to have an appetite for this evening."

"Well," answered the waiter-proprietor, "I'm sorry, sir, but this is only a small hotel and we cannot offer you much choice. The things I have mentioned are the only ones we have cooked. We'll have roast beef tomorrow noon."

I felt inclined to get up and leave the place to dine elsewhere. But as I afterwards discovered, it was lucky for me that I accepted what was offered as there was no other dining place in the little burg. I had to be satisfied with what I could get. As roast lamb didn't agree with me, and as the other dish was not to my liking, I made a meal of eggs and buttered toast. That evening, I had an attack of indigestion.

This brings us to the point we desire to make. There are various types of indigestion. There is a mental indigestion as well as a physical one. Some literature is so heavy that we cannot take much of it at one sitting without danger of incurring an attack of mental indigestion. Happy is the man who has a library in which there is a variety of mental food, light and heavy, ready to appease his mental hunger in a sane and satisfactory manner. The same idea applies to music. The possessor of a Playerpiano may have in his library of player rolls, a variety to supply every demand of his music hunger. If he has, he is wise. He can therewith obtain the music in variety and correct proportion to satisfy his appetite without fear of suffering from musical indigestion.

The Playerpiano can supply the kind of music you want when you want it.

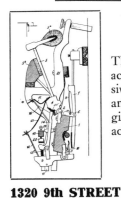

The Dynachord *Art Expression Player*

The Spirit of the Master

is at the piano when the DYNACHORD re-creates for you the playing of the world's greatest piano virtuoso.

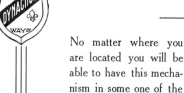

No matter where you are located you will be able to have this mechanism in some one of the 40 high grade makes

we are now united with in a progressive selling campaign.

Write us for the story and catalog "G."

The DYNACHORD makes your store *alive*, your men *alive*, and your business *alive*.

THE AMPHION CO.
SYRACUSE, N. Y.

Makers of Amphion Accessible Player Actions

The Seeburg Line

The Most Complete Line of Its Kind in the World

PIANO TRUCKS
in 9 Styles
PIANO HOISTS
The BEST Known
Ask about them

Self Lifting Piano Truck Co.
FINDLAY, OHIO

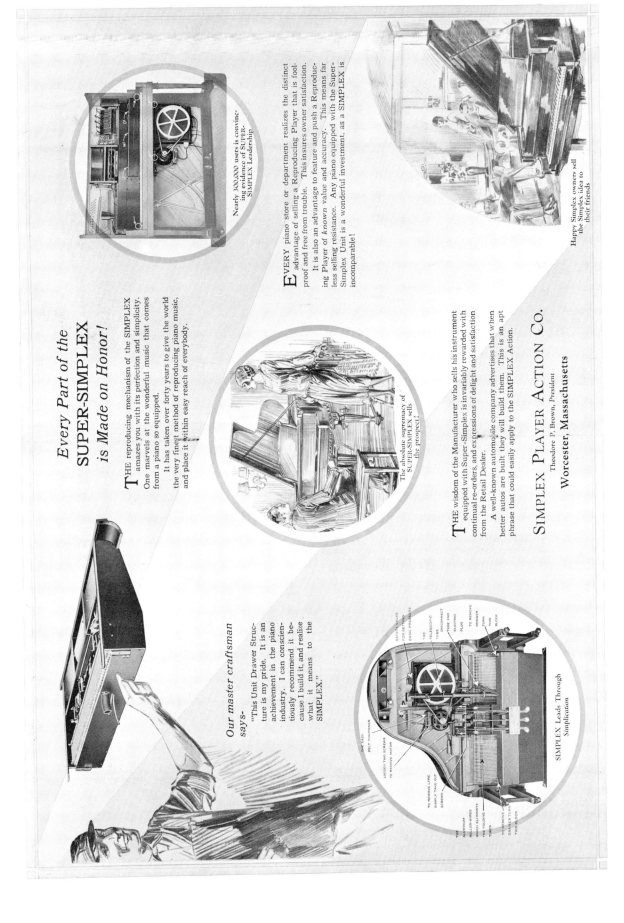

Every Part of the SUPER-SIMPLEX is Made on Honor!

THE reproducing mechanism of the SIMPLEX amazes you with its perfection and simplicity. One marvels at the wonderful music that comes from a piano so equipped.

It has taken over forty years to give the world the very finest method of reproducing piano music, and place it within easy reach of everybody.

Nearly 300,000 users is convincing evidence of SUPER-SIMPLEX Leadership

EVERY piano store or department realizes the distinct advantage of selling a Reproducing Player that is foolproof and free from trouble. This insures owner satisfaction.

It is also an advantage to feature and push a Reproducing Player of *known* value and accuracy. This means far less selling resistance. Any piano equipped with the Super-Simplex Unit is a wonderful investment, as a SIMPLEX is incomparable!

Happy Simplex owners sell the Simplex idea to their friends

Our master craftsman says—

"This Unit Drawer Structure is my pride. It is an achievement in the piano industry. I can conscientiously recommend it because I build it, and realize what it means to the SIMPLEX."

The absolute supremacy of SUPER-SIMPLEX sells the prospect!

THE wisdom of the Manufacturer who sells his instrument equipped with Super-Simplex is invariably rewarded with continual re-orders, and expressions of delight and satisfaction from the Retail Dealer.

A well-known automobile company advertises that when better autos are built they will build them. This is an apt phrase that could easily apply to the SIMPLEX Action.

SIMPLEX PLAYER ACTION CO.

Theodore P. Brown, *President*

Worcester, Massachusetts

SIMPLEX Leads Through Simplification

Bibliography

Bowers, Q. David. *Encyclopedia of Automatic Musical Instruments*. The Vestal Press, Vestal, N. Y. 1972.

Bowers, Q. David. *A Guidebook of Automatic Musical Instruments,* Vol. I and II. The Vestal Press, Vestal, N. Y. 1967.

Bowers, Q. David. *Put Another Nickel In.* The Vestal Press, Vestal, N. Y. 1965.

Buchner, Dr. Alexander. *Mechanical Musical Instruments.* Batchworth Press, London, England. n.d. (c. 1955)

dcWaard, Romke. *From Music Boxes to Street Organs.* English Language edition by The Vestal Press, Vestal, N. Y. 1966.

Dolge, Alfred. *Pianos and Their Makers.* Covina, California, 1911 and 1913.

Givens, Larry. *Rebuilding the Player Piano.* The Vestal Press, Vestal, N. Y. 1963.

Givens, Larry. *Re-Enacting The Artist.* The Vestal Press, Vestal, N. Y. 1970.

Loesser, Arthur. *Men, Women, and Pianos.* Simon & Schuster, New York, N. Y. 1954.

McTammany, John. *The Technical History of the Player.* Musical Courier Co., New York, N. Y. 1915. Reprinted by the Vestal Press, Vestal, N. Y. 1971.

Michel, N. E. *Historical Pianos.* Published by the author; Pico Rivera, California, 1969.

Michel, N. E. *Michel's Piano Atlas.* Published by the author. Later versions published by Bob Pierce, Long Beach, California.

Ord-Hume, Arthur W. J. G. *Player Piano.* A. S. Barnes & Co., Cranbury, N. J. 1970.

Roehl, Harvey N. *The Player Piano—an Historical Scrapbook.* Century House, Watkins Glen, N. Y. 1958.

Roehl, Harvey N. *Player Pianos and Music Boxes (Keys to a Musical Past)* Vestal Press, Vestal, N. Y. 1967.

Van Atta, Harrison Louis. *The Piano and Player Piano.* Published by the author, Dayton, Ohio. 1914.

"The AMICA." News bulletin of the Automatic Musical Instrument Collectors Association.

"The Bulletin of the Musical Box Society International." Periodical of the Musical Box Society International.

"Fox's Music Trade Directory of the United States."

"The Music Trade Indicator."

"The Key Frame." Journal of the Fair Organ Preservation Society.

"The Music Box." Journal of the Musical Box Society of Great Britain.

"The Music Trade Review."

"The Music Trades."

"The Piano and Organ Purchaser's Guide."

"The Presto."

"Scientific American."

"The Tuner's Journal."

Index